BETWEEN TYRANNY AND ANARCHY

SOCIAL SCIENCE HISTORY

Edited by
Stephen Haber and David W. Brady

Armando Razo, *Social Foundations of Limited Dictatorship: Networks and Private Protection During Mexico's Early Industrialization*

Stephen Haber, Douglass C. North, and Barry R. Weingast, editors, *Political Institutions and Financial Development*

David W. Brady and Mathew D. McCubbins, *Process, Party, and Policy Making: New Advances in the Study of the History of Congress*

Anne G. Hanley, *Native Capital: Financial Institutions and Economic Development in São Paulo, Brazil, 1850 to 1920*

Fernando Rocchi, *Chimneys in the Desert: Argentina During the Export Boom Years, 1870 to 1930*

J. G. Manning and Ian Morris, *The Ancient Economy: Evidence and Models*

Daniel Lederman, *The Political Economy of Protection*

William Summerhill, *Order Against Progress*

Samuel Kernell, *James Madison: The Theory and Practice of Republican Government*

Francisco Vidal Luna and Herbert S. Klein, *Slavery and the Economy of São Paulo, 1750 to 1850*

Noel Maurer, *The Power and the Money*

David W. Brady and Mathew D. McCubbins, *Party, Process, and Political Change in Congress*

Jeffrey Bortz and Stephen Haber, *The Mexican Economy, 1870 to 1930*

Edward Beatty, *Institutions and Investment*

Jeremy Baskes, *Indians, Merchants, and Markets*

BETWEEN TYRANNY AND ANARCHY

A History of Democracy in Latin America, 1800–2006

PAUL W. DRAKE

STANFORD UNIVERSITY PRESS

Stanford, California

Stanford University Press
Stanford, California

Printed in the United States of America on acid-free,
archival-quality paper

Library of Congress Cataloging-in-Publication Data

Drake, Paul W., 1944–
    Between tyranny and anarchy : a history of democracy in
Latin America, 1800–2006 / Paul W. Drake.
        p. cm. — (Social science history)
    Includes bibliographical references and index.
    ISBN 978-0-8047-6001-0 (cloth : alk. paper) —
ISBN 978-0-8047-6002-7 (pbk. : alk. paper)
    1. Democracy—Latin America—History—19th century.
2. Democracy—Latin America—History—20th century.
3. Latin America—Politics and government—19th century.
4. Latin America—Politics and government—20th century.
I. Title.   II. Series: Social science history.
    JL966.D73 2009
    320.98—dc22   2008038350

Typeset by Publishers' Design and Production Services, Inc.
in 10.5/13 Bembo

To Josh, Liz, and Katie Drake

CONTENTS

PREFACE

When I told people I was writing a history of democracy in Latin America, I encountered some skeptical reactions. One person joked, "Well, that will certainly be a short book." Another asked, "Is there any such thing?"

This book is longer than they (or I) expected. It shows that those questions set too high a standard for Latin America compared to the rest of the world. As a countercurrent to a deserved reputation for almost five centuries of overwhelming authoritarianism, the region exhibits a protracted and profound history of struggles for democracy. True, the result is mainly a tale of thwarted aspirations and dashed dreams, but it is also a journey toward progress.[1]

I was drawn to this topic by the tidal wave of democratization that took place from the late 1970s to the 2000s. Many people welcomed that tsunami in the aftermath of the previous harsh dictatorships. It showed that democracy could prosper in Latin America, that previous experiences with that political system may have been underestimated, that there should be significant antecedents for the present paradigm, and that if democratic institutions are so worthy of study now they must have been in the past. Indeed, most of the concerns about democracy in recent years are not new, but they are issues that have consumed the region ever since independence.

In the last two decades, a new generation of graduate students in political science also lured me into this subject. Trained in the discipline in the new institutionalism and rational choice theory, they asked me to help them study democratic institutions in contemporary Latin America. As a seasoned Latin Americanist, I of course warned them that this endeavor was a colossal waste of time. Any fool knew that democratic institutions in the region rarely functioned properly and seldom lasted long. However, as those rules and organizations increasingly survived and elicited compliance from the 1980s to the 2000s, I had to go along with my students' desires to probe such issues.

But then I ran into another problem. When the students discovered how political institutions functioned currently, they naturally asked me how that compared with their operation in earlier periods. This forced me to admit that I really knew very little about the matter. My cohort of historians and political scientists had not paid much attention to the question due to the often deplorable record of democracy in the region. Realizing that maybe democratic institutions were more important than I had thought, I decided that their history was a topic ripe for exploration. As an historian in a political science department, I found the project intriguing.

This book makes three broad contributions to understanding the evolution of Latin American democracy. First, it provides a comprehensive history of the region's efforts at democracy over two centuries in multiple countries. Second, it shows that most general theories of democracy can not adequately explain its trajectory in Latin America without a deep analysis of the historical context and causes. Third, it takes an interdisciplinary approach by weaving together the normally separated research on Latin American democracy by historians and political scientists.

By connecting the pioneering but seldom integrated work by historians and political scientists, this study links the past and the present across two disciplines. Although mainly historical in structure and methodology, it incorporates and addresses many of the current issues about democracy in political science. It bridges the two disciplines by emphasizing an institutional, rather than a sociocultural, approach to the history of democracy. It establishes that the ideas, behaviors, and institutions typical of Latin American democracies have deep roots.

An interpretive synthesis is, by nature, based mainly on secondary sources. This book owes an enormous debt to a treasure trove of older and newer literature. Four genres proved exceptionally useful. First, many sometimes overlooked classic books by both historians and political scientists still provided valuable insights. Second, another fruitful place to dig was largely forgotten academic writings from the 1950s to the 1970s, when political studies were shifting from descriptive, narrative, and institutional approaches to quantitative, theoretical, and behavioral methods. Third, the recent outburst of democratization has inspired an avalanche of sophisticated theoretical and empirical analyses by modern political scientists. Fourth, a new generation of historians has produced ground-breaking research on what democratic politics meant to ordinary people in bygone years, especially through elections.

This book offers an original combination and reinterpretation of these four bodies of work. It also rests on primary materials, including constitutions, laws, data on elections, polls, and coups, and statements by political actors, thinkers, and observers. The footnotes reference these items and indicate the extensive key literature.

For analytical purposes, this book organizes countries mainly by geography from north to south. It uses that format because the sub-regions exhibited special characteristics and experiences with democracy. Historically, Mexico, Central America (except for the democratic oasis of Costa Rica), the Caribbean, and the Central Andes suffered far more authoritarianism than did the relatively democratic Northern Andes (especially Colombia) and Southern Cone (Chile, Argentina, and Uruguay).

From the nineteenth through the twentieth centuries, striking continuities prevailed in the countries most and least likely to be democratic. This book concentrates on those South American republics with the most extensive history with embryonic, oligarchic, restricted, or full democracies. These countries also provided a great variety of regimes, trials and tribulations, and bibliography.

While emphasizing general trends, this study applies its concepts and questions to numerous other Latin American countries. It employs diverse examples from all sub-regions to illustrate patterns and deviations. In many instances, institutions did not move forward in unison or congeal to form a democratic regime. Nevertheless, isolated advances, such as constitutional or electoral innovations, merit examination. For these purposes, the chapters draw examples mainly from Peru and Brazil, and to a lesser extent Mexico, Ecuador, and Bolivia. They devote little attention to the small and historically undemocratic countries in most of Central America and the Caribbean, with the exception of Costa Rica.

The cases examined intensively also reflect the quantity and quality of scholarly literature. The farther back in time, the more uneven the coverage, particularly for the minor countries. Therefore, the chapters up to the 1930s must rely heavily on scattered, partial, and monographic information to unveil historical trends.

The abundant multi-national data on institutions for the period from the 1980s to the 2000s, and to a lesser extent for the 1930s to the 1970s, are simply not available for earlier decades. Consequently, it is impossible to construct reliable, long-run, systematic, comprehensive, comparative cross-national tables on regimes, institutions, and practices for the deep past. Nevertheless, pulling together case studies from those distant years sheds invaluable light on the ancestors of contemporary Latin American democracies.[2]

This book arranges all the above materials in chapters by historical eras characterized by distinctive experiences with democracy. Beforehand, the two introductory chapters provide a critical overview of democratic theory, practice, history, and institutions in Latin America from 1800 to 2006. They also summarize the essential conclusions of this study.

Thereafter, each chronological chapter first examines a particular period's history of democratic trends, causes of success or failure, and ideas about democracy. Then each chapter uses the framework, though not the methods, of contemporary political science to concentrate on the development of political institutions: constitutions, centralism, presidents, legislatures, judiciaries, elections, and political parties. Among institutions, this volume privileges elections because they were the most important measure of and force behind the growth of democracy, particularly for the common people.

Chapter 3 covers the independence period—skimming the colonial political legacy of three hundred years, and then exploring the subsequent frustrations in forging new republics from the 1810s through the 1820s. Chapter 4 excavates the archaeology of democracy amidst the rubble of the post-independence authoritarian and semi-democratic governments. It also investigates the blossoming of a few efforts at constructing stable constitutional orders from the 1820s through the 1870s.

Chapter 5 examines the much sturdier oligarchic republics from the 1880s through the 1920s, during Latin America's first great epoch of liberalism. Most of those highly elitist, protected democracies collapsed during the Great Depression of the 1930s. Chapter 6 assesses the heyday of popular democracies from the 1930s up to the 1970s, when populism incorporated many average citizens into legal participation, until exceptionally repressive dictatorships terminated that upsurge of the working classes.

Following the authoritarian regimes of the 1960s and 1970s, Chapter 7 reaches a climax with the tsunami of neoliberal democratization from the late 1970s to the early 2000s. That unparalleled wave built upon the legacy of two hundred years of struggles for democracy. That high point concludes an unfinished story of not only many disappointments but also extraordinary achievements with democracy. Chapter 7 closes with an assessment of today's challenge of how to make the latest protected democracies really serve the disadvantaged popular majority they claim to represent. Finally, Chapter 8 reviews in a brief compass the construction of Latin American democracies over two centuries.

As I traced this history, I received tremendous help from writings by and conversations with other scholars, both professors and graduate students, in Latin America and Europe as well as in the United States. I am especially thankful to my research assistants, Scott Morgenstern, Elisabeth Hilbink, and Druscilla Scribner. I am also immensely grateful to them as well as Eric Hershberg, Ivan Jaksic, Brian Loveman, Carmen McEvoy, Gerardo Munck, Peter Smith, and Peter Winn for reading and commenting on all or parts of the manuscript.

As has been true for over forty years, my wife, Susan, also contributed scintillating insights and unwavering support. I am eternally beholden to her. This book is dedicated to our children.

Map of Latin America

Chapter 1

The Theory and History of Latin American Democracy, 1800–2006

The title of this book comes, appropriately, from Simon Bolívar. In the opening decades of the nineteenth century, the Liberator expressed his exasperation at forging a democratic republic that could withstand the opposing dangers of "tyranny and anarchy." Ever since then, his descendants have grappled with the classic dilemma of crafting a democracy that provides order without dictatorship, and liberty without disintegration.[1]

Juxtaposed to its venerable fame as a home for despotism, Latin America also boasts one of the planet's longest, deepest, and richest histories of experiments with democracy. Along with the United States, the region hosts "the oldest continuous republics of the contemporary world."[2] Occupying a unique niche between the West and the developing world, Latin America offers an extraordinary laboratory for examining democratic movements, ideas, and institutions. "In no other part of the world have more persistent efforts been made to preserve freedom under such unfavorable circumstances."[3]

Amidst a history dominated by dictators, Latin America's struggle for democracy—like its battles for economic development, social justice, and human rights—was a protracted, erratic, and painful process. From the beginning in the nineteenth century, they sowed seeds that took a long time to sprout, let alone flourish. In the long view, these flawed (and often futile) attempts to instill democratic values and rules bore fruit. Their early themes,

1

concepts, practices, and institutions continue to shape the successes and failures of democracy in the region even into the present day.

   In spite of all their shortcomings, the attempts at democracy that had
their start in the nineteenth century should not be underestimated. Ex-
plicitly or implicitly, observers inside and outside the region have too often
denigrated these episodes because of the plethora of authoritarian regimes.
This study unearths a more positive picture without slighting the severe deficiencies. Contrary to conventional wisdom, the countries leading the region in making democratic advances did not lag very far behind the United
States and Western Europe. Latin America's continuing battles to establish
and improve democracy have resembled similar problems confronted in
both richer and poorer nations alike.

   In comparison with the United States and Western Europe, Latin America's democratic history has been distinctive because of its fundamental dilemma: how to reconcile political systems that are theoretically committed
to legal equality with societies that are divided by extreme socioeconomic
inequalities. Too often, the polarized distribution of social power undermined the efficacy of democratic institutions. For two centuries, the Latin
American upper classes repeatedly resorted to tyranny out of dread that the
lower classes would unleash anarchy—or worse, revolution. Between the alternatives of dictatorship or disorder, Latin Americans developed two special
variants of democracy to cope with their exceptionally unequal societies—
one through exclusion and the other through inclusion.

   These competing models of *protected* versus *popular* democracy stressed
the content and outcome of democracy more than the intrinsic value of the
institutional procedures revered in Western Europe and the United States.
In Latin America, many elites preferred protected democracies, with strict
formal and informal limits on participation and programs for the unprivileged majority. By contrast, many reformers advocated popular democracies,
with an emphasis on a massive role for the working classes in selecting governments and deriving benefits from them. This book traces the trajectory
of these contested visions of democracy from the 1800s to the 2000s.

   To assess that evolution, this book asks when, where, and why has democracy existed and lasted in Latin America? What have been the concepts,
types, rules, regulations, institutions, and limits of those systems? And what
have been their triumphs and tragedies?

   Without a thorough examination of the historical causes, most existing
general theories of democracy can not adequately explain its failures, successes, and forms in Latin America. Whether one assesses the international,
economic, social, cultural, or institutional determinants of the existence and

quality of democracy, the historical context conditioned their regional and national impact. Historical factors largely accounted for Latin America's earliest struggles for democracy and cast a distinctive mold that has shaped its democracies ever since.

To provide historical background for the current issues in political science, this study pays special attention to the new institutionalism. This book agrees with that school of thought that democratic institutions made a difference—even in inhospitable settings, and even when governments turned them into a farce. Whether fully enforceable or not, ancient Latin American constitutions and laws established norms and practices, precedents and beliefs, hopes and expectations. Even when democratic institutions were woefully defective, they still operated in significant ways and laid the groundwork for the future.

From the 1810s to the 2000s, Latin American political institutions exhibited unstable and often unenforceable constitutions, extreme centralism, hyper-presidentialism, legislative Lilliputians, conservative and ineffective judiciaries, explosive elections, and ephemeral political parties. For all these features, varying institutional designs could facilitate the probability and performance of some democracies. However, since the basic institutions remained much the same for two centuries in nearly all the countries in Latin America, it is improbable that they accounted for big variations in democratic outcomes over time and place.

Despite their significance, institutions by themselves can not fully explain the arrival, survival, or depth of democracy in Latin America. The challenge for proponents of democracy consisted not only in writing the correct laws but also in exerting the power or persuasion to get the crucial social actors to obey them. The exceptionally unequal distribution of social power made it very difficult for those institutions to elicit compliance and function properly. Their success usually depended heavily on structural and historical conditions, as well as elite consensus in favor of some form of democracy.

Among these institutions, elections were the most important. They constituted the essential, if not sufficient, condition for creating democracy. In Latin America, democracy unfolded as a protracted history of making the government actually allow, reflect, and represent widespread citizen preferences as expressed in electoral outcomes. Even when corrupted and violated, the amazingly ubiquitous elections from the 1800s to the 2000s were fiercely contested, sometimes surprisingly open to mass participation, and crucial for legitimating governments. They proved vital to the gradual inculcation and institutionalization of democracy.

Theories of Democracy in Latin America

DEFINITIONS OF DEMOCRACY

In this study, the term *democracy* refers narrowly to the prevailing procedures of electoral political competition. This book basically uses a binary,
minimalist definition of democratic versus authoritarian political systems.
It is necessary to establish this dichotomy before analyzing the virtues and
defects of any subtypes.[4]

This classification scheme is relative in three senses. First, it employs the
standards appropriate to and prevalent in particular eras, since democratic
expectations escalated from the early nineteenth to the late twentieth centuries. Second, for any one time period, the governments labeled as democracies might not meet some absolute or maximalist criteria. However,
they were generally more freely elected, representative, constitutional, and
civilian-based than those dubbed dictatorial, which were more imposed, authoritarian, arbitrary, and military-dominated. Third, movement from one
broad regime type to the other indicated that a government became relatively but significantly more democratic or despotic than its predecessor.
Across time and space, there were many close calls and mixed breeds.[5]

This book's definition of *democracy* emphasizes institutions. To qualify as
a democracy, a political system had to select its key leaders through regular
elections that were reasonably participatory, free, and fair, by the standards of
the era. It also had to respect enough civil liberties to carry out these procedures. One country could be more democratic—allowing broader suffrage,
holding more honest elections, and protecting more civil liberties—than
another, but they both could be classified as minimally democratic in contrast with blatantly dictatorial alternatives.[6]

Some scholars also mention other requisites for democratic systems, such
as the rule of law, government accountability, civilian control over the military, and even some minimal degree of social and economic equality. These
indicators, however, were difficult to measure, established too high a barrier to entry, and, while important to the quality of democracy, were not
necessary to distinguish broadly democratic from non-democratic political
systems. Latin America should not be held to higher standards than other
regimes in the same time period.[7]

At least three types of regimes in Latin America met enough of the criteria for democracies to demarcate them from the authoritarian species. First,
in the nineteenth and early twentieth centuries, *constitutional* or *liberal oligar-
chies* or *republics* held regular elections (but with very limited participation),

excluded some key issues and agencies from public control, and limited civil liberties significantly.

Second, in the twentieth century, "restricted democracies" provided more open government on all dimensions than did aristocratic republics—but they did not deliver as much participation, liberty, or accountability as did "full democracies." In contrast with authoritarianism or oligarchic republicanism, even restricted democracies tended to curb or eliminate property or tax qualifications for voting, enfranchise a majority of literate adult males (resulting in at least 5% of the population casting ballots), hold regular and direct popular elections for the executive and/or legislature, respect the electoral results, respond to elected officials, and defend basic civil liberties. They still were prone to ban certain parties and to succumb to frequent military interventions.

Third, in order to rise (increasingly in the twentieth century, particularly from the 1970s onward) to the level of "full democracies," these governing systems had to also establish universal male suffrage (and eventually include females and younger people), ensure totally secret and free and fair elections, protect more civil liberties, and respond more fully to the wishes of voters. In many parts of the world, countries generally progressed from types one to two to three, though with many breakdowns and reversions along the way.[8]

Table 1.1 shows the evolution in Latin America, listing countries according to their first experience of reasonably stable (though not necessarily uninterrupted) democracy that dominated an era. Minor and short-term regimes have been omitted. While there is room to quarrel with some of these precise dates, the placement of a regime in an era is widely accepted by most scholars. For different authors, the dates chosen for this table could refer to when a regime was constitutionalized, installed, or really took effect as a republic. For example, Argentina's oligarchic republic could be dated from the constitution of 1853, the taking of power in 1862, or the national institutionalization in 1880. At the same time, Costa Rica could be entered with the passage of the constitution of 1871, or the electoral stabilization in 1889. Since the best choice is usually a combination of constitutionalism and effective rule, this table places Argentina in 1862, and Costa Rica in 1889. The most unreliable and debatable dates are for the beginning of the oligarchic republics in the nineteenth century, both because of a more turbulent history and a less extensive scholarship prior to the 1930s. Many disputes continue about the more recent full democracies, which are categorized here mainly by institutional criteria—not by the more idealized indicators of performance and quality.[9]

TABLE I.I

Major Latin American democratic regimes, 1810–2006

Country	Oligarchic republic	Restricted democracy	Full democracy
Chile	1833–1920	1920–1924	1932–1973; 1990–2006
Peru	1860–1919	1939–1948	1980–1991; 2000–2006
Argentina	1862–1912	1946–1955	1912–1930; 1983–2006
Bolivia	1884–1930		1952–1964; 1982–2006
Ecuador	1884–1925	1948–1961	1979–2006
Colombia	1886–1936	1936–1952	1958–2006
El Salvador	1886–1931	1983–1993	1993–2006
Costa Rica	1889–1947		1948–2006
Uruguay	1890–1903	1903–1919	1919–1933; 1939–1973; 1984–2006
Brazil	1891–1930		1945–1964; 1985–2006
Honduras	1895–1919		1982–2006
Panama	1904–1967	1990–1993	1994–2006
Guatemala		1986–1995	1945–1954; 1996–2000
Venezuela			1958–2006
Dom. Repub.			1970–2006
Nicaragua		1984–1989	1990–2006
Paraguay			1993–2006
Haiti		1995–2006	
Mexico			2000–2006

CAUSES OF DEMOCRACY

International Factors Since democratic trends among countries outside and inside Latin America constituted international events, they must have had international causes (unless they were pure coincidences). The first modern wave of international democratization occurred from the 1820s to the 1920s, followed by a reverse flow from the 1920s to the 1940s. The second democratic surge swept through from the 1940s to the 1960s, succeeded by a rollback from the late 1950s to the mid-1970s. Then the third global overflow of democracy cascaded from the mid-1970s to the 2000s, without ebbing back so far. In very broad terms, Latin America participated increasingly in these inundations.   .

Prior to these flood tides, no Western nations qualified as democratic in 1750. Then the American and French revolutions unleashed the first democratic outpouring. The rough criteria for this period were that half the adult males were eligible to vote and that the chief executive was elected periodically. Following the wars of independence, a few Latin American countries met or came close to this standard from time to time. However, they were especially prone to illegal behavior and regime collapse.

After erasing property qualifications and instituting universal male suffrage, the United States came on board in 1828, although excluding slaves.

By the 1920s, over thirty countries had reached the same stage, usually including voting by secret ballot. The most prominent were several European nations (most significantly Great Britain, France, Switzerland, Italy, and Ireland) and Argentina, although Costa Rica, Chile, and Uruguay also fit the criteria except for the size of the electorate.

After the tide went out during the 1920s and 1930s, the second forward wave washed ashore briefly from World War II to the 1960s. The beneficiaries included West Germany, Italy, Austria, Japan, South Korea, Turkey, and Greece, as well as several Latin American countries, at least temporarily: Guatemala, Brazil, Argentina, Costa Rica, Ecuador, Bolivia, Peru, Colombia, Venezuela, and the Dominican Republic. The Latin American cases were still subject to frequent deviations and breakdowns. Decolonization in Asia and Africa also produced a few shaky democracies.

Thereafter, the second global authoritarian riptide inundated Latin America. By the mid-1970s, one-third of the thirty-two democracies that had been alive in the world in 1958 had died. Whereas nine democracies had flourished in South America in 1960, only those in Colombia and Venezuela survived by the end of 1973.

In the third democratic flood beginning in the mid-1970s, over 30 democracies supplanted dictatorships in Europe, Asia, and Latin America. The tsunami even swept away communist regimes in Europe. Rising higher than ever before, that tidal wave lifted approximately sixty countries, or almost half the nations in the world, to democratic status. Only about half that number had been democratic at the previous peak in 1922, but they had also accounted for over 45 percent of the states in the world at that time.[10]

In this long view of history, *diffusion* was a powerful instigator of democracy, both from outside Latin America and within Latin America. Huntington wrote, "New democracies are thus less the result of cumulative, necessary, predictable, and systematic developments than of historical busts and booms, global opinion climates, shifting opportunities, and contingent preferences." As evidenced by regional reactions to these international currents, external forces provided crucial impetus for regime changes and democratization in Latin America. At times, currents from overseas furthered democratization in Latin America, which then spread from one country to another. Over two centuries, that contagion enveloped more and more countries. Those foreign factors included strategic, economic, and intellectual impulses, whether arriving as events, trends, influences, or policies. They exerted the most impact when they dovetailed with the preferences of domestic winning political groups.[11]

In the even longer view from the late 1400s to the early 2000s, Latin America experienced three seismic regime changes, all facilitated by international forces. The first great transformation transpired during the conquest at the turn of the fifteenth and sixteenth centuries. The Spanish and Portuguese invaders replaced the indigenous rulers with their own in only four decades. Warfare in Europe detonated the second cataclysm at the start of the nineteenth century. Through the battles for independence, the Latin Americans supplanted external absolutism with republics in less than two decades. They crafted their new governments largely from United States, French, and Spanish blueprints.

Later in the nineteenth century, oligarchic republicanism in Latin America reflected the stabilization of the export economies and the imitation of political systems in the United States and Western Europe. Another regional regime change of lesser magnitude marched through with the military coups in the 1930s in the aftermath of the Great Depression. An even smaller ripple brought the brief opening to democracy and the left in the mid-1940s at the end of World War II.

The third major tumbling of dominoes occurred from the late 1970s to the 2000s. The foreign debt crisis and other international trends accelerated Latin America's democratic tsunami, bringing down nearly all the authoritarian regimes in a little over two decades. U.S. preferences for representative democracies held more sway than ever before as it exerted unparalleled hegemony as the sole superpower.[12] Table 1.2 shows the historical regime trends in Latin America from the 1400s to the 2000s.

From the 1800s to the 2000s, international economic factors influenced political possibilities and patterns. In the middle of the nineteenth century, they reinforced export structures that fortified landed barons, the class usually most opposed to open democracy. The economically predominant British seldom cared much about Latin America's internal political systems. As an open international trading and lending system stabilized toward the end of the 1800s, Latin American landowners felt secure enough to consolidate protected democracies in the form of aristocratic republics. The Great Depression's disruption of global trade and finance at the start of the 1930s discredited the oligarchic system of rule and facilitated dictatorships. The Depression and World War II also boosted import-substituting industrialization, which expanded the bourgeoisie, the middle sectors, and urban labor—all seeking political inclusion, sometimes through democratic means.

In the twentieth century, the new external economic behemoth, the United States, vacillated in its regime preferences. From the 1890s to the 1920s, it used force to install republicanism (however superficial and evanes-

TABLE 1.2
Historical regime trends in Latin America, 1400s–2000s

Era	Regime trend
1400s–1500s	Iberian conquest
1500s–1800s	Iberian empires
1810s–1820s	Independent republics
1820s–1870s	Caudillo dictatorships
1880s–1920s	Oligarchic republics
1930s	Military dictatorships
1940s–1970s	Popular democracies
1980s–2000s	Neoliberal democracies

cent) in Central America and the Caribbean. From the 1930s to the 1940s, it backed away from meddling in domestic politics in the region and tolerated despotism. Then Washington briefly sympathized with democracy in the wake of World War II. During the Cold War, the Colossus of the North sometimes promoted democracy but frequently backed anti-communist military dictatorships. When the second international debt debacle undermined dictatorships in the 1980s, it cleared the way for the latest stampede of democracies, usually endorsed by the United States.[13]

Domestic Factors: Economic Although international forces must be examined to explain concurrent democratization in multiple countries, their impact depended on domestic factors within those countries. Some posited preconditions, such as certain values (e.g., Protestantism), cultures (e.g., Anglo-Saxon), social structures (e.g., weak landowners versus a strong bourgeoisie), civil societies (e.g., vibrant voluntary associations), or economic configurations (e.g., lack of dependency) have generally not fared well under scholarly scrutiny. Although these factors may have facilitated democracy under certain circumstances, they did not provide satisfactory explanations for variations in democracy among countries or eras. Latin American nations with similar cultural traditions, social patterns, and economic circumstances had quite different experiences with democracy. Despite their significant contributions, most structural theories fell into disrepute in the 1980s, when democratization, to varying degrees, suddenly engulfed the region—not to mention other parts of the world—with seeming disregard for divergent cultural, social, or economic conditions. Consequently, this study emphasizes institutional analyses within historical contexts rather than a structural or sociocultural approach.[14]

The structural economic condition that has stood up best under the onslaught of research is that a higher level of capitalist socioeconomic development has been conducive to democracy, and dire poverty has not. The sturdiest democracies in the modern world have tended to have high per capita incomes combined with elevated levels of literacy, industrialization, and urbanization. These advances generated both the social groups to press for inclusion and the wherewithal to satisfy demands. Although this correlation between modernization and democracy has held up well for large groups of countries—particularly at the extreme high and low levels of income—it has not been determinate for individual cases.

The modernization thesis that more socioeconomically developed countries were more likely to be democratic has not fit Latin America as well as the rest of the globe, but it has stood up fairly well historically within the region, even during the nineteenth century. From 1900 through the 1930s, the Latin American countries with higher GDP per capita were more likely to become democratic, especially in the Southern Cone (Chile, Argentina, and Uruguay). From the 1940s to the 1970s, that pattern continued, with the at least temporary addition of democracies in Brazil, Colombia, Costa Rica, and to a lesser extent Venezuela and Peru. Meanwhile, the poorest countries in Central America, the Caribbean, and the Central Andes usually enjoyed much less success with democracy.[15]

Domestic Factors: Social and Cultural   Although international and economic factors played some role in encouraging and sustaining democracy, national actors were also essential, sometimes in the form of social classes.[16] In Latin America, all social classes historically exhibited some ambivalence about democracy. The landed oligarchy rarely supported unrestricted democratization, although sometimes it backed limited democratic measures, usually to increase its own base of support. One example came from the rural conservative elites who endorsed suffrage for literate males in Chile in 1874 to reduce the control over the electorate of the incumbent government. Another instance found the agricultural oligarchs of Colombia installing republicanism with safeguards for minority representation in 1910 to preserve the peace after the War of a Thousand Days. Still another case featured the highland conservatives in Ecuador becoming the first group in Latin America to implement female suffrage, doing so in 1929 to preserve their electoral base by bringing pro-clerical women to the voting booths.[17]

As in Europe, the bourgeoisie in Latin America did not take command of democratization, although it cooperated in countries like Chile, Colombia, and Uruguay. In most cases, urban economic elites were either too weak or too linked to the rural landowners to bring about democracy on their own. The growing urban middle sectors—however unreliable and divided—

sometimes allied with dissident elites or upstart workers to install democracies. In some cases, the middle classes rallied the workers to pressure for openings from the upper class but then turned against further working-class advances, at times supporting military coups.[18]

In all countries, the role of elites proved crucial to the rise or fall of democracy. Social power relationships more than institutional rules determined political behavior and outcomes. These two spheres interacted. It was important to get the institutions right, but until the upper classes and their allies accepted the laws, they would not function properly.

Latin American elites long resisted fully democratic institutions because glaring inequalities filled them with trepidation about the under classes. However, when the well-to-do concluded that it was in their self-interest and did not jeopardize their security, the upper and middle strata incorporated the subalterns into subordinate participation in democracy. The dominant groups admitted the unprivileged under four conditions: (1) when their mobilization of the lower classes against counter-elites helped resolve intra-elite conflicts; (2) when the masses' inclusion in and acceptance of the system gave it more legitimacy and stability with less costly repression; (3) when the ruling classes believed they could maximize gains or minimize losses through democratization; and (4) when their inclusiveness pleased powerful foreign observers.[19]

When the elites accepted democracy in Latin America, as well as elsewhere, they imposed procedural and substantive limits. This paradox illustrated "the dilemma that stabilization of formal democracy appears to require serious restrictions on substantive democracy because of the need for protection of elite interests." The less democracies threatened upper and middle-class assets and perquisites with socioeconomic reforms for the unprivileged, the more likely they were to exist and endure. The less elections mattered, the more likely elections were to occur.[20]

Until the late twentieth century, the armed forces and the Roman Catholic Church served the upper class and impeded democracy. Military coups d'état toppled democracies, as well as dictatorships, from independence onward. They became a regular feature of the political system. From 1823 to 1966, 351 coups removed presidents by force or threat of force. They occurred with great frequency from the 1840s through the 1850s, followed by a period of stability reaching low points of coups in the 1880s and 1920s. From the 1850s to the 1900s, the incidence of coups correlated fairly well with downturns in international trade.

From 1900 through 2000, at least 167 successful coups ousted governments (though not necessarily democracies), for an average of 1.6 coups per year or 8.8 per country, with a high of 15 in Bolivia and a low of 1 in Uruguay. The rate declined over the century, hitting bottom from 1990 on. In the twentieth century, the greatest numbers took place during the pressures on the oligarchic order from 1906 to 1919 and during the crisis spawned by the Great Depression from 1930 to 1939. For the subordinate classes, "the strategic problem of transition is to get to democracy without being either killed by those who have arms or starved by those who control productive resources."[21]

Throughout most of Latin American history, the Roman Catholic Church also obstructed the development of democracy by siding with the rich and mighty. From the conquest onward, the Church facilitated the social and political control of the under classes. Only beginning in the early 1960s did it contribute significantly to democracy by strengthening civil society, opposing military dictatorships, defending human rights, and supporting social reform for the poor. [22]

In contrast with Europe, the smaller working class played less of a role in democratization in Latin America. It had the greatest impact in the most urbanized, industrialized countries: Argentina, Uruguay, and Chile. It mainly propelled early democratization as a destabilizing labor force and as a backer of middle-class movements. Elitist Latin American democratic transitions in the late nineteenth and early twentieth centuries usually did not involve laborers to any large extent. Instead, those regime changes typically resulted from either elite calculations about expanding electoral support or pressures for inclusion from excluded upper- and middle-class groups. However, some of those privileged sectors also hoped that democratization would defuse and co-opt disruptive working-class movements.

By the early twentieth century, labor's ability to demand political participation as well as social justice increased as it grew in the cities. During that century, it also threw its lot in with successful multi-class revolutionary movements promising democratization in Mexico (1910), Bolivia (1952), Cuba (1959), and Nicaragua (1979). From the 1930s through the 2000s, workers became a bigger force to reckon with. Although normally supporting democracy as well as populist and leftist candidates, they sometimes backed authoritarian populists or revolutionaries.

During the tsunami, the organized working class significantly promoted democratization. Thereafter, the shrinkage of organized labor slashed its leverage on those neoliberal, protected democracies. However large or small its role in particular countries, the labor movement was usually one of the social actors most oppressed by rightwing authoritarianism, and most committed to democracy—especially the popular variety.[23]

The higher the level of effective representation of the lower classes and their demands, the less likely and stable have democracies been in Latin America, although they were more democratic in terms of popular participation and rewards. Up to the 1930s, the oligarchic republics granted little representation to the popular classes. Consequently, those limited democracies were quite durable, albeit not very widespread. From the 1930s to the 1970s, representation of the poor and their needs accelerated as did the number of democracies, but durability declined. From the 1970s to the 2000s, governments deemphasized mobilization, representation, and mollification of the underserved, while democracies became more numerous and long-lasting. Given the extremely inequitable distribution of social power, protected democracies exceeded their popular competitors in longevity.[24]

During these eras, Latin American electoral democracies varied along two main dimensions: contestation and participation. Some allowed a great deal of debate over fundamental differences of opinion, but only among a small group of voters, elected officials, and stakeholders. Others kept explosive issues off the agenda but permitted widespread electoral inclusion of citizens. The broader the space for contestation and participation, the more open and democratic but less durable the political system.

Historically, Latin America exhibited high contestation and low participation in the post-independence period from the 1820s to the 1870s, low contestation and low participation under oligarchic republics from the 1880s to the 1920s, high contestation and high participation during the zenith of populism from the 1930s to the 1970s, and low contestation and high participation under neoliberalism from the 1980s to the 1990s. When very high levels of contestation and conflict coincided between the government and its opponents, then each was likely to try to exclude the other. This phenomenon occurred in oligarchic battles over the state in most of the nineteenth century and in clashes between elites and masses in the twentieth century. As a result, numerous dictatorships banned unacceptable players, be they regional chieftains in the nineteenth century or leftist populists in the twentieth.[25] Table 1.3 shows broad chronological levels of contestation, participation, and regime durability.

Just as class conflicts may explain the likelihood and character of democracy, so might ethnic friction. Theoretically, countries with the least severe ethnic, racial, or linguistic cleavages should have had a better chance of installing and preserving democracy. They seemed more likely to be socially compatible and peaceful. Their ruling classes felt less apprehensive that democratic openness would unleash ethnic competition and strife. Conversely, more diverse populations heightened the racist paranoia and hostility of the

TABLE I.3
Historical evolution of contestation, participation, and durability

Regimes by era	Contestation	Participation	Durability
1820s–1870s	High	Low	Low
1880s–1920s	Low	Low	High
1930s–1970s	High	High	Low
1980s–2000s	Low	High	High

SOURCE: Based on Hartlyn and Valenzuela, "Democracy"; Dahl, *Polyarchy*, 4–5, 14–16; Smith, *Democracy*, 313–326.

upper strata, rendering them less willing to expand political participation. Even though ethnic fissures seldom erupted in Latin American politics, they deeply divided some societies.

In the long run, greater ethnic and racial homogeneity correlated fairly well with greater success for democracies in Chile, Argentina, Uruguay, Costa Rica, Colombia, and Venezuela—although Argentina showed that demographic uniformity was not a sufficient condition for stable democracy. Conversely, greater ethnic and racial heterogeneity correlated well with lesser democratic success in Mexico, Central America (except Costa Rica), the Caribbean, Ecuador, Peru, Bolivia, Paraguay, and Brazil, principally because elites were wary of extending democratic rights to indigenous, African American, and mixed peoples.

The more homogeneous countries also tended to have higher incomes. Some were ambiguous cases—for example Mexico, Cuba, and Brazil with relatively high incomes but also high heterogeneity—with only Brazil faring even moderately well with democracy. In all democracies, a contradiction persevered between the myth of legal equality and the reality of socioeconomic inequality. When that gap became extreme, as in the more heterogeneous and underdeveloped countries of Latin America, sustaining democratic legality became more difficult.[26]

Domestic Factors: Historical   History, as laid forth in this book, provides a powerful explanation for the general evolution of democracy in Latin America and for the varying trajectories of particular countries. Those countries with the most experience with democracy enjoyed the highest probability of becoming and staying democratic. The continuity from the nineteenth through the twentieth centuries in the sub-regions and countries most and least likely to be democratic lends credence to this hypothesis. The most likely were always in South America—especially Colombia and the Southern Cone, but not the Central Andes or Paraguay. The least likely remained in Mexico, Central America (except Costa Rica), and the Caribbean. Only a combination of history and social science can fully explain why and how the more experienced countries got on the democratic track in the first place.[27]

The authoritarian colonial legacy—political, institutional, social, and cultural—from Iberia hampered the development of democracy, most notably in the first decades of the nineteenth century. That heritage—along with poverty, illiteracy, and inequality—made rapid democratic success unlikely anywhere in the region. However, that common birthright can not explain political variation within or among the Latin American countries, especially in the long run and particularly in the exceptional positive cases.

Nor can the degree of Spanish colonial domination fully account for the subsequent fate of democracy. It is noteworthy that the continental leadership of independence came from the outlying colonies of Venezuela, Colombia, and Argentina, not the imperial centers of Mexico and Peru. Subsequently healthy republics like Colombia, Chile, Uruguay, and Argentina emerged from the periphery of the empire, but so did rickety and seldom democratic states like Venezuela and Paraguay.

Those countries—Mexico and Peru—that had constituted the core of the Indian and Spanish empires experienced crippling problems establishing democracies, as did their satellites in Central America and the Central Andes. However, countries in the Caribbean—not counting their English-speaking neighbors—with no great Indian or imperial legacy fared just as poorly. Countries heavily reliant on slavery—notably the Caribbean and Brazil—also tended to encounter more obstacles installing democracy. Both colonial and racial/ethnic legacies militated against democratic success.

The wars of independence and their aftermath also left Spanish America ill-equipped to found stable republics. The removal of the crown created a legitimacy vacuum. The years of fratricide and the resulting strength of contending private and public armies ravaged the new countries. So did tensions between the capital city and the outlying provinces. It took decades of civil discord before most of these countries could bring about enough order to construct functioning governments, "since the conflict of parties has been not infrequently transferred from the chamber to the camp, and the issue decided not by counting heads but by breaking them."[28]

From the 1810s to the 1870s, authoritarianism ran rampant. In the rubble left by men on horseback ("caudillos"), an archaeology of democracy is necessary to excavate the relics of rudimentary precursors, precedents, and aspirations. Although normally failing, the democratic experiments in those years laid the foundations for the later political systems. In those decades, many of the institutional designs and behavior patterns set the mold into the 2000s.

Furthermore, those trials and tribulations resulted in the first episodes of partial success at republicanism in a few countries. They began to travel on a road to democracy that would serve them well in the future, a virtuous path dependence. After many false starts and detours, they got on a learning curve of practicing democracy. Eventually, their elites and non-elites would come to accept it as the best system for resolving political conflicts without bloodshed.[29]

Restricted or full democratization may be more successful following a lengthy period of restrained oligarchic competition, the most that could be expected in the nineteenth century. As that protected system took hold in some countries in the second half of the 1800s, it allowed for the inculcation of democratic practices among elites and some lower social strata before the government threw the arena open to massive participation. Thus, the new participants could be socialized gradually into democratic behavior and might not try to eject the older players.

Over time, the decades of stable oligarchic republicanism in the late nineteenth and early twentieth centuries facilitated more inclusive democratic successes in Chile and Uruguay, and to a lesser extent in Colombia and Costa Rica. However, that staging did not guarantee a smooth or benign evolution. Those countries also suffered democratic breakdowns. Meanwhile, Argentina failed to stay on track from oligarchic republicanism to restricted and then full democracy until after weathering decades of intermittent authoritarianism.[30]

Such gradual sequencing was possible from independence to World War II, but rarely thereafter. Once countries established full democracy, they became unlikely to return to oligarchic or restricted democracy, as well as mild authoritarianism. Accelerating demands from workers and peasants for simultaneous participation and contestation—for political rights and social justice—underlay many of the disruptions from the 1940s to the 1970s. In that period, once certain issues, rights, and contenders burst onto the political stage, it became difficult to kick them off without extreme coercion under a dictatorship.[31]

From the nineteenth to the twentieth centuries, Latin American democracies varied over time and space as to who could participate, who could govern, how they could govern, and over what they could govern. Logically but not linearly, that evolution led toward greater inclusiveness in the ballot box and in the halls of government, greater protection for civil liberties, greater responsiveness to citizen expectations, and greater breadth of issues in government purview. With numerous exceptions and qualifications, this trajectory characterized the history of popular and populist democracy from the 1930s to the 1970s, when the lower classes gained access to government and its resources. Then a rash of military takeovers choked off their ascent.

Following extraordinarily repressive authoritarian regimes in the 1960s and 1970s, democratization with neoliberalism engulfed the region from the 1970s to the 2000s. During the tsunami, more Latin American countries became democratic than ever before, to enthusiastic acclaim at home and abroad. However, they adopted contradictory democracies. Formally democratic governments took power and improved widespread participation in elections and offices. But at the same time, they often employed technocrats to constrain accountability, restricted civil liberties, discouraged working-class activism, and, above all, banished major social issues, such as income and land redistribution, from the public agenda. For the marginalized majority, these restraints bred increasing frustration with protected democracies that allowed for their participation but not for satisfaction of their needs.

To an extent, the new democracies privileged form over substance. They restored the previous procedural advances of the mid-twentieth century (e.g., voting rights for women and illiterates) but returned to the substantive limitations of the nineteenth century (e.g, minimal state interference with the market, private property, or the overall distribution of economic and social power). In large part, governments erected these boundaries on policies to persuade the socioeconomic elites and their military allies, as well as the United States, to accept the resurrection of democratic institutions. By the turn of the century, lower-class protests against these neoliberal economic and political models catapulted several new leftists to the presidency. Once again, they used democratic mechanisms to address poverty and inequality.[32]

Protected versus Popular Concepts of Democracy

Two other factors that accounted for the frequency and character of democracy in Latin America were ideas and institutions. From independence onward, the two main schools of thought favored either *protected* or *popular* democracies. The former often criticized standard Western democracy from the right, as a dangerous opening to mediocrity, anarchy, or revolution. The latter did so from the left, as an oligarchic, tyrannical, and reactionary deception of the unprivileged. Both these variants of democracy reacted to the issue of mass participation and benefits in highly stratified societies. The first group erected formal and informal barriers, while the second opened pathways. Neither school stressed narrow legal political equality as enshrined in liberal, procedural, representative democracy, associated with the U.S. founding fathers, particularly Thomas Jefferson. Proponents of this classic liberal democracy wedged between the two opposites, but came closer to the protected model.

The distinction between protected and popular democracies referred both to the institutional rules and, above all, the social content of oligarchic republics, restricted democracies, and full democracies. Given the escalating legal inclusiveness of these three institutional types, protected democracies appeared in all three, but popular democracies only arose in restricted and, most commonly, full democratic regimes. Both the rules and, more directly, the distribution and deployment of socioeconomic power determined whether those restricted and full democracies gravitated toward the protected or popular formulation. Through extralegal economic, social, ideological, and military leverage, the rich and well-born usually shaped how the institutions were used.

Given the privileges of the dominant classes, a preference for protected democracy prevailed most of the time. This priority for elitist order became a recurrent anthem on the right, from Venezuelan Simon Bolívar in the 1820s, to Chilean Diego Portales in the 1830s, to Argentines Juan Bautista Alberdi and Domingo Faustino Sarmiento in the 1850s, to Uruguayan José Enrique Rodó in the 1900s, to Chilean Augusto Pinochet and his plans in the 1980s for a democracy constrained by authoritarian features. By contrast, popular democracy became a lasting refrain on the left from Mexican Miguel Hidalgo in the 1810s, to the Mexican revolutionaries in the 1910s, to Peruvian Victor Raul Haya de la Torre in the 1930s, to the Guatemalan revolutionaries and Argentine Juan Peron and Venezuelan Romulo Betancourt in the 1940s, to the National Revolutionary Movement in Bolivia in the 1950s, to Cuban Fidel Castro in the 1960s, to Chilean Salvador Allende and the Nicaraguan Sandinistas in the 1970s, to Peruvian Alan Garcia in the 1980s, to Venezuelan Hugo Chávez and Bolivian Evo Morales and Ecuadorean Rafael Correa in the 2000s. They placed a greater emphasis on mass mobilization dedicated to social equality.[33]

Either variety could become paternalistic or even authoritarian. The rightist version sometimes led to limited, oligarchic, elitist democracies to keep the masses in check (e.g., Portales in Chile), or it frequently became more reactionary in conservative dictatorships to repress the working classes (e.g., Pinochet in Chile). The leftist brand often produced populist, mass, or social democracies to incorporate the poor (e.g., Betancourt in Venezuela and Allende in Chile), or, in rare cases, it became more radical in popular dictatorships to repress the elites (e.g., the revolutionaries in Mexico and Cuba).

Both poles became more extreme by the 1960s and 1970s, as the lower classes escalated their demands for direct representation and benefits. This polarization generated rightwing protected (e.g., Pinochet) and, much less commonly, leftwing popular (e.g., Castro) autocracies. Then the right and the left settled into an uneasy truce or stalemate from the 1980s to the 2000s. The tsunami resulted in contradictory protected democracies that enveloped all social strata but discouraged populism, mass mobilization, and social reform.

Under the popular category, the leaders usually forged direct, personal, unmediated bonds with the working classes, transcending the representative institutions hallowed in liberal democracy. Although most of them channeled those popular mobilizations into democratic institutions, a few funneled them into authoritarian systems. Revolutionaries like those in Mexico and Cuba sometimes rallied popular support in the name of democracy and then converted it into a base for autocratic rule. Some populists, like Getulio Vargas in Brazil and Juan Peron in Argentina, operated in both democratic and authoritarian modes. This ambivalence indicated their greater interest in mass incorporation than in procedural democracy per se:

> in Latin America the democratic ethos has been much closer to the egalitarian, communitarian, integrative ideal than to the libertarian, individualistic one. Democratization has been understood in the collective historical memory more as a process of incorporating and constituting a collectivity—that is, more as social democratization or 'fundamental democratization'—than as the building of government institutions or political democratization. The idea of democracy is associated more with the constitution of collective identities, the reduction of inequalities, and social integration and cohesion, than with the liberal ethos and electoral returns.[34]

This polarization between protected and popular views of democracy resembled the duel between *elite* and *folk* cultures described by historian E. Bradford Burns. He saw the latter as a demand for autonomous social equality. He found it erupting during the independence period mainly in the Haitian (e.g., Toussaint L'Ouverture) and Mexican insurrections (e.g., Miguel Hidalgo and Jose Maria Morelos), in the nineteenth century behind certain charismatic and dictatorial "populist caudillos" (e.g., Jose Gaspar Rodriguez de Francia in Paraguay and Juan Manuel de Rosas in

Argentina) who identified with the common people, and in the twentieth century revolutions in Mexico, Guatemala, Bolivia, Cuba, and Nicaragua. Many of the movements praised by Burns, however, did not commit to representative democracy. Nevertheless, in the twentieth century social revolutions, many of their supporters championed the cause of electoral democracy, and all the revolutions promised democratic government when fighting for power.[35]

Historian Arthur P. Whitaker made a comparable distinction between *conservative democracy* and *radical democracy*. In the years during and after the wars of independence, the radicals wanted to include the impoverished majority immediately through bullets and ballots, while the conservatives preferred republics guided by a small elite until the common people became civilized enough for self-government. The elitists claimed to be carrying on the anti-Jacobin legacy of Bolívar. As the nineteenth century progressed, they came to dominate, rejecting the liberal idealism spawned in Europe and the United States and imbibed by some Latin Americans in the late-eighteenth and early-nineteenth centuries. The rightwingers advocated protected democracy to adapt Western political thought to Latin American realities.

As the debate wore on, the two camps added economic issues to their dispute. In the latter decades of the nineteenth century, Whitaker's conservatives came to propose stern rule by a privileged elite in the political sphere, combined with free enterprise in the economic arena, very similar to the position of authoritarian capitalists in the twentieth century. The late nineteenth century conservatives—some known as *Positivists*—claimed that material growth under very open economic democracy but very exclusionary political democracy would eventually raise the lower social orders up to a level of culture and education adequate for political participation.

By the early decades of the twentieth century, however, Whitaker's radicals pointed out that the protected oligarchic model increased the gap between rich and poor, alienated the vast majority, and perpetuated itself. Therefore they called for wide open political democracy and for state intervention to promote socioeconomic equality. They shifted the emphasis from political to socioeconomic democracy, a position that came to be identified with leftists, populists, and popular democracy.[36]

By the 1960s and the 1970s, some advocates of the radical version moved farther left to proclaim socialist revolution. Meanwhile some proponents of the conservative variety shifted farther right to support reactionary authoritarian and free-market regimes. The heyday of popular democracies ended on September 11, 1973, with the overthrow of President Allende in Chile, who went farther than any other democratic leader to promote socialism.

Then throughout most of Latin America, the rightwing authoritarians imposed dictatorships to demolish popular democracy and pave the way to a return of protected democracy.

After the restoration of democracy from the late 1970s to the 2000s, the iconic liberal, representative model of the United States and Western Europe attracted more adherents than ever before. Many Latin Americans saw that system as a way to avoid rightist or leftist extremes. Most governments cleaved to a procedural, institutional, formal version of democracy, designed to downplay mass activation and socioeconomic redistribution. As in the past, progressives complained that the rebirth of a version of protected democracy once again left the poor behind. In reaction, popular democracy reemerged behind such figures as Hugo Chávez and Evo Morales, though less radical than some of their predecessors in the 1960s and 1970s.[37]

Conclusion

From the 1800s to the 2000s, many Latin Americans struggled to construct democracies or at least republics in an inauspicious environment of authoritarianism, poverty, and inequality. Although encountering many more defeats than victories, they slowly gained ground against daunting odds. Their original intellectual and institutional efforts set the region on a course it has followed ever since. The founders cast an indelible dye.

The leaders grappled with how to build democracies that could withstand both tyranny and anarchy. They faced their biggest challenge in how to achieve both order and liberty in societies divided by extreme inequities based on class, ethnic, and racial prejudices. They responded to this dilemma by favoring protected or popular democracies. Over two centuries, those two visions clashed in regimes that evolved from oligarchic republics to restricted democracies to full democracies. In the process, some of Latin America's more advanced democracies caught up with the vanguard in the United States and Europe.

To explain the Latin Americans' frequent failures and infrequent successes—especially in a particular country—requires a combination of structural and contingent analyses. The first approach establishes the limits on and probabilities of democracy under certain international and domestic socioeconomic conditions. The second examines historical circumstances, ideas, institutions, actors, and actions. However, the long view shows that underlying conditions still had historical and continuing relevance.[38]

From these dual perspectives, Latin American democracy has been most likely to succeed in a favorable international climate, in the more developed countries, with larger middle and working classes and more homogeneous populations. From an historical perspective, democracies have had better prospects with a weaker imperial legacy from both the indigenous and Spanish conquerors, with a period of oligarchic republicanism preceding mass politics, and with a longer track record of democratic practice and learning. Under those benevolent circumstances, the agency of socially powerful elites and other relevant national actors has had a relatively better chance of installing, preserving, and enhancing democracy, especially the protected variety.

Their triumphs usually depended on a propitious confluence of international and domestic structural underpinnings, historical legacies and events, elite consensus and calculations, and political engineering. In this context, the choices among alternative blueprints for democratic institutions could contribute significantly to success or failure. The next chapter traces the historical evolution of those institutions.

Chapter 2

The Historical Evolution of Latin American Democratic Institutions, 1800–2006

From independence to the present, Latin American political institutions made a substantial difference for the development of democracy. Even in the often rough and tumble nineteenth century, constitutions represented more than just façades for arbitrary dictators. Legal rules and advances sometimes became more important than they may have seemed at the moment of their enactment. As time wore on, laws that were not always obeyed eventually accumulated legitimacy.

Whether fully operable or not, institutions and their laws established standards, boundaries, customs, and aspirations. Democrats could appeal to them and use their breakage to accuse an abusive regime of illegitimacy. They also could build upon those foundations in subsequent democratic periods. Under the best of circumstances, the institutional architecture could also convince all the major political forces to lay down their arms because the legal system would guarantee "fair and effective" competition within acceptable limits.[1]

This chapter addresses the following questions. Where did these institutions come from? How did they function? How did they endure and evolve over time? And most importantly, how did they help or hinder democracy?

Although the region's democratic institutions have been very unstable, their basic features have persisted for two hundred years. Some of their foundational characteristics made Latin American democracy more difficult, while others adjusted foreign models to local conditions. External analysts have long criticized these institutions for exhibiting excessive constitutional frailty, presidentialism, centralism, anemic legislatures and judiciaries, unfair elections, and disorganized political parties. Institutional defects can explain some important initial and continuing shortcomings of Latin American democracies. However, since the essential outlines of most of those institutions have changed little among decades or countries, it is unclear how they would account for significant variations in behavior.

One key question is under what conditions can alternative institutional arrangements make a difference? Perhaps under propitious international, socioeconomic, and historical circumstances, the proper institutions have the best chance of improving the likelihood (and especially the operation) of democracy. International factors are relevant, because they give the more promising cases a better chance of succeeding in a particular context and time period. Getting the institutions right might have a bigger impact in a relatively developed country like Chile more than in an impoverished one like Haiti. They might also make a larger contribution in a country with a long tradition of constitutional democratic experience like Chile as opposed to a perennially authoritarian setting like Haiti. In addition, institutions do more to explain the quality of a democracy than its mere existence.

Unfortunately, there is not enough evidence about the impact of various types of political institutions—constitutions, presidents, legislatures, judiciaries, elections, and political parties—to establish which designs will facilitate democracies in particular countries. Scholars have not reached sufficient conclusive consensus on the best institutions or their optimal features. Moreover, debates continue about tradeoffs and appropriate combinations among institutions. At least in Latin America, however, the balance of conventional wisdom and the historical record suggests that the following tentative and simplified dichotomy might distinguish some institutional traits that have been more or less likely to contribute to open, representative, accountable, and stable democratic operations.[2]

Table 2.1 shows dichotomous alternatives for democratic institutions. Many of the classifications of characteristics in this table are questionable, such as federalism versus centralism. It is hard to generalize, and the best choices vary by country. This table omits more controversial criteria, such as whether elections should be voluntary or obligatory and with open or closed lists, and whether political parties should be two or more in number, personalistic or programmatic, and ideological or catch-all. At the very least, the table serves as a guide to the alternative institutional designs discussed and attempted in Latin America. Despite ample room for disagreement, most observers of Latin American democratic institutions have made

TABLE 2.1
Dichotomous alternatives for democratic institutions

	More conducive to democracy in Latin America	Less conducive to democracy in Latin America
Constitutions		
Origins	Assembly, congress, or plebiscite	Decree
Durability	Long	Short
Civil liberties	Strong	Weak
Socioeconomic rights	Strong	Weak
Organization	Federalist	Centralist
Local government	Elected and strong	Appointed and weak
Presidents		
Election	Direct	Indirect
	Majority	Plurality
Reelection	No	Yes
Eligibility	Broad	Narrow
Powers	Narrow	Broad
Decrees	Rare	Frequent
Regimes of exception	Difficult and rare	Easy and frequent
Cabinet accountability	Congress	President
Control of military	Strong	Weak
Legislatures		
Election	Direct	Indirect
Reelection	Yes	No
Apportionment	Proportional	Disproportional
Eligibility	Broad	Narrow
Powers	Broad	Narrow
Organization	Strong	Weak
	Bicameral	Unicameral
Judiciaries		
Appointment	Mixed	President
Independence	Strong	Weak
Powers	Strong	Weak
Judicial review	Strong	Weak
Defense of constitutional democracy	Strong	Weak
Defense of individual, social, and human rights	Strong	Weak
Organization	Strong	Weak
Accessibility	Broad	Narrow
Elections		
Suffrage	Broad	Narrow
Scheduling	Regular	Irregular
	Concurrent	Staggered
Procedures	Free, fair, honest, and respected	Unfree, unfair, dishonest, and disrespected
Voting	Secret	Public
Plebiscites/referenda	Yes	No
Parties		
Types	Unrestricted	Restricted
Number	Two or more	One or none
Organization	Strong	Weak
	Democratic	Authoritarian
Finances	Public	Private
Primaries	Yes	No
Durability	Long	Short

judgments similar to those in the table. Most of the institutions have historically exhibited most of the traits in the right-hand column. Most reformers
have tried to move these institutions from the right to the left column, and
over time Latin America has made progress in that direction.[3]

This book will show how these institutional issues have been debated
and evolved in the region. Many institutional facets have remained fairly
frozen over the centuries, especially for presidents, legislatures, judiciaries,
and political parties. Other aspects have become significantly more democratic, above all elections. Constitutions still display many of their early attributes, but they have been adopted more in public forums, extended their
lifetime, and added more individual and socioeconomic rights. The organization of government has remained overwhelming centralist, but a few
gains have been made by provinces and municipalities.

Presidents have remained overpowering, but their elections have switched
from indirect to direct and from plurality to majority. Their eligibility requirements have been reduced. The ancient ban on reelection became enshrined, until some relaxation in recent years. In that same time period,
presidential control over the military finally increased.

Legislatures have continued to be weak, despite some recent improvements. They are still malapportioned. Nevertheless, the representatives have
become directly elected, with few eligibility requirements.

Among government institutions, the judiciaries have experienced
the least changes toward strengthening democracy. They have remained
dependent on the other branches of government, although presidential
domination of their appointments has declined. Largely inaccessible to
the majority of the population, they are still ineffectual defenders of individual, social, and human rights. Most importantly, the courts have yet to
become vital reviewers of constitutionality or bulwarks of constitutional
democracy.

In many ways the essence of democracy, elections have made the greatest
strides of all political institutions. Electoral advancements provide the key
reason Latin America has become more democratic. Although some political parties and party systems have matured, they have remained deficient in
many regards.

REVOLVING CONSTITUTIONS

Running from least to most democratic methods, Latin Americans employed three main procedures for giving birth to constitutions: presidential
imposition by decree, congressional drafting, or preparation by an elected
constitutional assembly. Sometimes plebiscites confirmed these creations.

Countries frequently adopted these charters in the aftermath of an extra-constitutional overthrow of the previous government.[4]

Especially in the nineteenth century (but continuing in the twentieth), the president simply announced most constitutions. Because these constitutions were typically crafted by a tiny elite, they were usually lofty, idealized, theoretical, juridical documents removed from the practical politics of everyday life. They were seldom designed by clashing, compromising interest groups in a convention representing national realities and conflicts. Increasingly in the twentieth century, such inclusive wheeling and dealing began to shape constitutions, most famously in Mexico after the 1910 revolution. Those more democratic procedures produced constitutions more closely reflecting the real diversity of competing groups. Consequently, those texts emphasized socioeconomic rights, consonant with visions of popular democracy.[5]

The most astonishing feature of Latin American constitutions was their number. From independence to 2006, the twenty Latin American countries adopted over two hundred fifty constitutions, an average of over twelve per country. The Dominican Republic, Venezuela, and Haiti led with well over twenty each, with Ecuador and Bolivia close behind at nineteen and fifteen. Over two centuries, the region adopted an average of over one constitution per year. The highest volatility occurred during the post-independence years from 1827 through 1879, and the lowest occurred during the tsunami from 1977 to 2006. To some extent, more constitutional instability prevailed because massive amendments sometimes significantly transformed the documents.

From another perspective, a much lower rate of turnover took place in the major countries after the middle decades of the nineteenth century. Latin America adopted a disproportionate number of its constitutions in the chaotic and authoritarian years from the beginning of independence through the 1870s. From the start through the twentieth century, the poorer countries with the least democratic success concocted many of these documents. Dictators found it easier than democrats to proclaim new constitutions. Many constitutions were very short lived or never really implemented. Furthermore, most constitutions actually differed little from each other, even from their predecessors. Although constitutions came and went rapidly, the basic institutions of governments changed little, including centralism, separation of powers, presidentialism, weak legislatures and judiciaries, elections, and other virtually immutable features.[6]

Despite the large number of constitutions, many lasted for decades. Notably in the more developed countries with more successful democratic experiences, several constitutional regimes proved far more durable than some of their counterparts in Europe. The more stable cases included, chrono-logically, Brazil from 1824 to 1891 (albeit a constitutional monarchy); Uruguay from 1830 to 1918; Chile from 1833 to 1925 (despite a brief civil war in 1891), and from 1932 to 1973; Argentina from 1853 to 1949 (and the 1853 constitution was soon restored and lasted ever thereafter); Mexico from 1857 to 1917, and then its successor from 1917 onward; Peru from 1867 to 1920; Paraguay from 1870 to 1940; Costa Rica from 1871 to 1917, and then from 1949 to the present; Guatemala from 1879 to 1945; Bolivia from 1880 to 1938; El Salvador from 1886 to 1939; and Colombia from 1886 to 1991.[7]

Historically, the more successful democratic countries tended to adopt fewer constitutions, including Argentina, Uruguay, Chile, and Costa Rica. The traditionally more authoritarian countries usually wrote many more constitutions, including Honduras, El Salvador, Nicaragua, Bolivia, Ecuador, Haiti, Venezuela, and the Dominican Republic. However, exceptions cropped up to these general patterns.

Some normally authoritarian countries installed a small number of constitutions. Panama and Cuba produced only a handful because they did not get started until the twentieth century. Paraguay, Mexico, and Guatemala needed few constitutions to underwrite long-term authoritarian regimes. By contrast, Colombia and, to a lesser extent Peru, experienced relative success with democracy along with fairly numerous constitutions, but they approved the vast majority of those documents from independence through the post–independence decades.[8]

Why did the Latin Americans compose so many constitutions, especially when the content often changed little? They mainly did so to legitimize new governments in the absence of widespread loyalty to the political system, particularly when the newcomers had taken power through extralegal means. The announcement of a new constitution disparaged the previous ruler and anointed the new one. The turnover in constitutions reflected the instability of governments and regimes. Rather than being the bedrock of government as in the United States, constitutions served the purpose of allowing new political forces and rulers to christen and express themselves. Although an enduring constitution provided more stability, it was not necessarily a more democratic instrument.

Constitutions also proliferated because the authors often made them difficult to amend. This tied the hands of their successors, who therefore replaced the document. Most Latin American judiciaries did not have the power of their United States brethren to interpret the constitution or declare government actions unconstitutional, which allowed the United States

TABLE 2.2
Latin American constitutions, 1800–2006

Country	1800–1826	1827–1879	1880–1929	1930–1976	1977–2006	Total
Panama	0	0	1	2	1	4
Argentina	3	1	0	1	0	5
Paraguay	1	2	0	2	1	6
Uruguay	0	1	1	4	1	7
Cuba	0	0	2	4	1	7
Brazil	1	0	1	4	1	7
Mexico	2	5	1	0	0	8
Chile	5	2	1	0	1	9
Costa Rica	1	6	1	1	0	9
Guatemala	1	3	0	3	2	9
Peru	2	7	1	1	1	12
Colombia	2	8	1	0	1	12
Honduras	1	4	5	3	1	14
El Salvador	1	5	3	4	1	14
Nicaragua	2	2	4	4	2	14
Bolivia	1	9	1	4	0	15
Ecuador	0	10	4	4	1	19
Haiti	6	6	3	8	1	24
Venezuela	3	5	10	6	1	25
Dominican Republic	0	14	10	7	0	31
Total	32	90	50	62	17	251
Average per country	1.9	5.0	2.5	3.1	0.9	12.6
Average per year	1.3	1.7	1.0	1.3	0.6	1.2

NOTE: This table shows the number of constitutions by era, ranked by countries from least to most total. For the years of adoption of each constitution, see Rosenn, "The Success," from which this table is adapted.

charter to evolve without massive amendments or replacements. United States invaders added some constitutions by imposition in the Caribbean and Central America, particularly from the 1890s to the 1930s. Over time, Latin Americans also issued new constitutions to take into account local political, social, and economic changes (such as the rise of the labor movement) and international advances (such as human rights). For example, they recognized the power of the caudillos and the oligarchy in the nineteenth century, and of new social actors and political parties in the twentieth.[9]

From independence onward, Latin Americans borrowed many constitutional provisions from their neighbors and from overseas, especially the United States, France, and Spain. U.S. influence declined slightly in the twentieth century, when socioeconomic rights came to the fore. Although many of these importations fit poorly with national realities and so were dysfunctional or inoperable, others were valuable and were adapted to local conditions. The Latin Americans did not just photocopy institutions from elsewhere. Even institutions grafted from external models, such as the U.S. presidency and legislature, were altered to function differently in the region.

Lawmakers modified foreign liberal principles to take into account their authoritarian traditions from the colonial period and their national conditions. They added such features as extreme centralism, exceptionally powerful presidents, and states of siege. These combinations of foreign and domestic designs set up a tension between liberalism and authoritarianism that continued to the present day. However, the Latin Americans also introduced distinctive democratic innovations, including *amparo* (the judicial protection of individual liberties, similar to habeas corpus) and social rights.[10]

From the beginning in the first half of the nineteenth century, the more conservative constitutions emphasized protection of elites. The more radical variety stressed majoritarian participation of the popular classes. Both differed somewhat from liberal constitutions dedicated to individual rights and limitations on government authority, closer to the United States' template. In practice, the Latin Americans blended these protected and popular ideal types in their charters but tended to tilt toward one conceptualization or the other.

In the nineteenth century and thereafter, the predominant protected democracies normally drew fairly tight limits on who could participate, who could govern, and how they could govern. These constitutions placed greater faith in centralism, awe-inspiring presidents with wide latitude to override civil liberties and to impose states of exception, frail legislatures dominated by aristocratic senates, an aloof judiciary, a praetorian military charged with upholding the constitution and national stability, and indirect and restricted elections. Prime examples included the early Andean constitutions influenced by the thinking of Bolívar and the Chilean constitution of 1833. More importantly, many of the bulwarks for the well-to-do and well-armed were informal rules, for example later banning extreme populists or leftists from office and forbidding policies such as the significant redistribution of property, income, or wealth.

The rarer radical blueprints favored republicanism, federalism, and limitations on the president as well as the judiciary and the armed forces. These plans also envisioned a more assertive house of representatives, usually buttressed by direct elections with wider participation. Jose Maria Morelos' proposed constitution of 1814 for Mexico approximated this approach. The early nineteenth century radicals also sometimes advocated social change, notably abolition of slavery and even implementation of land reform. Their sentiments gained greater currency during the upsurge of popular democracy from the 1930s to the 1970s.

Finally, the also marginal liberal constitutionalists argued that their intermediate alternative was more likely to avert both tyranny and anarchy. They opposed domination by either an unfettered president or majority. They preferred a limited state, checks and balances among the branches of government, judicial review, and strong civil liberties and individual rights such as religious freedom. Their vision did not carry much weight until the neoliberal democratic tsunami from the 1970s to the 2000s.[11]

From the nineteenth to the twentieth centuries, the constitutions and other political institutions reflected these opposing concepts. However, the two camps diverged less on institutional designs and more on how those institutions were used. The allocation and exercise of social power primarily determined whether those institutions served protected or popular purposes.

Especially during most of the nineteenth century, frequent variations in constitutions had only a marginal impact on the way government actually operated. Although laws were not totally irrelevant, they often did not cause authoritarian executive dominance, intrusions on civil liberties, military insubordination, weak congresses and courts, fraudulent elections, or other nagging political realities. Time and again, Latin Americans overturned and disobeyed their constitutions for many reasons.

The colonial era bequeathed a history of authoritarianism and inexperience with constitutional representative self-government. It also left a heritage of government offices viewed as private sinecures rather than public services, inconsistent and ambiguous legislation, weakness of the rule of law (especially in outlying areas), and endemic corruption.

The wars of independence unleashed a crisis of regimes with dubious legitimacy, predatory militarism and caudillism, and regional disputes. Not reflecting the real social distribution of power, the new institutions also contained flaws. Leaders found the excessively idealistic and detailed constitutions hard to implement, especially such foreign provisions as independent legislatures and judiciaries. Moreover, few effective protections existed for civil liberties. As seen in former colonies elsewhere in the world struggling for democratization in the twentieth century, Latin America's difficulties carrying out liberal constitutions were scarcely surprising.[12]

To understand the paradox of Latin Americans writing so many constitutions but heeding so few of them, it is helpful to make a distinction between the *nominal* and the *real* constitution. The nominal constitution was the full written version, whereas the real constitution was the written and unwritten provisions that were truly in operation—such as the written powers of the president to govern and the unwritten power of the military to overthrow illegitimate and incompetent governments. Most of the nominal constitution was also real, and increasingly so over time. A gap between law and practice was huge but not unique to Latin Americans, who nevertheless remained highly legalistic and quick to appeal to the authority of the constitution and other legal codes.[13]

Although constitutions were not faithfully followed, they were not dead letters, either. They pleased intellectuals and foreigners, protected the interests of the ruling elites, embodied genuine ideals and goals, sanctified governments, provided guidelines for governance much of the time, admonished illegal actions by government opponents (such as conspiring with the armed forces to overthrow the administration), and set limits on political behavior beyond which many leaders were reluctant to go. Even when frequently violated, constitutions established norms that became widely and increasingly embraced. They provided a recipe for government between caudillos. They were important enough that civil wars raged over their more controversial provisions, such as relations between the capital and the provinces or the state and the Church.

Even most dictators felt required to rationalize why they had temporarily suspended the constitution, to promise to restore or replace it as soon as possible, to pay it lip-service, and to honor some of its provisions. Authoritarians found it convenient to at least genuflect before the constitution and democracy to please both domestic and foreign audiences. Furthermore, some presidents were wary of breaking the constitution too brazenly. Excessive illegality could give their opponents an excuse to call for constitutional promises to be kept or for rebellion or military intervention to defend the constitution.

Even if often honored in the breach, these constitutions need to be taken into account. They embodied political thought and aspirations, revealed problems their authors were trying to solve, and gained traction over time. Moreover, even the earliest and ephemeral constitutions established founding principles and issues that continued into the 2000s.[14]

CENTRALISM OVER DECENTRALISM

One of the most disputed sections of any Latin American constitution, especially in the nineteenth century, was the issue of centralism versus federalism. This debate reflected the battles pitting the capital city against the provinces. Many theorists have argued that decentralized nodes of power—be they states, municipalities, interest groups, private property holders, or voluntary associations—provided a cornerstone of democracy. They deterred the power of the central government. However, most Latin American leaders opted for intense centralization, usually derived from the French system. In their view, they needed a domineering national government to hold together and govern the unruly new republics. They preferred to err on the side of tyranny rather than anarchy.[15]

Even in the few federal systems in Latin America, the central government remained far stronger than in the progenitor United States, both in the constitution and in reality. "Centrifugal federalism" in the United States and Canada differed from "centripetal federalism" in Argentina, Mexico, and other parts of Latin America. The former two countries devolved significant powers to the states, whereas the latter gave them some concessions to bind them to the overpowering central government. In other words, the Latin American cases constituted "centralized federalism."[16]

Compared to U.S. federalism, the Latin American variety gave the central government greater constitutional say over civil, penal, procedural, commercial, labor, education, and other laws. It possessed exceptional legal powers to intervene in provincial governments, usually to preserve order, republicanism, or sovereignty, all vaguely defined to favor officials and policies preferred by the national rulers. For example in Argentina, the central authority intervened to change provincial governments 20 times from 1853 to 1860, 101 times from 1860 to 1930, and 145 times from 1930 to 1943, after which President Juan Peron intensified the practice.

For most of their existence, four Latin American governments claimed to be federalist: Brazil, Argentina, Mexico, and Venezuela. Federalism only functioned to a small extent in the first two, less so in the second two. Mainly in the decade following independence, many other countries experimented with federalism or at least some form of decentralization, but seldom for long and never with any great success.[17]

Especially in the centralized systems but also in the federal ones, provincial and municipal governments remained anemic. Typically, beneath the central government were provinces ruled by governors, normally without state legislatures, and municipal councils and mayors, more comparable to county than city officials in the United States. None of these positions included much power or purse, with the partial exception of Brazil. Central governments controlled most taxes, even when they passed some revenues down to the states. Particularly in the unitary republics, local institutions were usually seen, as in the colonial period, as branches of the central government rather than as representatives of outlying constituencies. Central appointment of all provincial bodies became the rule, except in a handful of cases. Indeed, many of these posts were simply patronage plums at the whim of the president.[18]

Following independence, municipal government evolved into two organs, one a council (usually elected), and one an executive (usually appointed). Over time, most municipal governments became elected institutions, increasingly by proportional representation. In contrast with the United States and Europe, local suffrage rights were often extended to resident foreigners. Lying at the bottom of a very centralized national hierarchy of public offices, municipal authorities usually enjoyed few resources or powers. They only began to benefit from serious decentralization in the 1980s and 1990s.[19]

PRESIDENTIAL POTENTATES

In Spanish America, hyper-presidentialism derived from the legacy of indigenous emperors, colonial royal absolutism, governing attempts during the independence years, and reactions to the tumult of the post-independence years. The crown's personalization of executive power took on new form with the military leaders during and after the wars of independence. In the constitutions and even more in actuality, the presidents assumed awesome powers over all other political institutions. In the nineteenth century, strongmen experienced the greatest success stabilizing the new political systems over regional and local bosses.

From the beginning, Latin American constitutions endowed the presidency with more authority than its U.S. model. At the same time, the drafters tried to strike a balance between giving the executive enough power to be dynamic and enough restrictions to be democratic. Constitutions varied between two models or mixed them. Most emphasized order by leaning toward majestic executives with long terms in office, ample control of appointments, extensive powers, vague extraordinary faculties, and acquiescent provinces, legislatures and judiciaries. A minority preferred democratic controls by gravitating toward constrained executives with short terms and no reelection, some congressional control over the cabinet, narrow and precise powers and extraordinary faculties, and countervailing governors, legislatures and judiciaries.[20]

Constitutions also required presidents to have higher qualifications than legislators. These stipulations usually included native citizenship, advanced age, and some economic and educational achievements. The criteria took the male gender for granted. Sometimes they excluded certain occupations, such as the clergy.

In most cases, constitutions also specified the form of presidential election. Although countries frequently employed indirect methods in the early decades, they increasingly opted for direct popular election. Direct election provided voters with a clearly identifiable leader to represent them and to be accountable for government performance. It gave that office the aura of speaking for the sovereign people over other institutions. One of the few exceptions was the indirect system in Argentina, incorporated from the United States by the 1853 constitution and eliminated in 1974 in favor of the direct election of the candidate with an absolute majority.

Historically, Latin American presidents won office as first-past-the-post, whether with an absolute or a relative majority. In the twentieth century, the plurality system for electing the president favored catch-all parties or personalism to gather up as many votes as possible. This propensity offset the tendency for proportional representation to promote myriad parties in congressional contests. During the democratic tsunami from the 1970s to the 2000s, many countries instituted presidential runoffs for the top two vote-getters to try to assure a majority president and reduce the problem of party fragmentation and multiple candidates. After numerous contenders clashed in the first round, those runoffs favored coalitions around centrist candidates.

Powerful from the days of independence onward, presidents grew more domineering over time, both formally and informally. Constitutions gave them elaborate authority, and customs gave them even more—authority which often exceeded legal rights. Presidents generally exercised nearly un-inhibited appointment powers, since most countries lacked effective civil service regulations. In highly centralized governments, presidents even named provincial governors and municipal officials. In contrast with the United States' system, presidents in Latin America did not have to obtain congressional approval for their cabinet officers, although some constitutions allowed the legislators to interrogate, chastise, and even oust cabinet ministers, as well as vote on nominees for lesser offices.

Presidents encroached on the other branches of government. They subjugated the congress with their right to initiate, accelerate, execute, and totally or partially veto legislation. They particularly dominated the budget. In addition, they thoroughly controlled foreign affairs and most military matters. In the twentieth century, presidents accumulated extensive social and economic responsibilities. Furthermore, they weighed heavily on the court system through appointments and intimidation. At the same time, they presided over a highly centralized state, with few provincial or municipal checks on their actions.[21]

Presidents also called on extraordinary powers to rule by decree and even transgress civil liberties. Virtually all constitutions contained clauses allowing them to suspend some of the constitutional rights of the citizenry during emergencies. Presidents widely abused these regimes of exception as juridical figleafs for authoritarian rule. Time and again, they invoked these powers and sidestepped any restrictions. For example, they circumvented legislative approval by acting when the congress was in recess and extended the time limits on a period of exceptionalism by declaring new periods in succession.[22]

To counter the presidents' daunting powers and their penchant for dictatorial behavior, lawmakers enacted constraints. These included limits on the length and number of presidential terms (the latter appearing by the 1820s) long before in the United States. Constitutions usually outlawed either immediate reelection or any reelection in attempts to prevent *continuismo*.

No reelection allowed presidents to govern in a headstrong manner for a short period of time, because they did not feel compelled to continue to please the voters. However, their mandate could also evaporate quickly as they became lame ducks—even within their own party—partway through their term. Largely because of these drawbacks and pressures from popular presidents, a few countries relaxed this prohibition in the 1990s.[23]

Lawmakers also sought to tie the hands of presidents by spelling out civil liberties. Following the examples of France and the United States, constitutions guaranteed civil rights, including freedom of speech, assembly, press, and eventually religion. Although often trampled, these guarantees became more secure from the nineteenth to the twentieth centuries.[24]

Other attempts to erect limits on presidentialism included buttressing the legislature. Politicians tried establishing congressional influence over cabinet ministers through interrogation, censure, and impeachment, requiring congressional approval for more government appointments, mandating congressional permission for the president to leave the country during or immediately after the term in office, and forming congressional oversight committees to monitor the executive branch when the legislature was not in session. Other typically futile devices encompassed ruling that the cabinet had to concur with and sign off on presidential decisions, empowering the judicial and provincial branches, creating comptroller generals, and installing merit systems in the civil service. Most constitutions also provided for accusations and trials of presidents, following the U.S. provisions for impeachment. However, legislators found these procedures very difficult to carry out and rarely used them until the tsunami.

More drastic measures included unsuccessful adoptions of a plural executive by the Venezuelans in 1811, the Peruvians in 1823, and the Uruguayans in 1952. A couple of partial and unsatisfactory experiments with quasi-parliamentary regimes making congress the superior branch took place in

Brazil (to a small extent during 1839 to 1889 and briefly during 1961 to 1963) and Chile (1891 to 1924). But no deterrent to presidential excesses proved as effective as a coup d'état or the threat of one.[25]

Although presidents intimidated the other agencies of government, they exhibited less ability to implement policies and shape the nation. The state itself, despite expansion from the 1930s to the 1970s, was always quite limited in its capacity to penetrate and control the territory and society. In contrast with their United States counterpart, many Latin American presidents were more superior over other political institutions but less dominant over the nation in carrying out programs.[26]

LEGISLATIVE LILLIPUTIANS

Throughout most decades and countries, Latin Americans hosted legislative Lilliputians compared to the U.S. Leviathan.[27] This difference persisted even though they always followed the U.S. model of a separation of powers between the president and the congress. Their constitutions typically gave the legislatures duties and powers comparable to but less than their U.S. template. Those charters thoroughly spelled out the legislators' responsibilities and capabilities so as to clarify which functions did not belong to the executive or judicial branches. They did so because there had been no such assembly in the colonial period. Given that lack of experience, the congress always had difficulty defining and playing its role.[28]

The constitutions normally created bicameral congresses with a senate and house patterned after the United States. However, some unitary governments in small countries established unicameral systems, including Guatemala, El Salvador, Honduras, Costa Rica, Panama, Haiti, and Paraguay. Under Hugo Chávez, Venezuela also switched to unicameralism. Rulers usually installed that system to save money and personnel, as well as, in some instances, to make it easier for overbearing presidents to control a shrunken legislature.

As with other democratic institutions, establishing a vibrant tradition helped lay the foundation for future success. This was a much more challenging task for legislatures than for executives. Although congresses began operating in nearly all countries from independence onward, they seldom convened regularly in the early nineteenth century—with the main exceptions of Brazil from 1826 to 1889, and Chile from 1831 to 1924. In the latter half of the nineteenth century, they functioned with increasing regularity; for example in Uruguay from 1860 to 1973, Peru from 1860 to 1920, Argentina from 1861 to 1929, Costa Rica beginning in 1871, Colombia starting in 1876, Guatemala from 1876 to 1944, Bolivia from 1890 to 1938, and Brazil from 1891 to 1930. Since even ongoing congresses usually met for only brief periods each year, many of them appointed "permanent committees" composed of members from both chambers to keep an eye on the executive branch between sessions. They worried in particular about presidents imposing a state of exception.

Most constitutions required legislators to be natural-born citizens with a minimal period of residence in the country prior to their election, although not always in the district they represented. In most bicameral systems, the senators had to be older than the deputies, though both could usually be younger than their U.S. counterparts. The laws usually excluded from the legislature government officials and their close relatives and contractors, clergy, the armed forces, and convicts.

Senators were usually chosen by region, deputies by population within a region. In a couple of cases, senators were picked by other entities such as the provincial legislature, but deputies were almost always selected by popular vote, increasingly by proportional representation. A few constitutions provided for corporatist representation of functional interest groups in the legislature or other government agencies.[29]

Most constitutions did not intend for the congress to be as feckless or passive, obstreperous or obsequious, as it usually became. Following large parts of the U.S. model, they normally granted the legislators some authority over writing constitutions and their amendments, making laws, regulating provincial and municipal governments, monitoring travel and misconduct by the president, interrogating ministers, imposing states of exception, appointing high-level judges, ambassadors, ecclesiastical officials, and military officers, and overseeing electoral rules and disputes. On paper, the legislatures also took some responsibility for government procedures, fiscal affairs, commerce, regulatory codes, the armed forces, treaties, and declarations of war.

Contrary to their constitutional mandate, legislators rarely made laws. Instead they usually responded to the executive branch as either obedient lackeys or destructive adversaries. Most assemblies mainly rubber-stamped and legitimated bills proposed by the president. In practice, they seldom made policy, but sometimes they checked executive behavior and obstructed presidential legislation. Legislatures also served as a sounding board, a forum for public opinion, a source of pork for their districts, and a training ground for higher office. Over time, the congress exercised more of its assigned duties, especially in the countries that developed the strongest democracies. The legislature was seldom irrelevant because it could bicker with the chief executive and trigger coups d'état. Therefore, presidents and the military often thought the assembly was important enough to shut it down.[30]

The congress' weakness vis-à-vis the executive branch stemmed not only from its inferior constitutional powers but also from traditions of executive dominance. It suffered from the president's ability to call on the military and police, to go over the heads of the legislators to appeal to the public, and to influence their election. Moreover, the congress struggled with the small number of skilled legislators in poor countries with high rates of illiteracy, the lack of resources, and the ineffectiveness of political parties. Another problem was extreme legislative malapportionment, favoring overrepresentation of rural, conservative elites.[31]

Frequently the dominant party in the legislature gave the opposition virtually no rights or room to operate. Therefore the minority often resorted to obstructionism, boycotts, and violence. In a moment of extreme frustration, one member of the opposition in the Honduran legislature set the building on fire.[32]

JUDICIAL INADEQUACY

The main problems with the Latin American judiciary were its lack of independence, inability to review constitutional issues, and inadequate defense of constitutional democracy and human rights. At best, the judges favored protected over popular democracy. To an extent, U.S. criticisms of the Latin American courts for not upholding the constitution and its promises of liberty may have confused Anglo Saxon and Roman law, since that was not necessarily the courts' responsibility.

Latin America built its judicial systems on the Roman civil-law tradition, inherited from the mother countries. That legacy dictated that laws were supposed to mean precisely what they said and not to be interpreted loosely by any judicial institution, although laws that were vague or contradictory did allow for flexible readings. The judiciaries relied on detailed codes rather than prior court decisions. They saw their major responsibility as applying the laws, not upholding liberal values and institutions.

In general, the judiciaries capitulated to the executive branch, and even to the congress. The colonial heritage and the adaptations made in the independence and national periods partly accounted for judicial inadequacy in the new republics. Under Spanish rule, there had been no fully independent judiciary. After independence, the other government branches and autonomous elites kept the judiciary at bay and often refused to heed its decisions.

A supreme court headed the judicial systems in all the independent republics. Over time, most incorporated a broader version of the Anglo Saxon practice of habeas corpus (known as *amparo*) and a few some limited judicial review of the constitutionality of government acts. The U.S. system most influenced the federalist countries, particularly Argentina, whose courts even cited U.S. decisions as precedents.

Liberals criticized the judiciaries for being subservient to the other branches, for serving the state over the public, for ignoring abuses of democratic and human rights, for catering to the powerful, for denying access and justice to the poor, and for engaging in corruption. In all fairness, it should be remembered that achieving independent courts committed to democracy and enforcing their decisions to protect the constitution and liberal rights were also arduous and lengthy tasks in the United States. In Latin America, the horrendous dictatorships of the 1960s and 1970s and the rebirth of democracy in the 1980s and 1990s finally motivated most countries to tackle the need for fundamental reform of the judiciary. It still had a long way to go to become a cornerstone of democracy.[33]

UBIQUITOUS ELECTIONS

From the throes of independence onward, Latin Americans held amazingly widespread and frequent elections. In most countries, they quickly became de rigueur for installing and legitimating governments, even for many of the administrations actually established by force. The ubiquity of elections was surprising given their novelty and their susceptibility to manipulation. As in other parts of the world in the nineteenth century, participation was usually quite limited. In some remarkable cases, however, more Latin Americans—from more social strata—took part more than might be expected for the era, even in the nineteenth century.

Despite their flaws and their vulnerability to military coups, elections persisted, proliferated, and increasingly became the paths to power over two centuries. From the 1850s to the 1990s, every decade witnessed thirty-five to forty-five presidential elections, except for the 1970s, which only convened fourteen, almost as low as the twelve in the 1840s. Over time and many hurdles, elections became more democratic and efficacious in terms of the franchise, the methods, and the results. This book will explore which people voted, how they did so, and what that civic act meant to them and the political system.[34]

Even limited and corrupt elections brought people into the political arena as both participants and observers. They taught Latin Americans from all social tiers the ideal and expectation, if not the perfect practice, of becoming citizens, exercising sovereignty, and obtaining representation through voting. Through and beyond the balloting, elections fostered political socialization, values, beliefs, communication, education, debates, collective action, assembly, mobilization, and partisanship.

As they became routine and ritualized, elections engrained mores and customs that laid the foundation for more democratic rules and behavior in the future. From the beginning in the early nineteenth century, Latin Americans from most walks of life expressed their desire to vote, complained about grave defects in the process, and struggled to improve the implementation of elections. In the long haul, their electoral aspirations and efforts overcame formidable authoritarian obstacles to make their countries much more democratic.

Elections are not the only institutions crucial to democracy, but they are the most important. Free, fair, and participatory elections are the sine qua non for all the other features of democracy. They provide the necessary but insufficient condition for democracy to exist and make a difference. Therefore this study of the evolution of institutions gives pride of place to elections.

Latin America excelled at elections, often unfree, unfair, and narrow, but sometimes astonishingly open from the beginning (and increasingly so in the twentieth century). Their history shows broad inclusion alternating with restrictive exclusion, a struggle between popular and protected democracy. After many false starts, genuinely honest and representative elections gained ground. They eventually became the norm, especially as enfranchisement accelerated from the 1930s to the 2000s.

Among Latin Americans, their debates about elections addressed four key steps. First, they grappled with the question of who could vote. They chose criteria such as citizenship, gender, age, independence, economics, occupation, education, status, and ideology. Second, they wrestled with the issues of how they would vote. They expressed their preferences in regular or irregular and concurrent or staggered elections, with or without registration, in public or in secret, indirectly or directly, voluntarily or obligatorily, with ballots supplied by partisans or by the government, and under fair or fraudulent procedures. Third, they decided for whom or what they would vote, for which offices, with what proportionality between the population and those elected, for parties or candidates, for candidates selected by the parties or the voters, and for issues presented indirectly or directly in referenda. Fourth, they argued about how the votes would be counted and accepted. For every step, they also discussed how to prevent chicanery and dishonesty, which pervaded the process until the latter decades of the twentieth century.[35]

On the question of who could vote, some scholars would deny the democratic label to any polity falling short of universal suffrage. Although that absolute metric is ideal, it would eliminate most countries from the broad democratic, as opposed to authoritarian, camp until very recently. By that measure, the United States would have to be considered as something other than democratic before women (1920s) and blacks (1960s) were given full voting rights. Instead, this book recognizes reasonably democratic systems judged by the standards of an era and then notes how limited their franchises were by those standards as well as absolute criteria. If suffrage was extremely confined, then a regime might have to be dubbed oligarchic republican or restricted, but it still might be more democratic than an overt dictatorship in the epoch. In most respects, democracy was an evolutionary question of degrees, not of absolutes.[36]

In Latin America, democracy matured, slowly and erratically, as a long march toward more scrupulous, inclusive, authentic, and binding elections. Rather than a linear progression, however, in parts of the region the road led from unexpectedly broad electoral participation early in the nineteenth century to later constriction of the franchise and then to unparalleled amplification in the twentieth century. In the United States and parts of Western Europe, suffrage also sometimes contracted as well as expanded.

Overall from the nineteenth to the twentieth centuries, democracies in Latin America and elsewhere made suffrage more universal, although retaining some limitations for citizenship, age, and civil status. Gradually, governments reduced or eliminated restrictions based on gender, age, religion, race, class, income, property, education, and status. Generally in Latin America, legal suffrage progressed from eliminating economic to gender to literacy requirements, while lowering age limits. By the end of the twentieth century, most governments had also stopped withholding voting rights from political and ideological undesirables. Over time, not only the franchise but also political offices, parties, and policies became more inclusive.[37]

Universal male suffrage began in France and Switzerland in 1848 and spread throughout Western Europe, Australia, Canada, and Japan by 1925. Most countries jumped on board in the first two decades of the twentieth century. Universal female suffrage, bringing about total universal suffrage, began in 1893 in New Zealand and then diffused more gradually, with spurts after World War I and II, until finally Portugal came around in 1974. Almost the last industrialized country to achieve full universal suffrage was the United States, which did not reach there until 1971 because of inhibitions on African American voting. At least in law if not in practice, the Latin Americans did not trail far behind Europe.[38]

On age, the normal limit worldwide remained twenty-one years of age into the 1960s. Latin America got ahead of the curve. Uruguay pioneered by setting eighteen for married men (twenty for bachelors) in 1830 and then for everyone in 1918. Following Argentina in 1863 (and again in 1912), Paraguay, the Dominican Republic, El Salvador, and Guatemala legally dropped the age to eighteen in the 1870s and 1880s, and Brazil, Venezuela, El Salvador, and Bolivia did so from the 1930s to the 1950s. In the 1970s, most of the other Latin American countries followed suit. By the late 1980s, Cuba and Nicaragua instituted the lowest voting age (sixteen) in the region, following social revolutions.[39]

From the nineteenth through most of the twentieth century, many countries excluded illiterates. Latin American lawmakers hotly debated the issue, because this restriction often helped progressive urban movements by constraining the peasant voting base of conservative rural bosses. Legally, the earliest to enfranchise illiterates in the nineteenth century were Mexico in 1857, the Dominican Republic in 1865, Paraguay in 1870, El Salvador in 1883, Nicaragua in 1893, and Honduras in 1894, but some of them never really applied the law or reversed course thereafter. Uruguay's constitution denied illiterates the franchise in the nineteenth century, but actually any man who could sign his name could vote; then the 1918 constitution removed the literacy requirement. Some countries did so much later. For example, Chile finally admitted illiterates in 1970, Ecuador in 1978, Peru in 1979, and Brazil in 1988.[40]

Table 2.3 shows the first official Latin American adoptions of universal voting rights for men, women, eighteen-year-olds, and illiterates, without any pretense that reality always followed the law. The countries are listed in the chronological order of their legalization of universal male suffrage. Scholars disagree on some of the dates. For example, a good case can be made for universal male suffrage actually taking hold in Argentina in 1912, Chile in 1925, and Colombia in 1936, even though the laws first arrived in the earlier years listed in the table. Although legalization was an important first step, country-by-country studies are necessary to determine when all these suffrage rights really took effect, especially for the nineteenth century and the less democratic countries.[41]

Most early Latin American constitutions also denied the vote to dependents. Lawmakers feared that these people could not freely express their opinions, especially when voting took place in public, because of their legal, social, economic, or occupational servitude. This reasoning sometimes justified the exclusion of women, young people, illiterates, slaves, salary and wage earners, and members of the armed forces.

Latin Americans long debated whether the military was eligible to participate. In the aftermath of the independence wars, many countries assumed that soldiers were the most deserving citizens of all and obviously

TABLE 2.3
Legal introduction of electoral participation

| Country | Universal suffrage | | | |
	Male	Female	Age 18	Illiterates
Colombia	1853	1957	1853	1936
Argentina	1857	1951	1863	1912
Mexico	1857	1954	1973	1857
Venezuela	1857	1946	1946	1946
Ecuador	1861	1929	1978	1978
Dominican Republic	1865	1942	1873	1865
Paraguay	1870	1963	1870	1870
Chile	1874	1949	1970	1970
Guatemala	1879	1945	1887	1945
El Salvador	1883	1939	1886	1883
Brazil	1891	1932	1932	1988
Nicaragua	1893	1957	1979	1893
Honduras	1894	1954	1924	1894
Panama	1904	1941	1972	1904
Costa Rica	1913	1949	1971	1913
Uruguay	1918	1934	1918	1918
Haiti	1918	1950	—	—
Peru	1931	1955	1979	1979
Cuba	1934	1934	1976	1901
Bolivia	1952	1952	1952	1952

should vote. However, some leaders always argued that the armed services should be excluded because they were supposed to be obedient to their civilian and military superiors and to be neutral between political partisans. For example in Colombia, this debate raged for decades, usually with troops exercising the vote and being mobilized by the opposing political parties, until lawmakers terminated their suffrage in 1930. Many officers had long opposed the military voting, not only because of professionalism but also because the government frequently expected the armed forces to safeguard the electoral process.[42]

In terms of how to vote, for whom, and with what results, Latin American elections gradually became more regular, secret, direct, obligatory, participatory, equal, and free and fair. On adoption of the secret ballot, the region trailed the United States and Europe, but more in practice than in law. At least officially, Colombia led Latin America in 1853, followed by Mexico, Ecuador, the Dominican Republic, Nicaragua, and Honduras later in the nineteenth century. Then Paraguay in 1911, Argentina in 1912, Uruguay in 1918, and Chile and Costa Rica in 1925 joined the early starters. Most of the rest of the countries came around from the 1930s through the 1950s. Over time, the Latin Americans increasingly tallied the ballots honestly and respected the results.[43]

By world standards, Latin America has had high rates of voter turnout. The most distinctive Latin American voting procedure was to make it mandatory. European obligatory voting started in Belgium in 1903, and then spread to a few other countries by the 1920s. It became common in proportional electoral systems supposed to replicate national opinion in the legislature. Latin Americans adopted required voting first in 1844 in Costa Rica, next in 1894 in Honduras, from the 1910s through the 1920s in seven more countries, and from the 1930s through the 1960s almost everywhere else. They enacted this system to bolster participation, national integration, and government legitimacy, while reducing abstention and especially boycotts.

Most studies show that eligible voters turn out in the highest percentages where voting is compulsory and nonvoting incurs penalties. These laws increase participation by perhaps an average of 10 percent. The problem in Latin America was that governments seldom carried out the penalties. For example, when Uruguay enforced such a law for the 1971 election, turnout jumped from 67 percent to 84 percent. Electoral participation also rose with socioeconomic modernization, proportional representation, and watershed elections, such as those for the transitions from authoritarianism to democracy during the tsunami. This book will highlight key elections that produced democratic breakthroughs.[44]

Historically, most of Latin America opted for plurality or majority elections of presidents and proportional representation (PR) elections of congressional candidates. They implemented proportional representation first in Costa Rica in 1893, Argentina in 1912, Uruguay in 1918, and Colombia in 1925. Almost all the other countries chimed in from the 1930s to the 1960s.

Most scholars have concluded that plurality voting provides greater government stability whereas PR generates more representativeness. The plurality system for electing congresspersons tends to encourage two-party systems concentrating on the centrist, median voter and to discourage smaller parties, especially extremists. In Latin America and other fragmented societies, PR is more conducive to multiple parties, often maintaining fairly rigid social, economic, ideological, or regional identities. PR can even induce these parties to exacerbate differences in order to solidify their constituency against competitors. Therefore, as seen in Latin America, PR systems may not be as beneficial as plurality ones for producing strong, decisive, centrist, compromising, and durable democracies.[45]

A common type of proportional representation in Western Europe and Latin America was the list system. Which political party won how many

seats was determined by its number of votes, usually divided by some formula to translate votes into seats, the most common of which was the
d'Hondt method, which slightly benefited larger parties. An essential prerequisite for someone getting elected was securing a place on the party
roster of candidates. Which candidates on those lists captured the seats was
determined by the party rank ordering them and the voters just marking
a list, or by the voters designating not only a list but also their preferred
candidates on the list.

In the more common *closed list PR*, voters could select only the party,
giving it great authority. In the less common *open list PR*, voters picked
a party and one or more of its candidates, according parties less domination. Countries usually adopted one kind of list or the other depending on
whether they were trying to empower parties or voters.[46] In recent years,
the vast majority of Latin America became more democratic by legalizing
and increasingly employing direct democracy in the form of plebiscites and
referenda. Countries convened these direct elections normally to approve
constitutions or constitutional reforms (e.g., Uruguay, Chile, Ecuador) but
also to decide on recalls (Venezuela), privatizations (Uruguay and Ecuador),
and international disputes (Argentina). Although rarely used, provisions for
popular legislative initiatives were also written into a majority of the constitutions.[47] Table 2.4 displays the first passage of laws, not necessarily the implementation of practices, for secret voting, obligatory voting, proportional

TABLE 2.4
Legal introduction of electoral procedures

Country	Secret voting	Obligatory voting	Proportional representation	Referenda
Colombia	1853	—	1925	1991
Argentina	1912	1912	1912	1994
Mexico	1857	1917	1977	—
Venezuela	1946	1958	1946	1999
Ecuador	1861	1929	1946	1979
Dom. Rep.	1865	1966	1962	—
Paraguay	1911	1940	1947	1992
Chile	1874	1915	1925	1989
Guatemala	1956	1965	1956	1985
El Salvador	1950	1950	1950	1983
Nicaragua	1893	1984	1962	1984
Honduras	1894	1894	1957	2004
Panama	—	1928	1980	1978
Costa Rica	1925	1844	1893	2002
Uruguay	1918	1924	1918	1967
Peru	1931	1931	1931	1993
Brazil	1932	1932	1932	1988
Bolivia	—	1924	1956	2004

TABLE 2.5
Democratic landmarks in Latin America

Landmarks	1827–1879	1880–1929	1930–1976	1977–2006	Total
Regimes					
Oligarchic republics	3	9	—	—	12
Restricted democracies	—	2	4	5	11
Full democracies	—	2	9	15	26
Subtotal	1	15	13	20	49
Electoral participation					
Universal male suffrage	9	8	3	—	20
Universal female suffrage	—	1	19	—	20
Age 18	4	4	8	3	19
Illiterates	3	8	5	3	19
Subtotal	16	21	35	6	78
Electoral procedures					
Secret voting	5	6	5	—	16
Referenda	—	—	1	15	16
Subtotal	5	6	6	15	32
Total	22	42	54	41	159

representation, and direct democracy or referenda in Latin America. The countries are arrayed in the same order as in Table 2.3 on suffrage rights. The table here leaves out rarely democratic Haiti and Cuba because their data is unavailable or unreliable.[48]

Table 2.5 aggregates some of the data from Tables 2.3 and 2.4 to display the introduction of democratic landmarks in Latin America by the eras used in this book's chapters. The first section on regimes shows the increasing numbers of democracies, especially full democracies, established over time, peaking during the tsunami. The second section on legal electoral participation reveals the steady and dramatic expansion over the decades, climaxing with the adoption of female suffrage from 1929 to 1963. The third section on legal electoral procedures indicates that secret voting arrived gradually up through the populist period, while referenda came on in a rush during the tsunami.

MULTIPLE AND FEEBLE POLITICAL PARTIES

Although usually not formal legal institutions like the entities discussed above, political parties provided crucial linkages between citizens and government. In Latin America, the few healthiest democracies tended to have the strongest parties and party systems. In the more numerous weaker democracies, one of the biggest institutional deficiencies was feeble parties. In general, flimsy parties and party systems held back Latin American democracy from the 1850s to the 2000s.

This defect was particularly damaging because truly democratic political parties helped preserve democracies. From the 1880s onward, the governments or their opponents became less likely to terminate Latin American democracies when all the major political parties remained steadfast in their support of democracy. When some of those parties began calling for authoritarian solutions, then dictatorship was often not far off.[49]

This book makes a simple distinction between political parties and party systems. A political party is basically any identifiable organization running candidates for government offices. Whether an association can be classified as a party may depend on how structured and sturdy it is, although scholars sometimes have applied other criteria about leadership, membership, size, scope, programs, and internal and external democratic behavior. From the nineteenth to the twentieth centuries in the West, parties modernized and met more of these expectations.

The basic definition of a political party allowed even some Latin American personalistic campaigners with undisciplined and sporadically engaged followers to be included so long as they used some ongoing organization with a recognizable label. However, the character of parties was highly problematic in the region, where many were fragile, ephemeral, elitist, patrimonial, clientelistic, centralized, and undemocratic internally and externally. In exaggerated form, these shortcomings reflected the generally greater weakness of parties in presidential than in parliamentary systems.[50]

Parties and party systems have really only existed in the modern world since about the middle of the nineteenth century, so Latin America did not lag far behind. As elsewhere in the world, the party panoply reflected national history, underlying cleavages, and electoral rules. In Europe and Latin America, the six main party cleavages tended to be religious, regional (usually center-periphery), rural-urban, ethnic-cultural-linguistic, socioeconomic (based on sector or class), or ideological. In the course of modernization, European and Latin American party systems typically developed around the following divisions in the following sequence: (1) Center-Periphery; (2) State-Church; (3) Land-Industry and Rural-Urban; and (4) Owner-Worker.[51]

In the chronological and sociological process of incorporation of rising social sectors during national development, a key distinction was whether new groups were absorbed into existing parties or new parties. In contrast with multiparty systems, two-party systems made the emergence of fresh parties more difficult. Once any party spectrum was filled out along all dimensions and encompassed virtually all adult citizens, it became very daunting to change that alignment in Europe and the United States, but not in Latin America, where parties were more evanescent.[52]

Individual parties existed in different kinds of party systems and might be conservative, liberal, Christian Democrat, populist, socialist, communist, and so forth. In Latin America, the leading parties tended to be catch-all and clientelistic rather than intensely based on class or ideology. Among types of parties, Conservatives and Liberals usually took shape first in the nineteenth century. They exhibited minimal differences since both mainly represented factions of the upper class, as well as their regions and followers. In contrast with Liberals, Conservatives tended to identify with the Church, rural elites, and centralization. In the twentieth century, some of these traditional parties withered and even disappeared, but others endured.

In the late nineteenth and early twentieth centuries, moderate, pragmatic, reformist centrist parties arose. They usually rallied dissident elites and the urban middle classes. If they were able to compromise and forge broad coalitions, they could hold multiparty democracies together. Examples included the secular Radical parties in Chile and Argentina and the Catholic Christian Democrats in Chile, El Salvador, Peru, and Venezuela.

In the twentieth century—especially from the 1930s to the 1970s—populist parties appeared. They distinguished themselves by charismatic personalistic leadership, heterogeneous and vertical social makeup concentrated on urban workers, and a reformist program to promote nationalistic industrialization and a welfare state. Some of the most prominent cases included the American Popular Revolutionary Alliance in Peru, the Socialists in Chile from the 1930s to the 1950s, Democratic Action in Venezuela, the Peronists in Argentina, and some of the parties spawned by Getulio Vargas in Brazil.

A third type that came on stage in the twentieth century was revolutionary parties. They usually grew out of the labor movement and became small Marxist or Communist organizations. The few large and powerful revolutionary parties emerged out of social revolutions against dictators and reflected the character of that movement. They served not just as electoral vehicles but also as mass mobilization organizations for the state. Examples included the revolutionary parties of Mexico, Bolivia, Cuba, and Nicaragua.[53]

Party systems refer to the number of dominant parties. That array might feature none (countries ruled simply by military or personalistic dictators, principally in the nineteenth century), one (usually in the aftermath of twentieth-century revolutions), two (rare, but stable in Colombia and Uruguay from the nineteenth through most of the twentieth centuries), or multiple (almost all Latin American countries in the twentieth century). Systems with higher numbers of competitive parties gravitated toward greater instability.[54]

In one-party systems, the dominant party regularly won a large majority of the votes and offices, establishing an effective monopoly over government for a long period of time. Most significant party politics took place within the hegemon, wherein the factions resembled a subterranean multiparty system. These singular parties arose most often in post-revolutionary situations, but they could also emerge under authoritarian caudillos, as in Paraguay under Alfredo Stroessner and Nicaragua under the Somoza dynasty. Sometimes other parties existed to express dissent and confer legitimacy, but they found it nearly impossible to displace the ruling party.

In two-party systems, the top contenders were relatively evenly matched, although one usually prevailed for many years at a time. Both leading parties tended to reach toward the center, appeal to a multi-class base, and propose similar moderate programs. Third parties found it difficult to challenge these umbrella organizations for power.

In multiparty systems, three or more main parties competed and coalesced because they could not command an ongoing majority by themselves. These parties based themselves more on ideology and class, and they usually underscored their differences from each other. Multiple parties could still provide stable government if they could avoid polarization and forge compromises around centrist positions.[55]

Conclusion

From the early 1800s to the early 2000s, Latin America's democratic institutions increasingly became entrenched. The original problems, issues, and motivations—such as instability, inequality, and authoritarianism—that gave birth to these institutions persisted. Therefore continuities in their fundamental features exceeded alterations. Over time, what changed and improved most was their ability to garner the consent of the governed and thus withstand the threats of tyranny and anarchy.

Early on, these democratic institutions sank deep roots. The architects cobbled them together from foreign and domestic sources, adapting external models to internal traditions and conditions. In many respects, the institutions reflected the dominant vision of protected rather than popular democracies. Partly for that reason, many of their features inhibited democratic success. The poor performance of these institutions and democracy after independence stemmed both from legal shortcomings and from authoritarian behavior spawned by historical traditions and conditions, including the highly inequitable distribution of social power.

Over time, all these institutions made some progress in a direction more conducive to democracy. However, constitutions, presidents, legislatures, and especially judiciaries improved much less than elections. Almost keeping pace legally with more developed Western countries, electoral advances mainly drove democracy forward. Meanwhile, political parties and party systems remained one of the weakest features of Latin American democracies.

Over two hundred years, almost all the Latin American countries progressed from authoritarian to democratic forms of government, some more than others. By the beginning of the twenty-first century, democratic systems prevailed as never before. Although all of them staked some claim to being formal democracies, they varied enormously in virtues and vices. They all faced the remaining Herculean tasks of improving their durability and quality, especially their relevance to the popular classes. The following chapters explain how the region scaled the long climb to the current summit.

Chapter 3

The Bolivarian Legacy:
Struggles Toward Democracy
During the Wars for Independence,
1800s–1820s

After three centuries of submission to the Iberian crowns, Latin America erupted in an enormous fight for freedom—from both the mother country and from absolutism. The Creoles triumphed in one of the earliest and greatest struggles for liberty in modern world history. That battle cost fifteen years and untold thousands of lives. Except in Cuba, the liberators rapidly achieved their primary objective of independence, eventually giving birth in the early nineteenth century to eighteen new countries: Mexico, Guatemala, Honduras, El Salvador, Nicaragua, Costa Rica, Haiti, the Dominican Republic, Venezuela, Colombia, Ecuador, Peru, Bolivia, Chile, Argentina, Uruguay, Paraguay, and Brazil.[1]

The liberators enjoyed much less success with their secondary objective of forging stable republics, or at least constitutional monarchies. Nevertheless, in launching the first republics (however limited and fragile), they took a prerequisite giant stride toward democracy. They founded the largest number of republics up to that time on the planet. They created an unparalleled laboratory for experiments in democracy, as defined in the era. At least in their declarations and aspirations, the leaders of independence made republicanism the template for the future, the seedbed for democracy.

The history of these foundational years explains why the independence leaders adopted republicanism, why they gave it a distinctive institutional architecture that has prevailed ever since, and why it floundered in the early years. Republics, normally oligarchic, were the highest form of democracy feasible in these years. The historical record also reveals the emergence of a continuing split between visions of popular and protected democracy. At the same time, it shows how the initial political institutions forecast the future: unstable and often inoperable constitutions grafted from abroad, extreme centralism, hyper-presidentialism, lackluster legislatures, illiberal and ineffective judiciaries, and prolific elections. By the 1820s, the only institution not yet present was political parties.

At first, some of those pioneering elections included extraordinary participation by common people, which quickly provoked retrenchment by the upper classes. At most, the ruling groups tolerated protected, not popular, democracies. Although the liberators failed to erect sturdy democracies, their experiments with self-government inscribed indelible guidelines. They left to their descendants the task of convincing the people with money and guns to abide by the rules.

Independence and republican rule resulted from the need in Spain and Spanish America—and eventually Portugal and Brazil—to devise ruling bodies in the absence of the king. In 1808 the French under Joseph Bonaparte overthrew Ferdinand VII of Spain. Resisting the invaders, local juntas on the peninsula seized control in accord with the Spanish tradition that power devolved to the people when the monarch exited. Thus, local elites took a first, halting step toward representative self-government in the mother country. In short order, Creoles followed suit in the New World.[2]

The only prior establishment of independence occurred in 1804 in Haiti. In 1809, Spanish royal forces stamped out initial attempts at self-governance in Bolivia, Ecuador, and Colombia. In 1810, juntas claiming to rule in Ferdinand's stead took over several countries. The most radical uprising in 1810 boiled over in Mexico under Miguel Hidalgo, whose execution in 1811 turned over his movement to Jose Maria Morelos, who carried on until 1815.

Also in 1810, Spain created a national congress—the Cortes—to represent both Old and New World Spaniards, resulting in the Constitution of 1812. The 1812 Cortes of Càdiz, briefly restored in 1820, bequeathed a liberal tradition of parliamentary rule to Spanish America. In 1811, Venezuela became the first independent American republic, only to succumb to the royalists in 1812. Further revolts in Venezuela and Colombia ensued. Sovereignty reverted to the Crown when the restoration of Ferdinand in 1814 crushed the Cortes. Both Venezuela and Colombia fell back under Spanish control by 1815, as did most of the colonies, except for Argentina and isolated Paraguay. Thereafter Spanish reassertion of absolutism ignited a successful fight for full-fledged independence and republicanism in the colonies.[3]

Appealing to Creoles disillusioned with the return of the king, the great liberators then marched Spanish America to independence from 1817 until 1825. Simón Bolívar from the north and José de San Martín from the south ripped colonies from Spain's grasp and then converged on Peru. Meanwhile in Spain itself, peninsular liberals recaptured power in 1820 and restored a constitutional monarchy under the Constitution of 1812. They hoped to win back the colonies through conciliation.

Although some Creoles hailed the return of the constitution, for many others, including liberals, reconciliation with Spain came too late. For more conservative Creoles, the liberal turn in Spain converted them to independence. Chile secured independence in 1818, Gran Colombia in 1819, Central America in 1823, Peru in 1824, and Bolivia in 1825. Meanwhile, Mexico (1821) and Brazil achieved independence and became monarchies in 1822, although the former empire only lasted until 1823. After the major military campaigns climaxed in Peru and Bolivia, Uruguay obtained independence from Brazil in 1828, Venezuela and Ecuador from Colombia in 1829 and 1830.

Every time they wrested a Spanish American holding away from the mother country, the liberators declared it a republic. However, except in monarchical Brazil, the aftermath of independence brought conflict and chaos. By the end of the 1820s, virtually all the new republics had collapsed into civil war or dictatorship, anarchy or tyranny. Spanish authoritarianism had been succeeded by a homegrown variety.[4]

From 1810 through the 1820s, republican systems fared poorly for several reasons. First, the Creoles had scant experience with self-government, let alone republicanism, which many of them did not value. They bore the weight of three hundred years of political, social, and religious authoritarianism. Both before and during the colonial period, Spain maintained undemocratic governing structures.[5]

Second, social legacies from the colonial period also undercut even very limited democracy. Given severe racial and class inequalities, elite fears of mass upheaval compelled many of them to prefer authoritarianism over republicanism. Where colonial rule relied on exploitation of large indigenous or slave populations, that cleavage carried on past independence and hindered democratic prospects, most notably in Mexico, Central America, the Caribbean, the Central Andes (Ecuador, Peru, Bolivia), and Brazil. At the same time, the poverty, illiteracy, and oppression of the under classes rendered them nearly impotent as citizens. However, the significance of the colonial legacy can be cast in doubt because the independent countries discarded most colonial institutions, militarism grew out of the wars for independence more than the imperial experience, some countries succeeded at republican rule while others failed, and a few overlay their colonial heritage with later waves of immigration.[6]

Third, residues from the independence years also hobbled rudimentary democracies. International and especially civil wars shattered the incipient nations, leaving them at the mercy of public and private armies. Explosive conflicts between capital cities and provinces, Church and state, conservatives and liberals, and warlords (*caudillos*) generated chronic instability. At the same time, economic hardships kept governments poor and ineffective. The feeble state could not control the national territory, let alone its inhabitants.[7]

Despite formidable obstacles and failures, some of the modern world's first new nations registered a few initial political achievements. Formal imperial domination and absolutism vanished. At a minimum, independence and small steps toward republicanism created greater potential for democracy than had existed in the colonial period. However theoretical, contested, and flawed, liberal elected, representative, constitutional republics became the only lasting legitimate legal form of government.

Although true citizenship remained a distant dream for most Latin Americans, at least the creole oligarchy took charge from the peninsular Spaniards. Some mestizos also broke into political life. Slavery shackled and shadowed African Americans for decades to come, but legal bondage began to erode. While the indigenous peoples remained repressed—in many cases worse off than before independence—some of them at the margin became supporters of politicians, often caudillos. In most cases, law and society still excluded women from the public arena, but a few exerted influence beyond what had been possible in the colonial era. In the penumbra of tremendous disappointments and shortcomings, a legacy of republican ambitions and possibilities began to take shape.[8]

Foreign forces supplied little help. Although the United States encouraged emulation of its infant democracy, the dominant external power, Great Britain, placed no premium on republicanism. The United States hailed the creation of independent republics in Latin America, partly out of idealism but mainly out of desires for commercial access and for strategic exclusion of European powers from the Americas. Washington did not have the power to affect the outcome of the wars of independence, but it did make a contribution by beginning to recognize the new states diplomatically in 1822.

The liberal notion of defending the republics of the Americas against the despotisms of Europe infused the U.S. Monroe Doctrine of 1823. But that manifesto primarily sought to preserve the New World from the strategic and economic designs of the Old World. The United States revealed its lack of exclusive commitment to republicanism with its recognition of the monarchies in Mexico in 1822 and Brazil in 1824. Great Britain followed suit by recognizing the new states in 1825, without regard to their form of government. Like the Latin Americans and the British, the North Americans evinced more interest in independence than in democracy.[9]

The Origins of Dreams and Doubts About Democracy

The centuries-long debate between authoritarianism and democracy in Latin America began with Spain and Portugal implanting authoritarianism during the colonial period. Preceding and during the independence battles, foreign ideas about democracy and republicanism seeped into Latin America. The Enlightenment, with its emphasis on natural rights, and the revolutions in the United States and France influenced the Spanish and Portuguese colonists. In some ways, those two revolutions embodied the distinction between protected and popular views of democratic government.

Among Latin Americans in the era, the term *republic* usually referred to the representative U.S. system, while *democracy* typically implied the more direct Jacobin episode. In general, their leaders preferred, at most, the U.S. model, not the socially explosive French. As the premier precursor of independence Francisco de Miranda said in 1799, "We have before our eyes two great examples, the American and the French revolutions. Let us prudently imitate the first and carefully shun the second."[10]

During the independence period, some Latin Americans embraced the *Western Hemisphere Idea*. According to this notion, the peoples of the Americas shared a common identity setting them apart from the rest of the world—particularly Europe. As Latin America borrowed many political concepts from the United States, some leaders both north and south began to argue that republicanism unified the New World. For example, the Mexican intellectual and politician Lucas Alaman in 1826 claimed that among the American countries, "the similarity of their political institutions has bound them even more closely together, strengthening in them the dominion of just and liberal principles."[11]

This idea of a republican or democratic hemisphere had a rocky future, but frequently reemerged in later years, whether during World Wars I and II, the Cold War, or the euphoria of the tidal wave of democratization from the 1980s into the 2000s. Sincerely or cynically, leaders repeatedly invoked this unifying symbol in contrast with tyrannies elsewhere on the planet, whether in opposition to the Holy Alliance, the Axis, or the Soviet Union.

The United States sometimes used the rallying cry to promote its political values and domination south of the border. At times, Latin America echoed that refrain to appeal for U.S. support of democracy or other objectives. Often both sides applied the democratic label to dubious cases and to cover up less noble strategic and economic objectives. Beneath the sometimes Machiavellian manipulation of the concept, there remained, nevertheless, a wellspring of truth that many people in the United States and Latin America did share some core political beliefs, however imperfectly realized.[12]

From European and U.S. intellectuals, the Latin Americans adopted the concepts of natural rights and social contract. However, they were not just importing exotic ideas. Although no operative concept of political equality existed in the colonial period, some people, most famously Bartolome de Las Casas, had argued that everyone—including Indians and Africans—was equal before God. This concept opened the door for later Enlightenment beliefs about possessing equal human rights before the state.[13]

Moreover, some colonial practices contained the seeds of democratic possibilities. The Spanish empire maintained the notion that everyone was a citizen with the right to petition political authorities all the way up to the throne. In theory, all citizens deserved a hearing from the system, as seen in the vast legal records from the period and the setting aside of one day a week for the Viceroy to listen to grievances from any of his subjects. The slogan "long live the king, down with bad government" also presumed that citizens had a right to denounce and bring down lesser officials that failed to conduct themselves toward the populace in a way the crown would approve. In addition, the system of corporatist legislation established highly unequal duties and privileges but also recognized that most groups had some rights. Furthermore, the participation of local elites in the municipal council (*cabildo*) set a precedent for representation, if not democracy.[14]

Prior to the eighteenth century, Spanish neo-scholastic thought argued that all political authority rested on the consent of the people conferred through a social contract. This theory comported with the Spanish medieval tradition of regional and local rights. Francisco Suarez, a seventeenth-century Jesuit, and other late scholasticists contended that the people invested that power in a civil authority. Thereafter, the designated rulers retained that power unless the contract was violated—for example by descending into tyranny and abuse. In Spain, this contract theoretically existed between the Crown and the kingdoms, provinces, and colonies, to whom sovereignty reverted with the disappearance of the monarch.

Once in office, the kings did not govern with the people, or of and by the people, but with the authority originally allocated to them by the people.

When that ruler vanished at the start of the wars of independence, the people had the right to reclaim and reassert their sovereignty, as seen in the uprising of the town councils. Then, using natural rights arguments, both the Peninsulars in Spain and the Creoles in America professed the authority to delegate political legitimacy to some new ruler or system, at least until the crown returned. Such ideas did not necessarily lead to democracy, but they did make it conceivable.[15]

In a typical example, the Chilean junta in 1810 vowed loyalty to the ousted Ferdinand, but the Creoles' quest for governing mechanisms in his absence spawned embryonic republican principles. Their contention that sovereignty devolved to the people during the king's exile opened up the possibility that the people might delegate that power to someone else. The more reformist spokespersons argued that the interim government had to represent the people, to guarantee certain rights, to convoke an assembly, and to design a constitution, if only to organize authority in the meantime. To exercise and preserve those natural rights, the sovereign people of Chile eventually rejected the restored king and agreed to a social contract with a representative and constitutional government.[16]

Whatever the doubts, debates, and disasters, Latin America—from independence throughout the rest of the nineteenth century—generally subscribed to a classic "liberal" model of development, similar to that of the United States. In principle, this foundational myth entailed constitutional, representative republics and sometimes laissez-faire economies. After some early monarchical tendencies, so-called conservatives as well as self-proclaimed liberals adhered to this republican philosophy, albeit with differences in implementation. The broad republican political ideology became so prevalent that even the frequent dictators usually claimed to be operating within the democratic constitution or merely suspending it temporarily to cope with emergencies.[17]

As more Creoles turned against their Iberian masters, independence initially became a more unifying concept than republicanism. Indeed, most of the formal declarations of independence said little about the type of government to be installed. When victory was in their grasp, the Latin Americans intensified their debate over the replacement regime. Not counting outright dictatorship, which was more a fact of life than a school of thought, three main political proposals emerged during the independence period: monarchism, with the constitutional variety being an advancement over absolutism, and liberal versus conservative versions of republicanism.[18]

Frequently, the independence movements behaved in illiberal ways, despite their proclamations, and many of their leaders were not champions of democracy. Especially in the early years, some Latin Americans favored monarchism, albeit usually advocating constitutional and republican limits on the crown. They logically expressed this preference, since monarchy prevailed in Europe, and England's constitutional variety appeared highly successful. The second greatest independence leader, Argentina's San Martín, essentially espoused monarchism, rejected by the dominant liberator, Venezuela's Bolívar.[19]

Among the direct precursors of Spanish American independence, Miranda of Venezuela stood out as perhaps the most important activist. His commitment to democracy was restrained and conservative at best. While hailing Rousseau's concepts of popular sovereignty and human rights, Miranda preferred a constitutional monarchy for Spanish America, ideally presided over by the Inca dynasty, an idea whose time had not come. Appalled by the French Revolution, he admired the political system of Britain more than any other European blueprint.

In agreement with Montesquieu's advocacy of a separation of powers, Miranda also recommended a centralized government, a bicameral legislature with the lower house elected by literate male property owners, a judiciary selected by the monarch, and a board of censors to monitor legislation. Although he believed in a protected democracy, he expressed more sympathy for dramatic social than political change, advocating the emancipation of slaves. Some of Miranda's political ideas surfaced in the short-lived Venezuelan Constitution of 1811, when he briefly governed Caracas before dying as a prisoner in Spain in 1816.[20]

Another prominent precursor of independence was Argentina's Manuel Belgrano. He believed that political and economic liberty, particularly free trade, should go together. After Argentina won its independence, Belgrano despaired of democracy there and argued for government by aristocrats and a king. He suggested the restoration of the Inca ruler, in a desperate quest for legitimate autochthonous royalty.

Amidst the debates over how to reconstruct a national government in the wake of Ferdinand VII's removal in 1808, Spanish advocates of limited popular sovereignty and a partially elected congress also made an impact on political thinkers in the colonies. These currents emerged in the Cortes of Cádiz from 1810 to 1813. It included representatives of both America and Spain, elected in various ways by local juntas and governing bodies. The Cortes' Constitution of 1812 still recognized the ultimate authority of the crown. It attempted to establish a balance between royalty and liberty, between a king and a national assembly. Although the restoration of Ferdinand soon capsized a constitutional monarchy, these Spanish whiffs of liberalism nonetheless added an endogenous patina to the cause of representative government in Spanish America.[21]

The short-lived Spanish Constitution of 1812 contained some remarkably liberal features. Its provisions vaulted the Hispanic world into the vanguard internationally of many democratic rights. It gave Americans equal representation with Spaniards. This constitutional monarchy created three branches of government, with the unicameral legislature dominant, the crown secondary, and the judiciary tertiary. It established freedom of the press. It also recognized Indians and mestizos, though not Africans, as citizens. In a bold move, the constitution conferred on all males, except Africans, suffrage rights with no literacy or property qualifications, a more liberal standard than prevailed in the United States, France, or England at the time. After this benchmark by the Peninsulars, it became difficult for Creole elites to grant their compatriots lesser rights.[22]

In terms of implementation in the New World, Haiti became the first rebel to establish a brief monarchy. Although a few independence leaders sought European royalty to assume a throne in their countries, the Creole Agustín de Iturbide became the most successful Spanish American monarchist, crowned emperor of Mexico in 1822 (but deposed in 1823). He envisioned a monarchy constrained by the provisions of the Spanish Constitution of Cadiz of 1812. Unable to establish the legitimacy of locally manufactured royalty, Iturbide saw the centralism of his system provoke its rapid downfall, toppled by regional resistance.[23]

Brazil followed the most monarchist path of all, holding fast until 1889. It succeeded because it enjoyed the legitimacy of the Portuguese royal house. After the Portuguese king transferred his throne briefly to the colony during the Napoleonic wars, his son, Dom Pedro, stayed on to found the independent Brazilian constitutional monarchy in 1822. Ruling with the support of the conservative Brazilian elites, the emperor Pedro I held the giant country together.[24]

As civil strife tore asunder most of the rest of Latin America, the legitimacy vacuum bequeathed by independence proved harder to fill. Republicanism held sway after projects to import or fabricate a monarch fell through. However, the new nation-builders found little experience in the world or at home with the republican form of government. Most Creoles equated a republic with democracy, but they exhibited only a vague understanding of both concepts as some alternative to monarchy, tyranny or anarchy.

At a minimum, most of them agreed that leaders should derive their legitimacy from elections rather than from royal lineage or divine right. The neophyte governments floundered in the face of sub-national authorities with greater power and legitimacy: the military, the caudillos, the landowners, and the Church. As in the United States, the general who had won the war of independence often became the first president.[25]

Many of the liberators advocated elected, representative, constitutional republics. In typical cases, the main leaders in both Uruguay and Chile rejected monarchism or despotism in favor of republicanism. The Chileans believed that their republic needed to be guarded against two dangers: tyranny or anarchy. They thought the former could be avoided through the division of powers, the latter through restrictions on democratic participation until education could enlighten the popular classes. All their electoral laws from 1810 to 1833 included property and literacy qualifications excluding the vast majority, a recipe for an oligarchic republic.[26]

During the wars for independence, two main strands of democratic or republican thought evolved. The more liberal variety prevailed in the early years, partly discredited by some of the initial failures of republican government. The more conservative approach dominated by the end of the independence era. This general transformation could be seen in the evolution of Bolívar's thinking in the direction of increasingly protected, elitist democracies.[27]

Liberal idealism convulsed Spanish American politics from independence onward. If the Creoles had been merely opportunistic, it would have been far easier for authorities to control them through corruption or coercion, but some groups continued to struggle for liberty. They emphasized individual freedom from the state. Partly emulating the United States, the liberals stressed three key ideas that alienated conservatives: political limitations on the Church, expansion of the suffrage, and constraints on the central government and its president, often through federalism.[28]

Colombian lawyer Antonio Nariño emerged as an influential precursor of independence and liberal republicanism at the end of the colonial period. Influenced by Voltaire, Rousseau, and Montesquieu, he translated and distributed the French *Declaration of the Rights of Man and of the Citizen*. Another early liberal, Argentine Mariano Moreno, praised Rousseau's political, but not religious, ideas. He expressed enthusiasm about constitutional republicanism but wariness about chaos and upheaval from the under classes.[29]

The liberal and conservative dread that popular democracy could veer off into social revolution stemmed from revulsion at mass uprisings. The upper classes were appalled by some radical precursors of independence who rebelled against the Spaniards in the late eighteenth century. Most disturbing were the self-proclaimed Inca Tupac Amaru in Peru and Bolivia, who galvanized an indigenous revolt in 1780, and, to a lesser extent, the creole Comuneros in Colombia. However, these rebels exhibited ambivalence at best about independence and no commitment to democracy. Instead, they complained about unjust local administration. Moreover, the Indian followers of Tupac Amaru mainly campaigned for social change through popular insurgency. The Latin American elites also shuddered at the early rebellion of Toussaint L'Ouverture of Haiti, who aroused the blacks to oppose slavery and French colonialism from 1791 to 1803, but espoused no coherent political philosophy.[30]

From the point of view of the Creoles, two of the most terrifying radical independence leaders arose in Mexico, but even they were dubious democrats. Apparently influenced by the French Revolution and particularly Rousseau, Father Miguel Hidalgo y Costilla favored independence from Spain as well as some social reforms. Detonating a mass upheaval of peasants in 1810 until his death in 1811, he promised to abolish slavery and Indian tribute payments, as well as to restore some Indian community lands. Although coming the closest to spearheading a social revolution of any independence leader in Spanish America, Hidalgo never spelled out his preferred form of government. He did, however, panic the Creoles at the prospect of class and race warfare by mestizos and Indians once authority at the top broke down.[31]

Picking up Hidalgo's baton, Father Jose Maria Morelos fought on for Mexican independence from 1811 until his similar execution in 1815. Like Hidalgo, he advocated an end to slavery and to Indian tribute payments. He also endorsed popular sovereignty, represented by a congress. However, Morelos never explained precisely what kind of government he would have created.[32]

In contrast with the liberals or the advocates of popular democracy, the conservatives preferred a highly protected democracy. By championing "democracy," most leaders of independence envisioned equal rights for creole elites to control and hold political offices long monopolized by Peninsulars, not equal rights among all citizens to select and run the government. Conservative republicans believed in a paternalistic democracy wherein most of the population would cede the right and responsibility of managing state affairs to a privileged few.[33]

Conservatives did not subscribe to any ideals of Jefferson or Rousseau for the general population, but only for their own individualistic liberty away from the national government. They argued that the common people did have freedom, not to change the central government, but to pursue their individual lives as they saw fit in an open economy and society. The predominance of this perspective among many conservatives throughout much of Latin American history led one commentator to the exaggerated conclusion that, "Democratic government in the North American or European sense has not been established in Spanish America because its establishment has not been either sought or attempted."[34]

Like the liberals, the conservatives fancied a republic, but they were more fearful that too much democracy, federalism, and anti-clericalism would unleash political, geographic, and social divisions that would devastate the young countries. Therefore, they stressed an official Catholic faith, strong central government, a powerful president, a staunch military, and minimal popular participation outside their control. In their view, the new regime should preserve many authoritarian aspects of the colonial political system under the mantle of republicanism. Their increasing domination as the battles against Spain drew to a close prompted one cynic to lament that, "The War of Independence was the most conservative revolution which has ever occurred."[35]

In accord with much of Spanish America, Chile's liberal years in the 1820s disintegrated into a conservative reaction. Chile differed in that the conservatives established in the 1830s a stable, constitutional, oligarchic republic, symbolized by one of its architects, Diego Portales. In a letter in 1822, Portales forecasted the protected, tutelary republic he would help erect in the 1830s:

> Democracy, which self-deceived men proclaim so much, is an absurdity in countries like those of America, which are full of vices, and whose citizens completely lack the virtue necessary for a true Republic. Nor is Monarchy the American ideal; if we come out of one terrible monarchy to go into another, what do we gain? The Republic is the system we must adopt; but do you know how I conceive it for these countries?—a strong, centralizing government, whose members are genuine examples of virtue and patriotism, and thus set the citizens on the straight path of order and the virtues. When they have attained a degree of morality, then we can have the completely liberal sort of Government, free and full of ideals, in which all the citizens can take part.[36]

The most important liberator and political thinker of the independence era, Bolívar, personified the evolution from liberalism to conservatism. He wrenched from Spain's hands Venezuela, Colombia, Ecuador, Peru, and Bolivia, his namesake. Both an idealist and a realist, his thinking was influenced by the Roman Republic, European travels and writings (especially the French Enlightenment), British political institutions, the United States, the Spanish Constitution of 1812, and the bitter experience of republican rule in the new states of Spanish America.

At least rhetorically, Bolívar always bemoaned unconstitutional dictatorship and promoted a democratic republic, including limited civil liberties such as free elections, speech, and press, a moderately effective congress, and an independent judiciary. He also favored hemispheric defense of democracies. Unlike some contemporary proponents of democracy, he relied on a centralized government with a domineering presidency and opposed greater powers for the legislature or regional and local offices.[37]

During the independence wars, Bolívar became more terrified of anarchy than tyranny. He evolved into a proponent of some form of "classical republicanism," increasingly more aristocratic than democratic. In the early years of the independence struggle (1810 to 1813), Bolívar subordinated political plans to the need for order and unity to fight against the Spaniards. Throughout his military and political career, he wrestled with the desire to devise a limited form of republicanism for a people with no experience with it. Bolívar recommended hybrid forms of government, such as a constitutional unitary, centralized, elitist republic with a lifetime president, intended to progress toward greater democracy as the people gradually acquired republican virtues. As with so many of his successors, Bolívar labored to strike a balance between representation and efficiency. His military victories and his political vision lasted, but his detailed political engineering did not.[38]

Bolívar penned a pithy statement of his political beliefs in the so-called *Jamaica Letter* of 1815. He concluded that the failures of the first independent republics in Venezuela and Colombia showed that excessively democratic, libertarian, and federalist systems were inappropriate for Latin America. He attributed these disasters to lack of historical preparation for democracy and to severely fragmented geographies, polities, and societies. Bolívar urged, ". . . let us not adopt the best system of government, but the one that is most viable. . . ." He still preferred republics rather than monarchies for the future states of Latin America, partly because the former were less likely to wage war on their neighbors.[39]

Bolívar increasingly believed that the Spanish Americans, with their Iberian colonial heritage, were not ready for U.S. democracy: "Is it conceivable that a people but recently freed from its chains can ascend into the sphere of liberty without melting its wings like Icarus and plunging into the abyss?" His answer was the need to nurture democratic possibilities for the future under "the kindly guardianship of paternal governments."[40]

Bolívar gave the fullest expression to his political views in the Angostura address of 1819 in Venezuela. He argued, "Venezuela had, has, and should have a republican government. Its principles should be the sovereignty of the people, division of powers, civil liberty, proscription of slavery, and the abolition of monarchy and privileges." The Liberator concluded that the admirable U.S. model was inapplicable to Spanish America, with its lack of democratic background and its enormous social inequalities: "perfectly representative institutions are not suited to our character." He sought a delicate equilibrium between "moderation of the popular will and limitation of public authority."[41]

For Gran Colombia, the Liberator proposed a mixed system in which seats in the lower house would be elected but those in the senate would be inherited. Looming over the congress would be an awesome chief executive, presiding over a unitary republic. In contrast to what he would subsequently recommend in Bolivia, Bolívar called for frequent presidential elections to prevent continuism. Colombia's constitution makers followed little of his specific advice, though in 1830 they reacted to his dictatorial rule by adopting the only two-year presidencies in Latin America.[42]

Bolívar designed an even more restricted democracy for Bolivia. He attempted to avert the polar evils of despotism or dissolution, the first epitomized by the rule of Spain for three centuries and the second by the disintegration of Venezuela's first independent republic in 1812. Outlining principles that should guide their crafting of a constitution to the constituent congress of Bolivia in 1826, he warned: "**Legislators!** Your duty compels you to avoid a struggle with two monstrous enemies, who, although they are themselves ever locked in mortal combat, will attack you at once. **Tyranny** and **anarchy** constitute an immense sea of oppression encircling a tiny island of freedom. . . ." Bolívar recommended a lifetime president who would select his successor and a tricameral legislature, the third body being a Chamber of Censors to exert moral authority, although he opposed any official religion. The Bolivians did not adhere to his convoluted plan.[43]

Increasingly dismissing the egalitarian dreams of liberal or popular democracy as utopian, Bolívar ended up advocating an oligarchic republic with very limited participation and very centralized quasi-authoritarian institutions. His formula foreshadowed many ingredients of the conservative systems adopted in Chile in the 1830s and many other countries thereafter. Even Bolívar's dictatorships in democratic dress failed miserably, most notably in Bolivia and Peru when they briefly adopted his heavy-handed constitutions and their lifetime presidencies.[44]

Hoping to achieve both liberty and stability, the Liberator attained neither. Despondent at all the political catastrophes, he wrote in 1826, "I am convinced to the very marrow of my bones that only a clever despotism can govern in America." Although Bolívar sometimes ruled as a dictator, he refused to become an emperor. His dream that some kind of constrained republicanism might take root in Latin America withered. Surveying the violence and disarray wracking the region in 1829, he lamented, "Treaties are only pieces of paper; constitutions mere books; elections open combat; liberty is anarchy, and life itself a torment." Near his death in 1830, Bolívar concluded, "America is ungovernable to us. He who serves the revolution plows the sea."[45]

Premature Political Institutions

EARLY CONSTITUTIONS

Despite numerous versions and variations, the initial and subsequent constitutions stood out for their similarity, partly because they drew inspiration from the same foreign models. In every country from 1810 through the 1820s, after securing independence the leaders quickly approved a national constitution. Convened in various ways, usually constitutional conventions adopted these charters. Many regions and subregions also temporarily claimed the right to be new states with their own constitution. Even if the national charter did not elicit full obedience, its existence proclaimed a country's birth, sovereignty, and republicanism. Constitutions served as declarations of aspirations as well as documents for immediate implementation.[46]

In this period of trial and error, the framers sought a balance between liberty and efficiency, freedom and order, ideology and pragmatism. Whether out of idealism, wishful thinking, or the desire to specify novel principles, the founders became much more verbose than the U.S. constitution writers about spelling out the essentials of democracy. The Spanish American constitution's insistence on elaborating the rights of citizens suggested that the drafters knew how anemic those rights were and how difficult they would be to guarantee. The crafters may also have been insisting too much because they and their compatriots really harbored grave doubts about these principles.

To an extent, the constitutional architects viewed republicanism as a default solution because they lacked plausible alternatives. "The North Americans of the days of Washington were republicans by conviction and choice; the Spanish Americans of the days of Bolívar were republicans by compulsion. The former joyously embraced an opportunity when offered; the latter bowed somewhat sadly to necessity."[47] As a result, "Nowhere are constitutions more elaborate—or less observed."[48]

The Latin American constitutions formed part of the international West-ern trend away from the absolutist state to one limited by law in order to protect the rights of individuals and communities. In designing their char-ters, the Latin Americans followed in the footsteps of foreigners, especially the United States, France, and Spain. At least on paper, they mainly copied from the United States the separation of powers into three branches, presi-dentialism, the bicameral congress, the bill of rights, and sometimes federal-ism. In a few cases, the concepts of habeas corpus and judicial review also made an impact, but not much. The U.S. influence—especially federalism—appeared greatest in Mexico, Venezuela, and, above all, Argentina. French thought, particularly the Constitution of 1791, shaped notions of human rights as well ideas such as centralism, municipal organization, a council of state, congressional interpellation of ministers, proportional representation, legislation by decree, and, most significantly, states of emergency and excep-tion to suspend constitutional rights.[49]

At the same time, Latin America's pioneering constitutions incorporated many Spanish elements, including prior colonial laws, so long as they did not conflict too much with republicanism. The Spanish Constitution of 1812 also molded Spanish America. From that source, the Creoles com-monly transcribed the basic organization of the nation and the constitution, Catholicism as the official religion, limited government, three branches with checks and balances, the individual vote and representation, and in-direct elections to congress. Many leaders in the colonies saw that Span-ish document, however, as too close to French radicalism, particularly in its enfranchisement of the entire adult male population, with no property restrictions.[50]

By the 1820s, most constitutions prescribed centralized republics modeled after the 1812 Constitution of Cádiz, even though it proposed a limited mon-archy. Only a few countries opted for the Napoleonic regime favored by Bolí-var. In the first category fell those of Mexico (1824, although it was strongly federalist), Venezuela (1830), Colombia (1821, 1830, 1832), Peru (1823, 1828), Chile (1828), Argentina (1826), and Uruguay (1830). Like the Spanish, the Creoles were trying to adapt Anglo and French liberalism to their history, society, culture, and power relations. Whereas the Cádiz model distrusted the common people outside elections and concentrated power in the hands of alternating elites, the Bolivarians preferred even more autocratic restrictions to avoid electoral and political instability, such as presidents or senators for life. The latter also gave the military exceptional prerogatives and downplayed civil liberties. In most countries in the era, neither of these models succeeded. None of the constitutions adopted immediately after independence except

Uruguay's (1830 to 1918) lasted into the twentieth century, although many of their features reappeared time and again.[51]

CENTRALISM OVER FEDERALISM

The constitutional issue of centralism versus federalism generated intense controversy. The proponents of centralization—mainly in the capital cities—argued that it strengthened the novice national government, facilitated the war against Spain, required fewer qualified public officials, discouraged regionalism and localism, fortified control over rebellious provinces, and provided greater efficiency, uniformity, order, and equity. The advocates of decentralization—mainly in the provinces—countered that their plan encouraged democratic participation, prevented despotism by the central government, promoted efficient and effective provincial and local self-rule, recognized the reality of geographic distances and infrastructural deficiencies, acknowledged entrenched regional and municipal differences, and convinced recalcitrant zones to stay within the new nation. Behind these two positions sometimes lurked conflicting economic realities, for example with the core preferring free trade with Europe and the periphery opting for protection.[52]

Many of the early constitutions replicated the federalist provisions of the U.S. charter, but that system seldom worked in reality. It collided with the embedded power disparities between the capital cities and the provinces. After years of struggle between the two camps and numerous fiascos by federalists, centralism came to dominate in most of Latin America. Most leaders came to agree with Bolívar's rejection of U.S. federalism: "Such a system is no more than organized anarchy, or, at best, a law that implicitly decrees the obligation to dissolve and ruin the state with all its members. It would be better, I think, for South America to adopt the Koran rather than the United States' form of government, although the latter is the best in the world."[53]

The unitary result resurrected the orientation of the Spanish colonial government. It had been extremely centralist in organization, although its effective scope had often been limited to the capital cities, leaving substantial latitude to the outlying areas. The judicial jurisdictions of the *audiencias* beneath the Spanish viceroyalties bequeathed the outlines of many of the new republics. The intendancies created in Spanish America in the late colonial period by the Bourbons as intermediate governing bodies often became the new provinces and the champions of federalism after independence.[54]

In part, the assertion of municipal and provincial autonomy through the wars of independence constituted a reaction against the centralizing Bourbon reforms of the eighteenth century, and a return to traditional Spanish and Spanish American localism. Against that trend, the post-independence national rulers typically came to favor centralism (in reality if not on paper) to exert control over recalcitrant provinces. Consequently, the opponents of the new governments regularly attacked them in the name of federalism but usually governed as centralists once in power. Local conditions—not the degree of U.S. influence—mainly determined whether the new political systems became unitary or federalist. Whichever system prevailed in the constitution, the fledgling governments found it very difficult to overcome the peoples' devotion to local liberty and local authorities, much as in Spain itself.[55]

Clashes between centralists and federalists devastated even republics that became fairly successful later in the nineteenth century. In a somewhat typical but extended case, constitutions rotated rapidly in Colombia mainly as a result of furious battles between centralists and federalists. Of the ten constitutions between 1811 and 1886, six installed centralism and four federalism. The first constitution of 1811 instituted a "federal association." It reserved to the provinces all powers not delegated to the central government, a recognition that Bogotá wielded little clout over the outlying regions. The charter said almost nothing about the organization of the national government except that all authority rested in a congress elected by the provinces. Designed to organize the country for war, the centralizing constitution of 1821 vowed "to establish a form of government which will insure the benefits of liberty, property, and equality in so far as it is possible to a Nation beginning its political career and still struggling for its independence. . . ." Colombia did not settle this issue until the enduring and largely centralist constitution of 1886 forged a compromise.[56]

The early constitutions of Argentina also did not prosper principally because of the fratricide over centralism versus federalism. From the beginning, the provinces thwarted attempts by the city and province of Buenos Aires to establish a centralized government headed by a so-called "director." Proposals for a monarchy or for a decentralized federalist system also foundered. Some early constitutions—like that of 1819—tried to resolve the issue through fairly undemocratic measures, concentrating power in the hands of an indirectly chosen chief executive. The Constitution of 1826 established a centralized republic run by a president in the capital of Buenos Aires. Immediately federalists and provincial leaders denounced this short-lived constitution, while they claimed to represent more democratic impulses.

Civil wars ravaged Argentina until the putative federalist Juan Manuel de Rosas imposed order through a centralizing dictatorship in the 1830s. Amidst recurrent strife, stable constitutional government did not take hold until the 1850s. Whereas the Colombians finally established peace through compromise with a centralist constitution allowing for some federalist prerogatives, the Argentines did so with a federalist constitution incorporating counterbalancing centralist powers.[57]

Roiled by the same issue, Chile engaged in four unsuccessful attempts to hammer out constitutional order from independence in 1818 to 1828. The last effort at a liberal federalist constitution in 1828 failed to win acceptance. All these experiments crumbled because they produced either centralist tyranny or federalist anarchy—unleashing repeated donnybrooks among factions and provinces. The conservatives finally imposed order by force of arms in 1830, and implanted a sturdy centralist constitution in 1833. Many larger and more heterogeneous countries took much longer to put this dispute to rest.[58]

Although ruled by a central monarch, Brazil was de facto the most decentralized new country, also reflecting its colonial past. Leaner and more regionalized than the Spanish system, the Portuguese empire had also exhibited no well-defined democratic traits. The governors and captain-generals of the provinces came to exert almost as much authority as the viceroy. As in Spanish America, municipal councils in Brazil provided the governing entity most identified with local elite interests. After independence, the official centralized hierarchy remained much the same, as did the unofficial vigor of regionalism and localism.[59]

The Spaniards had established municipalities (*municipios*) and municipal councils (*cabildos*) as instruments of conquest. The town council had occupied the bottom of the Spanish system. It exerted no more authority in the colonial period than would municipal government after independence. From the sixteenth through the eighteenth centuries, it lost power as the sale of its offices brought more and more Creoles into these positions.

The cabildo was not a democratic institution, but it may have signified some limited participation and representation, as well as opportunities for corruption, for the local upper class. The Bourbon reforms attenuated the role of the town councils, but then those bodies reasserted themselves during the struggles for independence. Open council meetings—cabildos abiertos—often issued the first declarations of independence. After this brief outburst of local autonomy, the municipalities exerted little power.[60]

Following independence, many municipal governments retained the form of Spanish institutions, with mayors (*alcaldes*) and council members (*regidores*), but with very narrow authority. Local government lost ground, subordinated by the provinces or the central administration. In some countries, centralists increasingly appointed the officials for both the provinces and municipalities. In the new republics, municipal governments became notoriously impoverished, lethargic, ineffectual, corrupt, abusive, and undemocratic, dominated by local kingpins.[61]

REGAL PRESIDENTS

Both the Indian—especially the Aztec and Inca states—and Spanish empires bequeathed a legacy of executive dominance in politics. Spain's absolutist crown melded secular and religious authority. The king embodied and personified the state before independence as the president would thereafter. Moreover, office holders in the New World saw themselves as representing the king, not the people. Since those bureaucrats secured their offices either as a reward for service to the crown or through purchase, they viewed those posts as private property from which to extract status and profit, one of the roots of corruption. Although beholden to the king, they bent the legal rules to achieve their objectives. Nothing in the colonial political hierarchy augured well for public-spirited democracy thereafter.[62]

In the New World, the viceroy concentrated enormous powers in his hands. He not only ruled over his kingdom as the representative of the crown but also served as captain general and president of the *audiencia*, one of the antecedents of subsequent judicial subservience to the chief executive in the independent republics. Originally appointed for life, viceroys later had their terms shortened to three and then five years. Setting precedents for the subsequent republican presidents, they oversaw all administrative offices, carried out legislative and judicial functions, and managed military and ecclesiastical affairs.[63]

During the course of the colonial period, the royal political system gradually and slightly checked and balanced the viceroy's powers. Four institutions always limited viceregal latitude: the crown and its agencies in Spain, the *audiencia*, the *visita*, and the *residencia*. The difficulties of distance and communication constrained the crown's theoretically absolute ability to control the viceroy. However, the king played institutions off against each other by maintaining an uneven balance of powers among the multiple entities with overlapping functions, even though there was a clear ranking of authority.

The *audiencia* and its officials conflicted with the viceroy over judicial, legislative, and administrative matters, including fiscalization, and they could complain directly to the crown. The monarch could dispatch secret visits (*visita*) at any time to investigate the viceroy's conduct while in office. The king also ordered public hearings (*residencias*) about a viceregal term just ended. The toddler republics adapted some of these mechanisms to try to restrain presidents. Although reactions against Bourbon centralization led some early constitution drafters to favor hobbled presidents and federalism, the failures of the initial republican governments turned the tide in favor of unleashed chief executives presiding over unitary states.[64]

According to an Ecuadorean maxim, independence brought "the last day of despotism and the first day of the same thing." During and after the wars of independence, the military leaders exerted overwhelming executive authority. Four models of executive power emerged: monarchist from Iberian and other European models (Haiti, Mexico, and Brazil), collegial from France (various early constitutions and juntas, with no lasting effect), lifetime presidential from Bolívar (the short-lived Bolivian Constitution of 1826), and limited presidential from the United States (most countries).[65]

Believing that the monarchy helped stabilize the British system, Bolívar hoped to craft a republican surrogate. To contend with civil strife in fragmented societies, he envisioned a centralized, powerful chief executive, superior to the other branches of government but moderately constrained by them. He recommended this *democratic ceasarism* in various forms to the Peruvians, Colombians, Venezuelans, and Bolivians.[66]

As he became disillusioned with liberalism, Bolívar proposed to Bolivia his most extreme version of the president. That executive would rule for life, and would designate a vice president as successor. Fearing that presidential elections instigated anarchy, Bolívar presented his plan for the Bolivian constitution in these terms: "The President of the Republic will come to be in our Constitution like a sun that, firm in its center, gives life to the universe. This supreme authority should be perpetual, because in systems without hierarchies one needs more than in others a fixed point around which revolve the Magistrates and the citizens, the men and the things. 'Give me a fixed point'—said an ancient one—'and I will move the world.'"[67]

Although the Spanish Americans copied the outline of their standard presidential system from the U.S. constitution, that document was quite vague about the powers of the office. Consequently, many Creoles—for example in the Mexican Constitution of 1824—turned to the Spanish Constitution of 1812 for its itemization of the powers of the regent to be exercised in the name of the king. For example, the very early constitutions in Spanish America borrowed their allocation to the executive of the authority to submit legislation to the congress, to propose the budget, and to conduct foreign affairs. In law and practice, Spanish American presidents exceeded their U.S. counterpart not only with these agenda-setting, legislating, and vetoing powers but also with greater appointive leeway, including naming judges, governors, and sometimes municipal officials, albeit often with the consent of congress. The trail-blazing constitutions also generally granted the presidents control over the armed forces, although that proved difficult to effectuate.[68]

Presidents in Spanish America also became stronger than those in the United States because most of the constitutions tied the Roman Catholic Church to the state. This provision carried on the Inca, Aztec, and Iberian tradition of blending the state and the official religion in the ruling figure. Spanish American presidents also exceeded those in Washington because they assumed, or tried to assume, the patronage powers over the Catholic Church that had belonged previously to the crown. Furthermore, the first presidents often took on extraordinary powers to solve extraordinary problems, such as winning the war of independence, establishing peace among civil factions thereafter, and creating a new state from whole cloth. Far more than in the United States or in its constitution, they maintained exceptional authority to suspend civil liberties and override the other branches of government during emergencies.[69]

From the beginning, the Spanish American presidents possessed more authority than their North American forebears to govern internally and externally with fewer restrictions from congress. The caudillistic, militaristic origins and behavior of the early Spanish American presidents compounded this tendency. They frequently went far beyond their constitutional powers and often became outright dictators. Although repeatedly undemocratic in their treatment of formal institutions, some caudillos informally embodied to their followers *popular sovereignty* or *primitive democracy*.[70]

Like most countries, Chile suffered from overbearing early presidents. Once in power for six years (1817 to 1823), the founding father, Bernardo O'Higgins, worried much more about disorder than despotism, and basically governed as a dictator. Like many autocratic rulers in Latin America, he argued that true representative government would have to come later. Mainly governing within the rules he had established, O'Higgins became one of many examples in the region of legal authoritarianism.

The constitution of 1818, drafted by a commission appointed by the Supreme Director, O'Higgins, gave him sweeping powers. For example, he could appoint local heads of government, judges, and the five members of the senate. When the usually compliant members of the senate conflicted with the president, he shut it down. After fashioning another constitution to sanctify his authoritarian practices in 1822, O'Higgins was driven from office in 1823, fleeing into exile in Peru. His successors designed a new constitution in 1823, but dictators effectively ruled Chile.[71]

Peru's early constitutions also had little impact on the autocratic behavior of its sovereigns. Like their Chilean and Ecuadorean neighbors, some Peruvians initially argued in favor of a constitutional monarchy. They pointed out this was the only form of government the Creoles had ever known and the one most easily understood by the Indians. Thereafter, the Peruvians struggled to forge an orderly republic.

The Peruvian constitution of 1822 provided for a powerful four-year presidency and a unicameral congress. It had no immediate relevance because congress made Bolívar a dictator in 1824 until he resigned to go to Colombia in 1826. In typical fashion, the new Peruvian constitution of 1828 created a robust president chosen by an electoral college, a bicameral legislature, an independent judiciary, and local officials selected by the president. This constitution also had minimal significance, because armed force governed Peru. Subsequent constitutions came and went almost as rapidly as rulers.[72]

As another example, the Colombian constitution of 1821 also prescribed a domineering chief executive, inspired by the quasi-authoritarian views of Bolívar. However, it included more restrictions. The president possessed great powers, especially during emergencies, but he was to be advised by a Council of Government and his laws required the signature of the appropriate government minister. The central government totally subordinated the provinces and municipalities and named their officials. The president also overshadowed the bicameral legislature. On paper, the congress enjoyed extensive powers, but it only met for three months a year. The president and congress appointed the justices of the supreme court, and jury trials were recommended. All citizens supposedly had equal rights, including freedom of the press and freedom from abuse by the government. The four-year president could only be reelected once without an intervening term by someone else.[73]

As seen in Colombia, nearly all constitutions tried to constrain the chief executive, usually in vain. Most Draconian were some early fleeting experiments—notably in Venezuela, Colombia, Peru, Chile, and Argentina—with plural executives weaker than congress. Lawmakers proposed these executive triumvirates not only to curtail authoritarianism but also to avoid succession crises. These arrangements may have served as precursors of the later ruling juntas of the three commanders-in-chief of the armed forces.[74]

Limits on presidential reelection appeared extremely early, reflecting well-grounded fears of perpetuation in office. For the Congress of Angostura in Venezuela in 1819, Bolívar considered a four-year presidency with reelection permitted as in the U.S. constitution but then decided to recommend the possibility of only one reelection. The Congress settled on six years with no immediate reelection. In 1824, the Mexican Constitution barred the president from immediate reelection. This was not just an issue spawned by the later abuses of tyrants like Porfirio Díaz, who reigned from 1876 to 1911, when the Mexican Revolution erupted in the name of "no reelection."[75]

Most of the early constitutions set other limits on the chief executive, such as oversight by a council of state, co-signing of decrees by ministers, and counterbalancing legislatures including permanent committees to act in their absence. Steeped in nineteenth-century liberalism, many constitutions also guaranteed citizens' rights against presidential intrusion. For example, Chile's early charters officially protected individuals from government persecution and mistreatment, such as unlawful arrest or torture. They also preserved property rights, promised equality before the law (but not in society), and shielded civil liberties, particularly freedom of expression, within limits. But constitution writers were not ready to enshrine religious freedom in Chile or most of Latin America.[76]

Although some of the early constitutions spelled out elaborate civil liberties, others gave them less attention than did the United States or hedged them with numerous qualifiers. For example, Mexico's constitution of 1824 said little about civil rights or equality under the law. Instead, it recognized special corporatist privileges for the military and the Church. While the call for freedom of the press and expression constituted a sea change in Latin America from colonial times, it remained severely limited by law and practice. As one of Argentina's more progressive leaders, Moreno, phrased it, "At last we perceive that the masses of the people will exist in shameful barbarism if they are not given complete liberty to speak on any matter . . . as long as it is not in opposition to the holy truths of our august religion and the decisions of the government, which are always worthy of our greatest respect."[77]

In sum, in law and even more in execution, presidents overwhelmingly dominated the first independent governments. Legal attempts to hem in their powers spoke to real problems but not real solutions. Some constitutional inhibitions occasionally made a difference, especially over time, but they failed to tame presidentialism significantly.

LIMITED LEGISLATURES

The constitution makers expected congress to become the primary institution restraining the president. However, its early weakness remained another foundational legacy that persisted over time, despite gradual gains. After independence, conflicts between the executive and the legislature frequently led to presidents closing the congress. Other times, these clashes triggered military ejections of the president. Although the assembly wielded at least enough power to annoy the chief executive, the latter usually came out on top.[78]

An independent representative congress had no tradition among either the Indians or the Creoles: Of the three branches, the legislative proved the hardest to establish because it had not existed in the colonial period, when government offices combined legislative and executive functions. The only partial exceptions were the Spanish American representatives selected for the Cortes of Cádiz and for the cabildos at the local level. Although the founding fathers borrowed the trappings of the U.S. congress, they also incorporated traits from the open town council from the colonial and independence periods, now expanded to become a national institution.

After the fall of the king in 1808, many Spanish American cabildos transformed themselves into *cabildos abiertos* to involve more Creoles in deliberations about self-government. In imitation of the local collective governments that had arisen in Spain when Ferdinand departed, many cabildos formed *juntas* to, at least temporarily, exercise the sovereign will of the people. Not previously elected, the cabildo members historically represented their locality, not the population as a whole. Like the subsequent legislatures, these first assemblies of elites gathered together infrequently to issue general opinions on pressing issues, to draw up the constitution, to assign administrative tasks to government officials, or to pick an independence leader, like San Martín. They did not become standing lawmaking bodies to monitor and dominate the government or the chief executive, to whom they actually delegated the responsibility for running the government.[79]

Even in the beginning years of the new republics, the legislatures were puny but not completely irrelevant. At the very least, the founders set forth principles, procedures, and promises for the legislative bodies that shaped their futures. Although the constitutions generally bestowed much stronger powers on the presidents than on the legislatures, they also gave the congress potent attributes. The lassitude of the legislatures was due more to the abuses by the chief executives than to the design of the constitutions. The legislators' ineffectiveness showed that the way institutions evolved in a national setting was often more important than the characteristics assigned to them in the law.[80]

Most of the early Latin American constitutions accorded considerable responsibilities to the assembly, in some cases even calling it the locus of sovereignty. However, the legislators met infrequently—sometimes only a handful of months every year or two—and exerted little authority versus the president. In the early years, many congressmen refused to serve because of the costs of traveling to and working in the capital, which indicated that the opportunities for both salaries and graft were small. Despite their lack of experience, time, power, and resources, some early congresses actually worked diligently to carry out their pioneering duties. Others mired in haggling among themselves and with the executive branch.[81]

Whether preferring monarchy or presidentialism, neither San Martín nor Bolívar showed great respect for a democratic legislature, although they did advocate a strong and independent judiciary. At the Congress of Angostura in Venezuela in 1819, Bolívar proposed a bicameral congress with the house elected directly and the senate, to provide stability and continuity, populated by heredity, modeled after the Roman Senate and the British House of Lords. Bolívar thought the unelected senators should include the military liberators of the country. Thus it would provide a safeguard against shifts in public opinion or in the behavior of the other branches of government.

The congresses to which Bolívar submitted his constitutional plans proved to be more democratic than the Liberator. At Angostura, the delegates reduced the senate terms to life-long rather than hereditary. And at the Congress of Cúcuta in Colombia in 1821, the members made both houses subject to popular election in a legislature more powerful than the president.[82]

Bolívar's Bolivian constitution of 1826 also created an unusual legislature. He proposed a House of Tribunes, a House of Senators, and a House of Censors. He expected the Tribunes to concentrate on fiscal, military, and foreign affairs, the Senators on judicial, ecclesiastical, and constitutional issues, and the Censors on the implementation of the constitution, laws, and treaties. In 1831, the Bolivians replaced this constitution with a more standard organizational chart setting up a four-year presidency, a senate, a house, and a judiciary.[83]

Even in Brazil's hereditary monarchy, the constitution of 1824 established a functioning congress made up of a chamber of deputies and a senate. In its first years of existence, the legislature demonstrated that it was not totally inferior by frequently quarreling with the emperor. However, it would take many decades before Latin American assemblies began to approach their potential.[84]

JUDICIAL CONTINUITIES

More than any other political institution after independence, the judiciaries carried forward numerous colonial practices, some lasting into the twenty-first century. For many years, the Creoles left the Spanish system of courts and justice largely intact. Legacies included a civil or Roman law tradition, the blurring of judicial and political functions, a corporate and insular corps of judges, judicial dependence on the executive branch, and a formidable extra-judicial staff of court clerks and notaries public who thwarted legal efficiency and change. Furthermore, the rule of law had been very uneven and particularly lax in outlying areas, which generated mistrust and disrespect of the legal system.[85]

The institutions and procedures of the Spanish system of administration relied heavily on judicial devices and on legally trained officials. The empire was governed by several codes of law, all to some extent valid, and often conflicting, the interpretation of which lay in the hands of a Kafkaesque judiciary. The king sat at the apex of this system. He served as both the source of the law and the chief of judges, adjudicating among competing interests.

The crown divided the viceroyalties into *audiencias* in the principal city of each of the important provinces. These offices provided the core of the administrative-judicial system. They functioned as courts of appeal and as cabinet councils for the viceroys, performing administrative, legislative and judicial functions. They protected what few rights colonists and Indians enjoyed under the king's law. More than any other institutions, the audiencias restrained the arbitrary use of power by viceroys or captains-general, although remaining subordinate to them. The practices of the audiencias and the courts beneath them influenced the judiciaries of the new republics more than did the U.S. model.[86]

After independence, the judiciary actually became less independent from the government administration and less effective than it had been in the colonial period. Now the courts had to cope with an expanded workload, minuscule resources, and the need to sort out which Spanish laws still applied. They also faced overreaching chief executives, congresses, and armed forces, who, along with elites and caudillos, resisted legal restraints.

Bolívar recommended the U.S. judicial system because he admired its independence. He also called for trial by jury, as did the Mexican liberal, José Maria Luis Mora, but it did not catch on in Latin America. The exotic U.S. concept of judicial review of the constitution also functioned poorly if at all. Finding it very difficult to reconcile Spanish traditions with U.S. imports, judges usually opted for formulas from the past. In most countries, the judiciary did not play a significant role in politics or democracy until well into the twentieth century, when it still lagged behind other institutions.[87]

PIONEERING ELECTIONS

The new democratic institution that functioned best was elections, despite their shortcomings and the domination of caudillos. Whether those elections were broad or narrow, fair or fraudulent, respected or violated, their practices influenced political precedents, traditions, expectations, culture, identity, representation, and, eventually, power relations. Even those beneath the upper class sometimes participated in elections in surprising numbers and apparently attached significance to voting.

The early importance of elections surfaced in their widespread occurrence from the independence years onward. At the very start of the skirmishes for independence, elections in the empire catapulted Spain and its colonies into the forefront of electoral experience in the greater European world. Thereafter, up to a point, even Latin American conservatives and many dictators recognized the utility and legitimacy of elections, however contrived and however disconnected from more powerful institutions and forces that really determined national governance.[88]

From the beginning, elections became major sources of civic action, debates, uncertainty, instability, violence, coups, and, at times, opportunity. In spite of egregious flaws, early elections sometimes served as rare outlets for popular mobilization, aspirations, and expression, as opportunities for contending elites to galvanize mass supporters through ballots instead of bullets, as cauldrons of politicization, as seedbeds of an electoral culture, as pressure points to open up the political system, as a means to select or at least ratify leaders, and as vital parts of an ostensibly republican governing structure. In some cases, electoral rules and even practices were at least as democratic as in other parts of the contemporaneous Western world. In some countries, however, suffrage advances made in the early nineteenth century suffered subsequent reversals.[89]

When the monarchy first disappeared with Ferdinand, Spaniards and Spanish Americans initially theorized that sovereignty reverted to the will of the people. Barring brute force or direct democracy, they decided to express that will through elections in a representative regime. However unsatisfactory elections were in their conduct, the Creoles could find no other consensual and relatively peaceful way to select and legitimize their interim or independent governments.[90]

Thus, Spanish American elections began in a transition phase—before an independent state existed (for example in Argentina). In the province of Buenos Aires, the elections from 1810 to 1820 selected cabildo members, governors, and deputies to juntas or assemblies or congresses. The regulations adopted by the Argentines for these elections built upon those dictated by Spain to elect American deputies to the ruling Junta and the Cortes between 1809 and 1810.

Those first elections under Spain and then the Argentines limited participants to the "principal and most healthy residents" among free adult males in the municipality. They normally defined voters in Buenos Aires as free male citizens, native and resident, over twenty-five years old, property owners or gainfully employed, and not salaried servants. Having these elections managed by the cabildos reflected the Spanish concept of the representation of corporate groups (e.g., cities), not of individuals. However, great debates ensued immediately arguing for individual representation and inclusion of voters in the countryside. Most of these early elections were decided by a plurality and by voting in public.[91]

As in Argentina, most of Venezuela's first elections were indirect. In 1810, twenty-five-year-old men with at least 2,000 pesos in movable property elected electors to choose the deputies for the Cortes in Spain. These stipulations contained more restrictions than the criteria in the peninsula, which imposed no property requirements. Given low life expectancy, the Venezuelans also set a high age barrier.

One precursor of Venezuelan independence, Miranda, envisioned elections for provincial assemblies that would form a federal government, uniting all of Latin America. The participants would be all those born of free mothers and fathers as well as those born overseas who became established and married in America. His countryman, Bolívar, expressed skepticism about loosely or improperly conducted elections, as he witnessed in the first Venezuelan republic. He complained that the common people exhibited too much ignorance to vote correctly. Bolívar accused urban schemers of just using the elections to favor their own factions or parties and to install incompetent and corrupt officials. He feared that unguarded democracy would unleash racial conflict from below. Bolívar also thought freedom of the press had gone too far in fomenting dissent. He averted those problems in the second republic by ruling as a military dictator.[92]

In 1810, the cabildo of Santiago issued a call to all the other cabildos in Chile to send representatives to a congress. The regulations duplicated those the Spanish crown had historically established for the Cortes. Chile's unicameral congress would contain representatives from each of its twenty-five provinces, with the larger populations having more deputies, for a total of thirty-six. Voters or deputies had to be over twenty-five years old. The call recommended that those elected should possess sufficient money to pay their own costs for this service, since the cabildos managed few public funds. Most of these elections, the first in Chilean history, came off smoothly.[93]

Founded in 1810, the Cortes of Cádiz asked all the provinces in Spain and overseas to elect delegates. Although a democratic departure from recent practices, these notions of sovereignty, representation, and elections also harkened back to some traditional Spanish customs, laws, and beliefs, for example in the cabildos. Breaking new ground, the Cortes furthered the transformations in Spain and Spanish America by beginning to shift away from the historical concept of representation of territorial communities, estates, and corporate groups to individuals. These innovations emanating from the Cortes engendered a new definition of the body politic and thus the electorate.[94]

The Constitution of Cádiz inaugurated elections in most of the Hispanic world by granting municipalities the right to elect leaders. This right accentuated the colonial tradition of relative municipal autonomy. Thus, it authenticated and fortified the resistance of many Spanish American communities to domination by officials of the empire or of the newly formed nation-states and their capital cities. Communal electoral rights contributed to the fragmentation and ungovernability of Spanish America during and after independence. National leaders struggled to capture these municipal electoral expressions to legitimate central over local authority.[95]

From 1812 to 1814, Spanish Americans elected representatives for the municipalities, the provinces, and the Cortes. The elections for the city councils transpired under the most democratic procedures. Preceding the balloting, officials unveiled the constitution to the public and took a census to determine the electorate. In many elections, the main contests pitted upper-class Peninsulars against upper-class Creoles, the latter winning most of the time.

In all these types of elections, voters included not only the upper strata but also middle and lower-class male mestizos, Indians, and illiterates, giving many people their first taste of democratic politics. Some authorities actually annulled elections that prevented indigenous males from voting. Officials withheld the franchise from African Americans, domestic servants, women, criminals, and the regular clergy in orders, although secular clergy could vote. Women family heads had traditionally voted in a few Spanish elections, but now the organizers denied that right. Nevertheless, the Spaniards established extraordinarily inclusive criteria for the era. Under those Spanish rules, the municipality of Quito, for example, calculated in 1813 a huge eligible voting population of four hundred thousand people.[96]

Although influential, the Cortes laid down electoral criteria ambiguous enough to allow for local interpretation in the colonies. In response to the 1812 constitution, Mexico City officials arranged municipal and Cortes elections in that same year. They established very few regulations on who could vote or who could be elected, not even the minimum voting age. Nevertheless, they presumed that voters would be community residents and self-supporting. They instructed voters to select delegates, who would in turn choose electors. At the initial parish level, voters expressed themselves orally in public. At the higher level, delegates voted in writing, suggesting that the authorities expected them to be literate.

In these municipal elections, voters turned out in abundance. Indeed, in some parishes, ballots exceeded the number of eligible voters, meaning male residents except for Africans, debtors, unemployed, convicts, or domestic servants. Two parties campaigned for their candidates: the *autonomists* who favored home rule under the 1812 constitution and the *loyalists* who preferred the traditional royal system. In Mexico City, the voters elected only autonomists, inspiring some victorious crowds to chant anti-Spaniard slogans. The loyalists charged fraud, citing prefabricated ballots, multiple voting, and ineligible voters.

From the beginning, elections sparked enthusiasm, conflict, and turbulence. Mexican electoral officials admitted that they had enforced few restrictions on free male residents voting. They confessed little ability to impose racial or occupational requirements. Priests and others herded vagrants to the polls. Thousands of male voters swarmed the polls, including vast numbers of the poorest Mexicans. Many of them apparently took the term *popular sovereignty* to heart.

Elections provided occasions not only for casting votes but also for demonstrating mass political concerns in the streets. Contending elite factions mobilized the underclasses for their own advancement. Tumultuous elections with expanding suffrage in the 1820s convinced some Mexican elites that the lower classes exerted too much influence at the voting sites. In a backlash against popular democracy, the rulers imposed income restrictions by the 1830s.[97]

In the Andes, the need to adhere to the Constitution of Cadiz and the Cortes' call for elections, without clear instructions as to how they were to be conducted, generated debates over who should vote, over who were citizens. Every audiencia had to decide who could vote and how. They grappled with the main issue, for example in Quito, of whether Indians had the same suffrage rights as Spaniards.

In 1813, the audiencia of Quito decided that women could not vote, but that bastards, illiterates, and clergy could. It also ruled against Indians who were *dependents*, a category excluded by the constitution. This term normally meant *domestic servants*, but the Quitenos extended it to include Native Americans working on the haciendas in a state of servitude. Since the officials defined this category of servitude vaguely and enforced it unevenly, a majority of indigenous men received the right to vote. The audiencia disallowed some elections that barred indigenous peoples from the polls. This enfranchisement constituted a leap forward in defining citizens with equal rights before the law.[98]

Meanwhile, Chile drew up its first full-fledged electoral regulations to try to elect a congress in 1813. Voters or deputies had to be twenty-three-year-old men, able to read and write, employed, and earning a minimum salary. From 1813 to 1830, voting varied between public declarations and secret ballots.[99]

Portuguese liberals borrowed from the Spanish constitution of 1812 and from Spanish electoral practices when they called in 1821 for elections in Portugal and Brazil for deputies to a Cortes in the mother country. Although Brazil had known some elections for the offices of the municipal chambers in the colonial period, the first national elections for representatives to the state occurred with these indirect elections to the Cortes. This enfranchisement of male citizens marked a first step toward a new liberal political order. Excluding slaves, the requirements expected citizens to be at least twenty-five years of age if not married and to possess some status and property. Voters included clergy, military, bureaucrats, agriculturalists, professionals, merchants, and artisans.

After Pedro I broke away from the Cortes in 1822, Brazil followed the Portuguese electoral precedent by holding its own indirect elections for deputies to a constituent convention. The constitution of 1824 kept indirect elections with escalating property qualifications for voters and electors. From 1824 on, voters also elected county council members, as they had in the colonial period, though now with a much broader electorate.[100]

After the influence of the liberal Cádiz suffrage standards faded, the Spanish Americans tightened the suffrage to establish protected democracies. From the Cádiz-inspired elections into the 1820s, early elections in independent Latin America did not normally express the broad popular will. Instead, they typically became very narrow exercises in participation, instruments of social control by patron-client mechanisms, manipulation, or force, extremely fraudulent contests, and legitimation devices for oligarchic or dictatorial regimes. Local élites, landowners, caudillos, the Church, and government officials often orchestrated, co-opted, or coerced voters. When elections threatened to uncork social pressures from beneath, the ruling groups constricted or repressed those contests.[101]

Élites controlled these elections in five ways. First, they restricted the suffrage. Second, they established rules for candidates excluding all but the privileged few. Third, they installed systems of indirect representation, wherein those elected formed electoral colleges of aristocrats to select the final winners. Fourth, national and local bosses corralled or cajoled a slightly broader pool of voters, sometimes including the poor. Fifth, the élites committed extravagant fraud.[102]

The Latin Americans espoused two predominant views of participation, one favorable to mass mobilization and the other to mass marginalization. Some of the early leaders most sympathetic toward popular participation emerged among the supposedly uncivilized caudillos who identified with and rallied the lower classes. Although often violent and authoritarian, some of these strong men also furthered democratic expectations. At times they promoted widening the suffrage to allow for direct popular election of presidents.

By contrast with the Spanish constitution of 1812, most Spanish American independence leaders shied away from enfranchising the entire adult male population with no property restrictions. They believed the common people should not participate in electoral decisions until they became more educated, cultured, and indeed leavened with immigrants from Europe. Until then, the elites intended to govern in the name of the people. This assumption conditioned not only suffrage requirements but also the even higher property and income qualifications for holding office.[103]

The Latin Americans wrote fairly uniform suffrage laws. They often applied the word *sana* (meaning "sound, healthy, sane, wise") to those who should vote. This nomenclature may have stemmed from internal Church practice where the votes of the higher, better educated, saintlier clergy counted more in the selection of ecclesiastical officials. It clearly signified that mainly the enlightened upper crust, not the ignorant, rustic, coarse common people, should be voting for leaders.[104]

Although most of the new constitutions promised universal suffrage for free adult males, they usually introduced qualifications. The rulers normally conferred political rights on only *active* citizens, apparently meaning gainfully and independently employed or self-supporting. They also commonly required property holdings for voting, for instance in the Venezuelan First Republic's suffrage law of 1811. They also typically made literacy a qualification, as in the Chilean electoral regulations of 1822, excluding perhaps 90 percent of the population in most of Latin America. They frequently eliminated "dependents," banishing domestic servants, indigents, debtors, and slaves. All these restrictions together left as few as 6 percent of males or 3 percent of the total population eligible to vote. An even smaller percentage qualified for election to office.

Despite these limitations, the Latin Americans permitted, on paper and sometimes in practice, at least as many people—if not more—to vote than in the United States, England, or France, all of which enforced similar restrictions in the era. Some of the Latin American lawmakers gave the literacy requirements (e.g., in the constitutions of Chile in 1822 and Bolivia in 1826) several years to take effect so that men could learn to read and write. Over the years, the expansion of literacy would open the voting booth—when it operated—to more and more people.[105]

By the standards of the era in the Western world, Gran Colombia held an unusually orderly and reasonably democratic election for deputies to the Congress of Cucuta in 1821. Eligible voters included all males with 500 pesos (roughly equivalent to five hundred U.S. dollars) in real property or a profession or trade, as well as soldiers (including foreigners). The rules excluded the *honorable poor* because of their poverty, illiteracy, and susceptibility to manipulation by the Church. The Congress defended property qualifications on the grounds that "a rigorously democratic election does not suit us, will not suit us for many years . . . and perhaps will never be preferable. . . ." The election transpired without notable mischief and sent mainly priests, lawyers, and landowners to the congress.

The Colombian constitution of 1821 made all elections indirect and public, with arms prohibited. Reflecting gender, class, and racial stratification, it subjected voters to the usual sex (implicitly male), age (married or twenty-one years old), economic (owning property worth one hundred pesos or having an occupation, but not a dependent one as a day-laborer or servant), and educational (literate, but with ten years until 1840 to fulfill this requirement) restrictions. These regulations excluded at least 80 percent of the population. According to the law, selling or buying votes would forfeit the right to the franchise.

In a hierarchy of requirements typical in Latin America, Colombian voters chose electors, who needed even more exalted credentials. They had to possess twenty-five years, literacy, property worth five hundred pesos or an annual income worth three hundred pesos or a scientific degree. They selected the representatives (who had to be twenty-five, literate, owners of property worth two thousand pesos or an annual income worth five hundred pesos from landed property or be a professor of science), senators (who had to be thirty years of age, literate, with property worth four thousand pesos or an annual landed income of five hundred pesos or a professor of science), vice-president, and president (the latter two had to have the same qualifications as senators).[106]

In addition to suffrage restrictions, the Latin American elites further insulated themselves from popular sovereignty by carrying on the U.S. and Cadiz tradition of indirect elections well into the twentieth century. For Bolivia, Bolívar recommended that every ten citizens would elect one elector. The citizen and the elector did not have to own property, but they did have to be literate and possess a trade. He excluded day-laborers and domestic servants by occupation, the majority of the population by literacy. He expected the electors in their provincial electoral colleges to select some national legislators, governors, mayors, judges, and priests.[107]

The ruling class also protected themselves from electoral uncertainties by fiddling with the mechanisms, participants, and results. Adversaries commonly lodged charges of tampering, both because many politicians cheated and because accusations could discredit one's opponent. For example, often in Peru two parallel elections took place in a district, with both sides crying theft and submitting the conflicting results to congress for a decision by the national powers. Throughout Latin America, corruption was easy because voting was often done verbally in public, as was common in the opening decades of republican life in the United States. Open balloting allowed those bosses buying or coercing votes to make sure that voters kept their word. Fraud also thrived because of frequently vague national electoral regulations. They allowed actual electoral practices to vary enormously from place to place within countries, fostering fierce local donnybrooks over the conduct of elections.[108]

Conclusion

After all the bloodshed, independence launched Latin America on a rocky start toward democracy. Nevertheless, those initial efforts, ideas, and institutions started the region on a path it has traveled ever since. The founders labored to forge republics amidst the legacies of authoritarianism and inequality from the colonial and independence periods. From the earliest half-steps toward independence through the 1820s, they evolved in an increasingly conservative direction.

The new political institutions usually adhered to the Bolivarian spirit of a protected democracy. Although modeled after the United States, France, and Spain, the fledgling, fleeting, but influential constitutions also contained innovative features that concentrated powers in the hands of the elites, the president, and the central government. The regal presidents overshadowed the other branches of government but found it harder to impose their will over the national territory and inhabitants. The architects of the new regimes gave short shrift to legislatures and judiciaries.

Elections provided the most ground-breaking institutions. They occurred frequently, established crucial good and bad precedents for democracy, and sometimes enrolled surprisingly ample strata of the population. In one of the initial tussles between popular and protected democracy, many common people surged to the polls until the ruling class drove them back with restrictions, fraud, and repression. The battle for the future was joined.

The liberators accomplished the prerequisites and first steps toward democracy, but they left the Spanish American republics in shambles by the end of the 1820s. For decades thereafter, the efforts at democracy or at least republicanism experienced many more defeats than victories. Nevertheless, the end of formal colonialism and the birth of infant republics laid the groundwork for both the failures and successes of the years to come. Most of the world had not even begun the journey.

Chapter 4

The Archaeology of Democracy After Independence, 1820s–1870s

In the aftermath of independence, most Latin American attempts at democracy encountered frustration and failure. Amidst the ruins of these efforts, an archaeology of democracy can excavate the broken pots of proto-democratic civilizations, the shards of shattered institutions, the remains of ancient constitutions, the sarcophagi of buried leaders, and the relics of bygone voting sites. By digging in the more successful countries, it can also dust off the building blocks of the future. An historical archaeology can unearth the few pyramids to democracy that endured. Just as the Spaniards established continuity by mounting their cathedrals on top of the Indian temples, so the later leaders of democracy would erect their structures on the bases of these republican monuments. The less successful countries would find it harder to construct subsequent democratic edifices on the rubble of the post–independence period.[1]

From the 1820s to the 1870s, instability, conflict, and despotism dashed the democratic hopes from the independence years. While Brazil enjoyed the relative stability of its empire, tyranny and anarchy convulsed Spanish America. Between coercion and chaos, democracy stood on shaky ground in the former Spanish colonies. Countless dictatorships alternated with collapsing constitutions and governments. Many Liberals as well as Conservatives dreaded anarchy more than tyranny. They repeatedly supported elitist dictatorships out of their fear that popular democracy could lead to disorder or to popular authoritarianism behind demagogic caudillos.

Despite the frequent reign of autocracy, Latin Americans registered a few gains in a democratic direction. Republicanism remained the dominant political aspiration and virtually the only intellectual justification for the right to rule. A fundamental contradiction evolved between the elites' official liberal discourse and their marginalization of the vast majority of inhabitants.

A few countries experienced institutional improvements—more often on paper than in practice—although at least the laws left a legacy for the future. A handful actually made a little practical progress in constitutional stability, presidential restraint, congressional assertiveness, the exercise of civil liberties and a free press, and the incipient organization of political parties. Most remarkable was the expansion of elections and suffrage, followed by contraction of the franchise. However, all the institutions remained fragile, including the constitution, the central government, local government, the president, the congress, the judiciary, the national armed forces, the electoral system, political parties, and the press. In most cases, institutions made gains individually or partially, not as integrated cogs in a smoothly functioning republican system of government.

The weak national, formal governments confronted often stronger subnational, informal forces, such as regional barons, caudillos, the Church, and the rogue military. The state really only exercised authority over a small part of the national territory and population. For even semi-democratic rule, the most that could be expected was constitutional, civilian government by the oligarchy, and even that rarely succeeded. Sturdy elitist constitutional government usually required a fortuitous combination of economic growth, institutional engineering, consensus within the upper strata, and determined leadership presiding over order after victories in domestic or international warfare.

Constitutional governments faced several problems: (1) they lacked undisputed legitimacy and the widespread consent of elites; (2) both the government and the opposition frequently disobeyed the constitutional rules and violated civil liberties; (3) governments did not enjoy anywhere near a monopoly on the organized means of armed force; (4) they lacked fiscal resources, which exacerbated instability; (5) compared to the overbearing president and military, the other institutions of government were even more frail and dysfunctional; (6) in many cases, neither the government nor the opposition played fair in elections or heeded their results; and (7) political parties remained embryonic and unprogrammatic.[2]

Chronologically, the early burst of liberalism during independence gave way to a cycle of warfare, conservatism, and despotism from the 1830s to the 1840s. Then during the middle of the nineteenth century, the rise of the export economies brought greater political constitutional tranquility. Republicanism revived, and a second wave of liberal reformism crested. After an era of Conservative prevalence, Liberals rose again and pruned the powers of the Church, the military, and the caudillos, while also freeing the slaves. When government revenues swelled, the official armed forces became more capable of enforcing order, rising numbers of government employees became eligible for the franchise, and electoral politics became more competitive to gain access to state resources. As the increasingly wealthy upper strata asserted their control over the central government, they forged either authoritarian or republican systems of oligarchic rule.[3]

In the post-independence decades, three types of regimes predominated, in descending order of frequency: unstable dictatorships and republics (e.g., Bolivia), stable dictatorships (e.g., Paraguay), and stable republics (e.g., Chile). Some countries installed partial oligarchic republics that lacked key features, coherence, and durability. For example, they often failed to sustain the constitution, regular elections, or the regime, and they frequently turned many of the institutions into a farce.

A few countries established solid and ongoing (albeit sometimes interrupted) constitutional, elected, representative oligarchic forms of competition. Taking hold before massive participation became the norm, they tended to have the most success with long-run democratic stability. Early developers of sturdy oligarchic democratic institutions and practices, however aristocratic and flawed, included Chile, Argentina, Colombia, and (to a lesser extent) Uruguay, Costa Rica, and Brazil. By contrast, cases with little successful democratic experience even in the framework of oligarchic republics abounded in Mexico, Central America, the Caribbean, and the Andes.[4]

Analysts have offered several interpretations for the dismal episodes with democratic or republican government in these years. In the 1830s, Alexis de Tocqueville discounted geography as an explanation for the success of democracy in the United States compared to its southern neighbors. He reasoned that similar insulation from Europe, vast open spaces, and bountiful natural resources prevailed in Latin America: "... in what portion of the globe shall we find more fertile plains, mightier rivers, or more unexplored and inexhaustible riches, than in South America? Yet South America has been unable to maintain democratic institutions. If the welfare of nations depended on their being placed in a remote position, with an unbounded space of habitable territory before them, the Spaniards of South America would have no reason to complain of their fate .... There are, however, no nations upon the face of the earth more miserable than those of South America."[5]

Although geography may have mattered little, economic order and growth clearly rendered stable governments of some kind more likely. Durable regimes increasingly succeeded in Latin America after the mid-century upturn in exports. Along with poverty, huge social inequalities made broadly shared semi-democratic politics unlikely. Sharp divisions by gender, class, and race excluded most people from participation and left many elites leery of broadening the franchise.

As in the rest of the world, formal political activities banned women. The concentration of land, income, and wealth, accentuated by slavery, debt peonage, illiteracy, and penury, kept the overwhelming majority of the population from a significant role in political institutions. In this period, most countries abolished slavery, although Brazil remained the most glaring exception. Among legally free peoples, the Indians suffered the most ostracism from political participation.

Whereas many of his fellow Liberals accused the Roman Catholic Church of being the biggest obstacle to republicanism, Argentina's Domingo Sarmiento blamed the inferior Spanish and mestizo races, not just the indigenous peoples. His racism led this Liberal and others to recommend European immigration as the best hope for democracy. To the dismay of many oligarchs and with the connivance of others, the popular classes, despite their repression and disadvantages, sometimes encountered subordinate ways of taking part in politics, including voting, demonstrating, rioting, and joining armed bands.[6]

Negative political legacies from the colonial and independence periods compounded socioeconomic hindrances. The protracted wars for independence bequeathed continued civil wars, political turbulence, and dictatorships. In general, both the military and the Church supported authoritarianism. Private armies often deployed more firepower than the national armed forces.

Sometimes the only semblance of democracy was what might be labeled *democracy by violence*. This usually meant so-called democracy by caudillos, who hijacked popular democratic impulses in an authoritarian direction. Local and provincial bosses personified, represented, and roused their peasant followers in struggles against the sway of other provinces and of the central core. As much as mobilizing the masses, the caudillos exercised social control over them. These strongmen channeled lower-class grievances into patron-client relations or repressed them. They rallied and exploited the poor to legitimize their rule or to intimidate their opponents. In the battles between liberals and conservatives, the latter usually relied most on these warlords and their informal authority over the lower classes and the state. However, most elites were appalled by popular caudillos.[7]

Some caudillos not only manipulated but also authentically represented the popular groups. Many peasants, cowboys, miners, and other workers resented the upper class and its republican model of protected democracy. They asserted their own culture and desires for participation and liberation through their armed paladins. Argentine intellectual José Luis Romero referred to this identification of the common people with men on horseback as "inorganic democracy," a violent expression of popular sovereignty and equality. In mid-nineteenth-century Argentina, Liberal leader Juan Bautista Alberdi also lamented that the caudillos were "the will of the popular masses . . . the immediate organ and arm of the people . . . the caudillos are democracy." In the guise of caudillo democracy, taking up arms for a warlord planted one of the roots of popular as opposed to protected democracy. However, this caudillo variety usually took the form of popular authoritarianism.[8]

By and large, the Roman Catholic Church sided with Conservatives, the military, and the oligarchy in favor of rightwing authoritarian rule. For some Liberals, like Francisco Bilbao in Chile, the Church's clash with republicanism produced the fundamental conflict of the early nineteenth century, for the former represented dogma and the latter free reason. Nevertheless, during elections, clergy stood out as some of the most active mobilizers of voters. They did so normally for Conservatives, thus disenchanting Liberals with popular democracy. In many countries over the course of the nineteenth century, the Liberals gradually whittled down the secular powers of the Church.[9]

Democratic Principles versus Practices

Despite these impediments and the predominance of despotism, democratic ideas survived in some quarters. Nearly all political leaders, whether on the left or the right, subscribed (at least rhetorically) to some form of liberalism, usually in the mold of protected democracies. Almost no alternative defensible model to classic liberalism existed in official discourse. Most political thinkers still advocated some version of republicanism, even while they placed the highest priority in these anarchic years on order, both for security and for economic growth. Most liberals—as well as conservatives—feared anarchy more than tyranny. Although rarely successful before mid-century, their vision of liberalism became very limited and at best tepidly democratic, often more dedicated to liberal economic than political precepts.

In principle, most intellectuals believed in democracy, meaning that sovereignty resided in the people, and that legal equality was desirable. In practice, they favored government by the elites. Neither in the nineteenth nor the twentieth century did Liberals necessarily lead the way in promoting the addition of groups like the poor, the illiterates, and the women to the electoral rolls. They worried that those supposedly less independent voters might be corralled by the Church for the Conservatives.[10]

Even more than during the independence years, political planners far preferred the U.S. over the French Jacobin model of revolution. In the 1830s and 1840s, Latin American Liberals continued to praise the U.S. political system in the abstract but increasingly bemoaned its inapplicability to a far different society below the border. They pointed to their countries' colonial heritage, Roman Catholic Church, armed bands, illiteracy, and stark social divisions—indeed national character—as obstacles to imitation of the United States. Although virtually all these thinkers adhered rhetorically to some form of liberal constitutionalism, they exhibited more interest in pragmatic blueprints for government than in philosophical treatises.[11]

After the liberators turned away from liberalism, Conservatives came to dominate political thought and practice in the 1830s and 1840s. They advocated a restoration of the colonial order in republican dress, resting the state's authority on the Church and the aristocracy. Their greatest success came with Diego Portales in Chile, who believed that Latin Americans needed a long period of education to prepare them for unfettered liberal republicanism.[12]

Liberalism received a new lease on life at mid-century. The overthrow of the French monarch in the Revolution of 1848 helped inspire romantic liberalism in parts of Latin America. This new generation of Liberals vowed to safeguard individual liberties by uprooting the vestiges of colonialism, including Indian tribute, African slavery, and the suffocating power of the Church and the armed forces. Sometimes these Liberal theoreticians and politicians also expanded federalism and civil liberties—such as freedom of the press, speech, and assembly. Most notably in Chile and Colombia, they sought to activate more popular participation in their oligarchic republics, particularly among urban artisans and partly through advocating suffrage expansion and direct elections.

Although French socialist rhetoric penetrated Latin America, the ideology attracted few followers. In reaction against such ideas, Conservatives pointed to the socialist threat in France as a warning against stirring up popular expectations and activism in Latin America. By the end of this period, French positivism exerted its influence, mostly in an anti-liberal and authoritarian direction, preaching "order and progress."[13]

By mid-century, there arose two main strands of liberal ideas in Latin America, exemplified in Mexico. The traditional school of thought sought to protect the individual from the state oppression of the colonial period by limiting government. This position led naturally to an emphasis on constitutional constraints on power, federalism, civil liberties, property rights, and laissez-faire. The newer point of view aimed to protect individuals from intimidation by corporate groups, particularly the Church and the armed forces. This propensity required a muscular secular state to rein in corporate groups. To stretch a point, this contrast resembled that between small-government nineteenth-century liberals and big-government New Deal twentieth-century liberals in the United States—the former trying to shield individuals from government abuse, and the latter trying to use government to save them from corporate exploitation.[14]

This distinction between anti-statist and anti-corporate liberalism characterized the evolution of Mexico's leading post-independence Liberal thinker, José María Luis Mora. Like many Liberals, he expressed caution or at least ambivalence about how egalitarian he wanted democracy to be. Mora tempered his liberalism to adjust to the political reality of bloodshed and anarchy after independence and to the sociological reality of deep divisions by class, race, and ethnicity. For example, he preferred property rights qualifications for all political participants and accepted centralist controls over federalism. In Mexico and elsewhere, many Liberals shied away from open democracy because that necessitated the participation of rural Indians. These Liberals believed in theoretical equality before the law but not practical equality in terms of political rights and citizenship.[15]

Despite such doubts, Mexico reached the zenith of mid-century Liberal reform in Latin America. Led by Benito Juárez, the Liberals won an epic struggle for *The Reform* against the Conservatives, the Church, and the French empire of Maximilian, from 1855 to 1872. Their constitution of 1857 embraced an end to Church and military *fueros* (privileges), a strong bill of rights, federalism, and universal male suffrage, though still through indirect elections for national offices.

However, these Mexican Liberals never had the inclination or opportunity to rule in a very democratic fashion. They disintegrated into the extended dictatorship of Porfirio Díaz (1876 to 1910), who seized office with the slogan "Effective Suffrage and No Reelection," the same cry that would drive him from power four decades later. Although Díaz approved a constitutional amendment banning immediate presidential reelection, it did not inhibit his lengthy rule.[16]

After tremendous civil wars, the Argentine Liberals also took power at mid-century, following the ouster of the dictator Juan Manuel de Rosas in 1852. Alongside Alberdi, Sarmiento provided the other towering Argentine Liberal political thinker of the nineteenth century. Also forged in the crucible of the struggle against Rosas, Sarmiento avidly admired the United States. These intellectuals believed in changing the culture of Argentina, because unlike the United States, where history and customs made democracy flower easily, they had inherited undemocratic traditions from the Spanish colonial period.

Like Alberdi and many others, Sarmiento thought making republicanism a success required improving the stock of natives, both through education and immigration. In Alberdi's famous phrase, "To govern is to populate," Sarmiento hoped the society would slowly mature to correspond to the political system. Until then, he envisioned a gap between the democratic constitution of 1853 and an undemocratic reality, presided over by an aristocratic republic.[17]

For Alberdi, liberalism in economics as well as in politics provided the key to progress. He believed political participation and suffrage had to be limited to avoid descending into anarchy (pre-Rosas) or tyranny (under Rosas), but that economic and civil liberties should be uninhibited. According to Alberdi, "Liberty, alive in the written text and mistreated in reality, will be for a long time the law of our political condition in America previously Spanish."

When it came to designing a constitution, Alberdi felt Portalian Chile offered a better model than the United States, above all for a strong, centralized presidency with the ability to maintain order. For example, he imported from Chile the state of exception allowing the suspension of the constitution and the rights it bestowed. Although federalism would be engraved in the 1853 Argentine constitution, Alberdi did not intend for it to really function until years of order insured that neither the central government nor the society would allow federalist practices to result in disunity. Therefore, the constitution allowed the federal government to intervene frequently in the provinces.[18]

Throughout nineteenth century Latin America, a fundamental contradiction persisted between an elite discourse of nationalism, liberalism, citizenship, and democracy in contrast with the effective exclusion of the vast majority of the population from political rights and participation. At times, the marginalized groups tried to appropriate these concepts and assert demands for inclusion. Their rebellions stoked upper-class dread that the word *democracy* could be captured and actually implemented by the inferior and dangerous classes. The rulers avoided this threat by erecting protected democracies or tyrannies.[19]

Precarious Political Institutions

CONTINGENT CONSTITUTIONS

Almost regardless of written provisions, the fate of most constitutions was contingent on consensus among contending elites. Conservative constitution writers worried more about anarchy, liberals about tyranny. Many drafters in both camps continued trying to meld colonial political traditions with republican institutions. More conservative constitutions installed thinly veiled quasi–authoritarian systems. More liberal constitutions, closer to that of the United States, frequently collided with intractable realities. However, those charters were not just capricious imports but also attempts to deal with those realities. For example, some of these basic laws of the land tried to curb the powers of the chief executives, the military, and the rebellious provinces.[20]

Constitutions came and went with startling celerity from the 1820s through the 1840s, and then became slightly more stable from mid-century onward. From the 1820s through the 1870s, over eighty constitutions littered the landscape. Over half appeared in just five countries. The Dominican Republic scored the highest with fourteen, while the Andean countries of Ecuador contributed ten, Bolivia nine, Colombia eight, and Peru seven.[21]

Among the very few durable and largely operative constitutions, Chile's epitomized the conservative variety; Argentina's the liberal. The Chilean constitution of 1833 became the earliest successful charter in Spanish America, lasting until 1925. It worked well for the upper class because it recognized Roman Catholicism as the official religion, protected private property, centralized power in the national government and the president, slighted civil liberties, provided for states of exception to suspend constitutional guarantees, launched a functioning legislature and court system, and restricted the franchise. Although Diego Portales inspired this conservative document, Mariano Egana mainly wrote it. He believed it would prevent "anarchy in the shadow or name of popular rule, liberal principles, republican government. . . ." The new political system gained legitimacy and support through a successful war against Peru and Bolivia in the 1830s and the growth of raw material exports.[22]

The Argentine constitution of 1853 became the longest lasting—though not without interruption—in Latin America. Wanting to emulate England

and the United States, the elites borrowed their constitution from the latter. Through that imitation, these cautious Liberals sought to become thoroughly enmeshed in the Atlantic economy. Later in the nineteenth century, the Argentine supreme court underscored their constitution's origin in the United States, particularly its federalist and judicial form: "The system of government that rules us is not our creation. We have found it in action, tested by long years of experience, and we have appropriated it."[23]

The Argentine constitution deviated from the U.S. template by requiring support for the Roman Catholic faith and adherence to it by both the president and vice president. On paper, it established a federalist system, but a more centralist reality soon developed. To overshadow caudillos and caciques, the charter created a president much more powerful than the congress or the courts, a departure from the U.S. model and a compliment to the Chilean. In 1852, Alberdi lauded the Chilean constitution of 1833 as "superior in its writing to all others in South America, sensible and profound in regards to the executive branch . . . a mixture of the best the colonial regime had with the best of the modern regime. . . ." Following the U.S. and Chilean examples, the Argentine constitution also installed a bicameral congress, making the senate the voice of the provinces and the house that of the people.

In contrast with its U.S. counterpart, the Argentines made their constitution easier to amend. It only required a two-thirds vote of congress to summon a constitutional convention. Nevertheless, the Argentines would amend their document much less than the United States, partly because government officials had a more relaxed view of its provisions and often stretched them far beyond their original intent or even ignored them. Violating the constitution seldom required changing it because the courts proved reluctant to declare acts unconstitutional.[24]

Outside Chile and Argentina, many Latin American constitutions did not elicit much adherence because they lacked widespread acceptance or enforceability. No such document could reign for long without the consent of the elites. Civil warriors often associated the constitution with their rivals. Therefore, they refused to obey it and then trashed it if they took power. Most often, the plethora of constitutions merely signified that the new rulers wished to replace the old charter rather than just reform it. They did so partly for symbolic and partisan purposes, without really changing many fundamental aspects of the document. These largely unenforced constitutions fit a larger pattern of a chasm between law and reality, partly because the reach of the state was so thin.[25]

The Uruguayan constitution of 1830 represented an intermediate case of legal authority. Approved by a constituent assembly, it lasted until 1918.

However, the caudillos who governed for most of the nineteenth century rode roughshod over many of this document's provisions.[26]

Costa Rica's constitution of 1871 was also durable but often inapplicable. Installed by a Liberal dictator, Tomás Guardia (1871 to 1882), it lasted until 1917. It created a domineering president and a unicameral congress. In contrast with Chile and Argentina, the government did not heed many of its provisions very closely.[27]

Even less enforceable was the kaleidoscope of paper constitutions in Peru, normally subservient to the rule of the military and despots. As in other countries, many of these documents served as succession constitutions to legitimate a change in government without much substantive change in the charter. Their authors in a constituent assembly usually anointed the new president, who often had already taken power through a coup. From the 1820s to the 1860s, these texts tended to follow the U.S. prototype, with an even stronger president, a bicameral congress, an independent judiciary, and a bold bill of rights, although normally without federalism. The first constitution in 1823 created a centralized government partly inspired by the French example.

Peru's basic charters gave the Roman Catholic faith official status. They usually denied the powerful president immediate reelection. They often installed a Council of State as a subset of the congress to monitor the president when the legislature was not in session—a feature found elsewhere in the region. They made most elections indirect, requiring voters to be literate and propertied. The short-lived document of 1856 was one of the most democratic, inspired by the European radicalism of 1848. The longest-lasting constitution appeared in 1860, which, although heavily amended, held on until 1920, and even then was only modified slightly.

Although conservative and similar to each other and most Latin American constitutions, Peru's documents seldom evoked much obedience. Their ineffectiveness demonstrated that constitutional provisions, although they mattered, could not, in and of themselves, determine success. In most countries, constitutional engineering prospered only when the dominant classes perceived it as legitimate and efficacious.[28]

CENTRALISM SUPERSEDES FEDERALISM

Regardless of what was written in a country's constitution, federalism increasingly lost out to centralism. When the Latin Americans tried federalism following independence, it usually collapsed into disorder. Many countries eventually resolved this dispute by opting for extreme centralism. Others compromised by instituting centralism while granting minor concessions to provincial and local authorities. A few settled the matter by establishing a fairly ineffective federalist system on paper to mollify the provinces but with a president so strong that centralism gradually prevailed. By various methods, most national governments forced provinces and municipalities to cede their ability to represent local constituents in any significant democratic way.[29]

Only five countries adopted the federal system and adhered to it in substantial aspects for lengthy periods of time: Argentina (1853 to the present), Mexico (1857 to the present), Colombia (1863 to 1885), Venezuela (1864 to the present), and later Brazil (1891 to 1937). During the monarchy, Brazil chose centralism from 1822 to 1831, then underwent an unstable experience with assertive provincial assemblies in the 1830s, and thereafter reimposed centralism until the advent of the republic in 1889. Even in these officially federalist systems, the central government overshadowed the provincial units far more than in the United States. The national government retained many more powers, particularly finances. Most notably, it exerted the right to full-scale intervention in provincial administration to maintain order, proper conduct, and loyal officials.[30]

CAUDILLO PRESIDENTS

In the age of caudillos, the president had to ride the tallest of all. In effect, the majestic presidents replaced the monarch. Despite increased attempts to trim their leverage, they continued to tower over the legislature and judiciary.[31]

When not simply seizing power by force, the chief executives were chosen or christened by direct popular election, indirect election, or congressional selection. The requirements for president usually included citizenship and an age limit, as well as the often unwritten rule of maleness. Most constitutions added other prerequisites. For example, the rather typical Costa Rican Constitution of 1871 required the president to be a citizen by birth (not naturalization), "secular," over thirty years old, an "active citizen," literate, and "the owner of property of a value not less than five hundred colones or with an annual income of not less than two hundred colones." Moreover, the president could not be related to the outgoing president as "ancestor, descendant, or brother," presumably to prevent dynasties. Nor could the officeholder be reelected for a consecutive second four-year term. As in some other countries, the constitution forbade the president from leaving the national territory without congressional permission for one year after a term in office, apparently to prevent him from absconding with the national treasury or raising an external army to attack his successor.[32]

The constitutions normally gave the presidents more power than in the United States, and their chief executives typically exceeded their legal authority. The authors created such awesome national leaders to try to bring other power contenders, such as the provinces and armed groups, to heel. For example, most constitutions named the president as commander-in-chief of the armed forces, and prohibited the military from political deliberations (usually in vain).

One attribute of the executive branch different from the United States was the standard constitutional feature providing for states of exception, such as a state of siege. It granted emergency powers to suspend the constitution or some of its guarantees in order to deal with foreign or domestic threats, mainly the latter, whether existing or anticipated. Its imposition by the president usually required some concurrence by other bodies, normally the congress, and some time limit. Often the rulers abused this feature to bypass congress and to extend their powers or tenure. Yet, constitution makers almost never deleted this provision and only debated its limitations. In nineteenth-century Spanish America, only the Colombian constitutions of 1853 and 1863 omitted regimes of exception.[33]

Many constitutions tried—normally to no avail—to restrain presidential power by forbidding immediate reelection. They also relied on enumerating civil liberties, which governments routinely transgressed in the nineteenth century. One of the most democratic in this regard was Peru's first constitution of 1822 to 1823. Although never fully operative, it sought to prevent dictatorship by creating a pallid president subordinate to the congress. The chief executive could be elected by the congress for four years but not reelected for two terms thereafter. This progressive constitution guaranteed extensive civil liberties, except for religious freedom. Colombia also tried to constrain presidents by limiting them to two-year terms.[34]

Chile designed one of the strongest presidencies in its constitution of 1833. Indirectly elected presidents served for five years, usually being reelected for a second term and then designating their successor. The chief executives dominated these elections through their appointments of all provincial and municipal officials.

In some respects, the Chilean president possessed even more powers than the captain general had in the colonial period. In a model that became typical in Latin America, he had ample *ordinary powers* over all the agencies and actions of the state, all the way down to the municipal level. More than the congress, the chief executive initiated laws. He could also veto legislation. In terms of citizens' protections against the president, the constitution mainly emphasized property rights, since the elites were more concerned about their economic than political privileges. While ignoring habeas corpus, it guaranteed freedom of expression and petition but not of association or assembly.

At the same time, the Chilean president possessed *extraordinary powers* to preserve order by suspending the constitution under a state of siege. It had to be approved by the congress or the Council of State, a provision used frequently in the nineteenth century. The president also wielded *extra-constitutional powers*, including managing all elections (such as who was allowed to register, vote, and count votes) and controlling the selection of most congressional candidates. For example, in 1843 the president named public employees as two-thirds of the members of congress. Many congressional representatives were also beholden to the president because they belonged to the armed forces or worked on government projects. The rest of the members tended to be notables who might have complained if excluded and who also owed their seats to the president.

However, Chile's Portalian president was not totally autonomous or omnipotent. As was typical in the post-independence years in Latin America, the constitution provided that the president would be advised by a Council of State, composed of dignitaries from the Church, the military, politics, and society. The constitution also stated that the president, like a monarch, could not be tried for any abuses of power while still in office. After having left the office for a while, however, he and his ministers could be judged for improprieties committed during his presidency, as during the *residencias* of the colonial period. Ever thereafter, Chilean constitutions preserved this accountability mechanism, which was used many times.

From the 1830s to the 1890s, especially from the 1860s onward, presidential authority eroded slowly in Chile. Congress, the judiciary, and political parties played an increasing role. Congressional powers gradually expanded, especially to interrogate (although not yet to censure or remove) cabinet ministers, an innovation borrowed from European parliaments to enhance fiscal oversight. This congressional assertiveness would peak after the overthrow of President José Manuel Balmaceda, resulting in the so-called Parliamentary Republic from 1891 to 1925. Meanwhile from the 1860s up to the 1890s, the Chileans also pruned presidential powers. They cut their terms down to five years with no immediate reelection, curtailed their stage-managing of congressional elections, restricted their ability to impose a state of siege and abridge civil liberties, added congressional representatives to the Council of State, barred public employees from holding deputy seats, and made the judiciary more independent.[35]

In Argentina, the 1853 constitution required the president and vice-president to hold the same qualifications as senators. They had to be native-born or the offspring of a native-born citizen, as well as a Roman Catholic. They could hold office for six years and then be reelected only after someone else's six-year term. Their salaries could not be changed during their tenure.

According to the 1853 constitution, the electors to pick the president and vice-president were elected directly in the same manner as deputies, echoing the U.S. electoral college system. As in the United States, the electors themselves became irrelevant over time, so that eventually the people effectively elected the chief executive directly. To be elected president and vice-president required an absolute majority of all votes. If no candidate garnered an absolute majority, then congress chose between the top two vote-getters. As in Chile, the central government in the nineteenth century actually rigged most elections in its favor.

Partly copied from the Chilean model, the Argentine president possessed substantial powers in the constitution. Alberdi intended this potent presidentialism to reflect Bolívar's advice: "The new States of America previously Spanish need kings with the name of president." He could intervene in the provinces and later acquired the ability to rule by decree, which became unusually common in Argentina. The chief executive took charge of the capital as well as the nation.

The Argentine president proposed and approved laws, named his cabinet and other top officials on his own, exercised national patronage powers over the selecting of bishops and the issuing of decrees by the Vatican, appointed the judges of all federal courts with the consent of the senate, commanded the armed forces, and wielded most of the other powers associated with the U.S. chief executive. He also exercised a line-item veto, and his vetoes were seldom overturned by the required two-thirds of both houses. Borrowing from the Chileans and the French, he could declare a state of siege with the consent of the senate or by himself briefly if congress was not in session.

The constitution limited the Argentine chief executive by providing that he could not leave the capital without congress's permission, perhaps to deter him from mounting a private army, defecting to a provincial rebellion, or looting the public purse. It also tried to curtail dictatorial behavior by establishing an extensive bill of rights, including freedom of religion and press and from slavery and torture. The constitution did not incorporate habeas corpus, but Argentina adopted it thereafter, seldom with much effect.[36]

Although it created a president strong enough to override provincial and local bosses, the 1853 constitution tried to prevent future dictators like Rosas by declaring: "Congress may not confer upon the national executive, nor the provincial legislatures upon the governors of the provinces, any extraordinary faculties, or the fullness of the public power, or grant them acts of submission or supremacy whereby the lives, the honor, or the property of Argentines are placed at the mercy of any government or person whatsoever. An irremediable nullity shall be inherent in acts of this nature, and such acts shall subject those who formulate them, consent thereto or sign them, to the liability and penalty of infamous traitors to their country." As elsewhere in Latin America, these legal attempts to safeguard democracy frequently failed to prevent authoritarian behavior by presidents.[37]

Regardless of their powers on paper and their supremacy over the legislature and judiciary, most Latin American presidents remained vulnerable to overthrow by armed usurpers. This threat provided the major check on arbitrary rulers. For an extreme example, over thirty presidents came and went in Mexico from 1833 to 1855, for an average tenure of barely over seven months. The notorious caudillo Antonio López de Santa Anna accounted for nine of those presidencies. Comparable instability prevailed in Central America and the Andes.[38]

LANGUID LEGISLATURES

In the nineteenth century, Latin American legislatures were feeble in the constitution and even worse in practice. However, they were not impotent, and some of them accrued powers as time went on. The requirements for legislators often allowed very young men to be elected. For example, the Costa Rican constitution of 1871 declared that deputies had to be "active" citizens by birth or naturalization, over twenty-one years old, literate, and "the owner of property of a value of not less than five hundred colones, or to have an annual income of not less than two hundred colones."[39]

In the Chilean government, the legislature was a distinctly secondary power compared to the president but not immaterial. Over time, it evolved into one of the hardiest legislatures in Latin America. For the bicameral congress, senators were indirectly elected by provincial assemblies for six years, deputies directly for three. Exercising its two main functions, congress approved all laws and monitored the legality of actions by the executive branch, especially financial transactions. In addition, the congress, not the courts, possessed the power to interpret the constitution.

However, the Chilean president bent the legislature to his will by controlling the congressional candidates. As a result, their elections were really just referenda on his nominees. From 1834 to 1861, the government had twenty senators per term, the opposition none, and the government claimed between fifty and fifty-eight deputies per term (except for one low term of forty-three), while the opposition boasted three or four (except for one term with twelve and another with fourteen). The large landowners frequently captured those legislative seats by cashing in their sway over the rural vote. For example, they accounted for 70 percent of the senators and 44 percent of the deputies in 1874.[40]

In Argentina, the subordinated congress also played a larger role than in most of Latin America. The 1853 constitution defined the qualifications and powers of legislators. Deputies were elected directly by plurality. They had to be twenty-five years old, an "active citizen" for four years, and a continuous resident of the province where elected for two years. They served for four years and could be reelected. Two senators were selected by plurality vote by each provincial legislature. They needed stiffer qualifications: thirty years of age, six years a citizen, two years of continuous residence in the province where elected, and an annual income of two thousand pesos. They served for nine years and for as many times as reelected. The constitution barred members of religious orders from being members of either house of congress. It gave the assembly extensive attributes, including drafting legislation, setting the annual budget, levying taxes, establishing a national bank and currency, enacting codes, approving treaties, declaring war or a state of siege, and a host of other capabilities similar to those accorded to the U.S. legislature. [41]

Despite grave deficiencies, legislatures exerted some prerogatives not only in Chile and Argentina but also in countries with less developed oligarchic republics. Even amidst civil upheavals, political turmoil, and revolving dictatorships, the Mexican legislature functioned with few interruptions from 1821 to 1847. It frequently feuded with the executive branch, although it echoed most Latin American congresses in ultimately succumbing to presidential authority.[42]

Brazil's independent Empire (1822 to 1889) developed a tradition of an institutionalized but submissive legislature. Voters indirectly elected the chamber of deputies, while the emperor appointed the senate. The legislators sometimes took issue with the monarch, but he thoroughly dominated by convening or dissolving the chamber and replacing recalcitrant members through elections he controlled.[43]

HYBRID JUDICIARIES

During the post-independence period, the most notable feature of the judiciary was its infirmity in the face of growing presidential power. Constitutions divided almost evenly on whether the president or the congress appointed judges, in some cases jointly. However, the legislature often deferred to presidential preferences. In contrast with the United States, few countries granted judges permanent tenure. The shorter defined terms gave the other branches greater sway over the judiciary, as did budgetary authority.[44]

During the second half of the 1800s, significant change took shape in the region's judiciaries as some constitutional governments stabilized and civil wars subsided.[45] The republics modified the colonial judicial structure slightly by introducing national supreme courts, reducing the former audiencias to just appellate bodies. For example, Argentina did not install its Supreme Court until 1862, when the Liberal victory ushered in a period of continuous constitutional government that lasted until 1930. The Court began to hear cases in 1863 under an act that established a federal judiciary and the power of judicial review fashioned after the United States. It became slightly more effective than most judiciaries in Latin America.[46]

Other key reforms in Latin America included the introduction of a strict separation of powers doctrine, new codes of law, polyglot forms of judicial review, and legal remedies to protect individual rights. Above all, governments sought to remove legislative and executive duties from courts and to restrict them to the administration of justice. French practices predominately influenced legal codes and concepts, while U.S. and to a lesser extent Spanish and French models heavily shaped constitutional thought. The former colonies began adopting the French separation of powers doctrine to protect the executive and legislative branches from immoderate judicial intrusion.[47]

Governments now relegated judges to the position of clerks mechanistically applying the law. They confined judges to the strict application, not interpretation, of the laws passed by the legislature. They converted the judiciaries into highly centralized bureaucracies with no accountability to, and virtually no linkages with, external social or political forces.[48]

The French separation of powers doctrine suggested that judicial decisions declaring an act of the legislature unconstitutional interfered improperly with congressional prerogatives. At the same time, the U.S. constitution encouraged the adoption of judicial review and a presidential system of government theoretically balanced by legislative and judicial power. All the new countries in Latin America blended ingredients from both systems, which never meshed well.

All Latin American constitutions recognized the legal supremacy of the constitution, but they offered no uniform theory or practice as to how to maintain it. The Spanish constitution of 1812 vested the power of review in the Cortes, the United States archetype gave it to the ordinary judiciary, and the later Austrian Constitution of 1920 and the Spanish Constitution of 1931 established special judicial bodies to exercise constitutional review.

Over time, Spanish American constitutions mixed various elements from all these sources. They also varied in the extent to which judicial decisions about constitutionality rendered a law null and void. After cobbling together some frail form of judicial review of legislation, countries also incorporated the writ of habeas corpus to protect individuals from state action contrary to the guarantees enumerated in national constitutions. They combined the U.S. principles of a rigid constitution and judicial review with the civil law limitations on judicial power.

Thereafter, legal systems seesawed back and forth between the French and U.S. models of public law. As a result, the Latin Americans failed to develop a coherent system capable of controlling the executive. The institutional isolation, rigid legal training, and mechanistic thinking surrounding the proper political role of the judiciary characteristic of civil law made the exercise of judicial review problematic and ineffective. For many decades, the judiciary never matured into a self-assertive branch of government, let alone a bastion of democracy.[49]

FROM POPULAR TO PROTECTED ELECTIONS

Given the severe difficulties of constructing democracies or at least republics in the turbulent and tyrannical post-independence period, the most surprising achievement was the holding of some exceptionally participatory elections. In some cases, at least as many subaltern groups voted as in more developed countries outside Latin America in the era. In the debate between popular versus protected democracies, the crucial issue of electoral participation always sparked controversy in the region. Although elites usually placed tight boundaries on the franchise in these years of heavily insulated republics, sometimes they permitted unexpectedly broad inclusion of the lower classes. Consequently, some of these early democratic practices bore significance for very diverse social strata, both at the time and for the years ahead.

For all its shortcomings, nineteenth century republicanism allowed some plebeians to take part in politics and to bargain with elites much more extensively and effectively than in the colonial period. By partially bridging the gap between officially democratic governments and the marginalized majority, elections helped hold these contradictory systems together. Inherently unequal electoral relations prevailed between the upper and lower classes, but those connections formed a two-way street. The common people also made demands in exchange for their support.

Even restricted and fraudulent elections inculcated in the under classes the importance of voting amidst liberal discourses. Politicians who cajoled illegal voters into casting ballots communicated to the poor the significance of suffrage as a mark of citizenship and as a legitimating mechanism for the government. Elections accomplished more than just selecting or sanctifying leaders. They provided political education and socialization in the mores of democracy. Although the results often disappointed the voters, the routine, ritualized voting process gave some of them a sense of belonging, rights, and partisanship. These events and practices fostered mass expectations for true democratic participation and representation in the future.

Despite occasional remarkable breadth, electoral expansion did not necessarily move forward in a linear way—instead, setbacks occurred as well as advances. Rather than responding to an upsurge from the less fortunate, the ruling groups normally made these decisions about broadening versus narrowing participation based on competition among themselves. They either widened the franchise to enlarge their base of support and legitimacy against their rivals or constricted it to deny their opponents constituents. However, the dominant classes also clamped down when they became alarmed that popular participation was mushrooming out of their control.[50]

Latin America did not strictly follow the idealized monotonic European model of gradual expansion of voting rights to incorporate more underprivileged citizens. Instead, most of the region began its electoral history with a very ample definition of the franchise. During and immediately after the struggles for independence, Latin Americans generally granted suffrage to all independent adult males. This initial conception drew closer to the French revolutionary view of citizenship than the Lockean propertied notion.

From the Bourbon and independence periods, the upper class had acquired a phobia about mass participation, especially when it erupted into upheavals from beneath. The rich and the powerful (who usually prevailed) wanted to avoid not only unbridled democracy or anarchy but also tyranny linked to the unprivileged. Some caudillos and caciques—the *cowboyocracy* —used universal suffrage, however fraudulent, to galvanize lower-class support. In reaction, elitist republicans came to prefer a highly restricted or controlled voting pool. This dichotomy between broad and narrow participation could be seen in Argentina in the evolution from the mobilizing caudillo Rosas to the restrictive republicans Sarmiento and Alberdi.

This trend away from popular democracy toward more protected democracy took hold across the region from the 1820s and 1830s onward. Conservatives tended to spearhead the reactionary adoption of more prerequisites, including literacy, property, income, and independent occupations. Many governments enacted a hierarchy of qualifications, rising from voters through electors to the elected. Some imposed indirect elections.

However, countries varied in scope and timing. After mobilization during the independence period, the region's second opening up of the suffrage often coincided with the mid-century rise in export growth. In law but seldom in reality and sometimes only temporarily, Colombia, Argentina, Mexico, Venezuela, Ecuador, the Dominican Republic, Paraguay, Chile, and Guatemala launched universal male suffrage from the 1850s to the 1870s. Argentina in 1863, Paraguay in 1870, and the Dominican Republic in 1873 supposedly gave the vote to eighteen-year olds. Ostensibly, illiterates received the vote in Mexico in 1857, the Dominican Republic in 1865, and Paraguay in 1870. Later in the nineteenth century, some leaders narrowed the franchise once more. Only from the 1930s onward would there develop a general, persistent pattern of suffrage expansion.[51]

In the post-independence decades in Latin America, the frequency, regularity, and intensity of elections demonstrated their importance. In most of the countries, local, regional, and national elections occurred repeatedly. The epidemic fraud and mayhem, as well as frequent coups, that accompanied voting also indicated the significance of elections. However, in some countries, voter turnout shrank because elections were so violent, corrupt, and dedicated to upper-class interests.

The elites invested so much time and effort in these electoral exercises because they wanted some show of popular support to authenticate their power, principles, and programs. This motivation especially affected Liberals, who emphasized their claim to rule through popular sovereignty. The essence of the liberal electoral dilemma was how to concoct elections broad enough to confer authority but narrow enough to maintain social control.

Grappling with a similar dilemma, leaders tried to craft elections honest enough to certify legitimacy but stacked enough to guarantee victory. Liberals also needed to manage elections so as to avert the Church and Conservatives from running away with the popular vote. Controlled voting resolved the dilemma between official adherence to liberalism and actual maintenance of oligarchic rule, a means of avoiding both anarchy and tyranny.[52]

Although some nineteenth century elections were more inclusionary and influential than their reputation might suggest, most remained elitist and flawed. Elections provided only one way of choosing office-holders, and often the last resort and the least determinate. Governments frequently convened elections just to ratify or consecrate office-holding, for example scheduling them after the president had taken power.

The upper class devised numerous strategies for manipulating elections. Restricting the franchise provided one common method of control. Even in countries where elections were effective, lawmakers usually permitted only a tiny percentage of the population to vote, mainly those who were male, adult, literate, propertied, and upper class. Sometimes electoral laws also excluded the clergy, military, and prisoners or anyone suspected of lacking *independence*. For example, the rather typical Bolivian constitutions of 1826, 1836, and 1839 limited the suffrage to resident literate males with property resulting from independent occupations outside domestic service, regulations that lasted until 1952. As a result, only about 2 percent to 3 percent of the population could vote in most Latin American elections in the nineteenth century.[53]

Even if some popular groups participated in the initial balloting, the oligarchy usually still choreographed the outcome by making elections indirect. That system required organized groups to recruit voters behind pre-selected electors for pre-selected candidates. These organizers served as the precursors of political parties, which did not normally emerge as ongoing institutions until the end of this period.[54]

For example, Peruvian Liberals during 1845 to 1860 tried to achieve their dual objectives of encouraging voting but discouraging voter empowerment by devising supremely complicated indirect elections. Consequently, the ruling elites could easily orchestrate or nullify the balloting. Those Peruvian governments maintained electoral control so that the lower classes, particularly the darker mestizos and Indians, would not take power into their own hands.[55]

Voting in public also normally hindered independent exercise of the franchise. For example, the Uruguayan constitution of 1830 said nothing about balloting procedures, but the electoral law in that same year established that voting was to be public. The voter had to sign a ballot that carried his name and address, which was verified by the Justice of the Peace and the Registration Commission. Uruguay did not make voting secret until 1916, and in that election, the government lost.[56]

Beyond electoral rules, governments engaged in pervasive legerdemain to slant voting outcomes. Even when convened on schedule, elections were rife with corruption, intimidation, and armed combat. Time and again, the government harassed, cowed, censored, cheated, or banned its opponents. If voters cast their ballots for the opposition, the authorities usually overturned the results. Since those in power seldom lost elections, a common way to produce turnover was through outside intervention—by the military and caudillos in Spanish America or by the emperor in Portuguese America—both of which became a regular part of the political system.[57]

Latin America often held elections that were hoaxes. For example in Argentina, Rosas distorted balloting to consecrate his dictatorship, even though the electoral law of 1821 guaranteed direct elections with universal male suffrage. With no literacy or property requirements, all twenty-year-old free males had the right to vote (although only twenty-five-year-old property owners could be elected). However, the government coerced voters into backing the official candidates by excluding undesirables and by demanding public declarations of the vote. In 1835, Rosas convoked elections in Buenos Aires to grant him dictatorial powers, which passed by a thundering 9,320 votes to 4. Nevertheless, many common people voted, reportedly out of fear or love of Rosas.[58]

Because many elections were so unfair, opponents of the government sometimes boycotted, a practice still seen today. They resorted to this tactic because they had no hope of winning, because they wanted to protest the rigging, because they wanted to delegitimize the process, because they wanted to destabilize the regime, or because they planned to rebel against the powerholders. Boycotting developed early in Colombia and Chile, later in Argentina.[59]

Through clientelism, patronage, and enforcement by local officials and bosses, governments also induced voters to sanctify the existing balance of power, not challenge it. Informal power structures, especially the landowners, the clergy, and the caudillos, assured that most voters conformed to the wishes of the privileged classes, regardless of the breadth of the franchise. Local authorities took advantage of vague electoral laws to determine themselves the scope of the electorate, which resulted in a wide variety of participation. Bosses used the lack of precise national rules to exclude normally eligible opponents or to include normally ineligible proponents. For example, the Costa Rican constitution of 1871 simply said that, "It is a duty of citizens to attend and vote in popular assemblies in which the suffrage is exercised."[60]

Brazil offered one example of a smoothly running patron-client system. Most of the time, it provided order without blatant coercion. The peaceful legitimacy of the political system rested not only on the authority of the emperor but also on the appearance of relatively honest elections for deputies.

Under Pedro II from 1840 to 1889, elections occurred frequently and regularly. Framed by the constitution of 1824 and some respect for individual liberties, these contests provided the trappings of a liberal representative democracy. Europeans hailed Brazil's emulation of their political systems. Other superficial similarities included turnover of Liberal and Conservative parties in a functioning bicameral congress and the emperor's cabinet. The emperor named 50 Senators for life, while the electoral colleges selected

120 Deputies. Although the monarch appointed the cabinet, it required the approval of the deputies.

Brazil's elections did not determine directly who held seats in the legislature, let alone the chief executive. Voters selected elite electors who, through electoral colleges, picked the congressional deputies. The key officials who ensured that elections turned out as the government desired were the provincial presidents, appointed by the prime minister. The government allowed opponents to participate and, infrequently, to win.

The voting took place to prove the legitimate power of the local boss or landowner, usually called *colonels*. They formed part of the patron-client network that wove together nineteenth-century Brazilian politics from the top to the bottom. Although power flowed primarily from the center to the periphery, the colonels also exerted some leverage in the political arena. By delivering the expected vote for the virtually unchangeable ruling groups, the patron convinced provincial and national authorities to offer government positions to him and his followers. Then those local officials helped him corral the vote, which they easily monitored since there was no secret ballot. The boss also maintained his supporters by providing them services, connections, and protection.

On the rare occasions when patronage, persuasion, and sleight of hand failed to motivate voters to behave properly, the Brazilian government resorted to the iron fist. It relied on the police, the national guard, and the armed forces. By the same token, challengers to the government's local loyalists could only break through this electoral stranglehold by generating enough support in order to use brute force or the threat of it. They demanded that they eventually have their votes recognized and be rewarded with some positions either locally or nationally. In response, the emperor sometimes made concessions.

When the Republic replaced the Empire in 1889, the patron-client electoral machinery continued. The subsequent system operated with greater leverage at the municipal and state level. No moderating power like the emperor existed at the national level to settle disputes or alternate officeholders.[61]

All the manipulations discussed above in Latin America's electoral systems should not obscure their less obvious virtues, which increased over time. Law and power relations restricted voting and its impact, while nefarious electoral practices instilled cynicism and abstention among some people. Nevertheless, voting gave a minority beyond the elites some taste of citizenship and participation.[62]

Even in these early decades of republicanism and especially from midcentury on, some countries made progress toward more democratic elections, at least on paper and sometimes in practice. Little by little, divisions among the upper classes opened the door to greater mass participation in politics, whether through electoral or military channels. The élites' enrollment of the commoners in these disputes was paternalistic, exploitative, and not intended to be democratic. Nonetheless it gradually broadened the network of political actors.[63]

Although some countries scaled back popular voting, some practiced it regularly for long periods of time. Argentina became one of the first Latin American countries to include voters beneath the upper stratum. Buenos Aires achieved an electoral history more open than the rest of the country. In the first elections in the province of Buenos Aires in 1821, out of a population of 60,000 men, only 328 cast ballots. Thereafter, while most of the rest of the provinces imposed economic or educational restrictions on the franchise, Buenos Aires adopted universal male suffrage for those twenty or older in 1821, far ahead of Western Europe. This law led to a huge expansion in voters from 100–300 from 1810 and 1821 to 2,000–3,000 from 1821 on. Those elected to the Buenos Aires provincial Sala de Representantes had to be property owners at least twenty-five years old.

That 1821 law also made the vote direct. In response, the elites promoted their lists of candidates and built electoral machines to deliver the vote. By the 1830s, the ruling group brought these conflicts under control by negotiating a unified list of candidates endorsed by the government. Rosas installed this system of management from the top down in 1830.[64]

Although sullied and brutalized, voting provided a legitimate rule-bounded game for resolving disputes among power contenders short of civil war. In most Buenos Aires elections up to the 1880s, all sides engaged in rampant fraud and fights. Party bosses from the top to the bottom chose the candidates and ran their campaigns through political clubs, newspapers, rallies, and voter mobilization. Partisans fiercely contested most elections. To ensure most victories for the government, caudillos and caciques, frequently from the bureaucracy, police, or army, recruited or intimidated voters. Deploying the poor as hooligans, thugs armed with guns and knives battled over control of electoral officials, registration, and voting tables. After the government counted the ballots, the losers usually charged wrongdoing, and the legislature usually declared the government the winner.

Under these circumstances, elections expressed political domination at least as much as citizenship or representation. Partly for this reason, voters turned out in low numbers. According to Sarmiento, for an election in Buenos Aires in the middle of the nineteenth century, there were 187,000 inhabitants, 12,000 potential voters (6 percent of the population), 2,400 actually registered (1.2 percent of the population), and 700 finally casting ballots (0.37 percent of the population, or 5 percent of eligible voters). Among eligible voters from the 1860s to the 1880s, usually no more than 10 percent cast ballots, or around 2 to 3 percent of the population. All social classes participated in the elections, but the voters mainly came from the lower strata of the working class, with a tendency toward youth. The rest of the population—including women and immigrants—followed the elections with great interest and demonstrated but could not vote.[65]

Setting the stage for national universal male suffrage, the Constitution of 1853 spelled out criteria for being elected but not for voting, which it left up to congress. In 1856, the legislature followed the example of the capital city and province of Buenos Aires by ruling that all seventeen-year-old males could be voters, with no economic or educational qualifications. With this momentous decision, the Liberals endowed Argentina legally with universal male suffrage in 1857, following Colombia in 1853 and matching Mexico and Venezuela in 1857. "It was true that participation was restricted to a small minority, but participation in elections does not appear to have been more restricted in Argentina than in Britain until the Reform Act of 1867 or the Netherlands until late in the century."[66]

Although trailblazing, that Argentine franchise did not give a strong voice to the citizenry because voting was neither direct nor secret. Moreover, turnout remained sparse, partly in reaction to pervasive deception, oppression, and physical combat, mainly by the ruling National Autonomist Party, dominated by landowners. As one newspaper stated baldly in 1864: "We know how to win elections. Whoever has the strength, takes over the polling stations, and whoever takes over the polling stations, wins the election." Since the party in power normally imposed its candidates' victories, the opposition frequently resorted to rebellion or abstention.

Although Argentine voters came from the full range of social strata, the percentage of adult males actually voting remained small. They were dissuaded by the elitist government, discouraged by the fraudulence of the process and the lack of benefits derived, and later overshadowed by waves of non-naturalized immigrants. Turnout fell from around 7 percent of the total population in the 1820s and 1830s to approximately 3 percent in 1874 and 2 percent in 1880. Despite illicit procedures and voter disenchantment, majoritarian national elections took place on a regular basis from 1862 until the military coup of 1930. Argentina compiled one of the most stable electoral histories in Latin America.[67]

From early on, electoral regularity and participation were also greater in Chile than might have been expected in Latin America or even Europe in the era. From 1823 until 1924 (when the military intervened on September 11, as it did again in 1973), Chileans took part in uninterrupted congressional and municipal elections every three years and presidential every five. Voters cast ballots directly for deputies, indirectly for senators and presidents. Although the 1833 constitution imposed economic and educational restrictions on adult (twenty-five years old or twenty-one if married, or just twenty-one after 1884) male suffrage, many middle and lower-class merchants, artisans, employees, military officers, and workers met those criteria and voted. Moreover, the government applied these requirements loosely to make sure its partisans could take part.

Although the secret ballot existed from the 1830s onward, politicians often violated it. Many Chileans sold their vote or succumbed to government pressure. Throughout the nineteenth century, the ruling party almost always won, partly by sponsoring candidates and meddling with the voting. Nevertheless, opponents fielded candidates and sometimes snatched a victory.[68]

From the 1830s to the 1860s, Chile's landed aristocracy ran basically a semi-authoritarian, protected democratic political system. Their view that the state mainly had to supply order was reflected in the president's (*the Grand Elector*) control over elections, as well as his limitations on freedom of assembly, association, and the press. The outgoing president also selected his successor, who always took the vast majority of electoral votes cast by the electors elected in the provinces.[69]

The Chilean president dominated elections through his grip on the municipalities, which took charge of all voting. The president prepared a list of official candidates for every municipal and congressional election. The intendants and governors made sure that most citizens only voted for the blessed candidates. They did so partly by juggling voter registration, the voting itself, and the tabulation of the votes.

However, the central government was shrewd enough to pick candidates who would attract as much support and as little opposition as possible at the local level or to embrace strong opposition candidates, not unlike one-party systems such as the Mexican PRI in the twentieth century. By rallying voters, the opposition seldom won elections, but it could convince the government to co-opt it and/or adopt some of its policy preferences. As in Argentina, opposition candidates often reacted to the advantages of the official candidates by protesting or abstaining, both before and after the 1874 reform.

Despite electoral prestidigitation by the government, Chile was fairly democratic by the standards of the 1870s. All major political offices were elected on a regular basis and not seized by other means. Substantial freedom existed to express oneself and to form political parties or proto-parties. Elections, parties, and the press became increasingly powerful political instruments, not only for the government but also the opposition. Many Chileans beyond the voters—including women—campaigned in elections.

Conservatives and other political groups excluded by the ruling Liberals instigated a significant electoral reform in 1874, similar to the breakthrough in 1912 in Argentina. Chile's reform did not result mainly from pressure from the outside but rather from a division inside the political system. The opposition sought to enhance congressional and local powers by expanding the electorate, particularly that segment under the sway of landowners rather than the president. The proponents wanted to give free reign to party competition and consolidation.

While keeping the vote secret, the new law dropped the income or wealth requirement for voters, awarding the franchise to all literate males over twenty-five years old. Given low life expectancy at the time, this restricted suffrage to the older segment of the population. Henceforth, senators were elected directly by provinces instead of by the entire republic, which also made presidential intervention more difficult. In addition, the 1874 reforms included the right to peaceful public assembly, a boon for the growing political parties, who appealed to all social strata.

This reform made Chile as democratic electorally as the most advanced countries in the era: the United States, France, and Switzerland. With less electoral regularity, fewer important offices subject to elections, and less voting secrecy, universal male suffrage also existed on paper in Greece, Paraguay, Uruguay, and Argentina, as well as Germany and Denmark with the exclusion of indigents.

As a result of the reform, Chilean candidates for president from 1876 on actually had to campaign for themselves and their congressional and municipal candidates. Elections became increasingly spirited contests between the opposition and the still intervening but more restrained government. The electorate doubled from 49,047 registered in 1873 (2.4 percent of the national population) to 106,194 in 1876 (5.12 percent of the population). It rose to 148,737 by 1878, accounting for almost 30 percent of males over twenty-five years of age and 90 percent of eligible voters (about 7 percent of the total population, rising to 8 percent in 1912).

The main growth in registered voters occurred in occupational categories beneath the upper crust of property and income. The biggest increase took place in the countryside among peasants, often under the tutelage of landowners. From 1872 to 1878, measuring national registered voters (not necessarily those voting) by occupation, showed property owners falling from 13 percent to 3 percent, professionals, merchants, employees, and other middle class groups dropping from 32 percent to 21 percent, agricultural workers rising from 34 percent to 48 percent, and artisans, miners, and other workers climbing from 25 percent to 29 percent. Although registration rose, voters casting ballots remained a small percentage of the total population: 1.3 percent (1873), 3.9 percent (1876), 4.7 percent (1879), 4.2 percent (1882), 3.2 percent (1885), and 3.5 percent (1888). From 1870 to 1888, abstention normally exceeded 30 percent and often topped 40 percent.

From the 1870s to the 1920s, the growth in the Chilean electorate mainly depended on the expansion of literacy. No dramatic rise in the suffrage occurred until women were given the vote in 1949. Nevertheless, the 1874 reform opened the electoral door to numerous workers, including many in the cities. Their urban union and party leaders did not demand that illiterates be allowed to vote but only that elections be honest, perhaps because illiterates predominated among rural or unorganized workers. Deceit and falsification blanketed the countryside, where illiterates could sneak into the polls by signing their names.

Thus, Chile became an evolutionary democracy in which contestation and participation expanded gradually through reforms. As opposed to cases in which democracy resulted from the abrupt overthrow of an authoritarian regime, this gradualism encouraged the growth of political stability and parties. The reform path facilitated the development of both leftwing and rightwing parties. Representing the upper classes, the latter's participation in the system particularly fortified stability, mainly against military coups.[70]

Although often seen as a democratic latecomer because of the empire, Brazil, in practice, also adopted nearly universal male suffrage very early, with no effective literacy or property restrictions. In the same period, it moved ahead of most of Latin America and Europe in requiring compulsory voting. The first constitution of 1824 established indirect elections for deputies, but direct elections for local officials took place from the 1840s to the 1880s. Those contests required voters to be national males twenty-five years old or only twenty-one if married, a priest, or a military officer. Excluding women, slaves, servants, and sons living with their fathers (all on the grounds of not being independent), voters could be illiterate but had to possess a minimum income (with higher property qualifications for electors). Nevertheless, that income requirement effectively barred few from participating, both because it was low and because it was not rigorously enforced. Local officials determined who actually got to vote.

As in some other Latin American countries in this time period, astonishing numbers and types of people participated in the first stage of Brazil's indirect elections. Many very poor people, unskilled workers, free men of color, and illiterates regularly took part in elections from the 1840s until the 1880s. Rising to 10 percent of the population in 1872, voters included about half the men old enough to vote. An impressive 51 percent of all free males at least twenty-one years old registered to vote by the early 1870s, a high figure by any international standard. It is not known exactly how many actually cast ballots. However, a large percentage probably did so, since the government registered them in order to produce a large turnout and made voting compulsory for registered voters, although it seldom imposed fines.[71]

Peru also allowed voters beneath the oligarchy to play a remarkable role, within the confines of the era. In the 1830s, the governing class restricted the franchise mainly to landowners, merchants, and clerics. However, all free literate resident adult male citizens above the age of twenty-one and owning property, paying taxes, or working as a public employee or secular cleric had the right to deposit votes in an urn in the district primaries. These criteria ushered in a small electorate beyond the upper class, including urban artisans and rural Indian farmers. These primary voters chose electors with higher income restrictions (around five hundred pesos) to provincial electoral colleges, which picked congressional deputies by secret ballot. A highly safe, elitist, indirect system, it permitted little competition and usually only one candidate.

In Peru prior to the 1851 presidential election, presidents were normally elected by congress (1823 to 1827) or by a trumped-up general vote ratifying a president already installed by military means, except for some provincial elections in 1833. Only a few presidents simply did not bother with elections. Elections also took place for assemblies to write constitutions. Electoral registration and regulations were manipulated and intentionally vague. In disputed elections, which were common, congress decided the winners, under the heavy influence of the sitting president.

When Peruvian elections were held at all, they were rough and fraudulent, apparently exceeding the distortions in Argentina and Chile. As elsewhere in the region, democratic electoral rituals, liberal discourses, and legal smokescreens masked and legitimated Peru's system of *constitutional authoritarianism*. The chief executive (the *supreme elector*) determined the final outcome.

Even in unclean elections, Peruvian candidates for president from the 1850s onward rallied mass support—especially in the cities—to strengthen their claim and to convince the outgoing president to choose them. Demonstrating their ability to put people in the streets and in the voting booths provided one way to settle contests among contending elites. It also extended upper-class control over the masses in public spaces. Although fueled by bribes, liquor, fiestas, and fisticuffs, that mobilization gave normally excluded citizens—especially wage laborers and artisans—some small sense of participating in national politics.

Greater conflict among Peruvian political elites led, as in some other parts of Latin America, to a broadening of the franchise. As elsewhere around mid-century, the rise and stabilization of the export economy swelled government coffers. In the 1840s and 1850s, soaring guano income rendered access to the state more valuable. Consequently, electoral politics became more attractive, competitive, and open, especially in congressional contests. At the same time, rising incomes and government employment generated more citizens eligible for the franchise, as did the abolition of African slavery in 1854.

Electoral reforms made all Peruvian taxpayers voters in the 1850 congressional elections. This change enrolled many middle-class professionals, merchants, artisans, and employees, as well as some workers, especially in the urban areas. The liberals hoped that this expansion of the electorate in the cities would offset the power of the landowners in the countryside, who tapped Indian and Asian voters. Enfranchisement increased the involvement of the popular classes in national politics, but it did not produce any popular movement in politics, something the liberals as well as the conservatives wanted desperately to avoid. In 1855, the government replaced the provincial electoral colleges with direct elections of congress. Voter participation escalated along with complaints of illegalities and brutalities.

In the 1870s, Peruvian elections became more national. Candidates and their organizations activated more voters from all regions and social classes to support their competitive bids for power. As in Argentina, they employed local electoral clubs, mob rule, and strong-arm tactics to prevail at hotly contested electoral sites. The Civil Party particularly recruited provincial elites, state employees, and artisans, and even nominated a handful of artisans as congressional candidates.

The political elites in Lima used these electoral exercises to weave regional notables into a national structure of political authority, to legitimize that system in a broader but still limited swath of the population, and to compete for power without engaging in civil war. They did not unleash unbridled democracy, but they did use semi-democratic mechanisms to reconcile aristocratic rule with official liberal principles. The upper classes hoped this incipient oligarchic republic would solidify political stability so that an export economy could grow.[72]

Colombia also adopted universal male suffrage in the constitution of 1853. Previously, on a merry-go-round of constitutions and electoral rules, the 1832 charter tried to expand democracy by defining the government as "republican, popular, representative, elected, and responsible." It also sought to defend civilian rule by declaring that, "The essential duty of the armed forces is obedience; they shall not have the power to deliberate." The military voted from independence until 1930, despite concerns that officers would command soldiers how to cast ballots.

The 1832 Constitution deleted the real property restriction for voters but kept occupational ("those having an assured income who are not employed by another as a domestic servant or as a day laborer") and educational (voters were given until 1850 to fulfill this requirement) criteria. Elections remained public and indirect, with voters choosing electors (who had to be literate but who had no economic qualifications) who selected presidents, vice-presidents, senators, representatives, and deputies to the provincial houses, thus making it likely that the entire government would be in the hands of the same party. When no candidate for president had a majority, the congress selected the winner. The law maintained escalating economic qualifications for these national officials.[73]

For many years, republican practices in Colombia remained narrow but steady. Beginning in 1832, presidential and congressional elections transpired every four years. Since the government delayed the literacy requirement for two decades and the economic restrictions only demanded some murky independence, artisans and small farmers voted in these elections. Contending elites competed for their support. Even the disenfranchised, like women and the poor, took part in campaigns and rallies. A fairly free partisan press followed public affairs. In exceptional cases, the anti-government candidate even won.[74]

Colombia's Liberal Constitution of 1853 recorded some striking advances. It separated Church and state, abolished slavery, decentralized government organization, removed the president's emergency powers, promoted jury trials, expanded freedom of the press and religion as well as other civil liberties, and enshrined universal male suffrage by erasing property and literacy qualifications for voting and holding office. It only required voters to be at least eighteen or married. It also lowered the age limit for political office to twenty-one years for everyone except thirty years for president and vice-president. And it made all voting direct and secret, including for president, vice-president, senator, representative, provincial deputy, governor, and even some judges.

Although Colombian Liberals spearheaded these reforms, some of them worried that universal male suffrage would benefit the Conservatives because the clergy would shepherd the votes of the illiterate lower classes. Nevertheless, Liberals hailed this constitutional breakthrough as a watershed for democracy. While it lasted less than a decade, this may have been the most progressive, democratic constitution of any consequence in Latin America in the nineteenth century.[75]

From the 1850s to the 1880s, Colombian males of all social classes voted repeatedly for municipal councilors, for state judges, deputies, and president, and for national deputies and president. Participants often turned out in high numbers, with some 40 percent of eligible voters taking part in the 1856 presidential election. Although fraud and fighting occurred regularly on election day, so did legal contestation. While some districts were monopolized by one party, others were genuinely competitive.

From the middle to the late nineteenth century, Colombia's electoral rules oscillated nationally and provincially. Sometimes they constricted the franchise to property owners and literates, sometimes they restored indirect elections. Elections were frequently perverted by the incumbents and abstained from by the opposition. When a party lost too many elections, it resorted to insurrection.

Although elections varied by time and place, they remained the epicenter of political events, involving some of the poorest as well as the richest Colombians. However improper, combative, elitist, and unfair, elections were held and contested routinely, serving as the normal route for anyone seeking office. Civilians, not the military, ruled. From 1863 to 1886, only one of eleven presidents took power by non-electoral means. In many respects, Colombia was just as republican and democratic as the United States or any other nation in Latin America or Europe in these years.[76]

Another Andean example of suffrage extension occurred in Ecuador, after a typical post-independence beginning with a tiny electorate. Independence in 1830 brought with it the country's first constitution and electoral rules. Along the lines in most of Latin America, the laws required voters to be males, twenty-two years old or married, owners of property worth three hundred pesos or professionals or tradesmen (not domestic servants or laborers, whose independence was doubted), and literate. For those citizens meeting these criteria, voting was obligatory and public, as well as indirect. They elected delegates to the cantonal electoral assembly, which elected town councils, mayors, deputies and senators. In turn, the deputies and senators elected the president and vice-president. All these tiers excluded women and the overwhelming majority of the population.[77]

In 1861, an electoral reform democratized Ecuador's franchise. Pro-clerical Conservatives backed this change to expand their popular base. Endorsing universal suffrage against property restrictions, the new law dropped economic requirements for voting and being elected. It introduced proportional representation for the election of deputies. It made elections direct and secret. From 1848 to 1894, the percentage of the population voting rose from .02 percent to 3.3 percent.

In spite of these improvements, complaints of endemic corruption continued to mar elections and sow cynicism about elite manipulations. Despite all the blemishes and abuses, the Ecuadorean example, like the others above, indicates that some of these elections were exceptionally participatory and meaningful for the era. They formed part of a democratic heritage and nurtured hopes for broader, cleaner elections in years to come.[78]

Even when progress toward a more inclusive franchise occurred, it was seldom cumulative or continuous. Several countries rescinded previous openings of the electorate. Unwelcome political competition could convince elites to tighten the rules, as the Conservatives did in Mexico City after taking power nationally in 1835. Their central government and governor imposed the first income restrictions on voting in 1836 because many artisans and laborers—including shoemakers, bricklayers, carpenters, and water carriers—had cast ballots for their opponents in the municipal elections of 1835 and earlier.

In previous municipal and congressional elections in Mexico City in the 1820s, voter turnout had peaked around 70 percent to 75 percent of the adult male population, an amazingly high percentage for the era. In Mexico City's municipal elections from 1829 to 1831, approximately 27 percent of the total male population had still voted. This figure far exceeded the suffrage permitted in France and England at the same time. In France in 1831 less than 25 percent of all males over twenty-one years of age enjoyed the right to participate in municipal elections, whereas in England in 1833 only some 4 percent of the total adult population could vote in borough council elections.

In 1836, the Mexican Conservatives cracked down on the suffrage by establishing a minimum annual income of one hundred pesos for voters and one thousand five-hundred pesos for congressional deputies. They did so because they were apprehensive about class conflict and about orchestration by their enemies of lower-class voting and mob action. Subsequently, declining electoral turnout resulted from both these obstacles and voter disillusionment with the efficacy of participation. Despite such restrictions on the franchise, competitive municipal and congressional elections continued throughout the first half of the nineteenth century and produced alternation among some office holders.[79]

Another example of suffrage upsurge followed by regression took place in
Colombia. The Liberal constitution of 1853 took a leap forward by installing direct elections with universal male suffrage. Subsequent constitutions in
the 1860s restored indirect elections and backed away from universal male
participation. They allowed voting rights to be set by the provinces, many of
which reinstituted literacy requirements. Some Liberals were not unhappy
about this reversion, since many illiterates had been backing Conservatives.
Moreover, Liberals in power proved just as guilty as Conservatives of rigging elections.[80]

In a similar retrogression in Peru in the 1860s, electoral contestation
prompted liberals to raise the economic qualifications for voting. They
compressed the franchise to reduce the constituency of conservative rural
landowners and bosses, who relied on Indian and indentured Asian voters.[81]
By the same token in Brazil in 1881, the elites' dread of voting by rising
numbers of urban workers and freed slaves produced a new electoral law
that enforced the previously lax property and income qualifications. Consequently, the number of voters fell from the astonishing figure of over 1
million to approximately 150,000.[82] After such backtracking, many ordinary
Latin Americans would have to wait decades to capture or recapture their
suffrage rights.

Nascent Political Parties

Idealized twentieth-century concepts of organized, structured, bureaucratic, enduring, programmatic mass political parties should not obscure
the extent to which infant parties worthy of the name emerged in a few
parts of Latin America in the latter half of the nineteenth century. They
should not be held to higher standards than parties elsewhere in the world
in the same era just because Latin America was less developed. These parties usually took shape as a pyramid of networks of patrons and clients, with
national caudillos stitching together alliances of local caciques forged at the
regional level. Sometimes the nuclei of parties crystallized in the legislature.
Neophyte proto-parties also arose out of the organizations—typically vertical, personalistic, patron-client mechanisms—formed to mobilize voters
for elections, not unlike urban machines in the United States in the same
epoch. Because of restrictions on the franchise, they were usually parties
of notables. Although dominated from the top down, they had to bargain
with their regional and local bosses to hold the network together.

These loose associations competed for political power through elections
and other avenues. Like all political parties up to the present, they sought

to win power in order to achieve personal or policy objectives. In contrast with the most modern and elaborate twentieth century parties, their main failings were their elitism, weak organization, short life span, and undemocratic behavior. However paternalistic, hierarchical, undisciplined, transitory, opportunistic, authoritarian, or unsuccessful, they met the rudimentary criteria for parties in an early stage of evolution, not unlike their contemporary counterparts in the United States and especially Europe.[83]

In the nineteenth century, a few political parties in Latin America progressed from nonexistent to embryonic, in a handful of cases maturing into durable organizations. Absent in some countries and frail in most, nascent political parties in the early decades usually represented familial, personalistic, regional, or Church-State cleavages within the upper class. Normally dubbed *Conservatives* or *Liberals*, the former tended to favor pro-clericalism and centralism, while the latter tilted toward anti-clericalism and federalism. These intra-elite divisions seldom created openings for the middle and lower classes to take charge, but they did cause political leaders to seek support from beneath.[84]

Political parties were generally weak, but over time, those countries with the strongest parties and party systems tended to evolve into the most robust democracies, including Chile, Colombia, Costa Rica, Uruguay, and Argentina. From mid-century onward, several parties grew into ongoing, patterned organizations with clear regulations and programs, at least in the more prosperous, urbanizing countries. Nevertheless, they still primarily represented patron-client, geographic, or religious groupings rather than sharply defined socioeconomic or class alignments.[85]

In the middle of the nineteenth century, Chile and Colombia provided the two leading country examples of functional political parties. In both cases, these parties lasted over a hundred years, comparable to their analogues in the United States or Europe. In Chile by the 1850s to the 1860s, the enduring Conservative, Liberal, and Radical parties—arrayed from pro- to anti-clerical positions—already regularly issued programs, ran in elections, and placed members in the congress and the presidency. They continued doing so—and usually defending democracy—throughout most of the twentieth century, when other major organizations joined the multiparty system.[86]

In Colombia in the second half of the nineteenth century, the Liberal and Conservative parties emerged as identifiable groups of political partisans that campaigned regularly in elections. Until the 1890s, they lacked the permanent national organizations with officers and conventions associated with modern political parties, but notables in congress and other offices provided informal leadership. These parties competed locally, regionally, and nationally. Although regionalism factionalized both parties, all provinces contained advocates of both groups.

Early in their development, Colombian Conservatives as well as Liberals commanded intense loyalties, more so than the military but less so than the Roman Catholic Church. Both parties relied on passionate support from all social strata, including the poor. The precocity and tenacity of these parties underpinned the lengthy success of liberal democracy in Colombia. These organizations provided resilient institutions before the arrival of mass politics, which they were able to absorb into the two-party system in the twentieth century.[87]

Even in Peru, where political institutions were less stable, political parties began to congeal in the 1860s and 1870s. They took shape through the chamber of deputies and through increasingly national electoral campaigns for president. Although no lasting parties or party system took hold, one organization, the Civil Party, became prominent from the 1870s into the twentieth century. Most of its leaders and members sought personal advancement more than programmatic accomplishments, but that has been true of many parties around the world. Nevertheless, the Civil Party's deputies often voted in congress as a block. Ruled from the top down, it was similar to other elitist parties that arose in places like Argentina to dominate the era of oligarchic republicanism at the end of the nineteenth century.[88]

Even in Brazil's constitutional monarchy, political parties began to crystallize. The Conservative and Liberal parties based themselves mainly on personalistic, patron–client ties, not on divergent social classes, ideologies or programs. Consequently, their positions and composition changed frequently. Highly factionalized and regionalized, they did not really represent cohesive, substantive, national parties in the modern sense, despite their appearance. Nevertheless, they became significant, ongoing organizations that met the minimum criteria for political parties by nineteenth-century standards in Latin America and much of Western Europe.[89]

Conclusion

During the first six decades after independence, both popular and protected democracy largely failed in Latin America. Time and again, dictators trampled essays in democracy. But particularly from mid-century onward, it made some small advances, at least by the Western metrics of the era. Although Liberals as well as Conservatives feared anarchy more than tyranny, they continued to advocate republicanism. In a few countries, stable republics emerged, however elitist.

A handful of constitutions held fast. Their implementation hinged on consensus within the upper class. Even the numerous short-lived charters laid down institutional patterns that persisted. They included valiant attempts to write laws to correct political misbehavior, but the harsh realities of vastly unequal social power subverted their efforts.

To accomplish the highest priority of establishing order, political institutions mainly followed the colonial and Bolivarian legacies. Centralism prevailed in law and reality. Also powerful in the constitutions and even more in practice were the caudillo presidents, who at least began to dominate their sub-national rivals. Legislatures remained anemic but made tiny gains. The redefined judiciaries blended colonial, United States, and French attributes that left them unsuited to review the constitutionality of acts by other branches of government or to uphold democracy. A smattering of political parties began to take shape and to recruit ordinary people.

A few institutions became more democratic and participatory than might be expected in a dark age dominated by warfare, caudillos, and dictators. However deformed and disappointing in their conduct and results, elections at times offered exceptional opportunities for political involvement and learning. The temporary upsurge of popular elections imparted to the lower classes a glimpse of broader democratic practices, possibilities, and potential. After the ruling groups sought protection by reversing their opening up of the suffrage, the disenfranchised majority would have to wait decades to resurrect and realize their democratic aspirations.

Imperfect and ephemeral as they usually were, these intellectual and institutional experiments sometimes reflected democratic beliefs and ambitions. In the post-independence period, they typically succumbed to authoritarian forces. Nevertheless, they paved the way for the first wave of constitutional democracy in Latin America from the 1880s to the 1920s.

Chapter 5

Oligarchic Republicanism,
1880s–1920s

In Latin America, the first era of classic liberal economics and politics reigned from the 1880s through the 1920s. In broad terms, it resembled the second era of essentially the same paradigm from the 1980s to the 2000s. In both periods, the globalization of open market systems co-incided with the stabilization of civilian, constitutional, elected, representative democracies—although fewer in the first instance than the second. In both episodes, globalization opened the way to rising U.S. influence in favor of these low-intensity, protected democracies. In the first epoch, the Colossus of the North exerted leverage mainly in the Caribbean Basin; in the second, throughout the hemisphere, as U.S. hegemony expanded.[1]

In both cases, the élites intended these democracies to be constrained, largely devoid of mass mobilization or redistributive social reforms. Because of the marginalization of the lower classes and their social issues, both experiences witnessed rising discontent with these procedural liberal democracies. This disenchantment recapitulated the longstanding debate in Latin America between protected and popular democracies.

The big difference between the two liberal epochs was the scope of legal electoral participation. A narrow oligarchy excluded most of the population in the first instance, but universal suffrage prevailed in the second. Because of the tight restrictions on voting and governance, this first fifty years of liberal orthodoxy in Latin America constituted oligarchic republicanism rather than full-fledged democracy.

"Oligarchical democracies" were "regimes in which presidents and national assemblies derived from open, if not fully fair, political competition for the support of limited electorates, according to prescribed constitutional rules and which were largely comparable to the restricted representative regimes in Europe of the same period."[2]

The major oligarchic constitutional republics in the late nineteenth and early twentieth centuries included Chile from 1833 to 1920, Argentina from 1862 to 1912, Colombia from 1886 to 1936, Uruguay from 1890 to 1903, and Brazil from 1891 to 1930. Among these historical democratic standouts, Uruguay exhibited the least preparation under a lengthy oligarchic republic, Colombia the most severe interruption of that type of regime during its war of a Thousand Days (1899 to 1902) and the subsequent dictatorship (1904 to 1909). Three of the most successful countries evolved into more open (albeit still somewhat restricted) democratic systems in the era: Chile from 1920 to 1924, Argentina from 1912 to 1930, and Uruguay from 1903 to 1933.

To a lesser extent, other more tipsy, more limited, more oligarchic and less republican examples of these regimes arose in Peru from 1860 to 1919, Bolivia from 1884 to 1930, Ecuador from 1884 to 1925, and Costa Rica from 1889 to 1947. Some less developed countries in Central America—notably Honduras from 1880 to 1931, El Salvador from 1886 to 1931, Honduras from 1895 to 1919, and Panama from 1904 to 1967—also hosted varieties of more rudimentary, restricted, and rocky oligarchic republics, but they receive almost no attention in this book. In contrast with the major cases, the scholarly information on these political systems is very thin, and most of the existing evidence indicates that they were much more authoritarian and elitist, much less democratic and institutionalized.[3]

From the late nineteenth through the early twentieth centuries, some of the major Latin American aristocratic republics actually exhibited democratic attributes and participation that came close to their counterparts in the United States and Europe. Argentines used the terms *republic* and *democracy* interchangeably as virtual synonyms for their political system. In many respects, Argentina's civilian, constitutional, electoral stability—based on universal male suffrage without economic or educational restrictions beginning in 1856—kept in step with or ahead of the Western world. Although significant shortcomings separated the most successful Latin American republics from the leaders in Europe, the contrast should not be overstated.

Prior to 1914 outside Latin America, only the United States, France, Portugal, and Switzerland hosted formal republics, while the rest of Europe usually maintained constitutional monarchies. Whatever the regime, the Europeans moved toward universal male suffrage—adopted first by France in

1848 and then sweeping most of Europe in the first two decades of the twentieth century. In these same years, the secret ballot spread more slowly from the United States in 1888 through some European countries, including France in 1913. However, many countries, such as Germany, still practiced the public oral vote. Proportional representation remained rare, only enacted in Belgium in 1899 and Sweden in 1909.[4]

From the 1880s through the 1920s in Latin America, the most significant change from the post-independence decades was the further stabilization and growth of the export economies and of civilian oligarchic rule, the climax of a trend that began around the middle of the nineteenth century. In some countries, the protection of civil liberties made even more progress than the expansion of electoral rights. New middle and working class groups asserted themselves in civil society before breaking into the electoral arena.

In general, participation and contestation belonged to an élite minority, but not exclusively. In some countries, governments reduced suffrage rights. Nevertheless, a few republics in the early twentieth century gradually propagated and institutionalized more democratic practices, admitting new social actors and political parties. These advances set the stage for an explosion of political mobilization after the Great Depression of the 1930s.[5]

On both sides of the turn of the century, the types of regimes continued to vary. However, a strong trajectory took hold toward stable, constitutional, civilian oligarchic rule, whether exercised by reasonably republican regimes or by fundamentally authoritarian ones. After a trip to South America in 1912, the British observer James Bryce concluded about their governments:

> Some of them are true republics in the European sense, countries in which the constitutional machinery is a reality and not a sham. Others are petty despotisms, created and maintained by military force. In the fairly large class which lies between these two groups, the machinery works, but more or less irregularly and imperfectly. The legislature has some influence as an expression of public opinion; the rights of individuals to personal safety and to property receive some respect; the application and enforcement of the law, though uncertain, are not subjected to the arbitrary will of the executive.

He judged that the most bona fide republics with true constitutional governments resided in Argentina and Chile.[6]

For the era, analysts often rank the most democratic countries as Argentina, Chile and Uruguay—with Colombia, Brazil and Costa Rica also making some lists. By the eve of World War I, oligarchic electoral republics existed in over half of the ten South American countries. In South America, the trend toward these republics spread so far that the regime changes sparked by the Great Depression mainly replaced civilian rule with dictatorships based on the armed forces. To a lesser extent, a similar pattern prevailed in El Salvador and Honduras.

Prior to the Great Crash of economies and political regimes, some countries—like Peru and Bolivia—had continued alternating between oligarchic republics and oligarchic despotisms. By contrast, stable, modernizing, oligarchic autocracies had ruled most of the time in places like Mexico and Venezuela. In some of the less developed countries in Central America and the Caribbean, more primitive military or *sultanistic* tyrannies persisted.[7]

From 1900 to 1930, military takeovers succeeded fifty-two times. They concentrated overwhelmingly in Central America, the Caribbean, and Paraguay. These coups usually marked no great change in regime. The most significant overthrows of oligarchic republics transpired in Chile and Ecuador in the mid-1920s.[8]

Whether ostensibly republican or blatantly dictatorial, many of these oligarchic regimes had to decide whether to include more of the increasingly discontented subordinate classes in the political system or to repress them. Efforts to maintain stability led to gradual incorporation of excluded groups, as in Argentina and, to a lesser extent, Uruguay and Chile, or to intensified oppression, as in Peru, Bolivia, and Central America. That latter strategy in Mexico detonated a social revolution in 1910. That upheaval ushered in new political participants, many of them from the middle class, working class, or peasantry. Occurring at approximately the same time in the second decade of the twentieth century, the inclusion of the unprivileged by peaceful means in Argentina and by violent eruptions in Mexico alerted ruling élites in some countries to open up institutional channels for dissent and in others to clamp down harder.[9]

One democratic appeal to the middle and working classes came from the early populists—charismatic leaders galvanizing the new urban groups behind reformist programs. The most successful presidential examples arose in two of the more advanced countries: Argentina under Hipólito Irigoyen (1916–1922 and 1928–1930) and Chile under Arturo Alessandri (1920–1924), although a case could also be made in Peru for Guillermo Billinghurst (1912–1914). They strode forth as precursors of the classic populists, who would emerge after the Great Depression blasted the oligarchy's exclusionary economic and political model.[10]

During the oligarchic era and thereafter, both internal and external observers continued to cite many of the same reasons for the so-called *pathology of democracy* in Latin America: geographic immensity and barriers; economic underdevelopment (including poverty, volatility of the external sector, and control of key economic areas by foreigners); social structure and inequality (latifundia and shortage of small landowners, lack of a hegemonic bourgeoisie, a small middle and working class, illiteracy, racial and ethnic disparities); political impediments (legacies from the colonial and independence periods, caudillos, other military groups, the Roman Catholic Church, and flaccid political institutions); and even alleged cultural inhibitions (including authoritarian and personalistic attitudes).[11]

After itemizing these debilitating factors, Bryce concluded: ". . . small wonder that legislatures were not honestly elected, that, when elected, they wasted time in vain debates and neglected business, that each party in turn drove out its opponents or cowed them by violence, that debts were recklessly contracted and left unpaid, that the government remained one not of laws, but of men, and those men mostly military adventurers at the head of armed bands."[12]

Although socioeconomic variables still made democracy difficult, some changes may have helped. From a modernization perspective, economic growth and social articulation, especially in the burgeoning cities, rendered the wealthier countries more suitable for democratic politics. As the middle and working classes grew in size and expressiveness, pressures mounted for their political inclusion. The more prosperous, urbanized countries often fared better with republicanism. Until the military coup of 1930, Argentina, with its gradual incorporation of new groups, seemed to fit best the model of socioeconomic modernization leading to political evolution to democracy.

Rather than promoting broad-based democracy, however, the élites established these oligarchic republics mainly to provide order for economic growth. That prosperity kept many of these political systems afloat until the Great Depression smashed their economic foundation, their image of efficiency, and their legitimacy. As a result, many in the middle and lower classes turned against these regimes, which the oligarchy often abandoned in favor of military dictatorships.[13]

International politics affected democracy in Latin America in contradictory ways. From the 1890s to the 1920s, the United States partly justified its frequent military interventions in the Caribbean, Central America, and Mexico in the name of exporting electoral democracies, or at least aristocratic republics. In the countries it occupied, the United States insisted on elections, wrote electoral laws and constitutions in the belief that institutions held the key to democratization, observed and supervised electoral behavior, and certified the winners.

However, Washington did not apply that policy—which was often inconsistent and insincere—to South America. Moreover, economic and security goals far outranked democracy promotion, which proved notoriously unsuccessful. The Colossus of the North cared more about stability than democracy. By the end of this era, a few of Latin America's most ruthless and tenacious tyrants held office in the very countries of Central America and the Caribbean where the United States had invested the most troops, time, and money to install a democratic façade. Indeed, throughout this epoch and the twentieth century, democracy or at least oligarchic republics had the earliest and most success where the United States had the least influence (South America) and the latest and least success where the United States had the most influence (Mexico, Central America, and the Caribbean).[14]

Allegedly fought to make the world safe for democracy, World War I briefly encouraged democratic impulses in Latin America, although Europe took essentially no interest in the makeup of Latin American governments. After the war and the revolutions in Russia and Mexico, the United States in the 1920s commenced backing away from democracy promotion. The U.S. government developed a policy of neutrality toward regime types or even support for rightwing dictatorships in Latin America as the lesser of two evils, despite its stated preference for democracies.[15]

From Positivism to Popular Nationalism

In the oligarchic period in Latin America, mainstream political thought evolved from nineteenth-century liberalism initially to positivism, then to conservative nationalism, and finally to popular nationalism or populism. In many ways, these ideas journeyed from protected democracy to popular democracy. At the same time, new radical ideologies entered from abroad.

In the latter decades of the nineteenth century, conservative intellectuals imported positivism. Laced with some tenets of social Darwinism, it seemed to promise that if the state supplied order, then the economy would provide growth. Thus society, in turn, would naturally mature into a developed entity capable of sustaining more democratic forms of government. From the viewpoint of the upper classes, that maturation required education and immigration to improve the stock of racially inferior natives. Until that evolution reached a high enough stage, these thinkers believed that oligarchic republics or even dictatorships would be necessary to maintain stability.

In the late nineteenth century, the two most famous Latin American symbols of this school of thought were the *cientificos* advising Mexican dictator

Porfirio Díaz and the national motto of *Order and Progress* emblazoned on
the flag of Brazil. This positivist outlook flowed naturally from conservative
and even liberal formulas for government that had festooned Latin America
since the wars of independence, when Bolívar and others called for paternalistic rule by the élites until the population was better prepared for self
government. Some of the same attitudes toward the unreliability of the common people rationalized authoritarian regimes, technocracies, and protected
democracies in Latin America for a century from the 1880s to the 1980s.[16]

The first counterattack against positivism and its infatuation with foreign
science took the form of idealism and conservative nationalism. Some of
their advocates praised venerable upper-class cultural and aesthetic qualities
as the essence of Latin American identity. These thinkers tended to exalt the
rule of the traditional Hispanic élites as a bulwark against ideas and immigrants from abroad. Then a reaction against this aristocratic or cultural nationalism set in, often labeled popular nationalism or populism. It extolled
the common people, including Indians, Africans, and Mestizos, as the core
of Latin America's identity and called for their elevation in the government
and economy.[17]

José Enrique Rodó, one of the most famous intellectuals in Uruguayan
and Latin American history, espoused conservative cultural nationalism at
the turn of the century. He reacted against positivism, U.S. imperialism, and
the flood of European immigrants. Although he condemned U.S. economic
and military expansion as well as its cultural vulgarity, he praised its limited
democracy. Like many Latin American thinkers since the days of independence, Rodó preferred a constricted democracy in which élites maintained
controls over the dangerous classes to avoid mediocrity or massification.[18]

Visions of protected versus popular democracy divided Mexico between
the conservatives in the dictatorship of Porfirio Díaz (1876–1910) and the
radicals in the Mexican Revolution (1910–1917). Both groups claimed to
favor democracy, but neither of them carried it out. Both the Díaz regime
and the revolt of Francisco Madero against it began in the name of liberalism, democracy, effective suffrage, and no reelection, but Mexico had to
wait almost a century for the fulfillment of those promises. Nevertheless, by
the time of the 1910 Revolution, Mexican liberals and radicals had come to
argue that democracy had to include social justice. Some of those revolutionaries championed the social, economic, and political uplift and incorporation of the under classes, sounding the chords of popular nationalism that
would soon resonate throughout the hemisphere.[19]

At the same time, some intellectuals in other countries also hoisted the
banner of popular nationalism. However, more often groups like the middle

sectors, students, workers, and populist politicians spearheaded the drive for popular democracy. For example, the Argentine student movement of 1918 set the standard for Latin America by advocating greater democracy within the university, within society, and within the political system. Even these rising friends of democracy, however, promoted a distinctly Latin American linkage of political democracy with class-based social reform, an outgrowth of the glaring inequalities in the region.[20]

Some imported ideologies gave even more emphasis to social equality—but not to liberal democracy. Anarchism, anarchosyndicalism, Marxism, socialism, and communism penetrated Latin America in these years. Their popularity showed how the neglect of social issues by oligarchic republicanism resulted in alienation from—rather than incorporation into—liberal democracy. The proliferation of these ideologies indicated that some of the social concerns of popular democracy could lead to anti-liberal or authoritarian solutions.

Among these movements, the only commitment to Western democracy arose among some socialists, partly in reaction against the Communists. In Argentina, Uruguay, and most of the time in Chile, socialists embraced the democratic route to social justice. Anarchism and anarchosyndicalism took hold in the labor movement more than among intellectuals. Around the turn of the century, those beliefs exhibited strength in Argentina and Chile among unions, in Mexico among precursors of the Revolution, and in Peru in the writings of Manuel González Prada. Eventually, Marxism in a broad sense had the greatest impact on political thought in Latin America from World War I through most of the Cold War. That trend rarely lent support to liberal democracy.[21]

Stabilizing Political Institutions

SOCIAL CONSTITUTIONALISM

Compared to the previous period, more constitutions endured for decades, as did some regimes. From the 1880s through the 1920s, the twenty countries produced fifty constitutions, a smaller number per country and per year than in the preceding epoch. The Dominican Republic accounted for one-fifth of the output with ten charters. Particularly in the less developed countries in Central America, the Caribbean, and the Andes, lawmakers continued to write and rewrite constitutions with consummate dedication and frequency. Such devotion suggested that the crafters thought these documents were or should be important. More of these charters or parts of them operated effectively, although many still did not.

Even when these documents served mainly as expressions of aspirations or pretensions, nearly all governments claimed legitimacy based on some constitution. Only rarely did a despot reign without vowing to honor, obey, or prepare a constitution. Rulers of all stripes often brandished these consecrating texts to impress opponents and foreigners. "The constitutions did not suit the facts, and the facts had to prevail against the constitutions, sometimes against their letter, usually against their spirit."[22]

One example of a typical sham constitution came into being in Peru in 1920. Augusto B. Leguía seized power by force in 1919 and replaced the 1860 constitution. Reflecting Latin American reformist ideals in these years, the charter of 1920 became more democratic than its predecessor on paper, although not in operation. Some of the provisions had applicability, like the maintenance of Roman Catholicism as the state religion, but many of the articles, especially the innovative ones, rang hollow. For example, the new document formally gave slightly more authority to outlying regions, but it retained a unitary, centralist system. Like its successor in 1933, it also accorded congress more power, for example to interrogate, censure, and remove cabinet officers. However, the chief executive remained overwhelmingly dominant in the 1920s and 1930s, when, in effect, dictatorships ruled Peru.

Like the Mexican Constitution of 1917, this Peruvian document broke new ground by incorporating social and economic guarantees for labor and Indians, and allowing government interference with property rights; however, the rulers seldom implemented these provisions. On paper, it took another step forward by making all elections direct; however, the government still restricted the franchise to literate adult males, mocked civil liberties, and perpetuated systemic electoral fraud. Other largely fictitious constitutions proliferated in poorer countries like the Dominican Republic.[23]

While many constitutions proved transitory and inconsequential, several durable and fairly functional charters remained intact, notably those of Argentina (1853), Costa Rica (1871), and Colombia (1886). Enduring successors replaced other long-standing documents. These included Mexico's which had lasted from 1857 to 1917, Uruguay's from 1830 to 1918, and Chile's from 1833 to 1925.[24]

In 1917, Mexico adopted the most path-breaking and influential constitution in early twentieth century Latin America. Arising out of a social revolution, that document inaugurated a new breed of social constitutions, thereafter a fixture of popular democracy throughout the region. It stretched the definition of democracy to include social and economic justice. It blazed new trails by adding social rights, especially for workers and peasants, and curbing private property rights, especially for foreigners. Written by a convention of revolutionaries, the charter declared that the government "shall be democratic, considering democracy not solely as a juridical structure and a political system, but as a system of life based on the continuous economic, social, and cultural improvement of the people."[25]

This constitution also raised the no reelection principle to new heights. It forbade the president to ever reoccupy that office. After the revolution, Mexico also denied members of congress and state legislatures consecutive terms, although they could return after an interval. Consequently, the presidency changed hands every six years, as did the senate, and the chamber of deputies every three years. However, the politicians only implemented the second half of the revolutionary battle cry of "effective suffrage and no reelection," since the revolutionary party came to dominate all elections, through fair means and foul. As a result, Mexico moved toward a popular democracy in terms of social reforms but retained a protected authoritarian system in terms of political practices.[26]

In the era, Uruguay provided the counterpoint to Mexico. Through peaceful democratic rather than violent revolutionary means, it achieved similar, though milder, social reforms and adopted a comparably progressive, though less advanced, constitution. Both countries claimed to be installing a political democracy, but Mexico lagged far behind Uruguay in honoring that commitment.[27]

Uruguay's José Batlle y Ordóñez provided a prime example of political democratization being combined with social reform. First elected president by the General Assembly in 1903, he demonstrated his devotion to democracy by not running again in 1907 because the constitution did not permit two consecutive turns in office. In his second term (1911–15), Batlle created the beginnings of Latin America's first welfare state, partly modeled after European examples. He also instituted political reforms to bring peace between the two dominant parties—his own Colorados and the opposition Blancos—and to emasculate the presidency. Thus he hoped to eliminate civil wars and dictatorships.

Batlle did not lead a middle and working class coalition, which was scarcely ready for such a venture in the opening years of the twentieth century. Rather, he engaged in pre-emptive or anticipatory reform and incorporation for those subordinate classes from an élite vantage point. As so often in Latin America, this reform emanated from above, not from below, akin to that of Sáeñz Pena in Argentina.[28]

Promoted by Batlle, Uruguay used secret balloting for the first time in 1916. Voters elected a constituent assembly that began revising the constitution of 1830 in 1917. The representatives succeeded because they forged a

coalition between the Colorados and Blancos, a typical compromise pact between the two parties to bring about major political changes. Batlle's brain-
child won approval in a plebiscite in 1917 by 84,992 against 4,030 ballots.

The revamped constitution made great strides in democratization. Promulgated in 1918 and implemented in 1919, it separated Church and State,
eliminated the death penalty, retained centralism but promised decentralized
authority for departments and municipalities elected by popular vote, and
installed habeas corpus. It created a weakened president elected by direct
vote of the people. It also mandated a bicameral congress with proportional
representation and guaranteed the second-largest party—the Blancos—one-
third of the seats in the legislature and the executive branch's National
Council. For elections, the constitution established obligatory inscription in
the civil registry, the secret ballot, no political activity by military or police
except voting, and no more literacy requirement for voters. Since Batlle
focused more on political than social reform, this document did not subject
property rights to social needs or include a list of social rights as seen in the
Mexican charter of 1917.[29]

Constitutional modernization transpired in Chile when the military—
contrary to its tradition, overthrew the Parliamentary Republic in 1924 to
1925, partly to break a deadlock between the president and congress. They
backed President Arturo Alessandri's reinvigoration of a presidential system.
He concocted a small committee to design the constitution of 1925. A national referendum overwhelmingly approved the document, although over
50 percent of the voters abstained, as all the political parties had urged in
their opposition to the new charter.

Defining the government as unitary, republican, and representative, the
1925 constitution contained many continuities with its 1833 predecessor—
such as presidential authority to suspend constitutional guarantees. However,
it introduced separation of Church and State, local provincial assemblies,
presidential control over ministerial appointments, greater executive influence over legislation, direct popular election of the president, proportional
election of senators and deputies, and a tribunal to monitor all elections.

In reaction to the military's interventions in 1924 and 1925, Chile's new
constitution also proclaimed that, "The public forces are essentially obedient. No armed body may deliberate." Perhaps somewhat wistfully, it added
that, "Every decision that the President of the Republic, the Chamber of
Deputies, the Senate, or the tribunals of justice may agree to in the presence or on demand of an army, an officer at the head of an armed force,
or of any assembly of people, with or without arms, and in disobedience of
the authorities, is null in law and cannot produce any effect." From 1927 to

1931, a rare military-based dictatorship ran the country, but from 1932 to 1973, democratic civilian governments breathed life into these sentiments from 1925.[30]

CENTRALIST COMPROMISES WITH DECENTRALISM

In most of Latin America, centralism gained ground, while granting a few concessions to decentralism. For example, Colombian President Rafael Núñez convened a special National Council in 1885 to replace the federalist constitution of 1863. He criticized that previous blueprint for failing to allow the central government to provide for political order and economic growth. The charter of 1886 established a centralist government, a potent president elected for six years by indirect vote with no immediate reelection, a bicameral congress, an independent judiciary, and a united Church and State. It stripped states of any autonomy and demoted them to departments managed by governors appointed by the president—but with directly elected assemblies. Many countries installed this split between appointed governors and elected assemblies in the provinces. In Colombia, municipal councils also existed, but mayors served as the agents of the governors.

This 1886 document succeeded because it not only ensconced centralism, but also allowed subnational units some authority. This compromise ended the interminable feuds between centralists and federalists. Henceforth, the central government determined all legislation and national policies, but the departments and the municipalities enjoyed some control over their implementation. In short, Colombia installed local government but not *local self-government*. Colombians called the new formula "political centralization and administrative decentralization." This constitution remained in force until 1991, albeit with significant revisions from time to time, becoming one of Latin America's landmark constitutions.[31]

Both Chile and Uruguay maintained extreme centralism with occasional gestures to decentralism. After some tepid decentralization to municipalities in this period, both would revert to centralization in the 1930s. Under the Parliamentary Republic from 1891 to 1925, Chile instituted local elections but retained one of the most centralized governments in Latin America. Although the 1925 constitution recognized regional resentments by providing for provincial assemblies, they never came into being. Instead, *intendants* appointed by the president administered the provinces. Beneath them, governors, also selected by the president, in consultation with the intendants, ruled over departments. At the lowest level, every four years voters elected municipal councils, which picked the alcalde, except in the larger cities, where the president named the mayor. Also highly centralist, Uruguay instituted modest political and fiscal decentralization in its 1918 constitution.[32]

In other cases, Peru's 1920 Constitution made its government as centralized as the French, with every regional and local body controlled from Lima.[33] The Mexican Constitution of 1917 resurrected the federalist promise of the 1857 Constitution, but in fact centralism came to prevail in subsequent decades.[34]

In contrast with the rest of Latin America, Brazil decentralized dramatically under the Old Republic (1889 to 1930). Following the military's overthrow of the empire in 1889, political power devolved to the leading provinces (called *states*). Heavily influenced by the examples of the United States and Argentina and the power realities in Brazil, the federalist constitution of 1891 replaced the centralist document of 1824. The new system known as the *Politics of the Governors* lasted until the centralizing revolution of Getúlio Vargas in the 1930s.[35]

OLIGARCHIC PRESIDENTS

Presidentialism still ruled the region, although some significant efforts tried to instill more checks and balances. Most constitutions required presidents to hold higher qualifications than other officeholders. According to Mexico's 1917 constitution, presidents had to be Mexicans by birth and sons of Mexican parents by birth, a pretty stiff requirement reflecting the nationalism of the revolution. They had to be over thirty-five years of age, to have resided in the country for the year leading up to election, to not belong to the clergy, to have left the army six months prior to election, to have departed any high government office six months before, and to have never been president previously. Followed closely, these stipulations aimed to curb clericalism, militarism, nepotism, continuism, and dictatorship.

Most Latin American constitutions maintained strong presidents. On paper and even more in practice, the authoritarian Mexican president, after 1917 as before, brandished some of the most ample powers in Latin America. For example, he named all civilian and military officers of the government, although he had to obtain senate approval for appointments to the diplomatic corps and the upper ranks of the armed services. He also needed congressional permission to leave the country. Nevertheless, the congress usually heeded his beck and call.

Theoretically, protections for civil liberties also constrained the Mexican president. However, the 1917 constitution replicated most of its counterparts throughout Latin America in vagueness and intricate qualifications, leaving generous room for insidious interpretations and abuses. For example, the section on freedom of speech was phrased, "The expression of ideas should not be subject to any judicial or administrative investigation, unless it offends good morals, infringes the rights of others, incites to crime, or disturbs the public order." Moreover, the constitution ceded to the president wide latitude to suspend civil liberties.[36]

To a lesser extent, the presidency also served as the dominant institution in late nineteenth century Argentina. Although legally limited in powers and tenure, and balanced somewhat by the legislature, judiciary, and provinces, the president ruled like royalty. Once elected, the chief executive exercised supreme authority, not because of his personality but because of his legal office. From 1853 to 1930, Argentina suffered none of the tyrannical or personalistic dictatorships seen thereafter.

Although the executive branch intervened shamelessly in elections and provinces, one great issue of republicanism in the nineteenth century—the guarantee of universal male suffrage as the legitimate basis of democratic government—had been resolved in Argentina. Moreover, the ruling party fortified that principle by overseeing a gradual transition to greater democracy. That process culminated in the electoral reform of 1912 and the end of the party's own monopoly on the presidency in 1916, almost a century before Mexico's one-party state achieved the same goal.[37]

In the oligarchic era, a few Latin American constitutions actually amplified presidential powers. Colombia's 1886 constitution fortified presidentialism. The president possessed great unbridled appointment authority—for example with his cabinet and governors—although the lower house had to concur with his choices for Attorney General and Comptroller General. He also exercised vast other powers, including a state of siege to cope with civil war or instability, a right rescinded previously by Liberals. This constitution also backtracked on prior Liberal establishment of freedom of the press, subjecting it to the requirements of "social order and public peace." However, the president could not leave the national territory during or for one year after his term without senate approval, a standard Latin American safeguard against executive malfeasance.[38]

Another example of significantly increasing presidential clout in these decades appeared in the 1920 constitution of Peru. Leguía amended it to allow the president to serve a second consecutive term. He became the first executive in Peruvian history to do so, winning reelection in 1924 by the stunning vote of 287,969 to 155. In effect a dictator, Leguía wielded even more ominous powers than those granted him in the constitution, until his overthrow in 1931.[39]

Although robust presidencies remained the rule in Latin America, oppressed regional, social, and political groups increasingly reacted against the authoritarian propensities of chief executives. These resentments surfaced not only in the Mexican Revolution of 1910 but also in other cases, such as the Argentine electoral turnover of 1916. From the 1880s to the 1920s, by far the greatest reductions in presidential powers occurred in Chile, Brazil, and Uruguay, although overweight presidents would return subsequently in all five countries.

Of the three cases of presidencies losing authority, Chile came first. By the time Chile elected José Manuel Balmaceda president in 1886, that office had already ceded substantial ground to the congress. The power of the legislature to question and censure (but not appoint or remove) ministers had become well established. Beginning in the 1860s, presidents took care to appoint cabinet members reflective of the majority in congress. When Balmaceda dared to fill ministries at variance with congressional preferences and tried to revive electoral intervention through picking candidates or rigging the voting, the legislature rebelled against the president.

Chile's civil war of 1891 pitted the president against the congress, where the maturing political parties predominated. The legislators ignited that conflict in 1891 by refusing to approve the president's budget unless he appointed a minister of the interior to their liking. The president responded by decreeing the extension of the 1890 budget bill. Almost all the political parties denounced him as a dictator and called for his removal. The civil war erupted with the navy siding with the congress and the army backing the president. As the tide turned against him, Balmaceda took refuge in the Argentine embassy until the date of the official end of his term in office, when he committed suicide.

Without writing a new constitution, the victors in 1891 created the unique Parliamentary Republic, which lasted until 1925. These reforms did not construct a true parliamentary system, but they did spawn a government dominated by parties and congresses rather than presidents. After the civil war, congressional censure of cabinet ministers required removal and occurred increasingly. From 1831 to 1861, the executive branch hosted 14 cabinets, from 1861 to 1891 it hosted 17, and from 1891 to 1924 it hosted 121 cabinets. In only a little over three decades, 530 ministers headed 6 ministries.

Constitutional reforms whittled down the Chilean presidency by changing his veto of legislation from forbidding such a law completely to prohibiting its consideration for a period of time. Furthermore, his diplomatic appointments henceforth required the concurrence of the senate. An informal change was that presidents no longer managed or interfered significantly with municipal and congressional elections. Now the municipalities and political parties ran those contests, often engaging in fraud and bribery of their own. In addition, presidents no longer picked their successors, now chosen by the political parties.

With increased powers vested in the parties, the congress, and the cabinet (especially the minister of the interior), the chief executive became largely ceremonial. The successful presidential candidate in 1891, Germán Riesco, promised in his campaign slogan, "I am not a threat to anyone." With laissez-faire leadership, the Parliamentary Republic neglected the so-called social question, referring to the unsatisfactory conditions of the increasingly obstreperous working class and, to a lesser extent, the middle class.

After lawmakers reinstated presidential supremacy in the Constitution of 1925, candidates had to be born in Chile, thirty years old, and qualified to be a deputy. After direct election, the chief executive served for six years with no immediate reelection. Victory required an absolute majority, or else the full congress had to choose between the top two candidates.

The 1925 constitution endowed the president with more powers than congress. On his own, the executive appointed ministers and top officials, as well as judges, intendants, governors, and mayors of the important cities. He could declare a state of siege briefly without congressional approval, but only if congress was not in session. The new charter also provided for a national plebiscite if the president and the congress could not agree on constitutional amendments. At the same time, the constitution tried to restrain the president by guaranteeing the usual civil liberties, such as freedom of religion, expression, assembly, movement, and petition.[40]

Similar to Chile in 1891, Brazil disempowered the chief executive, but it passed authority down to the provinces. Under the Politics of the Governors, the leading states not only ran their own affairs but also controlled the indirectly elected president. The electoral system remained very corrupt and small, with less than 4 percent of the population voting in presidential elections. Nevertheless, the chief executive still subordinated the bicameral legislature. And presidents frequently declared states of siege. As in Chile, this period witnessed a lack of national governmental direction or social reform, while the oligarchy presided over an essentially laissez-faire economy until the Great Depression capsized that system.[41]

To constrain drastically the chief executive in Uruguay, Batlle borrowed from Switzerland the concept of a collegial executive with a rotating president. Rather than adopting his proposal, the constituent assembly of 1917 diluted the presidency by making it share authority with a National Council of Administration. Instead of being chosen by the congress, the president would now be elected directly, but still for a four-year term with no immediate reelection. The Council's nine members were also elected directly, with the highest voted party getting two-thirds of the seats and the second party one-third, in order to promote bipartisan participation and support. The president was supposed to have mainly executive functions, the council administrative functions, a concept similar to the division of authority between the chief executive and the audiencia in the colonial period. Given the power and prestige of the president and the inevitable discord between the two offices, however, the council never really took off.[42]

LACKLUSTER BUT INVIGORATED LEGISLATURES

With the main exception of Chile under the Parliamentary Republic, legislatures remained frail in law and even more so in practice. Nevertheless, some improvements took place. Proportional representation appeared in the democratic leaders Costa Rica (1893), Argentina (1912), Uruguay (1918), and Chile (1925).

Most countries expected legislators to have some stature because they required higher qualifications than voters. For example, the Mexican constitution of 1917 established criteria intended to reduce the congressional role of the military, the central government, and the Church. Elected directly for three-year terms, deputies had to be citizens by birth, over twenty-five years old, residents of the state where elected, and not army or police officers, high government officials, or religious ministers. Elected directly for six-year terms, senators faced the same qualifications as deputies except that they had to be over thirty-five years of age. Although congress met regularly after the revolution, it remained almost completely subservient to the president.[43]

In similar fashion, the Peruvian legislature exemplified the general disabilities of that body in Latin America. As in the past, the constitution of 1920 made the congress bicameral. In a nod to calls for reform, that constitution eliminated property and education requirements for members of both houses. Senators as well as deputies were elected for five-year terms and could be reelected immediately. Although congress had existed since independence, it enjoyed very little prestige and accomplished even less. Riddled with partisanship, undisciplined parties, personalism, corruption, and local interests, it left most national business up to the executive branch. It seldom took any initiative, usually only discussing and rubberstamping presidential proposals.[44]

From the constitution of 1830 to the 1880s, the pallid Uruguayan congress gradually gained vigor, particularly to interpellate, censure, and jettison government ministers. Then presidents reasserted their authority and their ministers' autonomy from the 1890s until the constitution of 1918, which tried to check the chief executive. Thereafter congress intensified its scrutiny of cabinet officers, its debates over policies, and its other challenges to the executive branch. Its obstructionism angered President Gabriel Terra, who shut it down in a self-coup in 1933. Like other coups in the early twentieth century, such as Chile's in 1924 and Argentina's in 1930, this takeover partly responded to executive-legislative conflict, despite the conventional wisdom that congresses had little power. The coup also tracked the regional trend of reasserting executive authority.[45]

Although normally browbeaten by the executive branch, the Argentine congress from the 1890s onward was not completely servile. It influenced legislation, voiced public opinion, and bred future presidents and cabinet ministers. Hardly ever initiating laws, the directly elected deputies nevertheless shaped policies, principally by holding hearings of cabinet ministers, commenting on legislation, and delaying bills. As elections became more honest after 1912, the chamber of deputies and political parties waxed in strength, while the parties increasingly disciplined the voting of their legislative members. Chosen in pairs by provincial legislatures, senators fulfilled similar functions.

In addition to electoral reform expanding the franchise and favoring the majority, another Argentine innovation in 1912 moved away from absolute majoritarianism. It required that at least one-third of the deputies and the provincial legislators come from the party with the second highest number of votes. In elections, parties and then voters selected candidates for two-thirds of the seats, which went to the majority, while one-third accrued to the minority. This system favored larger parties and left many voters unrepresented but guaranteed that more than one party would hold office.

In part, this arrangement protected conservatives as democratization created opportunities for their more popular opponents. It resembled the electoral engineering carried out in the same period—by Batlle in Uruguay and Reyes in Colombia and in the 1980s by Pinochet in Chile. It lasted until Argentina installed full proportional representation in 1957.

In the chamber of deputies, the electoral reform of 1912 drastically reduced the percentage from the upper stratum from 1916 to 1930, falling from a majority to a minority of members. Although upper-class deputies belonged to all parties, they were more common among the Conservatives than among the Radicals, who accumulated increasing political strength up to the Great Depression. This downward social and political trend away from the oligarchy fostered a divergence between socioeconomic and political power. That split partly motivated the retaking of the government by the conservative élites through undemocratic means in the 1930s. By the same token, the lack of strong representation of the working class from 1900 to 1945 paved the way to the assertion of pro-labor Peronism thereafter.[46]

Even more than in Argentina, Colombia's legislature possessed some noteworthy functions throughout much of the nineteenth century. According to the 1886 constitution, a senator had to be a male citizen by birth, over thirty years old, with an annual income of 2,000 pesos, and to have held previously a high political office such as a cabinet member or a governor, or to have been a university professor for at least five years, or to have engaged in a liberal profession with a university degree. These restrictions left very few Colombians eligible to be senators. They were directly elected for six years and could be reelected indefinitely. Deputies merely had to be male citizens over twenty-five years of age who had never been sentenced to corporal punishment. Also directly elected, they served for indefinitely renewable four-year terms. To try to quash corruption, the constitution prohibited senators and deputies from transacting any business with the government, from having done so within six months of their election, and from increasing their salaries during their terms. As in previous constitutions, committing fraudulent electoral acts was grounds for loss of citizenship, with the severity of the penalty perhaps indicating the pervasiveness of the crime.

Colombia's 1886 constitution awarded the bicameral congress extensive lawmaking and codemaking powers. Laws could stem from either house of congress or the executive branch. Presidents could veto a bill in whole or in part, but they could be overridden by an absolute majority in congress. The legislature could also grant the chief executive temporary extraordinary powers to ensure the public good. The two houses of congress chose the justices of the supreme court from slates drawn up by the president.[47]

Overall, probably the most powerful congress in Latin America flexed its muscles in Chile, especially during the Parliamentary Republic. That system of congressional supremacy has been criticized for presidential lethargy, ministerial instability, clientelism and corruption, pork-barrel budgeting, and immobility and inattention to mounting socioeconomic problems. However, it has also been praised for nurturing a vibrant congress and political parties, for admitting new contenders without great violence, and for encouraging give-and-take among political élites. In contrast with Argentina and Brazil, powerful congressional parties developed before an extensive central bureaucracy and thus acquired a significant role in the distribution of resources between the state and locals. Even after the presidency eclipsed the congress from 1925 on, the latter retained a high level of importance rare in Latin America.

The 1925 Constitution prescribed proportional representation for both houses of congress. Both were elected directly, with deputies serving four years, and senators serving for eight years. Deputies and senators had to be citizens with voting rights, with no contracts with the government, and "never to have been sentenced for an offense punishable corporally." Senators needed to be thirty-five years old, but deputies apparently were not held to a minimum age requirement.

Although the congress no longer loomed over the president, it retained substantial powers, including giving the president permission to leave the national territory. The assembly approved taxes and the budget, but it could not raise expenditures without finding revenues to cover them, an attempt to bring inflation to heel. Laws could originate with either house or the president. If presidents vetoed a bill, they could be overridden by two-thirds of the congress. It remained politically, if not legally, difficult for a president to sustain a cabinet of which the legislature strongly disapproved. From the middle of the nineteenth century to the present, the exceptionally long record of relevance for the Chilean congress showed that tradition could build up a significant legislature, even in the inhospitable environment of Latin America.[48]

MANAGED ELECTIONS

However flawed and fraudulent on the part of both the rulers and the opposition, elections remained crucial elements in the political life of Latin America. They were widespread and frequent, even in the poorer countries. Surprisingly often, some of them encompassed all social strata. They legitimized the governments. They also set precedents for later, more profound democratization. Indeed, they formed such a regular and essential part of politics that even many of the civil wars, rebellions, and coups d'état occurred around elections, whether to change the rules and balance of power before the balloting or to alter the results thereafter.[49]

The pattern of oligarchic governments manufacturing elections and their results reflected an ambiguity that had emerged in the early days of the wars of independence. From the beginning in 1810, the élites vacillated as to whether representation should flow from the state, as in colonial times, or the individual citizens, as defined by republicanism. This contradiction survived as republican suffrage became the dominant mode of representation but governments interfered with elections to make sure that state interests and representation prevailed. In the oligarchic republics, the state, not the individual citizens, still really did most of the selecting.

Consequently, a tension persisted between republican ideology and statist reality, despite the evolution of more regular elections with increased citizen participation, competition, and expectations. The ruling groups saw this clash between more inclusive republicanism and persisting autocracy as a necessity for building the state and the economy. They sustained this arrangement through managed elections in order to reconcile yawning social inequality with the official formula of political equality. Thus they forged a sometimes cynical compromise between the hierarchy inherited from the colonial regime and the democracy heralded by the republican regime.

Meanwhile, classic liberals interpreted this inconsistency between republican electoral promises and practices as proof of the need to further restrain state domination of the individual. Mounting numbers of dissident élites perceived this disconnect as a cause for complaints and even rebellions. Subordinate groups expanded their social mobilization, political involvement, protests, and demands for genuine participation and representation. As a result, oligarchic republicanism increasingly risked illegitimacy and instability with its stage-managed elections. In the early twentieth century, countries tried to solve this problem in various ways, ranging from repression to reform to revolution.[50]

In general, most elections offered limited participation, indirect and public voting, pervasive cheating, and virtually guaranteed victory for the ruling groups. In this era, voters only accounted for an average of about 2 to 6 percent of the total population.[51] No clear trend emerged toward more inclusive, direct, honest, competitive elections. Instead, countries continued to move forward and backward on electoral practices, as élites changed strategies for engineering elections to maintain power. In almost every country, politicians debated whether to broaden the suffrage toward universality in order to make elections more legitimate and representative or to narrow it in order to retain control.

If any strong pattern existed, it was to roll back the scope of the franchise, most strikingly by excluding illiterates in Brazil and Peru. This contraction occurred partly out of fear of rising demands from the middle and working classes as well as from provincial barons for meaningful political participation. Rather than constricting the suffrage, Chile protected the secret vote but retained a tiny electorate. By contrast, Argentina stood out as the one clear pioneer and harbinger of the future by dramatically opening up the electoral arena.[52]

It is plausible that exceptionally ethnically divided societies with large indigenous populations were more likely to impose indirect elections with highly limited suffrage. In comparison with the Southern Cone, the Andean countries tended in that direction. However, no clear correlation held in Central America, where Guatemala, Honduras, and El Salvador emphasized direct elections, while Nicaragua and Costa Rica usually preferred indirect. Consequently, this hypothesis, like some other single-factor explanations for the adoption of political systems, did not stand up consistently. Instead, individual national political frictions, debates, and strategies seemed to determine political practices.[53]

Opening or closing the franchise usually resulted from internal competitions and calculations among the ruling groups. They mobilized their partisans both by changing the electoral prerequisites and violating them. Conservatives were almost as likely as Liberals to promote suffrage expansion in order to amplify their own base of support. Sometimes the rulers took lower class demands for participation into account, but sometimes they did not. In some cases, subalterns did not pressure for removal of the qualifications for voting but rather for their inclusion in the favored categories. For example in Bolivia, Indians implored the state for more primary education and artisans for recognition that they were not domestic workers so that they could meet the existing criteria for suffrage.[54]

In most cases, only citizens could be legal voters. Under some conditions, eligible citizens could be quite young. For example, in the 1886 Constitution of El Salvador, it proclaimed that, "All Salvadorians more than eighteen years of age, and those who are married or have obtained some literary degree, even though they have not reached that age, are citizens." In a legalistic attempt to abolish common nefarious practices, the constitution warned that citizenship could be lost if people sold their vote or tried to reelect a president immediately. Guatemala, Uruguay, and Honduras also lowered the voting age to eighteen.[55]

Like Peru, Brazil provided an example late in the nineteenth century (1881) of converting from indirect to direct legislative elections and of eliminating illiterate voters, combining a step forward with a step backward. As in most of Latin America, Brazil had erected a hierarchy in its multi-stage indirect elections, with each level normally requiring higher qualifications. For example, typically electors needed higher status than the first level of voters, and the representatives chosen by the electors were required to meet even loftier standards. The reformers argued that the adoption of a single set of suffrage criteria above those previously laid down for the first level of voters was consistent with going to direct elections.

By requiring literacy for all stages of the electoral process, the empire intended suffrage regression to reduce participation, particularly among the lower classes. The rulers allegedly aimed to squelch deceit and thuggery. Out of the total population, voters fell from 10 percent in 1872 to 1 percent in 1881, rising to 2 percent in 1894, 3 percent in 1898, 6 percent in 1930, and 13 percent in 1945.[56]

Peru furnished another major case of compressing the franchise in order to preserve élite control. In 1895, President Nicolás de Piérola altered the 1860 constitutional requirement that voters (resident national males 21 years old or married who were neither government officials nor members of the police or military) had to be either literate or head an enterprise, own property, or pay taxes. Instead of allowing these two alternative criteria, Piérola made literacy the only stipulation.

Out of approximately 3,000,000 total population, enforcement of this singular restriction eliminated roughly 2,000,000 Indians, as well as continuing to exclude women and minors, to leave perhaps 50,000 eligible voters. This measure mainly removed numerous illiterate indigenous landowners or taxpayers who had been voting throughout much of the nineteenth century. Given that most of the Indians resided in the mountains, this measure also formed part of the centralization of political power on the coast and in Lima.[57]

In the late nineteenth and early twentieth centuries, Peru exemplified a narrow oligarchic republic resting on the foundation of electoral trickery. The party in power continued to pull the strings on elections through artifice, falsification, and intimidation. Reforms proved futile, including President Guillermo Billinghurst's 1912 introduction of new electoral officials and oversight mechanisms to make elections less crooked.

By the 1920s, voters in Peru had to be active literate male citizens, 21 years old or married, and registered with the military, although active members of the armed forces and judiciary could not vote. Out of a national population of approximately 5,000,000, only 288,124 cast ballots in the presidential electoral simulacrum of 1924, or about 5 percent. By then, all voting was public and direct. Opponents of the government either did not bother to vote or saw their ballots not counted, although they received more representation in the congressional races than in the presidential contest.[58]

Joining Brazil and Peru in the 1880s, Colombia took two steps backward by constricting direct elections and suffrage. The 1886 constitution maintained direct elections for congressional representatives, electors, deputies to the departmental assemblies, and members of the municipal councils. But it undid the Liberal preference for broader direct elections by switching to indirect selection of the more important offices of president, vice-president, and senator, the first two chosen by electors, the third by department assemblies.

The 1886 constitution also rolled back earlier Liberal provisions for universal male suffrage, except for local elections. Henceforth all male active ("engaged in some lawful profession or occupation") citizens over twenty-one years of age could vote directly for municipal councils and department assemblies, but they also had to possess literacy and an annual income of 500 pesos or real property worth 1,500 pesos to vote for the house of representatives and electors. The constitution barred members of the armed forces from political deliberation, discussion, assembly, petition, and voting. It also banned priests from public offices, except for teaching and social work. Electoral shenanigans by all parties, not just the government, remained ubiquitous at all stages of the process.[59]

Because corruption and coercion permeated most Latin American elections, the size of the franchise did not guarantee citizens' ability to freely determine the winners. Bryce observed "that the better or worse political condition of these states has seldom turned upon the extent to which the suffrage had been granted, for in those where violent methods prevail, the result would be the same whether the number of voting citizens were great or small."[60] Even the most respectable civilian oligarchic republics retained electoral dominance through systematic guile and wiles carried out by patron-client networks. Although electoral bossism and fraud suffused Latin America and triggered complaints everywhere, it was difficult to know whether it was more epidemic in some countries than in others or in comparison with similar skullduggery in Europe and the United States in the era.

The patron-client systems for courting, harassing, and robbing voters varied from more centralized chains of bosses managed from the government on down (as in Argentina, Chile, and to an extent the thoroughly authoritarian case of Mexico under dictator Porfirio Díaz) to more decentralized independent machines competing at the provincial and local levels (as in Colombia, Peru, Bolivia, and Brazil). The former tended toward greater stability than the latter, although it was debatable which was more democratic. In countries with more institutionalized political systems, whether centralized or decentralized, organized fraud replaced naked force as a way of selecting leaders, which was at least a pale approximation of peaceful democracy.[61]

Under the 1886 Constitution and civilian rule, Colombia held elections and legislative sessions with regularity. However, the outcast Liberals complained of oppression and deception, as well as press censorship. Both political parties and especially government officials massaged registration rolls, voting requirements, balloting, and counting, with greatest abandon in the countryside. The central government prevailed by rewarding local leaders with patronage and pork. In response to this illegal exclusion from elected or appointed government offices, many Liberals abstained from voting or rebelled. Rather than preserving stability, this perverted system led to the War of the Thousand Days between Liberals and Conservatives in 1899 to 1902.[62]

The Old Republic in Brazil provided another exemplar of a constitutional civilian oligarchy propped up by largely bogus elections. In 1891, the political élites installed in the new constitution a decentralized, federalized democratic regime with universal and direct voting for all literate males at least twenty-one years old. This reform produced an increase of almost 300 percent in voters as a percentage of the population from the last legislative election under the empire in 1886 to the first full presidential election under the republic in 1898.

Without the secret ballot or neutral electoral oversight, however, local civilian *colonels* still warped the process. They did so usually in collusion with national and provincial authorities, through a complex web of patron-client relations and exchanges. They contorted registration, turnout, balloting, and tabulating so that the ruling groups almost always won. Such misbehavior most commonly occurred in the poorest regions under the aegis of large landowners. Some of these political juggernauts operated independently from the national government, with the governors exerting more authority over the colonels than they had under the empire. Although the president tried to replace the emperor as the moderating power among the governors, the more powerful states behaved like fiefdoms.[63]

In the same decades, electoral corruption also became more decentralized under Chile's Parliamentary Republic. Presidential manhandling of candidate lists and voting practices diminished following the civil war of 1891. Voter registration became easier and secrecy more respected, although abstention remained high. After 1891, vote buying and other finagling by parties increased, not as devices of government sabotage but as illegal craftiness by parties trying to beat each other, in a sense a more democratic form of fraud.

The electorate remained small because voters had to be male, twenty-one years of age, and literate. About half of those eligible did not register, and about half of those registered did not cast ballots, partly because of the complexities of registering and voting. In the parliamentary era, only about 5 percent of the population voted, about the same percentage as in Sweden but far less than the 10 to 25 percent turnout of the population in the United States, Britain, and France. Chilean parties mainly gathered votes through rural bosses and, increasingly, their urban counterparts. Successful candidates rewarded their vote collectors with government jobs, from which they in turn dispensed favors to their followers.

Nearly universal male suffrage, rising literacy, and urbanization had the unexpected consequence of increasing vote purchasing in Chile. As more parties competed to buy votes, the practice became somewhat more democratic. Most rural voters remained under the paternal eye of the landowners and local *caciques*, who often rounded up illiterates to vote illegally. At the same time, urban voters increasingly sold their votes. This gave the advantage to richer parties, but since all parties paid for votes, the voters could exercise their leverage and conscience to some extent. The spread of this electoral market led even working class parties to seek wealthy candidates who could afford the cost of voters.

As bidding drove that price up, however, more and more popular parties in the early twentieth century struggled against the tradition of bribing voters. These parties implored them to vote their programmatic self-interest. They also exhorted workers who accepted bribes from conservative parties to nonetheless cast their ballots for reformers. As parties and their candidates emphasized more programmatic, class, ideological, national, and personalistic appeals directly to voters, the power of bribery and bosses eventually waned, especially after World War I.[64]

Even under the reformer Batlle's first presidency at the start of the twentieth century, party apparatuses and their loyal local government agents continued to determine the conduct and outcome of Uruguayan elections. The army, the police, and government officials guaranteed that their underlings and private citizens normally cast their ballots for the anointed candidates. They monitored voter behavior fairly easily because the political parties provided the ballots to the voters, who signed and deposited them in public view. In addition, the parties usually organized voters through clubs and brought them to the polls. When necessary, the party and public bosses stuffed the ballot box and doctored the count. "An old gaucho proverb on politics said: 'The police chief's horse always wins the race.' "[65]

Beneath the most democratic veneer in Latin America, Argentina's political system also rested on dubious foundations. From the 1860s to the 1910s, widespread prestidigitation to keep the conservative rulers in power undermined and demeaned universal male suffrage. For that reason, the Radicals frequently boycotted elections and then tried to take everything for themselves after honest balloting was introduced in 1912.

Although other countries, such as Great Britain and the United States, tolerated electoral rascality, those practices seemed particularly blatant, flagrant, and frequent in Argentina, thereby corroding democratic legitimacy. The government often broke the rules in the registration of the voters, the casting of the ballots (done voluntarily and in public, though often forced or purchased), the tabulating of the votes, and the acceptance of the results by the legislatures. Thus the supposedly benign sequence between élites accepting restricted but valid democratic norms and then opening the gates to mass participation lacked safeguards.[66]

Individual voting in Argentina was not really that decisive because the rulers of the central government normally determined who got elected. They did so through management and distortion of elections, federal intervention in the provinces, designated succession to the presidency, and distribution of patronage and pork. From the stabilization of the government in 1880 until the electoral reform of 1912, the president, in effect, named his successor and the governors of the provinces. The governors and their allies in the central government ran the National Autonomist Party (PAN). The governors selected the senators, deputies, and provincial legislators. In turn, the provinces chose the electors for president and vice-president, similar to the U.S. indirect system. Moreover, an enduring coalition of provinces ensured that the official candidates always won in the electoral college by wide margins, usually between 79 to100 percent.

Through this system, the central government infringed on the only supposed federalist powers of the provinces, that of elections. Nevertheless, it did have to cooperate with the governors of the provinces to maintain its majority. The political élite was even more tightly knit together because governors—who, like presidents, could not be reelected immediately—frequently became senators, as did some ex-presidents, and senators also often became governors.

At the bottom of the inter-locking Argentine hierarchy, largely staged and fabricated elections guaranteed that most voters would choose the designated candidates for the provincial legislature, the electoral college, and the chamber of deputies. Some elections were competitive, while others were simply referenda on unopposed candidates. Some elections were honest, while others were tainted. Voter obedience was facilitated by limited suffrage and low turnout, which were repressed by the stunted participation of the huge population of immigrants. Therefore the opposition parties protested the entire electoral performance until the 1912 reform gave them a chance at victory.[67]

From 1880 to 1912, PAN—the ruling party and representative of the oligarchy—provided the façade of political liberalism to maintain order for the flourishing of economic liberalism. To do so, governments supervised and stole elections. As one observer noted about their predetermining elections, "In the deserted electoral registration offices one could hear nothing but the scratching pens of the government clerks writing imaginary names."[68] If the provincial results proved unsatisfactory, the congress could annul the election and call for a second chance to produce the correct outcome. As one disgruntled governor complained, "The only elector in Argentina is the President of the Republic, who elects the provincial governors, the legislatures, the National Congress, and his own successor."[69] President Miguel Juárez Celman (1886 to 1890) rationalized this twisted system on the grounds that, "To consult the people is always an error, since the people have only confused and muddy opinions."[70]

According to one critic of the PAN in 1914:

> It never had much faith in universal suffrage, nor in the republican form of government. In its judgment the People was not ready for the vote. Since it has been omnipotent for the last thirty years, it never occurred to it to limit the vote. It accepted all the great ideals of political liberty written in the books. It proclaimed the purity of the elections and universal suffrage, the impartiality of government, autonomy or the federalist principle, the free play of the institutions and many other things, all of which it had absolutely no belief in, and indeed feared as dangerous for internal peace and material progress . . . The government has a theory, which it rarely confesses, but which is its guiding idea, and this is the theory of the tutelary function of government or of governments in relation to the People. This concept of tutelage extends to the point of defending the People lest the government fall into bad hands. The tutelary idea, which is the same as that of the Church . . . is incompatible with the democratic idea and with representative forms of government.[71]

In all the non-military governments in the hemisphere, elections were perhaps least consequential in Mexico, even though held on a reliable schedule. Both before and after the 1910 Revolution, elections did not determine who took office in free, fair, competitive contests, although they supposedly generated legitimacy for the government. The ruling élites so tightly controlled voting from the top to the bottom that it did not even provoke political breakdowns as elsewhere in the Americas. Instead, the country endured essentially one-party rule from 1876 until 2000, although the parties changed during the Revolution and mass participation exploded.

It was noteworthy that Mexico and other countries held elections so punctually even though the results were often preordained. At least the electoral calendar minimized unscheduled civil strife. Even in authoritarian

Mexico before and after the 1910 Revolution, regular elections may have created some electoral habits and expectations as well as cynicism. After all, the Porfiriato's use of contaminated elections for legitimation established precedents for the opposition to galvanize rebels around the demand for truly free and fair elections.[72]

Elections also abounded in some other normally authoritarian countries. In Guatemala, counterfeit elections for president occurred fairly regularly from 1865 to 1941. In the nineteenth century, voters had to be literate and propertied adult males, as in most of Latin America. The authorities feared that the majority of the population was composed of "the ignorant masses . . . victims of insolent demagoguery." From 1865 to 1916, the reported percentage of the Guatemalan population voting varied between less than 1 percent and a maximum of 4 percent, rising in 1920 to 13 percent and in 1935 to 39 percent.[73] Also in Bolivia, another country seldom seen as a beacon of democracy, direct elections occurred frequently. Dominated by the privileged minority, the restricted electorate also included some voters from all social strata, whether legally or illegally.[74]

To an extent, these choreographed contests resembled "demonstration elections" that the United States cobbled together in countries it invaded in Central America, the Caribbean, and other parts of the world. Washington mainly staged these extrication elections to convince its own citizens that the marines could come home because democracy had been implanted. Many Latin American governments designed similar performances, not to allow citizens to choose leaders freely but to impress opponents and foreigners with the rulers' ability to conjure up majorities. These electoral Potemkin villages conferred a patina of internal and external legitimacy. Although dictators used these cooked-up elections to sanctify their undemocratic rule, it was significant that they found this authentication valuable. This political theatre suggested that electoral expectations were deeply rooted even if repeatedly violated.[75]

Despite all the defects discussed above, in many countries elections soon became more frequent, participatory, and democratic. Brazil in 1891, Costa Rica in 1913, and Uruguay in 1918 adopted universal male suffrage. In addition, between 1883 and 1918, El Salvador, Nicaragua, Honduras, Panama, and Haiti also legalized universal male suffrage in law (if not necessarily in reality). At least legally and temporarily, El Salvador in 1883, Nicaragua in 1893, Honduras in 1894, Cuba in 1901, Panama in 1904, Argentina in 1912, Costa Rica in 1913, and Uruguay in 1918 granted the vote to illiterates. Argentina in 1912, Uruguay in 1918, and Costa Rica in 1925 established secret voting. In addition, Nicaragua in 1893, Honduras in 1894, and Para-

guay in 1911 claimed to do so. From 1894 to 1929, compulsory voting arrived in Honduras, Argentina, Mexico, Uruguay, Panama, and Ecuador.

As a leading example of this general progress, Costa Rica implemented
local elections for previously nationally appointed municipal officials in
1909, direct voting in 1913, universal male suffrage with no literacy requirements in 1913, and the secret ballot in 1925. Partly as a result, the reported
percentage of the population voting in the regularly held every-four-years
presidential elections rose from less than 1 percent from 1872 to 1914, to 11
percent in 1919, and then between 15 percent and 17 percent from 1923
to 1940. However, this suffrage expansion had limited effect on electoral
results under the oligarchic republic from the 1880s to the early twentieth
century because fraud remained endemic. Nevertheless, sometimes the opposition won presidential elections.[76]

By far the most significant electoral reform in the era occurred in Argentina in 1912. In the previous period dominated by the conservative PAN,
civil society changed enormously, but the narrow voting public changed little. In and around Buenos Aires, the foreign born, who seldom naturalized,
far outnumbered the native born. Consequently, a majority of males over
the age of eighteen were not eligible to vote. Among those eligible in the
federal capital, from 1880 to the 1900s, turnout rose but remained usually
under 30 percent, still a respectable figure for the era in Latin America or
Europe. However, precise numbers were suspect because of cheating, which
discouraged higher turnout.[77]

For all its shortcomings, the limited electoral system enrolled registered
voters from all social classes. A sample of the registered electorate (potential voters) in Buenos Aires in 1896 showed that 45 percent came from the
working class, 42 percent from the middle class, and 13 percent from the
upper class. The average age was 30 years, the average percentage literate 93
percent. The literacy figure was quite high, since literates only accounted
for 78 percent of adult males in the city of Buenos Aires and only 44 percent of the voters in the province of Buenos Aires. In the city of Buenos
Aires, these voters participated in competitive elections that exhibited rising support—mainly from the upper and middle class—for the PAN's main
rival, the Radical Party.[78]

Even while Argentine elections remained somewhat restricted until
1912, civil liberties—freedom of the press, religion, education, association,
assembly, etc.—grew in amplitude. As a result, civil society became more
capable of exerting itself and of eventually demanding effective electoral
inclusion. Through the press, clubs, unions, street demonstrations, and rallies around elections, political participation without voting snowballed.

Ordinary people—including foreigners—became partial citizens in public spaces before they gained full access to political rights.

In the second half of the nineteenth century, some élites justified the distinction between deep civil liberties and shallow political liberties on the grounds of differences between the private and the public sphere. They discriminated between who was allowed to be free and who was allowed to govern. As envisioned by Alberdi, this gap between broad informal participation and narrow formal representation allowed civil society to mature while the oligarchic state presided over the order necessary for material progress.

This contradiction bred rising discontent with tutelary or protected democracy. A system that had been tolerable up to the 1870s became less so as immigrants, urban workers, and middle sectors grew in numbers and expectations. The widening gulf between professed liberal principles and managed elections with low levels of participation and high levels of violence and misdemeanors also dissatisfied many counter-élites.[79]

In response, the ruling groups put through the 1912 reform for several reasons. First, they wanted to continue the peaceful evolution of the political order that encouraged foreign investment, economic growth, and immigration. By improving the purity and sanctity of elections, the élites wanted to increase voter turnout to legitimize and solidify the existing political system. Second, the oligarchs hoped to incorporate and co-opt social and political dissidents. Thus they sought to adapt to changing sociopolitical conditions without being submerged by the rising numbers of immigrants and urban workers. They realized that the abstention of the Radicals and the threat of disruption and violence from them as well as working class and leftist movements endangered tranquility.

Third, the government believed that power-sharing would engender moderate and cohesive political parties committed to the republican system. Fourth, the Radical Party leaders appeared easy to mollify. They did not differ much from the ruling oligarchy in their social composition or their governing program. All they asked for was the political system to function as it promised. If the government would curtail pervasive fraud and coercion by bosses, the Radical Party could take office through the ballot box. Mainly representing some disaffected rural élites and urban middle and upper sectors, the Radicals reached consensus with the conservatives on this reform. Fifth, those in power thought they had a decent chance of hanging on under the new rules. In sum, the élites believed that the costs of exclusion exceeded those of inclusion.[80]

In 1912, in approximately the same time period as Sweden and the Netherlands, the Sáenz Peña law instituted meaningful universal male suffrage. It enacted universal, obligatory, and secret voting rights for all male citizens eighteen years or older. It created two main exceptions, members of the clergy and the army. It also mandated electoral courts to protect the new process.[81]

The new law made voting compulsory except for the aged and the illiterate. It absolved the latter out of fear that bosses would herd the unschooled masses into balloting their way. The reformers designed the obligatory vote to engage more citizens with the political system and to marginalize socialist, syndicalist, and anarchist movements. However, since the government seldom imposed penalties for not voting, the new rule probably did not fully explain the rising turnouts from 1912 to 1930.

After the Sáenz Peña law was instituted, participation also climbed because fraud became more difficult and rare. Political parties sent watchers to every polling place. In spite of severe penalties for misconduct, electoral theft remained a problem, especially in rural provinces.[82]

As a result of the new law, electoral turnout soared from 21 percent of all male citizens over eighteen years of age in 1910 to 69 percent in 1912 (this was 69% of registered voters but only 9% of the total population, given the nonvoting of immigrants, women, and children). The percentage of the population voting continued to grow thereafter as the percentage of foreigners in the population declined. Until the military coup of 1930, voter participation rose at least as high as in the United States and parts of Western Europe, peaking at 81 percent of registered voters in 1928 and dipping to 75 percent in 1930.[83]

Before and after the reform, voting penetrated all Argentine social strata because of the absence of property and literacy requirements. The voter registry for the capital of Buenos Aires in 1918 showed that the electorate, measured by occupations, comprised more upper (8%) and middle class (53%, mainly white-collar employees) than the urban population but also included the working class (38%). Most of those working class registered voters were skilled workers (72%). Since many workers were immigrants, their participation remained lower than that of the higher classes. Many registered voters were also illiterate (almost 50% outside Buenos Aires).[84]

Breaking the hold of the ruling party and the governors, the reform immediately led to the presidential victory of the Radical Party's Hipólito Yrigoyen in 1916. In that triumph, less than 10 percent of the population voted. Thereafter, the Radicals controlled the presidency until 1930. At the same time, a rising percentage of deputies came from that party and social sectors beneath the upper class. The conservatives retained the senate as well as many rural governments.

Within this increasingly representative system, the peaceful transfer of power to the Radical Party seemed to signal a consolidating democracy by the still fairly elitist standards of the era. All the indicators of socioeconomic modernization also made Argentina appear to be the ideal candidate for an evolving, stabilizing democracy in the 1920s. However, the Great Depression of 1930 ushered in an authoritarian, oligarchic retrenchment, ending Argentina's first modern democratic period that had begun in 1916. The restored conservatives resented their exclusion from the presidency, their decline among deputies, and the breakdown of the economy.[85]

The brief period of free elections from 1916 to 1930 preceded unfree elections with the Radicals and Communists proscribed from 1931 to 1943, free elections under Peronist domination from 1946 to 1955, and lack of electoral freedom with the Peronists and Communists outlawed from 1957 to 1973. From the first national electoral law in 1857 until the elections of 1973, only twenty-seven (23%) of those years witnessed free elections. This dreary record led one analyst to conclude that normally in Argentina those with sufficient military or economic power governed, decided when and how to hold elections, and tampered with those contests to make sure they retained power. In short, elections in and of themselves seldom determined who governed or how.[86]

By the late nineteenth century, Chile also exhibited most of the minimal criteria for an electoral democracy. It maintained a constitutional government chosen regularly at the ballot box under basic civil liberties. The electorate remained small, with only about 5 percent of the total population voting. Nevertheless, the electorate was heterogeneous enough to include working class voters and parties. However, the regime retained some authoritarian features because it manufactured official lists of candidates who won most of the time. They triumphed in elections that did not guarantee the secrecy of the balloting.

The electoral reform of 1890 ended this control by the presidency. It gave all candidates equal opportunities and all voters free and secret access to the ballot box, fortifying what had been promised in 1874. It also ensured an accurate count of the votes. These changes made fair competition among political parties for voters the key to victory for electing presidents, legislators, and municipal officials. The government implemented these reforms after the civil war ousted the interventionist President Balmaceda and established the so-called Parliamentary Republic in 1891. Until Chile gave the franchise to women (1949) and illiterates (1970), the 1890 innovation converted the political system into "a democracy with incomplete suffrage."[87]

In the opening decades of the twentieth century, the rise of middle and working class social and political actors spawned an electoral breakthrough in Chile similar to the one fostered by the Sáenz Peña reform in Argentina, even without any comparable change in the legal franchise. The emerging groups took advantage of existing rights for citizens, voters, and political parties, bequeathed by the aristocracy and the Parliamentary Republic, however corrupt. Whereas democratization in the nineteenth century emphasized the struggle for freedom from the state, democratization in the twentieth focused on the struggle for equality.

To deepen democracy now signified the amplification of social classes included directly or indirectly in Chile's process of government. For example, now workers' issues became salient in political debates, workers' parties appeared on the scene, a few workers and artisans reached the congress, and workers and other voters increasingly influenced who got elected and how they governed. They tried to hold elected officials accountable for their programmatic promises in their campaigns and in office.

Gradually, a protected oligarchic republic metamorphosed into an incipient popular democracy. In the 1920 presidential contest, the Chilean middle and working classes propelled the "revolt of the electorate," defeating the traditional ruling groups. The reformers' triumphant champion, populist pioneer Arturo Alessandri, vowed to reach out to the underprivileged so that "rapid evolution would avert revolution." However, his challenge led to the breakdown of the oligarchic republic in the military coup of 1924. Neither Chile nor Argentina was ready yet for mass politics.[88]

MODERNIZING POLITICAL PARTIES

Although political parties remained absent, evanescent, or puerile in many countries, they began to modernize in the more advanced republics, much as in the United States. The most remarkable successes transpired in Argentina, Chile, Colombia, and Uruguay. Into the 1880s in Buenos Aires, parties remained preeminently personal vehicles, dominated by notables and corrupt machines run by bosses. From the 1890s through the 1920s, they became more bureaucratic and programmatic, approximating modern political parties. Although personalism did not disappear, they echoed the U.S. model of permanent organizations with tightly controlled committees and conventions, where party leaders, governors, and local bosses normally chose nominees. They devised rules for party management and for candidate selection. Democratic participation within the parties expanded, notably from the middle class. The parties raised funds from members, especially the wealthiest, and they published newspapers. They engaged in less fraud and much less electoral violence.[89]

As in Chile and a few other countries in the era, the Argentine Radical Party and others began to introduce mass mobilization politics. After abstaining from elections for two decades, the Radicals took advantage of the 1912 electoral reform to rise to power. More Argentines from beneath the upper class ascended in political parties, national politics, and government offices. Instead of mainly élite manipulation, political campaigns increasingly became direct personalistic appeals by candidates, replete with face-to-face contact, speeches, rallies, propaganda, and pageantry. As seen with the charismatic Radical President Irigoyen, early populism was afoot, especially after the 1912 reform made popular voting more significant.[90]

Under the Parliamentary Republic, Chilean political parties grew in independent strength outside the legislature. In the early twentieth century, they also became more democratic, with mounting participation from modest social strata and less domination by notables. New parties representing the middle and working classes gained stature, as did those groups within older parties. With party officials increasingly elected, assemblies and conventions began to make party decisions formerly reserved to the very top leadership. They increasingly adopted detailed programs. In particular, the Radical Party rose to challenge the Liberals and Conservatives. The Radicals resembled their Argentine namesakes in appealing to disaffected regional as well as upper and middle class groups.[91]

After pitched battles between Colombia's entrenched two parties resulted in the horrendous War of the Thousand Days, General Rafael Reyes ruled from 1904 to 1909. He established peace by imposing compromise. Similar to Batlle in Uruguay, Reyes' Conservative administration also appointed Liberals to the government and passed a constitutional guarantee in 1905 of at least one-third legislative representation for the minority party.

From the early 1900s until the 1940s, political stability reigned under civilian rule. Civil liberties improved, elections and presidential turnover occurred on schedule, most governments included officials from both parties, and minority representation continued in the legislature. Even during the shock of the Great Depression, civility persisted when the Liberals finally captured the presidency electorally from the Conservatives. Based on understandings between two deeply rooted parties, Colombia developed one of the most durable elitist republics in Latin America.[92]

Uruguay's two dominant parties also became more institutionalized and peaceful. In 1872 and 1897, the Colorados temporarily settled the recurrent civil wars between the two camps by giving the Blancos a share of offices and spoils, a sort of consociationalism, not unlike Colombia. However, bloodshed did not really end until the two parties reached a more lasting accommodation during the second presidency of Batlle in 1911.[93]

Conclusion

In this era, both anarchy and tyranny declined, although dictatorships still governed many of the poorer countries. Especially in South America, liberal economies grew along with liberal polities. Several leading countries continued to be the most democratic and laid foundations for future success with that political system. They institutionalized protected democracies in the form of oligarchic republics. Although highly aristocratic, those republics exhibited many traits in common with similar regimes in the United States and Western Europe.

The contending forces of oligarchic stability and popular assertiveness affected political thought and institutions. The dominant classes justified paternalistic rule in the name of positivism, but the middle and working classes demanded inclusion under the banner of popular nationalism. Radical ideologies from overseas also advocated social justice for white- and blue-collar workers.

While constitutions became more durable and enforceable, social constitutionalism called for rights for the downtrodden. In Spanish America, centralism solidified, partly by making small concessions to decentralism. In Portuguese America, decentralization reigned supreme in the Old Republic.

Oligarchic presidents wielded great power in law and even more in practice. While some presidencies became even stronger than before, a few suffered temporary losses of their supremacy, partly to provinces and congresses. Civil liberties improved. Legislatures remained inferior to the chief executives but recorded small gains; a few adopted proportional representation. Judiciaries remained insignificant players in disputes among the other branches of government or debates about democracy and justice.

The most important democratic institutions, bountiful elections, became increasingly institutionalized affairs managed by the oligarchic republics. Those regimes manipulated voting to reconcile a discourse of political equality with extreme social inequality. However, that cynical game risked illegitimacy and instability by raising expectations and resentment from the middle and working classes.

The era featured no clear trend toward opening or closing elections. Some countries moved forward, others backward, depending on the calculations

of contending élites about their competitive advantages. While most electoral regulations maintained narrow suffrage, some permitted surprisingly
broad participation. At least in law, several countries lowered the voting age,
enacted universal male suffrage, enrolled illiterates, and instituted secret and
compulsory voting. In a few countries, political parties became more modern, institutionalized, and consequential. A handful also began to represent
middle and working class constituents in elections and government offices.

Just as the post-independence years planted seeds for export growth and
oligarchic republicanism, so the precursors of the 1930s to the 1970s era of
mass politics emerged from the 1880s to the 1920s. The oligarchy's stable
constitutional, electoral, representative system allowed democratic institutions, practices, and desires to develop. Continued economic and urban
growth generated rising middle and working class demands for inclusion.
Incipient populists rallied the underprivileged.

In response, some governments tried to resolve the growing contradiction
between their official commitment to democracy and their actual marginalization of the mobilizing majority through electoral restrictions, patron-client
networks, and fraud. Others reacted to popular pressures with repression or
partial incorporation. The difficulty of sustaining democracy without the
people paved the way to popular democracy in the next period.

When the classic liberal economic system of the 1880s to the 1920s collapsed in the 1930s, so did many of Latin America's classic liberal political systems. Whereas the debt crisis of the 1980s would undermine many
military dictatorships, the debt debacle of the 1930s scuttled many civilian
republics, however oligarchic. The limited advances made under those republics as well as the discrediting of their rule during the Great Crash set
the stage for the coming era of mass politics.

Although primarily authoritarian regimes seized power in the early thir-
ties, they soon faced unprecedented challenges from middle and working
class advocates of democratic social reform. In the next period from the
1930s to the 1970s, popular democracy would supersede protected democracy in several countries. Governments would rise to new heights of democracy, and then sink to new lows of tyranny.

Chapter 6

Populist Democracy, 1930s–1970s

In contrast with the era of oligarchic republicanism, protected democracy now gradually gave ground to popular democracy, usually in the form of populism. Neither protected democracies nor dictatorships disappeared from Latin America, but they increasingly contested control of the state with the new popular forces. In many countries, both social actors and political institutions moved toward popular democracy, yet the institutions lagged behind. Legislatures, judiciaries, and the armed forces proved most resistant to change, although even some of them became more receptive to the lower classes.

In tune with popular pressures, constitutions incorporated more individual and social rights. Presidents responded increasingly to mass constituencies and to the desires for national development. They expanded state programs for social welfare and economic modernization. Elections became more inclusive, participatory, secret, and honest. They encompassed many more women, younger people, illiterates, and urban and rural laborers. As a result, voting became more consequential for the marginalized majority. Political parties multiplied, adding many populists and leftists representing the working classes.

What changed more than the basic structure of political institutions was how those institutions were used. Popular leaders and followers tried to make these long-struggling democratic institutions live up to their ancient promises. Their efforts responded to the social changes accumulating since the late nineteenth century, especially in the mushrooming cities. Reformers took advantage of inherited models of constitutions, presidencies, legislatures, judiciaries, elections, and political parties to mobilize the middle and lower classes for participation and benefits.

Following the Great Depression's disruption of oligarchic rule, many Latin American countries eventually responded to the crises of participation, legitimation, growth, and distribution with a populist formula. It emphasized vertical, multi-class mobilization behind charismatic leaders committed to nationalistic import-substituting industrialization and a limited welfare state. This inclusionary popular nationalism extolled the common people, particularly urban workers, as the foundation of government authority.[1] From the 1930s to the late 1970s, democratic governments exhibiting fully or partially populist leadership styles, social coalitions, and/or reformist programs took office in the countries following, arrayed from the earliest to latest arrivals: Chile (1938–1948 and 1970–1973); Ecuador (1944–1948, 1952–1958, 1960–1961, and 1968–1972); Guatemala (1945–1954); Venezuela (1945–1948 and 1958–1963); Peru (1945–1948); Argentina (1946–1955 and 1973–1976); Brazil (1951–1964); and Bolivia (1952–1964).

While populism became the prevalent form of popular democracy, it also surfaced in inclusionary authoritarianism, for example under rare reformist military rulers in Peru from 1968 to 1975 and Ecuador from 1973 to 1976. Although most populist leaders channeled mass activation through electoral politics, a few relied on more traditional hierarchical methods, reminiscent of nineteenth century popular caudillos. Even a couple of elected populists sometimes behaved in authoritarian style once in office, notably Juan Perón in Argentina and José María Velasco Ibarra in Ecuador. Nevertheless, populism in general propelled democracy forward, both by encouraging democratic behavior and by enrolling lower class groups and their quest for social justice in political life.[2]

In response, the élites scrambled to co-opt or crush these movements. When the well-to-do feared that popular democracy jeopardized upper and middle class privileges, they imposed protected democracies or exclusionary authoritarianism. Some resorted to unusually barbaric dictatorships by the armed forces.

From the 1930s to the 1970s, no dominant regime pattern took hold. Although democratic institutions became broader and sturdier, they made neither steady nor even progress. Instead, democracy alternated with despotism. At the same time, a trajectory of polarization evolved. As many democracies became more populist and reformist, dictatorships became more repressive and reactionary.

From 1900 through 2000, nearly a majority of regimes in Latin America qualified as authoritarian rather than democratic, whether oligarchic, restricted, or full democracies. Autocracies accounted for a majority of regimes from 1900 to the 1970s, but more and more inclusive democracies replaced oligarchic republics from the 1930s to the 1970s. Then from 1978 to the 2000s, full democracies prevailed as a majority of all regimes. Throughout these decades, once a more open democracy replaced an oligarchic republic, the latter regime never returned, although dictatorships often stepped back in.[3]

Amidst these vicissitudes, the historically most democratic countries still tended to have the most success with that regime from the 1930s to the late 1970s. Restricted or fully democratic governments enjoyed the most years, in descending order, in Chile (1932–1973), Colombia (1930–1952 and 1958–1970s), Uruguay (1939–1973), Costa Rica (1948–1970s), and Venezuela (1945–1948 and 1958–1970s). Following close behind were Brazil (1945–1964), Ecuador (1948–1961), Argentina (1946–1955 and 1973–1976), Bolivia (1952–1964), Peru (1939–1948), and Guatemala (1945–1954).[4]

During these decades, Latin America had to adjust to three seismic global transformations: the Great Depression, World War II, and the Cold War. In the 1930s in the region, the depression mainly capsized oligarchic republics or protected democracies. This economic shock ushered in a dictatorial decade. Anti-democratic ideologies in Europe and the United States' Good Neighbor Policy's determination to tolerate all types of regimes south of the border reinforced authoritarianism.

From 1930 to 1934, thirteen successful coups rocked Latin America. From 1928 to 1930 and 1932 to 1934, the region switched from fourteen democracies (albeit oligarchic republics) and six dictatorships (exclusionary despotisms) to ten democracies and ten dictatorships. By the end of that decade, seven more coups took place, and Bolivia, Ecuador, Nicaragua, Paraguay, and Peru also moved firmly into the dictatorial camp. After initially suppressing populist movements, the right-wing authoritarians had to keep holding the lid on or begin to accommodate the effervescence from below. In the same period, most of Central America and the Caribbean fell to or remained under tyrants. Some of the most notorious and longest-lasting despots seized power in the countries that U.S. troops vacated, notably Anastasio Somoza in Nicaragua and Rafael Trujillo in the Dominican Republic. Mexico continued under the mild authoritarian rule of the revolutionary élites.

In the 1930s, Chile constituted one democratic exception. Having been oppressed by a dictator when the depression struck, the country then confronted demonstrations calling for a return to civilian rule. It switched back to its tradition of a democratic government in 1932 and stayed there until 1973. Colombia provided another bright spot. It reacted to the economic plunge by changing electorally from the Conservative to the Liberal parties in 1930 rather than trading in democracy for dictatorship.[5]

From 1946 to 1988 in the ten countries of South America, forty-seven regimes held power, twenty-six democratic and twenty-one authoritarian, the former reigning 59 percent of the forty-three years and the latter 41 percent.[6] In the 1940s and 1950s, optimism grew that democracy was spreading and lasting in large parts of the hemisphere. But dictators dashed those hopes repeatedly, first after the spike of democratization in the afterglow of World War II, second after the "twilight of the tyrants" in the 1950s, and third after the transient gains during the Alliance for Progress in the early 1960s. By the middle of the 1970s, the military had the region firmly under lock and key. According to one calculation, Latin American hosted eight democracies in 1950, six in 1955, twelve in 1959, and five in 1976. From 1950 to 1990, Latin American regimes suffered the most instability of all world areas; 141 countries around the globe experienced ninety-seven regime transitions, of which forty-four transpired in Latin America.[7]

As World War II came to a close, a springtime blossomed for democracy and the left in Latin America. Partly inspired by the victories of the Allies, elections and popular mobilization proliferated, frequently spearheaded by urban labor. In the mid-1940s, democracy—and in some cases social reform, often captained by populists—surged in many countries: Guatemala with the election of Juan José Arévalo in 1944, Argentina with the first election of Juan Perón in 1945, Brazil with the replacement of Getúlio Vargas by a democratic regime in 1945, Venezuela with the three-year government of Democratic Action from 1945 to 1948, Peru with the equally brief stint in office in the same years of the American Popular Revolutionary Alliance (APRA), Chile with the electoral win of Radical Gabriel González Videla and his Communist allies in 1946, Costa Rica with the triumph of the democratic forces in a civil war in 1948, and Ecuador with a rare democratic cycle from 1948 to 1961.

However, the Cold War—led by the United States and its conservative allies in the hemisphere—quickly snuffed out this progressive moment. The élites either constricted or closed most of the democratic and leftist openings before the end of the decade. Governments shifted to the right and repressed the left and labor, as well as many democrats. In the most violent reversals, the military captured the presidential palace in El Salvador, Peru, and Venezuela in 1948, Bolivia in 1951, Colombia in 1953, and Paraguay and Guatemala in 1954.[8]

The twilight of the tyrants in the 1950s proved equally transitory, although a majority of the countries qualified as democracies by 1960. The exits of the armed forces in Ecuador in 1948; the oligarchic Rosca in Bolivia in 1952; the increasingly authoritarian Perón in Argentina in 1955; the despots Anastasio Somoza in Nicaragua; Manuel Odria in Peru in 1956; Fulgencio Batista in Cuba in 1958 did not usher in lasting democracies, although the departures of dictators Gustavo Rojas Pinilla in Colombia and Marcos Pérez Jiménez in Venezuela in 1957 to 1958 did. The United States did not normally promote this outbreak of democratization, instead more often siding with the authoritarian forces.[9]

During his guerrilla insurgency in the 1950s, Fidel Castro vowed to restore the liberal democratic principles embedded in the Cuban Constitution of 1940. Once in office, he dismissed bourgeois democracy in favor of socialist democracy, or, simply put, communism. His triumph radicalized the Latin American left and turned many from a democratic to a violent struggle, just as Castro himself had found the electoral route blocked and so took up arms. His takeover, turn to the left, drastic economic and social reforms, and alignment with the Soviet Union fueled a sense of crisis among United States and Latin American policymakers in the 1960s. For those leaders, avoidance of revolution by promising social reforms temporarily replaced democracy as the premier issue. To prevent revolution by more forceful means, many dictators soon replaced democrats.[10]

From the 1960s to the 1970s, the United States rhetorically committed the Alliance for Progress to democracy and social reform. Initially, democracy registered a few gains with the elections of reformers like Fernando Belaúnde in Peru (1963) and Eduardo Frei in Chile (1964). However, conservative, anti-communist military coups succeeded in El Salvador and Ecuador in 1961, in Argentina and Peru in 1962, and in Guatemala, Ecuador, the Dominican Republic, and Honduras in 1963, usually with support from the United States.

As Washington came to prefer dictatorship to democracy as an antidote to revolution, tyrants gradually took back the rest of the region, often with U.S. backing. This march of the despots began with the leader Brazil and Bolivia in 1964, followed by Argentina in 1966, Peru and Panama in 1968, Ecuador and Honduras in 1972, and Uruguay and Chile in 1973, capped off by Argentina again in 1976. Only the democracies in Costa Rica, the Dominican Republic, Venezuela, and Colombia (although it adopted a civilian form of fairly restrictive rule) bucked the tyrannical trend.

Meanwhile long-standing dictatorships in Central America, the Caribbean, and Paraguay persisted, as did the one-party state in Mexico. International friends of Latin American democracy expressed the most dismay at the fall of some of its greatest showcases, especially Chile and Uruguay, and the ferocity of the new dictatorships, especially in the Southern Cone and Central America. For many observers, the 1930s to the 1970s rise of popular democracy effectively ended in the Chilean military coup against Allende, a devastating defeat for democracy as well as socialism.[11]

At least in Brazil, Uruguay, Chile, and Argentina, the overwhelming evidence from elections, polls, and even public mobilizations showed that polarization and support for authoritarianism among ordinary people remained far too low to account for the breakdown of democracy. Rather than the majority of citizens, economic, political and military élites, once again deserted and scrapped these democratic regimes. They exaggerated public turmoil and demands for an end to democracy in order to serve their own interests, as they had been doing since independence.[12]

These chronological trends responded to both external and internal currents. Some foreign factors, like the New Deal's domestic reforms, World War II's defeat of fascism, and the Roman Catholic Church's reorientation toward social justice and democracy in the 1960s, pulled in a democratic direction. Meanwhile, other international influences, like the Great Depression, the Cold War, and the Cuban Revolution, tugged toward authoritarianism.

Domestic transformations within Latin America also exerted contradictory pressures. Rising population, literacy, and urbanization brought more people into the political arena. Per capita income improved, as did industrialization. The growth of the middle class, university students, organized labor, and peasant unrest expanded political participation beneath the upper class. Means of communication, such as radio and television, spread beyond the élites to the unschooled, and the media became more sophisticated and independent.

Although some socioeconomic conditions for democracy improved, impediments remained. Monocultural reliance on the international economy and on revenues from the state coffers perpetuated the élites and left governments at the mercy of global economic cycles. Foreign investment still strengthened the ruling class and, in many cases, dictators. Widespread poverty and illiteracy kept millions from becoming true citizens, as did rigid social stratification, often rooted in racial, ethnic, and class discrimination. As it had for centuries, the inequitable system of land tenure blocked democratic participation by many rural workers, who still comprised a majority of the population of Latin America in the 1950s.[13]

Some U.S. authors still stooped to ethnocentric explanations for Latin American political behavior. As an example, one historian blamed political instability on "the mercurial temper of Latins" and urged upon them "a measure of self-discipline which they do not possess."[14] Racism colored some writers' views of the political landscape and the prospects for democracy. One U.S. scholar opined that Argentina should be a natural home for democracy because, "It is peopled by a predominantly white race. It is free from the deadweight of a heavy Indian population, the too-mercurial influence of the Negro, and the disturbing leaven of mixed peoples. . . ." This analyst also attributed Uruguay's democratic success partly to its "superior racial stock." These comments seemed particularly odd since Argentina and Uruguay exhibited similar ethnic compositions yet opposite predilections toward dictatorship or democracy in the era.[15]

Three major social science theories tried to explain the presence or absence of democracy in Latin America: modernization, dependency (and its bureaucratic authoritarianism variant), and corporatism (especially its cultural version). To oversimplify, modernization theory postulated that as underdeveloped countries became more capitalist, industrial, urban, and middle class, they should replicate the values and habits of the United States and Western Europe before them, thus becoming more democratic. To the contrary, dependency theory argued that so long as the Third World remained a subordinate part of the global capitalist system, it would likely stay mired in authoritarianism as a way to perpetuate the inferior position of those countries and their exploited classes. When the more advanced as well as impoverished nations of Latin America knuckled under to new dictatorships, the theory of bureaucratic authoritarianism contended that modernization had a propensity to lead to oppression, not democracy. In the more developed countries, the ruling élites and their foreign supporters suppressed demands from emerging social groups in order to maintain economic accumulation and growth.

Although modernization and dependency theories bordered on economic determinism, one brand of corporatism smacked of cultural determinism. It insisted that patrimonial attitudes and practices inherited from the Iberian and colonial past predisposed Latin America toward autocracies. All these theories contributed some important insights, but they proved too grandiose to account for regime changes among countries and over time. By the late 1970s, they all fell into disrepute.[16]

From the 1930s to the 1970s, several types of regimes arose in Latin America. Among dictatorships, only one constituted all-out totalitarianism (Cuba under Castro). At various times, the others comprised personal sultanistic despotisms (Nicaragua, Haiti, Paraguay), traditional exclusionary military dictatorships (Guatemala, Honduras, El Salvador, Panama, Cuba under Fulgencio Batista, Bolivia), reformist inclusionary military dictatorships

(Ecuador, Peru, Bolivia), noncompetitive civilian authoritarianisms (Mexico and the mixed case of Colombia), and exclusionary bureaucratic authoritarian systems (Chile, Uruguay, Argentina, Brazil). The closest to competitive, civilian democratic regimes existed from time to time in Guatemala, Costa Rica, Panama, the Dominican Republic, Venezuela, Colombia, Ecuador, Peru, Bolivia, Chile, Argentina, Uruguay, and Brazil. In terms of participation and policies for the masses, the inclusionary dictatorships exhibited some features in common with popular democracies, the exclusionary dictatorships with protected democracies.[17]

Beginning in 1945, political scientist Russell H. Fitzgibbon conducted opinion surveys every five years, asking U.S. experts to rate the state of democracy in Latin America. From the 1940s to the 1960s, the overall rating for the region improved slightly. In general, the country rankings changed very little. As they probably would have in many past decades, Costa Rica, Chile, and Uruguay always held the top three spots. Paraguay, the Dominican Republic, Haiti, Bolivia, Nicaragua, and Honduras consistently finished closest to the bottom. Although fairly accurate at the high and low ends, these Latin Americanist scholars' categorizations were less reliable for the countries between the top and the bottom, where the biggest change was the plunge by Cuba under Batista and Castro.[18]

Concepts of Popular Democracy

Latin American intellectuals and politicians increasingly spoke out in favor of sweeping social reform, but they divided over democratic or revolutionary methods. Some espoused ideas at odds with liberal democracy. Both the right and the left put classic democrats on the defensive, either for having done too much or too little for the poor. On the right, a few political thinkers favored traditional or corporatist authoritarianism, even imbibing fascist concepts from Europe. Partly in response to leftwing radicalism, some conservatives in the 1960s and 1970s argued for highly protected democracy or even dictatorship to safeguard capitalism, social stability, and political order. On the left, more Marxists, communists, and some dependency theorists came to prefer revolutionary dictatorships over popular democracies.[19]

Three schools of thought supported democracy and social reform, but sometimes opted for authoritarian models to achieve social justice. First, the Roman Catholic Church officially converted to democracy and social reform. Among Catholics, the Christian Democrats favored Western democracy. Some liberation theologians became more radical and even embraced revolution rather than representative democracy as the path to social redemption.[20]

The second train of thought backing democracy and social reform but sometimes justifying inclusionary authoritarianism was populism. Victor Raúl Haya de la Torre, leader of the American Popular Revolutionary Alliance (APRA) in Peru, stood out as the most famous intellectual advocate. Like Perón, he waxed more enthusiastic about identifying with and uplifting the common people than defending electoral democracy.[21]

The third intellectual construct that promoted social justice through democratic or dictatorial means was socialism. Especially after the Cuban Revolution, more socialist thinkers advocated armed insurrection over democratic means, although most Chilean socialists preferred the democratic path. Going far beyond popular caudillos in the nineteenth century, Castro redefined democracy in revolutionary and socioeconomic terms. In 1960, he propounded one of the most radical definitions of popular democracy by any leader of a country in Latin American history:

"*This* is democracy, where you, farmer, are given the land that we have recovered from usurious foreign hands . . . *This* is democracy, where you, worker, are guaranteed the right to work . . . where you, students, have the opportunity to win a university degree . . . where you, old man, have your sustenance guaranteed . . . where you, Cuban Negro, have the right to work . . . where the women acquire rights equal to those of all other citizens . . . Democracy is *this*, that which gives a gun to the farmers, gives a gun to the workers, gives a gun to the students, gives a gun to the women, gives a gun to the Negroes, gives a gun to the poor, and gives a gun to any other citizen who is willing to defend a just cause."[22]

The Impact of Popular Democracy on Political Institutions

SOCIALISTIC AND NATIONALISTIC CONSTITUTIONS

The basic content of constitutions, like that of other political institutions, changed little from the 1930s to the 1960s. At the same time, Latin Americans more frequently obeyed their constitutions. In contrast with the oligarchic era, this became another period of multiplying and unstable constitutions. In large part, their proliferation reflected attempts to take into account the rise of popular democracy and government responsibilities for national socioeconomic development.

From independence through the 1950s, the twenty Latin American republics adopted over 180 constitutions, for an average above nine apiece. The Dominican Republic led with twenty-nine, while latecomer Panama trailed with only three. Of the original republics forged early in the nineteenth century, the other top scorers included Venezuela with twenty-four, Haiti with twenty, and Ecuador with seventeen. By the end of the 1950s, Paraguay and Uruguay recorded the fewest constitutions at four each, the first country stable because it had been so dictatorial and the second because it had been so democratic. From the 1930s through the 1960s, Latin America generated nearly sixty constitutions. Per usual, the Dominican Republic (seven constitutions), Haiti (six), and Venezuela (six) set the pace.

Argentina still boasted the longest-lasting constitution (from 1853, preceded by only three other documents), although briefly replaced by Perón's constitution from 1949 to 1957. After ten previous charters, the Colombian constitution of 1886 also proved very durable, even though significantly amended in 1936, 1945, and 1968.[23]

Most Latin American constitutions still closely followed the U.S. blueprint. Nevertheless, they were usually longer and more detailed, not unlike state constitutions in the United States. A composite Latin American constitution for the 1950s would have run about 35 pages, or roughly three times the length of the U.S. document. One purpose of including greater specificity was to try to get Latin American governments to really follow what the constitutions intended rather than using broad-brush provisions, as in the U.S. charter. Another reason for the verbosity was the attempt to secure new social and economic rights through their exhaustive listing.[24]

These socioeconomic pledges illustrated the long-standing Latin American association of democracy with social justice, not just proper government procedures. From 1932 to 1960, all the Latin American countries except Mexico (which had started the trend in 1917), Chile (which had partially followed suit in 1925), and Haiti (which officially clung to 19th-century individualism) introduced constitutional sections on social rights. These guarantees were at least as advanced as similar provisions in the United States and Europe, although the Latin Americans mainly enforced them only in the urban areas. These reforms made the central governments and presidents more interventionist. New constitutions usually emphasized state responsibilities for labor, family, education, and, increasingly, economic welfare, development, and nationalism. The newest trend in group social rights addressed those for rural and indigenous peoples.[25]

Examples of this social constitutionalism included Peru's 1933 constitution adopting some nationalist and socialist ideas from the 1917 Mexican charter, such as government ownership of mineral rights and collective bargaining for workers.[26] The 1934 Uruguayan charter also guaranteed significant economic and social rights, particularly for trade unions and children.[27]

The 1936 constitutional reform in Colombia echoed many of its contemporaries by allowing for regulation or even expropriation of private property in the "public or social interest . . . for the purpose of rationalizing the production, distribution and consumption of riches, or of giving the worker just protection. . . ."[28] Argentines added sections on social and labor rights to their constitution under Perón in 1949, and again when they restored the 1853 document in 1957.[29]

Following World War II, some constitutions also introduced novelties in common with Europe. They absorbed international laws such as the Declaration of Human Rights, added economic rules and regulations, endorsed proportional representation, and inserted anti-fascist and, especially, anti-communist prohibitions against totalitarian or anti-democratic parties. They also expressed nationalism and anti-imperialism, including restrictions on economic rights for foreigners and extensions of territorial sovereignty to include the subsoil, sea, and air.[30]

The most significant and successful democratizing constitution in this period was Costa Rica's of 1949, following a rash of early documents and then two very stable charters in 1871 and 1917. In the wake of the civil war of 1948, the new constitution established the institutions for a vibrant and durable democracy. It set up an interventionist welfare state guaranteeing broad political as well as socioeconomic rights to its citizens. Although most of the provisions adhered to standard Latin American fare, it maintained a centralist system but with municipal elections, pruned the president's powers, buttressed congress, gave women the vote, and founded an exemplary electoral tribunal. Most momentous for democracy, the constitution abolished the armed forces.[31]

CENTRALISM FOR DEVELOPMENT

Leaders saw centralism as necessary to promote nationalism, national integration, and national development. They wanted to knit closer ties between the state and the subordinate classes. Throughout Latin America, central governments assumed vast new economic and social functions, not unlike New Deal liberalism in the United States. Rather than being oppressive, centralism sometimes furthered democratization. The overwhelming majority of constitutions retained or even bolstered unitary systems. Even the four federalist countries exhibited centralizing tendencies.[32]

As the cities snowballed in size, municipal government gained elected representation. By the mid-1950s, seventeen of the countries elected their town councils, and nine their mayors. Still, those officials languished in the shadow of the central or even provincial authorities. As the central government accumulated more power to lead national development, it actually stripped many municipalities of their previous functions. By the 1970s, municipal government barely survived, with little purpose or resources.[33]

POPULIST PRESIDENTS

Presidentialism intensified in order to lead national development and mass movements, although most of the fundamental, legal structure of that office stayed the same. Sometimes posing as champions of the common people, presidents clashed with other branches of government and with conservative social actors. Chief executives tried to move their nations forward with formidable powers over other institutions but with tenuous influence over socioeconomic forces, the military, U.S. interests, and their own security.[34]

From 1940 to 1976, Latin American presidents lasted in office less time on average than their foreign counterparts, even in other underdeveloped countries. They also exhibited a high percentage of unconstitutional transfers of power. Peru provided one extremely unstable case, hosting ninety-five presidents from 1821 until 1969, for an average of about one every year and a half.

Compared with the average in North Atlantic democracies, Latin American chief executives took power with much less ministerial experience. This occurred partly because presidents tended to be personalistic outsiders with thin party ties, making them less attuned to building coalitions, cooperating with congress, and relying on political parties to keep them in office. Another reason was that some countries prohibited recent high government officials from immediate election to the presidency.[35]

In the middle of the 1950s, all the Latin American constitutions insisted that presidents be native-born citizens who had resided in the country for a while prior to their election, partly so that recent exiles could not compete. Age requirements tended to be younger than in the United States, with one country (Nicaragua) requiring presidents to be at least twenty-five years of age, seven countries requiring presidents to be at least thirty years of age, nine requiring presidents to be at least thirty-five years of age, and only two countries requiring presidents to be at least forty years of age. Although vague, the Dominican constitution of 1947 indicated that the president only had to be eighteen or older. Some countries included economic, occupational, and educational stipulations. For example, Colombian presidents had to be citizens by birth, at least thirty years old, earning a minimum income of almost U.S. $1,000, and experienced in a previous high public post (or a university professor or a professional with a university degree, particularly wise qualifications).

Six countries barred presidents who had been on active duty in the armed forces for six months or a year previously. Eight outlawed the election of a priest, while Argentina and Paraguay demanded that the chief executive subscribe to Roman Catholicism. By the mid-1950s, Latin American presidents could serve one legal term from four to six years.

Presidents increasingly claimed popular mandates. By the mid-1940s, all the countries save three (Cuba, Haiti, and Argentina until 1949) directly elected their presidents. Most constitutions empowered the congress to select the president from among the top vote-getters in the absence of a majority winner. The Costa Rican Constitution of 1949 required a runoff if no candidate received 40 percent of the popular votes. Presidential elections commonly did not coincide with congressional contests, thus exacerbating relations between the executive and the legislature.[36]

The typical constitution contained a contradictory tendency to invest the presidency with enormous powers while also trying to hem it in with restrictions. Peru's 1933 constitution exemplified the glorification of an awe-inspiring president by proclaiming that officeholder "personifies the nation."[37] Colombia's President Alberto Lleras Camargo (1958–1962) quipped that a president had to be "a magician, prophet, redeemer, savior, and pacifier who can transform a ruined republic into a prosperous one, can make the prices of the things we export rise and the value of the things we consume drop."[38] He bemoaned the fact that, "Everything of importance for the citizenry, both in the way of fundamental norms and in social and economic matters has almost without exception been the product of extraordinary faculties authorized by the Congress to the executive or of decrees under the state of siege."[39]

Presidents generally possessed vast, autonomous appointment powers, since most countries still lacked effective civil service regulations. In no country did presidential cabinet appointments require legislative approval, although some constitutions allowed congress to interpellate them and even force them to resign. All the constitutions made the president the head of the armed forces, at least on paper. However, in many cases, the appointment of high officers by the president required congressional concurrence.[40]

Presidents still cowed the legislature. They seldom needed to use their item veto. The executive originated most bills, and that legislation usually sailed through congress unscathed. Even rarer than a veto was its override. Most presidents could issue laws—as well as their implementing regulations and instructions—by decree, particularly when congress was not in session, which was frequent. Most presidents also had the right to spend in excess of the budget approved by congress, especially in times of so-called emergencies.

The greatest extraordinary power was to govern during states of exception or siege.[41]

Even during the collaborative National Front, the Colombian president ruled by decree under a state of siege or emergency most of the time. From the 1950s to the 1980s, the bi-partisan coalition governments of the Front reigned, officially from 1958 to 1974 but unofficially and partially until 1990. Cooperation between the executive and legislative branches should have been high, but the factionalized parties in congress exasperated the president. He could impose states of exception so long as all the cabinet ministers agreed. However, congress did set some limits, most importantly that decrees did not retain force after the special state expired unless approved by the legislators.[42]

The constitutions placed Latin American presidents in an awkward position vis-à-vis the military. Normally the law forbade the armed forces to disobey civilian authorities or to deliberate on politics but authorized them to defend the constitution and order. On the main thrust of trying to exert civilian control over the military, the Nicaraguan charter of 1939 said that, "The army is a non-political institution. Its members in active service may not vote or exercise political activities of any kind."[43] In a further attempt to shield the legislature from military takeovers, the 1933 Peruvian constitution proclaimed that the armed services could not "encroach" on the congress and that the president had to provide whatever defensive force it requested.[44] The Bolivian constitution of 1938 warned that any armed group who tried to govern was guilty of sedition.[45]

The most radical and successful provision appeared in the Costa Rican constitution of 1949:

> The army as a permanent institution is proscribed. For vigilance and the preservation of the public order there will be the necessary police forces. Only through continental agreement or for the national defense may military forces be organized; in either case they shall always be subordinate to the civil power; they may not deliberate or make manifestations or declarations in individual or collective form.[46]

In most countries, constitutional attempts to thwart military intervention had little discernible impact, at least in the short run. From 1920 to 1960, the Latin American armed forces still staged seventy-eight successful coups d'état. The most frequent per country were nine (in Bolivia and Ecuador), seven (in Argentina and Paraguay), and six (in El Salvador and Guatemala). Only one each took place in Costa Rica, because it was so democratic, and Nicaragua, because it was so authoritarian.[47] Some scholars underestimated the continuing threat from the armed forces in seemingly consolidated democracies. Even after the election of Socialist Allende in 1970, a standard text on Latin American politics in 1971 noted that, "The army does not need to be considered as a separate power element in the political landscape of Chile, which is one of a small handful of Latin American states where military impact on politics is at ebb."[18]

Since most militaries continued to intrude in politics, the Latin Americans retained other provisions for dealing with that eventuality. The rights to asylum and the tradition of sending ousted opponents into exile, along with the reluctance to prosecute departing dictatorships for human rights violations, may have made coups more likely. At the same time, they may have made unconstitutional takeovers less bloody and less durable. Perhaps these practices increased the tyrant's willingness to tolerate his opponents and to step down under favorable conditions. These protections for the politically defeated were also quite rational in systems with low numbers of trained public officials, with frequent unscheduled and violent changes of government, and with today's victors often becoming tomorrow's vanquished.[49]

From 1932 to 1973, Chile provided a rare example of a multiparty presidential system with great stability. The president exercised the line-item veto and broad appointive powers, although the senate had to concur in many cases. Traditionally, the dominant executive mainly concentrated on broad national issues, the subordinate legislature on particularistic local questions, although both shaped national policies. The two branches feuded frequently, based on separate powers, elections, party compositions, ideologies, and agendas. From the 1950s onward, congressional elections shifted away from mainly pork barrel concerns to echo the national, ideological issues of presidential campaigns. Therefore compromise between the legislature and the executive became increasingly difficult. Meanwhile presidential power gradually expanded to provide leadership for national development. Those attributes peaked in the constitutional reform of 1969, put through by rightist and centrist politicians who never expected Allende to win the 1970 election.[50]

Even more than in Chile, Colombia supported a robust president looming over a congress dedicated principally to localistic, clientelistic services but also engaged in national policy debates. Although not quite as grandiose as in many other Latin American countries, the president's considerable power rested mainly on his ability to make most high-level appointments (including ministers, governors, and rectors) with no interference from congress, to staff most of the bureaucracy, and to command the armed forces. He also initiated most significant legislation, shaped laws through implementation, exercised the item veto, issued decrees, and ruled under states of exception. Increasingly, the executive presided over economic policies and agencies to boost national development, often in consultation with technocrats more than legislators.[51]

Even intensely democratic Uruguay bowed to the trend toward more activist presidents. In the aftermath of the Great Depression, an elected constitutional convention designed a new constitution, approved in a plebiscite in 1934. Eliminating the weak, cumbersome, conflictual, and controversial National Council of Administration, it restored a preeminent presidency.

In a brief reversal, Uruguay's 1952 constitution recreated a debilitated collegial executive confronting a muscular congress. Popular vote would elect the members of the National Council of Government for four years, with no immediate reelection permitted. The constitution guaranteed the runner-up party three of the nine seats. The top vote-getting representatives from the majority party would rotate the presidency of the council every year. Unlike the earlier hybrid system, now the Council would rule without a separate directly elected president. However, the unwieldy institution did not function smoothly.

In 1966, Uruguayan voters reinstated the previous presidential system in hopes that a dynamic chief executive could cope with economic problems. Those constitutional reforms created a powerful five-year presidency, with no immediate reelection. The officeholder also could not leave the national territory for more than forty-eight hours without senate approval. The president enjoyed full control over his cabinet, although its members could be interrogated by the congress.

For a brief moment, the balance of power between the Uruguayan executive and the legislature may have been the most even in Latin America. However, the 1966 reforms also enhanced the president's authority to rule under emergency laws. He deployed those abilities to subjugate the congress and pave the way to the military takeover with him in 1973.[52]

The most important legal constraint on Latin American presidents remained the prohibition against reelection. In the mid-1950s, all the constitutions banned immediate reelection except those of the Dominican Republic and Paraguay, both ruled by long-standing dictators. The Costa Rican constitution of 1949 required two terms between the election of the same person as president, as did the Venezuelan constitution of 1961 and the Cuban constitution of 1940.[53]

Some constitutions went to greater lengths to stymie *continuismo*. For example, the El Salvadoran and Guatemalan constitutions called for popular rebellion and intervention by the armed forces if any president violated the rule of alternation. After the ouster of the dictatorship of Jorge Ubico (1931 to 1944), the Guatemalan constitution of 1945 barred from the presidency clergy, active military, previous coup or insurrection leaders and their close relatives, previous high officials of de facto governments and their close relatives, and anyone who proposed or tried to interfere with the principle of alternation in the presidency, which was a six-year term, renewable only after a twelve-year interlude. The constitution also said that one of the fundamental duties of the apolitical, non-deliberative army was to defend alternation in the presidency, as well as fair elections, democracy, and the constitution. The Guatemalan and Costa Rican constitutions labeled any attempt at continuation as treason. In the same spirit, several constitutions also proscribed immediate presidential election for relatives or high public officials close to the president, so as to block indirect continuation.[54]

The Bolivian constitution of 1945 also went farther than most by establishing that not only presidents but also their vice presidents could not be elected president until after an intervening six-year term. Bolivia also banned from election to the presidency sitting cabinet ministers, members of the armed forces, clergy, close relatives, and contractors with the government. The president had to be elected by a popular majority or chosen by congress from among the top three vote-getters.[55]

In its 1946 constitution, Ecuador blocked the president and vice-president from becoming president or vice-president until four years after their four-year term. It also prohibited close relatives of presidents from succeeding them immediately. Rules against close relatives becoming president were common in smaller countries as in Central America. Some Latin American constitutions also excluded close relatives of the president from other public positions, such as congress. They also commonly imposed anti-corruption strictures, for example preventing congressional representatives from having dealings with state agencies.[56]

Some dictatorial presidents, including Rafael Trujillo in the Dominican Republic, Anastasio Somoza in Nicaragua, and Juan Vicente Gómez in Venezuela, found their way around these no-reelection restrictions. They ruled from behind the scenes, handpicked successors to govern in brief interim regimes, resorted to the courts, congress, or a phony plebiscite to extend their term, or amended, rewrote, suspended, or abolished the constitution. Although obviously violating the spirit of the constitution, it is telling that these continuist presidents often felt obliged to go through some legalistic conjuring to perpetuate themselves in office rather than just using brute force.[57]

Another common legal restriction on presidents involved travel so that the legislature could monitor their behavior. Along with many others, the

Ecuadorean constitution of 1946 prohibited their presidents from leaving the country during their tenure or for one year thereafter without congressional approval. Going abroad without such consent would forfeit their office. Presidents also could not exit the national capital for more than thirty consecutive days even within the country, though during those days they could continue to rule from anywhere in the national territory.[58]

Constitution writers also invented other provisions, often futile, to tether the chief executive. Some constitutions allocated additional powers to the cabinet, congress, or courts. Some relied on the Comptroller General, a new officer who ruled on the correctness of all budgetary outlays. Others introduced regulations on government administration and finances to try to curb arbitrariness and corruption.[59]

Other legal strategists sought to restrict the president's enormous powers to suspend constitutional guarantees during states of exception and siege. They required limits and congressional authorizations, beforehand if in session and afterward if not. Some lawmakers mandated signatures of cabinet officers for presidential acts above and beyond normal constitutional provisions, but ministers appointed freely by the president were unlikely to obstruct his wishes. Going even farther, the Bolivian constitution of 1938 declared, in vain, that "Neither the Congress nor any gathering of the people may grant to the chief executive extraordinary powers, the sum total of public authority, nor any power that will place the lives, the honor, and the property of Bolivians at the mercy of the government, or of any person."[60]

In an extreme case of attempts to handcuff the chief executive, the Ecuadorean constitution of 1946 invested congress with the right to remove the president for "permanent physical or mental incapacity," later employed against Abdalá Bucaram in 1997. Illustrating some of the problems with presidents, the constitution placed limits on their extraordinary powers during emergencies. It also expressly forbade them to violate the constitution and laws, to inhibit or dissolve congress, to interfere with the judiciary, to meddle in elections, or to govern from outside the country.[61]

Typically in the twentieth century, Latin American constitutions guaranteed their citizens crucial and detailed individual rights against oppression by the executive branch. These normally included property rights, equal protection of the law and due process, safeguards against government abuses of criminal or political laws, rights of amparo and/or habeas corpus, freedom of speech and writing (although with tricky clauses against slandering certain persons or disturbing social order), freedom of travel, freedom of religion (although some still embraced Roman Catholicism as the official faith), freedom of assembly and association, freedom to petition, the right to join political parties, the right not to be discriminated against on the grounds of race or religion, and the right of asylum. Constitutions also usually outlawed the death penalty. Although governments often transgressed basic civil liberties, they also increasingly respected them.[62]

Overall and over time, the Costa Rican constitution of 1949 established the weakest presidency in Latin America. It counterbalanced presidentialism with significant capacities for the unicameral legislature (notably the ability to censure ministers and investigate the executive branch, but without the right to immediate reelection), for the supreme court, and for other governing bodies. It deprived the president of a veto over the national budget, any ability to legislate by decree, emergency authority without the support of two-thirds of the congress, and reelection.[63]

Despite the monumental formal and informal powers of presidents, most were elected by a minority and held a minority of the seats in the legislature. Growing congressional oversight sometimes curtailed their authority. Pacts between the government and opposition constrained chief executives in some countries, principally Venezuela, Colombia, and Uruguay. At the same time, presidents faced threatening militaries. And even sincere democrats often expressed frustration at the challenges of national development, infrastructural deficiencies, small budgets, recalcitrant citizens and regions, disloyal élites and other opponents, unruly social movements, ideological foes, guerrilla bands, foreign meddlers, and other international and economic forces beyond their control.[64]

CONSERVATIVE CONGRESSES

In the mid-1950s, fourteen of the legislatures were bicameral—with senators and deputies—and six (Guatemala, Honduras, El Salvador, Costa Rica, Panama, and Paraguay) were unicameral. The criteria for legislators were similar to those for presidents, especially for senators, but not so stringent, especially for deputies. Qualifications for election to congress always required a minimum age, usually at least thirty years old for the senate and twenty-one for the lower house, and citizenship, normally native born. Other requirements varied, including no felony convictions but some prior professional or government experience in Colombia, military service in Bolivia, and an income threshold in Argentina.[65]

In the mid-1950s, voters directly elected most senators and deputies, although provincial assemblies selected senators in Argentina and Venezuela. In many countries, the distribution of seats still disproportionately favored the rural and conservative populations. Senators were typically elected by geographic district, much as in the United States, except for the functional senators in Ecuador, the senators who were ex-presidents and the runner-up in the previous presidential election in Nicaragua, and all the senators being elected at-large in Nicaragua and Uruguay. Senatorial terms ranged from four to eight years. Only Mexico and Costa Rica outlawed immediate reelection.

In most countries, voters elected deputies by population numbers (for example, one for every 50,000 inhabitants in a district) except that all were elected at-large in Nicaragua and Uruguay. Typically deputies were elected by proportional representation, adopted in twelve more countries in this period. Their terms varied from two to six years, usually longer than in the United States. Only Mexico, Costa Rica, and Guatemala disallowed immediate reelection. Most Latin American constitutions did not limit the reelection of congresspersons in hopes that they would accumulate leverage vis-à-vis the overbearing presidents.[66]

In these years, most scholars did not study Latin American legislatures. They criticized congresses that appeared to be conservative, élitist, puerile debating societies, either delaying or rubberstamping legislation, in countries needing vigorous presidential leadership for rapid national development. Looking for responsible decision-making congresses, researchers usually only highlighted Chile, Colombia, Uruguay, and Costa Rica, although they sometimes gave a nod to Venezuela, Brazil, and Peru.

Nevertheless, when political scientists took other functions into account—such as legitimation, criticism, recruitment, and socialization—they gave the Latin American legislatures slightly higher marks. And if they compared those congresses not with the leviathan in the United States but rather with their counterparts in Africa, Asia, and even Europe, they saw them as less pathetic. Analysts agreed that the most vigorous Latin American legislatures boasted a long tradition of relative autonomy and influence, lengthy legislative careers, adequate committee and staff structures, and healthy political parties capable of opposing the president.[67]

Although a few legislatures possessed positive features, most remained even weaker in reality than in the constitutions. They customarily only met for about four months per year, even then for only a few hours per day. In addition, they possessed tiny budgets and staffs. Members of congress were typically expected to donate a portion of their already small salaries to their political parties. Their work was undermined further by the opposition's practice of boycotting sessions. Worse, dictators usually closed the congress altogether, although some made partial exceptions, for example the first Carlos Ibanez government in Chile (1927–1931) and the military in Brazil (1964–1985). Authoritarian Mexico maintained one of the most slavish congresses, whose chamber of deputies from 1935 to 1964 approved unanimously per year between 59 percent and 100 percent of presidential projects.[68]

After World War II, constitutional changes aimed to strike a better balance between the legislative and executive branches. Reforms extended the length of legislative sessions and prohibited more former government officials from becoming congresspersons. In addition, some constitutions transferred a few powers—such as convoking an extraordinary session of congress—from the president to the legislators. Most legislatures possessed impeachment procedures, but they virtually never used them against a president until the 1990s.[69]

Although overpowered by the chief executives, congresses squabbled with them frequently. This friction sometimes triggered military coups, which usually cashiered both the president and the legislators. Only rarely did freely elected presidents enjoy the luxury of single-party majorities in both houses of congress. From 1900 to 1990, this combination only occurred in Uruguay (for twenty years), Venezuela (for thirteen years), Argentina (for ten years, mainly during the second and third Perónist presidencies), Costa Rica and Peru (for nine years), Colombia (for seven years, mainly in the 1940s), and the Dominican Republic (for four years). Most of the time, parties were too fragile or fragmented to guarantee a majority for their presidents.[70]

Peru, Argentina, and Brazil hosted fairly weak congresses. In the rather typical case of Peru, the 1933 constitution barred from congressional office members of the clergy and the armed forces. Voters directly elected both the senators (native-born and at least thirty-five years of age) and the deputies (native-born and at least twenty-five years of age). They elected them at the same time and length (six years) as president via proportional representation, and they could reelect them indefinitely. However, from the 1920s to the 1960s, turnover in congressional membership from one election to the next reached nearly 90 percent among deputies and nearly 70 percent among senators.

Although not powerful by U.S. standards, the Peruvian congress influenced the budget and presidential appointees more than some of its Latin American counterparts. It also fueled political instability and numerous military takeovers through its quarrels with the executive branch. From the 1930s to the 1960s, congress was undercut by the frequent military interventions and the equally frequent banishment of the largest political party, the populist American Popular Revolutionary Alliance.[71]

Argentina filled its nine-year senate terms with two people from each province and the Federal District. They were elected by plurality vote of the provincial legislatures except for the ones from the Federal District, who were chosen by popular vote. In 1949, the populist Perón established the direct election of senators, but his successors reinstated the indirect system. Both senators and deputies could be elected over and over.

Voters directly elected the deputies to four-year terms. In 1962, a new electoral law switched from the Sáenz Peña system of giving the first-place party two-thirds of the district's deputies and the second-place one-third to a d'Hondt system of proportional representation. The lawmakers intended this change to allow the Perónists to participate in congressional elections but give them little chance to win control because many minority interests would capture seats. Political parties determined who the congressional candidates were and how they would be listed on the ballot. Consequently, during 1958 to 1966, legislators normally followed dictates from their parties, not their constituents.

Under more authoritarian presidents, the stature of Argentina's congress declined from the oligarchic republic to the mid-twentieth century. It did not enjoy full interpellation rights with cabinet ministers. It could question but not remove them. The legislators rarely initiated or made major public policies. Instead, they at most criticized and modified legislation introduced by the executive branch. Congress at least trained the several presidents who served there. Despite the legislature's debilities, a poll in Buenos Aires province in 1963 found 78 percent of respondents saying they thought congress was important to moving the nation forward, a figure below that for universities but well above that for labor unions, political parties, or the military.[72]

Ever since independence, Brazil had always had a puny legislature. During his authoritarian period from 1930 to 1945, President Getúlio Vargas effectively eliminated the congress, even though it met briefly during 1934 to 1937. In the democracy from 1945 to 1964, lawmakers installed proportional representation for the lower house of congress and for state and municipal legislatures.

In Brazil's democracy, voters directly elected presidents and deputies for four years at the same time. They selected congressional representatives statewide in multi-member districts. Voters chose a party and a candidate within that party. Seats were awarded by the state's electoral quotient, the number of registered voters divided by the number of representatives. This system encouraged smaller parties to form electoral alliances to maximize their total vote and thus their number of quotients and seats. Each state also elected three senators for eight-year terms.

Both houses of Brazil's congress overrepresented states with smaller populations, giving rural and conservative groups exceptional weight. This bias set up intrinsic adversity between a congress more representative of the traditional agrarian areas and a chief executive more representative of the progressive urban concentrations. This dichotomy exacerbated the standoff that led to the fall of populist President João Goulart in 1964.

The legislature functioned in the shadow of the president. The frailty of the party system further sapped congress. Nevertheless, the Brazilian assembly wielded some powers. During 1961 to 1963, a semi-parliamentary system designed to weaken Goulart temporarily increased the authority of a prime minister and cabinet controlled by the more conservative chamber of deputies. Thereafter, the 1964 coup raised to new heights the sway of the president over congress.[73]

Chile and Colombia boasted two of the strongest congresses, buttressed by organized and assertive political parties. According to most outside observers, the Chilean legislature was the most capable in Latin America. It exerted so much influence because of its long history, often bucking the chief executive. From the 1930s to the 1970s, the president always faced an opposition majority in at least one of the houses of congress. That was one reason lawmakers elevated the presidency further over congress on the eve of Allende's surprise electoral victory, but his subsequent stalemate with the legislature helped detonate the military coup of 1973. Then Pinochet abolished the congress until 1990, consulting instead with the usually cooperative junta as the legislative power.

From the 1930s to the 1970s, the Chilean congress had ample powers to initiate, alter, or shoot down legislation. Although only the president could propose the annual budget, which congress could only legally reduce, it found circuitous ways to pump up expenditures. It possessed the constitutional right to grill and impeach cabinet ministers but not to name them. It also exerted considerable control over the bureaucracy and patronage, partly through case work for constituents to make government offices accountable.

The senate wielded authority partly because its membership remained fairly stable. In the 1960s, only 25 percent of the Colombian congress was reelected to a consecutive term, but 78 percent of the Chilean senate was returned. Chilean legislators also enjoyed far better staff support and committee structure than did their Colombian counterparts. Moreover, the Chilean members attended sessions and influenced policies much more regularly than did those in Colombia.[74]

Nevertheless, the Colombian congress also outshone most of the others in Latin America. However, the legislature became less salient, as the executive branch increasingly concentrated on accelerating economic development from the 1930s onward. Under the bi-partisan unity government of the National Front (1958–1974), the congress lost more leverage, when it did not launch any initiatives. That power-sharing agreement between the Liberals and Conservatives required a two-thirds majority in congress for any major legislation. Since two-thirds was very hard to obtain even under consociational agreements, the legislature delegated more decree powers to the president.

In 1968, majority rule returned to the congress, but it remained unimposing. That body still suffered from slender financing and staffing compared to the ballooning executive branch. Moreover, high turnover resulted in 64 percent of the victorious deputy candidates in 1968 being newcomers. The assembly was overshadowed not only by the president and the clientelistic Liberal and Conservative parties but also by weighty interest groups, such as the Roman Catholic Church, the military, the industrialists, and the coffee growers.

Despite these problems, the Colombian congress still wielded some influence. Although seldom shaping national policies during the Front, it recruited new players into the political process, integrated regional groups into national dialogue, distributed patronage and spoils throughout the nation, aired conflicts, and legitimized national government institutions and practices. It sometimes obstructed the president, for example by delaying or modifying legislation. The congress also exerted oversight through hearings with government officials.

Colombian legislators also enjoyed leverage through their parties. Congressional representatives tended to be subservient to their parties, especially the one controlling the presidency. A congressperson's future was determined more by party than by constituency. The national parties selected the candidates for all electoral contests and their place on the ballot. Since congressional seats went to the candidates listed highest on the ballot, parties maintained considerable discipline. For example, during 1961 to 1968, party cohesion in congressional votes normally ranged between 90 percent and 100 percent.[75]

FRUSTRATED JUDICIAL REFORMS

The growth in mass democracies highlighted the ineffectiveness of Latin American court systems. Antiquated legal codes from the mid-nineteenth century still emphasized rationalistic individualism, private property, and a limited state. They did not allow for mushrooming political participation, concern with egalitarianism, social and labor rights, and roles for the state. When reformers tried to improve judicial independence, legal education, accessibility, and defense of democratic rights, they encountered stiff resistance.

Some constitutions tried to augment the independence of the judiciary by taking appointments away from the president, giving judges lengthier terms, making dismissal from the bench more difficult, prohibiting the president from reducing judges' salaries, and forbidding judges from meddling in "politics." By the mid-1940s, only eight countries allowed presidents to select supreme court judges on their own. By 1957, the president, at least in law, could name supreme court judges without confirmation by congress only in Haiti, Chile, and Paraguay. The legislature alone picked supreme court judges in twelve countries, while both branches made the appointments in the rest. Many countries also delegated lower court appointments to the supreme court. Most countries still assigned supreme court judges temporary terms, in some cases as short or shorter than a presidency. In the 1950s, however, Mexico, Peru, Chile, Argentina, and Brazil appointed them for life.[76]

These reforms helped some judiciaries exhibit greater independence, as indicated by the ejection of judges by many authoritarian regimes. Although upholding the rule of law remained problematic, it was sustained more frequently now, particularly in the larger and more modern countries. Despite improvements, both democratic and authoritarian presidents still worked their will over the judiciary in many ways. They usually resorted to removing uncooperative judges or defining broadly political matters outside their jurisdiction. Chief executives also violated institutional autonomy by formally abrogating judicial independence, bypassing ordinary courts though the establishment of separate ones, transferring and reassigning judges, slashing their salaries, and refusing to enforce their decisions. Judicial subservience to presidents also resulted from the social and political realities of private corruption, clandestine repression, and economic insecurity.[77]

Most reformers also advocated a shift away from legal formalism, especially in law schools. Even with assistance from the United States, they enjoyed little success. These efforts formed part of the often futile attempts to make the courts more accessible to citizens of lower economic and social status.[78]

The advocates of protected democracy preferred courts to continue emphasizing property rights, while the champions of popular democracy urged them to start focusing on social rights. The Mexican constitution of 1917 inspired the regional development of individual and group constitutional guarantees. Its promises of social justice found expression in nearly all other Latin American constitutions between the 1930s and 1960s. To protect these guarantees, reformers created new judicial remedies, especially amparo. Judicial protection of individual and social rights, however, was hampered throughout the period by declarations of states of emergency, unconstitutional changes in government, growing politicization of the judiciary, and proliferation of special courts outside the jurisdiction and control of the ordinary judiciary.[79]

Despite some improvements in the courts' defense of individual and social rights, the overriding problem with the judiciary remained its failure to defend constitutional democracy. Judicial review to determine the constitutionality of government actions was frequently copied from the United States, but not in all countries and not in full. Even where this judicial practice existed in Latin America, courts used it more narrowly and ineffectually than in the United States. As had been true since independence, it was often unclear who had such authority, how far it went, or how it could be applied or enforced. Many Latin American countries did not really expect courts to uphold constitutional democracy or to resist dictatorship, particularly when the former could suspend the constitution legally to confront emergencies and the latter could drape their usurpation of power in legality. Frequently confronted with arbitrary behavior and de facto governments, courts were hard pressed to decide what acts were legal or illegal.

The executive branch viewed these exceptional periods as political questions beyond the jurisdiction of the supreme court. Moreover, the judiciary usually treated the laws promulgated by unconstitutional rulers as legitimate both during the existence of the regime and after its demise, even when a constitutional government followed a dictatorship. The separate sphere of the courts from political issues was reflected in that coup makers more often disbanded the congress than the courts, although they sometimes shuttered both.[80]

In Latin America, the Argentine judiciary probably ranked historically second only to the Chilean as an autonomous, forceful branch of government. Nevertheless, between 1930 and 1970, Argentine governments suspended constitutional guarantees approximately 45 percent of the time, limiting the ability of courts to respond to cases of rights transgressions. The supreme court recognized the de facto seizure of power on five separate occasions beginning in 1943. Like those in Brazil, El Salvador, and Peru, it also suffered wholesale purgings, being completely replaced by new regimes six times from 1946 on.[81]

During this period, however, judicial capitulation in the face of states of emergency and de facto regimes sometimes gave way to judicial resistance, notably in Argentina, where it was least expected. In general, such defiance remained infrequent and ineffective. In any country, confrontation was unusual because all Latin American courts generally recognized the legitimacy and legality of extralegal governments. Resistance normally proved futile, due not only to armed intimidation but also to the government's manipulation of law and constitutional provisions as well as judicial careers.[82]

When Pinochet deposed Allende in 1973, the Chilean supreme court immediately recognized the legality of the dictatorship and its laws. The court ignored the gross violations of human rights. The armed forces quickly boarded up the congress but left the judiciary largely intact. As in some other countries that experienced military rule, the governing junta suspended or amended key parts of the constitution and assumed the legal and legislative authority of the state. This takeover included the expansion of a system of military courts, over which the supreme court surrendered supervisory authority. By the end of the dictatorship, these military courts exercised jurisdiction over more civilians than over armed services personnel.[83]

From the 1960s to the 1980s, the Latin American courts compiled an abysmal record of protecting constitutions, constitutional democracies, and individual liberties. They offered little legal redress for severe human rights abuses committed under unusually savage military governments. These failings set the stage for a widespread rethinking and revamping of the administration of justice in the following democratic period.[84]

BREAKTHROUGH ELECTIONS

The upsurge of popular democracy permitted and propelled some of the most groundbreaking elections in Latin American history. Voters benefited from expanding access, rights and protections. Nevertheless, they remained hampered by somewhat limited suffrage, a few indirect elections, inefficient and biased electoral systems, corruption and chicanery, manipulation and intimidation by national and local bosses, interventionist militaries, and frail political parties. Although improving, voter effectiveness was also hindered by low levels of education, inadequate information, and glaring socioeconomic disparities.

Some governments still imposed the selection and election of a candidate through multiple shady means. These tactics included controlling registration, juggling nominations, allowing only one candidate, dominating the campaign and media, harassing the opposition, bribing or coercing voters, stuffing the ballot box, and miscounting the results. Although penalties existed for electoral misconduct, fraud and favoritism often besmirched the process, especially in the countryside. Nevertheless, electoral travesties declined thanks to rising urbanization, education, voter participation, and secret ballots.[85]

Amidst widespread democratization of the franchise, some qualifications on voting remained. By 1958, only Paraguay still denied women the national franchise, whereas ten countries had still withheld it by the mid-1940s. Although all countries had scotched property requirements, four (Peru, Ecuador, Chile, and Brazil) still banned illiterates. Peru and some other countries excluded clerics from balloting, while a majority barred the military from the voting booth. While disenfranchising the armed forces, the Ecuadorian constitution of 1946 obliged them to "guarantee the purity of the electoral function." Many countries expected the armed forces to maintain order and propriety during elections.[86]

Electoral reform crowned the trend to amplify and fortify democratic institutions. Many countries expanded suffrage, both by enfranchising new groups such as women, illiterates, and young people and by removing conditions such as income, property, or status. Latin American reformers also cut back qualifications (mainly age) for elected officials. They switched from indirect to direct elections and from majoritarian to proportional representation. In many cases, they made municipal officials elected instead of appointed.

From the perspective of the dictatorial 1970s, these legal advances appeared minor, but from the vantage point of the democratic 1980s, they looked valuable. However, the failure of these significant reforms from the 1930s to the 1960s to generate durable and deep democracies called into question the ability of lesser institutional engineering to achieve that goal from the 1970s to the 2000s. Although institutional changes were important, they could not accomplish all their objectives without fundamental alterations in the underlying structure of power and beliefs. Élites needed to accept the democratic rules of the game.[87]

By the mid-1950s, Latin American constitutions typically bestowed universal suffrage through obligatory and secret voting on all citizens over eighteen years of age, whether male or female, literate or illiterate, property owners or squatters, rich or poor. Equally significant, legal voting rights increasingly coincided with reality. As barriers to the franchise fell, some countries even allowed resident foreigners to vote in municipal elections on the grounds that they were members of the community, a notion of municipality going back to Iberia before the conquest of the New World.

From the 1930s to the 1970s, governments continued lowering the age requirement for suffrage. The Dominican Republic required eighteen years for regular voters but no minimum age for married persons, while Mexico, Honduras, Nicaragua, Costa Rica, and Peru dropped the minimum age to eighteen for married persons, and Nicaragua and Honduras did so for literates. All of Latin America adopted a lower voting age than the twenty-one years required in the United States.

In this era, the enfranchisement of women caused the most growth in the electorate, expanding the number of voters by 140 percent. Conservatives were as likely as progressives to bring about female suffrage, since they expected to capture most of their votes. Beginning with Ecuador in 1929, three more countries came on board in the 1930s, six in the 1940s, and eight in the 1950s, ending with Paraguay in 1963.

By the mid-1950s, almost all the Latin American countries had removed literacy requirements, while literacy rose in general. For example, in the wake of its 1944 democratic revolution, Guatemala gave the vote to illiterate males, enfranchising all men (thus enrolling many indigenous males) and literate women in the 1945 constitution. But after the upper class, armed forces, and United States extinguished that regime in 1954, Guatemala made voting public and more difficult for illiterates, barred illiterates from offices above the municipality, and still required female voters to be literate.[88]

By the mid-1950s, all the countries required registration to vote. At the same time, most mandated compulsory voting, although they seldom enforced it. Among country variations, Peru's 1933 constitution made voting compulsory up to age sixty. Paraguay assigned to all male citizens of at least eighteen years of age the duty to vote, unless they were criminals or in the military. The constitution of 1940 warned that "persons who preach or proclaim electoral abstention lose their rights as citizens without altering their obligations." The Cuban constitution of 1940 vowed that someone who failed to vote could not hold any public office for two years thereafter. Guatemala's 1945 constitutional enactment of obligatory voting left it optional for illiterates. Ecuador's constitution of 1946 made voting obligatory for men but not for women. Also in 1946, the Brazilian constitution compelled voting by both sexes, but exempted persons under the age of eighteen, illiterates, people not conversant in Portuguese, unemployed women, men over the age of sixty-five, and most enlisted soldiers. Although not prescribed in the constitution, the Argentine electoral system obligated all persons (including women from 1948 on) eighteen years and older to vote, except for criminals, insane people, clergy, members of the armed forces, and deserters from the military.[89]

Some of the highest turnouts in the world transpired in countries with legal penalties for not voting. From the late 1950s to the late 1970s, the participation of eligible voters in elections in ongoing democracies worldwide varied enormously from a low of 59 percent in the United States to a high of 94 percent in Italy. Latin American democracies tended to fall in the middle range from 70 percent to 80 percent. For example, the average turn-out of eligible voters in Chile and Uruguay reached 71 percent, in Costa Rica 73 percent, and in Venezuela 80 percent.[90]

From the 1930s to the 1980s, the percentage of the population participating in Latin American elections skyrocketed. In many cases, it doubled or tripled, after decades of gradual growth. For example, from 1930 to 1940 and 1970 to 1980, voters as a percentage of the population jumped from 20 percent to 61 percent in Uruguay, 12 percent to 52 percent in Argentina, 8 percent to 44 percent in Chile, 15 percent to 33 percent in Costa Rica, 3 percent to 25 percent in Ecuador, and 6 percent to 19 percent in Colombia. In the same period, those figures went from 24 percent to 47 percent in France, from 47 percent to 44 percent in Great Britain, from 40 percent to 43 percent in Canada, from 37 percent to 50 percent in Spain, and from 36 percent to 37 percent in the United States.[91]

In contrast with the United States, only Mexico, El Salvador, Nicaragua, Cuba, Venezuela, and Chile (after 1958) used official Australian ballots printed by the government. In the other fourteen countries, parties and candidates prepared the ballots, which made misbehavior easier and ticket splitting nearly impossible. Nearly all the countries formally guaranteed the secrecy of the balloting, but they did not always preserve it in practice.[92]

Some of the greatest excitement in Latin American elections still occurred after the ballots were cast and even after they were counted. Then intense bargaining often ensued between the winners and losers. The latter frequently threatened to cry foul, dismiss the results as bogus, and even promote destabilization, perhaps resulting in a military takeover. They demanded that the victors—usually the government—make concessions in the final tally, offices, policies, and other spoils. In this tense period, the contenders jockeyed to see who—the opposition, the oligarchy, the Church, the military, the labor unions, the student organizations, the media, or the foreign powers—would recognize the results as valid and at what price.[93]

To reduce these uncertainties, most Latin American countries devised special agencies to manage elections and deal with results and disputes. For example, the constitutions of Nicaragua in 1939, Cuba in 1940, and Brazil and Ecuador in 1946 created electoral tribunals and judges to oversee the entire electoral process. The Cuban constitution of 1940 instructed this body to be appointed by the courts and to exercise jurisdiction over parties and candidates as well as elections: "From the call for elections until the elected persons take office, the superior electoral tribunal shall have jurisdiction over the armed forces and over the police bodies for the sole purpose of guaranteeing the purity of the electoral function."[94]

In these years, proportional representation (PR) in elections for the legislature spread to a majority of the countries. For example, in congressional and municipal elections, Chile used a version of the D'Hondt system of proportional representation, in which voters chose one of several candidates on a party list. The votes for all candidates on the party list were combined to determine the number of seats won by the party, and those seats went to the candidates of that party with the most votes. As in other parts of Latin America, this meant that candidates ran against members of their own party as well as other parties. However, that feature did not seem to undercut political parties in Chile, as some theories would predict. Although the Socialists split often, other Chilean parties remained quite cohesive. This system favored identification with individual candidates more than in standard PR systems, while also giving parties an important role.[95]

In terms of electoral procedures, Latin America was catching up legally and statistically with the more industrialized democracies. However, the region still suffered by comparison because of the inconsistent rule of law and the virus of corruption. It also lagged behind the United States and Western Europe because of the frequent distortion and interruption of those electoral rights by non-elected powers, principally the dominant social classes and the armed forces, sometimes backed by the United States. Those élites were particularly disposed to shutting down these electoral systems when the winners threatened to use their victories to bring about major social redress, as reformers had done earlier in parts of Western Europe. Consequently, Latin American progressives confronted exceptional challenges in employing democratic politics to achieve significant strides toward social justice.[96]

Among the major countries, elections mattered least in selecting leaders in authoritarian Mexico. The civilian Party of the Institutionalized Revolution (PRI) always won every major election. Presidential and congressional elections occurred regularly on the same day. The official party's massive campaign served several purposes: assuring the expected victory, cowing the opposition, mobilizing voters, sending messages, establishing the personal authority of the incoming president, gathering information from the provinces and municipalities, impressing foreign observers, and generally legitimizing the government. The regime permitted little fair competition in either the conduct of the election or the counting of the ballots, although opposition parties slowly gained ground. From 1910 through 1940, the whopping official margin of victory for the president varied between 99 percent and 94 percent of the votes except for a low of 84 percent in 1924. From 1946 through 1964, those tallies dipped, ranging between 90 percent and 74 percent.[97]

In many other countries, elections took on more crucial importance than ever before, especially for the rise of populists and other reformers. Electoral triumphs for new political forces realigned the balance of power. They opened the way to more vital, popular democracies with increasing mass participation and social reforms.

In this time period, one of the first breakthroughs were the victories of the Colombian Liberals in the presidential elections of 1930 and 1934. Thereafter, they launched the Revolution on the March, a bland version of the general regional trend toward greater state involvement in the economy and society, usually backed by the middle and working classes. In 1958, the other transformative Colombian election brought the National Front to office, a coalition of Liberals and Conservatives dedicated to ending a rare military dictatorship and epidemic violence. Voters cast ballots directly for municipal council, departmental assembly, congress, and president.[98]

During the hemispheric democratic opening around the end of World War II, Guatemala elected a pro-labor, socialistic government headed by Juan José Arévalo in 1944. His elected successor, President Jacobo Arbenz, moved to redistribute land to peasants, including parcels from the United Fruit Company of the United States. Washington used the Central Intelligence Agency to back that government's overthrow in 1954, in one of its first covert anti-democratic interventions of the Cold War. Decades of dictatorship, civil war, and death ensued.[99]

One of the most influential populists in Latin American history, Juan Perón, won election to the presidency in Argentina in 1945, 1951, and later in 1973. Although elected honestly, he governed in an increasingly authoritarian style in the early 1950s, epitomizing delegative popular democracy. Accompanied up to the 1950s by his charismatic wife Evita, Perón instituted far-reaching reforms for nationalistic state protection of the industrializing economy and for rights for workers and women. He commanded a labor-based political party that remained the strongest in his country into the 2000s.

From the 1950s to the 1980s, Perónism and the armed services crossed swords to dominate Argentine politics. After the armed forces abandoned and overthrew Perón in the name of democracy in 1955, the country careened between democratic and authoritarian regimes. Following the military's ouster of Perón's new wife Isabel in 1976, they established an extraordinarily lethal dictatorship that lasted until 1983. According to the best evidence, most Argentines did not favor that authoritarian regime.[100]

Brazil also experienced fundamental realigning elections. In 1930, the electoral breakdown of the Old Republic ushered in the authoritarian regime of Vargas until his removal by the military in 1945. Under its fifth constitution, that of 1946, Brazil embarked on its first modern democratic experiment. The percentage of the total population voting soared from 1 percent at the end of the empire to 6 percent at the end of the Old Republic to 20 percent in 1962.

In 1950, voters returned Vargas to the presidency as the "father of the poor." He inaugurated a populist system that climaxed with the ascension of his protégé Goulart in 1960. The élites used President Goulart's rhetorical appeals to the downtrodden to justify the 1964 takeover by the anticommunist military, supported by the United States in the throes of the Cold War. Up to the coup, all polling and electoral data indicated that most Brazilians remained committed to democracy and centrist politics, but those on top had other preferences. The resulting dictatorship became a model for bureaucratic authoritarian regimes in South America until it restored democracy in 1985.[101]

Like many other countries, Costa Rica underwent democratization in the aftermath of World War II. Following a contested election and brief revolution in 1948, José Figueres convened an elected constituent assembly in 1949 to replace the constitution of 1871. The new charter launched a model democracy and welfare state. Figueres also founded the nation's most organized, programmatic, and popular political party, the National Liberation Party. The renovated and enduring democracy elected him president in 1953 and 1970.[102]

Another triumph for populism erupted when the Bolivian oligarchy, known as the *Rosca*, tried to steal the election of 1952. Protests by the National Revolutionary Movement (MNR), a populist amalgam of the middle sectors, workers, and peasants, escalated into a pitched battle. It resulted in the party's takeover and the Bolivian Revolution, which lasted from 1952 through successive elections until the military ejected them in 1964. While in office, the MNR extended the franchise to eighteen-year-olds, women, and illiterates. It promoted economic nationalism, labor rights, and land redistribution. The MNR attempted to replicate the statist economic and social reforms of the Mexican Revolution under one-party rule by the PRI, but this Bolivian variant did not manage to institutionalize itself. Nevertheless, it left a legacy of democracy, mass mobilization, and social justice to be revived in the future.[103]

In 1958, Venezuela, like its neighbor Colombia, terminated a dictatorship and christened a vibrant two-party democracy. Elected president in 1958, Rómulo Betancourt and his populist party of Democratic Action dominated. The government sowed the oil to bring about state intervention in the economy and social welfare.[104]

Perhaps the most famous and controversial election in Latin American history occurred in Chile in 1970. The narrow plurality victory of Allende took place in the most staunch and open democracy in the region. It produced the most revolutionary government ever in South America. Going far beyond standard populism, Allende's vow to create socialism through democratic means embodied hope for many leftists at home and abroad. In the cauldron of the Cold War, his redistribution of power and property to workers and peasants aroused equally fervent fears among his opponents in Chile and the United States.

Pinochet's 1973 blitzkrieg smashed democracy and socialism, regardless of the devotion to democracy of a resounding majority of Chileans. The death of Allende and his government, along with many of his supporters, showed that any democracy, however venerable, institutionalized, and deeply supported by its citizens, remained vulnerable to destruction by the military. The coup d'état dealt an enormous setback to Marxism, socialism, revolution and even democratic reform or populism, especially in Latin America and the Third World. The unprecedented ferocity of the coup intimidated progressives throughout the hemisphere and haunted the more timid and moderate democracies that would come later.[105]

POPULIST AND LEFTIST POLITICAL PARTIES

In most of Latin America, political parties remained little more than patron-client machines. They suffered from personalistic leadership and divisions, hierarchical organization, cronyism, programmatic vacuity, regional fragmentation, indiscipline and instability, deficient finances, government persecution, and military intervention. Parties usually chose candidates with no direct consultation with the voters, normally at conventions run by bosses, as was largely true in the United States before the expansion of the primary system. In most cases, parties viewed each other as enemy camps engaged in a winner-take-all, zero-sum battle for spoils. They rarely entertained any concept of a loyal opposition.

Nevertheless, political parties made progress and responded more to the unprivileged. In most cases, the sturdiest democracies hosted and benefited from the strongest parties and party systems. The most vibrant party systems rested on stable institutionalized parties that took coherent programmatic positions and incorporated virtually all the key segments of society.[106]

As in the United States, almost no national regulation of party organization or behavior existed historically in Latin America. This was true even though many constitutions subjected parties to special laws, which mainly allowed governments to rid themselves of parties they disliked. In these years, some constitutions increasingly regulated party organizations and behavior, both guaranteeing and limiting their rights. The limitations usually referred to international or ideological orientations, mainly to exclude communists, but the Panamanian constitution also banned parties based on sex, race, or religion.

Ahead of its time, the Cuban constitution of 1940 tried to prevent fly-by-night parties or candidates by requiring all parties to obtain at least 2 percent of the votes in every election and all candidates to run from said parties. That charter also ruled that, "The organization of political parties and associations is free. However, no political groupings of race, sex, or class may be formed."[107]

Latin America continued to display a variety of political party systems. At the same time, as in any polity, parties did not offer the only avenues to political influence, often taking a back seat to the military, the Church, business firms, landowners, labor unions, guerrillas, foreigners, and other interest groups. Among one-party dominant systems, some authoritarian governments tolerated only one party (for example in the Dominican Republic and Cuba) and some allowed only one party to win most of the time but permitted other parties to exist (Mexico).

Among competitive party systems, multiparty arrangements remained the most common. The most successful existed in Chile. Two-party systems with both capable of competing for a majority prevailed in Colombia, Venezuela, and Uruguay. Therein, one party normally dominated, most exceptionally the Colorados in Uruguay. The two main parties in all three countries persevered partly because they repeatedly forged power-sharing pacts with each other to avoid political breakdowns and the rise of political rivals. For many decades before Venezuela consolidated its party duopoly, Colombia and Uruguay joined Mexico and Chile in having the most vigorous enduring party systems in Latin America.[108]

However, robust political parties provided no guarantee against authoritarianism. Under resilient two-party systems, Colombia became more authoritarian in behavior during the National Front, while Uruguay succumbed in 1973 to a dictatorship that achieved notoriety for torture. In Latin America's hardiest multiparty system, increasingly ideological parties degenerated into "polarized pluralism," which helped cause the radicalization and breakdown of Chilean politics under President Allende. The disintegration of this system was an exceptional tragedy because "not only did Chile have the best record of constitutional government and free elections of any major Latin American country, but it also displayed the most highly structured party system of the continent."[109]

From the 1930s to the 1970s, new parties added to the traditional lineup of Conservatives, Liberals, secular centrist groups like the Radicals in Chile and Argentina, Socialists, Communists, and regional or personalistic vehicles. Within party spectrums, class and ideological cleavages became important alongside older religious or regional divisions. A few small fascist parties sprouted briefly in the 1930s. Much more importantly, new centrist reform parties dubbed Christian Democrats arose in several countries. They enjoyed the greatest success in Chile, Venezuela, El Salvador, and Peru.

Populist parties provided the most significant newcomers. They reflected the upsurge of the lower classes, especially organized labor. Usually dominated by personalistic electoral caudillos, these heterogeneous parties included the APRA in Peru, the Socialists in Chile from the 1930s to the 1950s, Democratic Action in Venezuela, the Perónists in Argentina, the MNR in Bolivia, the Brazilian Labor Party, and numerous smaller examples. In many cases, these populist parties generated not only expanded social participation and reform but also implacable resistance from élites, leading to polarization, stalemate, and breakdown.[110]

In the twentieth century, revolutionary parties also strode forth. Although powerful intermediaries between the state and society, they subordinated themselves to the government of the revolutionary élites. The heirs of the revolution commanded these parties in an authoritarian, vertical manner, mobilizing mainly workers and peasants. They claimed to be more than just another party, because they represented the revolution and the nation against excluded oligarchic enemies. They aspired to create hegemonic one-party systems, usually wiping out previous, historically fragile contenders. The revolutionary parties in Mexico and Cuba established their monopoly for a long period, but those in Bolivia and Nicaragua failed to maintain their grip on power.

Conclusion

From the 1930s to the 1970s, protected democracy temporarily ceded space to popular democracy, often captained by populists. Without discarding many of their traditional features, both political ideas and institutions reflected the demand for democracy to embrace social justice. The historically most democratic countries still led the way. Overall, however, no clear regime tendency took hold, as democracies alternated with dictatorships, either of which could be inclusionary or exclusionary. Both anarchy and especially tyranny continued to tear asunder democracies.

Among political institutions, constitutions multiplied and added social and economic guarantees to incorporate the unprivileged and national development. To serve these same purposes, central governments and presidencies expanded their size and power. Some chief executives increasingly respected civil liberties. Although gaining a little leverage, legislatures remained weak. Nevertheless, confrontations between conservative congresses and populist presidents frequently triggered military coups. Reformers made a few judiciaries more independent. But the courts revealed their lack of accessibility and their inability or unwillingness to defend human rights and constitutional democracy under dictatorships. In most cases, the strongest political parties and party systems sustained the hardiest democracies. While populist and leftist parties rose at the polls, they encountered defeat at the barracks.

Popular democracy achieved the greatest victories through elections. Reformers amplified the suffrage, enrolling vast numbers of women, illiterates, and young people, while deleting economic restrictions. Many countries installed direct elections, municipal elections, and proportional representation. The proliferation of voters, secret ballots, and electoral tribunals diminished fraud. These institutional advances facilitated breakthrough elections for the disadvantaged majority, which frightened the upper classes into abandoning democratic institutions.

In the context of the escalating Cold War of the 1960s and 1970s, both the left and the right increasingly turned against electoral democracy in Latin America. Inspired by Castro, many on the left argued that only undemocratic revolutionary means could bring about national development and social justice. Backed by the United States, many on the right feared that democracy was the antechamber rather than the antidote to revolution and so supported reactionary dictators.[111]

The military takeovers in Uruguay and Chile in 1973 produced the two most shocking losses for democracy. Most polling and electoral data indicated that the overwhelming majority of Uruguayans continued to favor democracy and moderate political positions up to the end, including 79 percent in late 1972. Surveys on the eve of the coup in Chile still showed that over two-thirds of the citizens opposed military intervention and rule. In both countries, the élites, not the masses, turned against these long-standing democratic regimes.[112]

After the dramatic democratic gains from the 1930s to the 1970s, the onslaught of a new dictatorial era in the 1960s and 1970s proved especially disappointing and sobering to democrats. The rightwing authoritarian forces mainly stamped out popular, populist, and leftist threats. In the most developed countries of the Southern Cone, events took a particularly grim turn as a new style of tyranny appeared. These bureaucratic authoritarian regimes became much more ruthless and long-lasting than previous auto cratic governments. It looked to some scholars as though modernization was leading to even worse despotisms, not democracies. It seemed to others that a deep-seated cultural propensity toward authoritarianism was reasserting itself.

Although structural or cultural arguments were hard to prove, one pattern remained indelibly clear. Once again, Latin America's conservative military and civilian élites had dispensed with democracy. The armed forces were key actors, but they did not act alone. In most of these latest cases, they did so with the backing of the hegemonic United States. They defeated democracy, but not for long. After the authoritarians delivered the harshest blows to popular democracy, a more cautious variety of protected democracy soon returned.[113]

Chapter 7

The Tsunami of Neoliberal Democracies, 1970s–2000s

Previous waves of democracy had rolled over Latin America, but never before had a tsunami flooded the entire region. From the late 1970s to the 2000s, Latin America became more democratic than ever before, but not because of any massive institutional engineering. The basic formal political rules and organizations for these democracies did not change much, but behavior did. Why did these enormous democratic regime transformations occur and endure?

Although the Latin Americans revised some constitutions and adopted several new ones, they maintained most of the key features from the past, along with an amplified emphasis on social rights. A majority of the political systems remained centralist rather than federalist. However, more decentralization than ever before, mainly to municipalities rather than provinces, became the biggest institutional innovation in the era.

Many political scientists advocated converting to parliamentary systems, but no country followed that advice. Presidents became even more powerful, despite the long-recommended fortification of not only sub-national governments but also legislatures and judiciaries. A few of the chief executives acquired the right to be reelected immediately. They exerted more control over the armed forces and almost never succumbed to military ouster. The new democracies restored civil liberties and human rights but continued to abuse them.

Still subordinate to presidents, legislatures and judiciaries nonetheless gained some stature, partly thanks to professionalization and foreign assistance. Also with the help of external consultants, elections became increasingly regular, inclusive, and honest, while the rules for voting stayed much the same. The biggest legal advance was the introduction of referenda and other forms of direct democracy. Political parties and multiparty systems proliferated and gained importance, yet remained fragile in most countries.

The new democracies surpassed their predecessors both in number and comportment. In terms of behavior, governments met higher standards than in the past in both assuming and exercising power. More presidents respected the constitutions and the rule of law. They imposed fewer and more restrained states of exception. Although some governments broke the rules and engaged in covert authoritarianism, virtually none established overt military dictatorships. When a few presidents fell because of pressures from the armed forces or social movements, their successors immediately restored constitutional procedures.[1]

Prior to the tsunami, the number of democracies in non-English-speaking Latin America hit the low watermark in 1978. The only widely recognized democratic regimes prevailed in Costa Rica, the Dominican Republic, Venezuela, and Colombia. None of those had existed without interruption since the end of World War II. The region deteriorated into one of the least democratic in the world.[2]

Suddenly from 1978 to 1992, transitions from authoritarianism to democracy cascaded over Latin America. Only Mexico and Cuba withstood that tidal wave. In both countries, a powerful official party ruled with revolutionary and nationalistic legitimacy, a solid, if shrinking, social base, and a tradition of resistance against U.S. political demands. The former finally completed its gradual transition with the election of Vicente Fox in 2000, while the latter held out under Fidel Castro.

Elsewhere in the region, democratization took place under three formats. First and most commonly, that process transpired under military tutelage or negotiation. It progressed from liberalization of an authoritarian regime to installation of a civilian democracy in Ecuador (1978–1979), Peru (through the 1979 Constitution and the 1980 election), Honduras (1980–1982), Bolivia (1982), El Salvador (1982–1984), Uruguay (1984), Brazil (1985), Guatemala (1985), Chile (1988–1990), and Paraguay (1989–1992). Second, Argentina returned to democracy in 1983 through the collapse of the military regime after its ill-fated war with Great Britain in the Malvinas/Falkland islands. Third, three transitions took place through the overthrow of the previous dictator. After destroying the Somoza autocracy in 1979, the

Sandinistas won the 1984 elections. Their attempt to establish a popular democracy under the hegemony of their revolutionary party ended with the victory of the opposition in the 1990 election. Haiti celebrated the downfall of the last of the Duvalier dynasty in 1986 and soon installed a restricted democracy in 1995. The United States invasion of Panama overthrew the dictator Manuel Antonio Noriega in 1989.

Although democracy spread unusually far in this period, continuities ran deep, both in the structure of democratic institutions and their most fertile locations. Neither the type of authoritarian regime nor the type of transition explained much about the subsequent type of democracy. Long-term historical factors and socioeconomic conditions exerted more influence. In the aftermath of the tsunami, the countries with the healthiest democracies exhibited the longest records of experience with democracy.

Rather than creating democracy from scratch, the more successful cases either revived democracy or maintained it. For example, Chile suffered from one of the most prolonged, effective, and brutal dictatorships. Pinochet controlled the transition and hobbled the restored democracy with authoritarian restrictions. Nevertheless, Chile quickly reestablished one of Latin America's most solid democracies based on its pre-authoritarian political traditions. In similar fashion, after forging a peace treaty with the dictatorship to guide the transition, Uruguay resurrected its prior long-standing democratic institutions. The continuing democracies in Costa Rica and, to a much lesser extent, Colombia also functioned better than most. With weaker democratic legacies and greater problems, Venezuela, Argentina, and Brazil performed less well but above average. In line with the least democratic historical antecedents, democracy remained rickety and riddled with authoritarian hangovers in Mexico and especially Central America, the Caribbean, the Central Andes, and Paraguay.[3]

For all its flaws, the Fitzgibbon survey of Latin American specialists every five years provided a continuous rough estimation of democracy in Latin America. From the highly authoritarian year of 1980 to the highly democratic year of 2000, the biggest improvements occurred in Uruguay, Chile, Argentina, and Brazil. The totals from all twelve surveys from 1945 to 2000 placed Costa Rica, Uruguay, and Chile at the top, and the Dominican Republic, Guatemala, Honduras, Bolivia, Paraguay, and Haiti at the bottom.[4]

At least from 1900 to 2000, democratic regimes exhibited as much durability as dictatorships, with each type lasting approximately twelve to thirteen years. Including many oligarchic republics, the most stable democracies had occurred from 1900 through the 1930s, averaging twenty-one years. From 1978 through 2000, democracies persisted an average of fifteen years, compared to fourteen years from 1940 to 1977. Democracies proved at least as hardy as dictatorships during the 1980s debt crisis. Throughout the century, however, instability remained common, with fifty-five regime changes between democratic and authoritarian systems.[5]

In the twentieth century, a few Latin American democracies were not extremely fragile but rather exceptionally durable. Since the 1930s, examples of long-lasting democracies include (chronologically): Chile, 1932 to 1973; Uruguay, 1939 to 1973; Brazil, 1945 to 1964; Costa Rica, 1948 to the present; Venezuela, 1958 to the present; Colombia, 1958 to the present; the Dominican Republic, 1970 to the present; and Ecuador, 1979 to the present. From 1979 to 1990, almost 90 percent of Latin America switched from authoritarian to democratic rule. Despite dire predictions and interruptions of constitutional government thereafter in Peru, Ecuador, Argentina, Venezuela, and Bolivia, not one country reverted to outright military dictatorship, except for a brief time in Haiti.[6]

Although tenacious, Latin American democracies from the 1980s to the 2000s were limited in several ways compared to their 1930s to the 1960s predecessors. While many became more democratic institutionally than the past variety, they tended to be less democratic socioeconomically and ideologically. Often inhibited by the nightmare of the previous dictatorships, advocates of social equality and leftwing ideologies lost ground. The extremely hierarchical structure of social power blocked more substantive changes toward democratic mobilization and benefits for the poor. Because of informal barriers to unbridled mass participation, representation, and demands, most of these institutionally *full democracies* became *protected* rather than *popular* democracies.

Most politicians marginalized organized labor and other social activists. The left participated with old or new labels, but not with its old ideas. Most leftists and other reformers evinced reluctance to deviate significantly from the broad parameters of the free-market, neoliberal economic model. They shied away from redistributive, nationalistic populism, let alone socialism. Instead, most governments reduced the state and social welfare programs. As a result, satisfaction with these sanitized democracies rose among the élites and declined among the unprivileged.[7]

From the 1970s up to the 2000s, populism in the classic sense largely disappeared in most presidential palaces. From the 1930s to the 1970s, that term had usually referred to a reformist, personalistic, often charismatic leader of a multi-class coalition emphasizing urban labor and advocating socioeconomic redistribution and nationalism. When scholars talked about *neopopulism* in the 1970s to the 2000s, they were normally just describing a personalistic political style, often practiced by outsiders. Disdaining and undermining institutions such as political parties, these politicians deployed that unmediated strategy to appeal directly to unorganized lower classes.

In contrast with classic *populism*, neopopulism was not as coherently useful as a concept. It included leaders from the right as well as the left and advocates as well as opponents of neoliberal economics. Although sometimes sounding like the populists of yore on the hustings, most of these politicians veered to the right once in office. As seen under so-called neopopulist neoliberal presidents Fernando Collor in Brazil, Carlos Menem in Argentina, and Alberto Fujimori in Peru, they exhibited virtually nothing in common with the classic populists except personalism, which they also used tepidly compared to the mass mobilization of their predecessors João Goulart, Juan Perón, and Victor Raúl Haya de la Torre. From the 1980s to the 2000s, the strategy, base, and policies of these neoliberals displayed almost no connection with the long-standing Latin American notion of popular democracy.

They also bore no substantive resemblance to other so-called neopopulists with no clear program, like Abdala Bucaram in Ecuador, or those opposed to neoliberalism at the end of this era, like the mavericks Hugo Chávez in Venezuela and Evo Morales in Bolivia. Although Chávez and Morales came closest to a classic definition of populism, neither of them relied heavily on organized labor. By 2006, it was too soon to tell if these Andean outliers would really implement some programs comparable to the nationalistic and redistributive socioeconomic policies more common from the 1930s to the 1970s.[8]

Despite improvements in their durability and operations, the tsunami democracies faced major challenges to their quality. Many democracies remained highly elitist, autocratic, centralized, presidential, personalistic, clientelistic, incompetent, and corrupt. They struggled to overcome trauma and fear from the dictatorships, root out authoritarian residues in institutions and attitudes, account for past human rights abuses, and bring the military under civilian control. Within the government, they still needed to strike the proper balance and accountability among the branches, enhance state capacities, and stamp out malfeasance. In their relations with society, they sometimes failed to enforce the rule of law, strengthen civil liberties, conduct clean elections, fortify political parties, and raise levels of support in public opinion. They also found it difficult to craft policies that would satisfy socioeconomic and regional vested interests and simultaneously achieve economic growth with equity. It remained unclear whether these regimes were consolidated and how they might become so.[9]

Above all, the deepening of democracy required a better job of representing and serving the lower classes. Somehow, these governments needed to address poverty and the highest levels of inequality on the planet without arousing the wrath of the privileged minority. Like all capitalist democracies, these administrations labored to impose their will over extremely powerful socioeconomic actors, both in the international and national arenas. In Latin America, foreign forces flexed exceptional strength, but domestic sectors still wielded the greatest authority. When Latin American political leaders were asked in 2002 who exercised the most power in their country, they ranked the national private business sector far ahead of political institutions, the former having grown in capacity under neoliberalism.[10]

In this era, the debate between protected and popular democracies did not differ much over the formal institutions, such as the extent of the suffrage. Both visions endorsed essentially the same institutional arrangements. Instead, they mainly clashed over the extent and quality of popular mobilization, participation, representation, and receipt of benefits. The two camps diverged over who exerted social power through or around the institutions.

The affluent abhorred a popular democracy that truly incorporated lower-class groups and demands, while the subalterns decried a protected democracy that effectively excluded their leaders and aspirations. Politicians confronted the challenge of devising a democracy that could embrace the disadvantaged without driving the wealthy to overturn it. In the absence of a solution to that conundrum, the comfortable classes and their protected democracies normally prevailed.

Largely because of the shortcomings of their governments, public support for democracy seldom rose very high. It eroded as the 1990s wore on, sometimes falling to dismally low levels. Since the new democracies still had a long way to go in developing sound institutions and meeting expectations, public opinion rendered highly critical judgments. The commitment of many Latin Americans to these political systems remained shallow and contingent on short-term outcomes.

More than a decade after democratization in most countries, a 1997 poll in South America and Mexico (still undemocratic) revealed that 62 percent of the respondents preferred democracy but 18 percent viewed authoritarianism as better on occasion. Only 36 percent expressed satisfaction with their democracy. While 16 percent said that democracy was fully established, 80 percent contended that many tasks remained to consummate a well functioning democracy. Among institutions, 71 percent of those polled registered confidence in the church, 49 percent the armed forces, 34 percent the judiciary, 37 percent the president, 33 percent the police, 33 percent the congress, and 26 percent the political parties. Only 30 percent believed the laws were obeyed, while 76 percent complained that there was no equality before the law. Sixty percent denounced the fraudulence of elections.

In this 1997 survey, the two historically strongest democracies in the Southern Cone—Chile and Uruguay—scored higher percentages, for example well above those for Argentina or Brazil. Although Chileans racked up similar percentages on some of the questions, they accorded political institutions higher marks: 42 percent expressed confidence in the judiciary, 61 percent in the president, 52 percent in the police, 54 percent in the congress, 35 percent in the political parties, and 68 percent in clean elections. Uruguayans also recorded higher than average percentages for political institutions and especially for a preference for democracy over authoritarianism (86 percent to 7 percent). Among Uruguayan respondents, 41 percent also thought that their democracy was fully established, 58 percent that their laws were obeyed, and only 47 percent that there was no equality before the law.[11]

In 1998 to 1999, massive surveys of political attitudes in the United States, Costa Rica, Mexico, and Chile found that most of these Latin Americans, in contrast with North Americans, conceptualized democracy much more in terms of socioeconomic wellbeing and equality, a viewpoint common to a vision of popular democracy. Mexicans and Chileans especially favored this outlook, whereas Costa Ricans placed closer to North Americans in their emphasis on democracy as a purely political good. 68 percent of the respondents in the United States, 54 percent in Costa Rica, 21 percent in Mexico, and 25 percent in Chile defined democracy as *liberty/freedom*. By contrast, 5 percent in the United States, 6 percent in Costa Rica, 21 percent in Mexico, and 18 percent in Chile identified democracy with *equality*. Respectively, 1 percent, 7 percent, 14 percent and 8 percent chose *welfare/progress*. In that same survey, on preference for democracy over other types of regimes, Costa Rica scored 84 percent, Mexico 51 percent, and Chile 53 percent.[12]

In 2000, region-wide polls still showed that a slight majority of Latin Americans always preferred democracy to authoritarianism, but that figure varied from a high of over 80 percent in Uruguay and Costa Rica to less than 40 percent in Brazil. Those respondents sometimes opting for authoritarianism averaged slightly below 20 percent, rising from 6 percent in Costa Rica to 39 percent in Paraguay. By contrast, dedication to democracy in the United States and Europe approximated the Uruguayan results.

This polling data also unveiled that satisfaction with the performance of democracy correlated strongly with preference for democracy in Latin America. Surveys further revealed great dissatisfaction with economic performance, corruption, and therefore with all the democratic political institutions, which fell beneath the armed forces and far beneath the church. The president outpolled the congress, judiciary, and the most disrespected of all, political parties.[13]

From 1995 to 2001, polls in every country uncovered a drop in the percentage of respondents always choosing democracy over all other forms of government. It fell 11 percent on average. On the question of satisfaction with democracy in 2001, only Costa Rica and Uruguay tallied close to 40 percent. When asked in 2001 to identify the most important trait of a democracy, respondents ranked elections first (26 percent), followed by an economic system with fair incomes for everyone (19 percent), equality before the law (16 percent), and freedom of speech (14 percent).

In the early 2000s, these increasingly negative opinions partly grew out of the economic recession at the turn of the century. In 2002, a public opinion survey discovered that just 56 percent of Latin Americans favored democracy over other forms of government, compared to 53 percent in Eastern Europe, 61 percent in East Asia, 69 percent in Africa, and 78 percent in the European Union. 55 percent of the Latin American respondents said they would accept authoritarianism that could cure economic ills. And 56 percent ranked economic development more important than democracy. Sizable minorities expressed support for presidents to ride roughshod over legal constraints. Over one-third thought that democracy could exist without legislatures, political parties, or independent media. Based on these responses, it appeared that about 43.0 percent of Latin Americans were committed democrats, 30.5 percent ambivalents, and 26.5 percent non-democrats.

From 2002 to 2003, support for democracy dipped from 56 percent to 53 percent, while satisfaction sank from 32 percent to 28 percent. Overall from 1997 to 2003, region-wide polls encountered support for democracy declining from 62 percent to 53 percent and satisfaction with democracy falling from 41 percent to 28 percent. Those disinclined to support democracy came disproportionately from the less educated groups.[14]

Although these numbers remained ominously low, they rebounded in 2005 and 2006, after the economies revived. The regional percentage preferring democracy climbed from 53 percent in 2005 to 58 percent in 2006. The 2006 figures reached a high of 77 percent in Uruguay compared with a low of 41 percent in Guatemala. The overall percentage expressing satisfaction with democracy rose from an average of 21 percent in 2001 to 31 percent in 2005 and to 38 percent in 2006. Those disparaging their elections as fraudulent slipped from 54 percent in 2005 to 49 percent in 2006. The polls tempered some evidence from elections and protests of mounting support for leftist critics of neoliberal economics. The 2006 survey found 44 percent of Latin Americans identifying with centrist, 32 percent with rightist, and only 24 percent with leftist political beliefs. On ranking current presidents in the Americas, they gave virtually the same lowest marks to Fidel Castro of Cuba, Alán García of Peru, Hugo Chávez of Venezuela, and George Bush of the United States.[15]

International and National Causes of the Tsunami

In some ways, it is easier to understand discontent with these democracies than it is to explain their phenomenal success at replacing dictatorships. Some institutional modifications may have solidified the tsunami, but more fundamental causes must have accounted for the wave itself, its size, and its longevity. Why did these democracies arrive, and why did they survive?

When so many political regimes moved in the same direction at the same time, individual national factors could not provide a plausible explanation. An historical cycle of change in regimes so vast, rapid, and uniform could not have been a coincidence. It could not have been merely the fortuitous result of myriad national, local, individual, and idiosyncratic conditions and decisions. Instead, the answer had to lie in the interactive transformation of broader external and internal forces and regimes.

Internationally, a rare confluence of forces moved in a democratic direction. If scholars focused on the results of direct, concrete, intentional, and official policies of foreign governments and agencies, external factors did not loom large in this wave of democratization. However, if they examined general currents and trends in the international arena, then outside influences looked more significant. Two types of international factors had to be taken into account. First, some global forces caused disorder, thus undermining dictators and strengthening their opponents. Second, other international currents made democratization and then its endurance the likely result of this turbulence.

In the global Third Wave of democratization, contagion by geographic clusters obviously recast Latin America as it had during independence and the end of World War II. The latest virus of democratization swept Southern Europe and Latin America from the 1970s through the 1980s and then Eastern Europe from the end of the Cold War in 1989 onward. The tsunami of democratization began with the downfall of the long-standing authoritarian regimes in Portugal (1974 to 1975) and Spain (1975 to 1979), as well as the briefer dictatorship in Greece (1974). The two Iberian transformations resonated loudly in Latin America, as had the displacement of their monarchs at the start of the nineteenth century.

This latest prairie fire of regime changes spread without any external power necessarily lighting or fanning the blaze intentionally. At the same time, conscious U.S. promotion of democracy in Latin America and the implosion of the Soviet regime in Eastern Europe provided part of the explanation. These diffuse and targeted external influences reached particular regions and countries in different ways. The diffuse factors traveled through demonstration effects and domestic learning, while the targeted factors arrived through public and private policies.[16]

Four clusters of international causes drove the democratic tsunami: economic, imperial, ideological, and domino factors. First, economic growth before and during the 1970s generated more complex societies demanding Western-style liberal economies and political systems. New technologies—especially cable television, fax machines, and personal computers and the internet—diffused such desires, helped people learn about successful democratization in other countries, and sapped the abilities of states to control their citizens.

Then the international recession and debt crisis of the early 1980s battered authoritarian regimes. It destroyed their image of economic efficiency and left them with shrinking resources, dwindling legitimacy, and mounting protests. During the 1980s and 1990s, the spread of neoliberalism and globalization undercut central governments, labor unions, leftists, and populists so that business executives and military officers saw democracy as less threatening and therefore worth keeping.

Besides economic factors, four of the most powerful entities in the world facilitated democratization by the start of the 1990s: the Vatican, the United States, Western Europe, and, in a neutral way, the former Soviet Union. The influence of the papacy on the Roman Catholic Church and the United States on the capitalists and the armed forces, pushed the three Latin American groups historically most prone to authoritarianism toward democracy. The end of the Soviet Union and the Cold War helped the Latin American democracies solidify without great rightwing fears of leftwing revolution or totalitarianism. Meanwhile, Western Europe and other international groups, including non-governmental organizations, joined the democratic chorus.

Of these imperial forces, the United States—as the sole remaining superpower from the late 1980s to the 2000s—exerted hegemony over Latin America as never before. It led the way in establishing an international context or regime favoring three interconnected codes of conduct. These three frameworks emphasized a security regime focused on the so-called war on

drugs and external enemies identified by the United States, an economic regime centered on neoliberalism promoted by the United States, and a political regime prescribing elected democracies endorsed by the United States.

All three regimes constrained the Latin American governments, their
sovereignty, and their maneuverability. The attempt to balance neoliberal
economic and political systems proved particularly frustrating. The limitations on the state imposed by the economic norms made it very difficult for
these shaky democracies to satisfy the social demands of their citizens, especially the poor. As a result, dissatisfaction with these democracies expressed
through polls, elections, and demonstrations mounted.[17]

Throughout the twentieth century, a superficial and uneven correlation
prevailed between political systems in Latin America and foreign policies of
the dominant power, the United States. During democratic eras in the region,
the U.S. government tended to support or at least accept many democracies. However, the connection between cause and effect remained unclear. In
most cases, the arrival of democracy in Latin America convinced the United
States to back it. In a few cases, U.S. promotion of democracy encouraged its
adoption in the region. And in still other cases, Washington helped destroy
democracy in Latin America through overt or covert methods.[18]

In this latest period, the United States played a contradictory role. Until
the late 1980s, the Cold War kept the United States sympathetic to anti-
communist dictators and leery of less vigilant democrats. After supporting military dictatorships in the 1960s and early 1970s, most infamously
in Brazil and Chile, Washington championed human rights and democracy under President Jimmy Carter in the late 1970s. The Colossus of the
North tried to take some credit for the surge of democratization in the
1980s and 1990s. Direct instruments employed by the United States to foment democracy included pronouncements by officials, annual reports on
human rights, economic, social, and technical assistance to democratizers,

TABLE 7.1

Latin American regimes and U.S. foreign policy, 1910s–2000s

Period	Dominant regime type in Latin America	Dominant U.S. foreign policy toward democracy
1910s–1920s	Democracy	Positive
1930s–1940s	Dictatorship	Neutral
1945–1948	Democracy	Positive
1948–1954	Dictatorship	Neutral/negative
1958–1963	Democracy	Positive
1964–1976	Dictatorship	Neutral/negative
1978–2006	Democracy	Positive

economic pressures, election observers, and even invasions in Grenada, Panama, and Haiti. However, in most cases, Washington essentially played a reactive role.

In the 1990s, while the United States endorsed most democracies, it exhibited more concern with promoting free markets and trade agreements. Meanwhile, international bodies like the Organization of American States became more active in defending democracy, with the OAS declaring a commitment in 1991. From 2001 on, the United States' War on Terror seemed unlikely to buttress democracy in Latin America.

In addition, ideologically, a renaissance of classic liberal economics and politics emanated from Washington and London, spearheaded by Reaganism and Thatcherism. At least as important was the universalization of the concept of human rights, including women's liberation. Finally, contagion spread democracy from one country to the next, making the subsequent fall of each dictatorship more likely. The new democracies pushed their neighbors to get on board. The democratizers next door learned the techniques for and the likelihood of toppling their own tyrant, while the authoritarians learned that democracy did not necessarily usher in communism, populism, economic disaster, social chaos, the reduction of national security, or the punishment of the armed forces.

By the same token, the global or regional context could endanger and even capsize these democracies in the future, as it has in the past. For example, economic depressions, wars, and anti-democratic ideologies could return to jeopardize these democracies. These regimes grappled with the challenge of constructing and consolidating democratic systems that could survive hostile international storms in the years to come.[19]

Although international factors were crucial for encouraging and sustaining democratization, national actors were also essential. During such a worldwide trend, domestic factors could determine the transmission, the reception, the translation, the character, the form, the pace, the timing, the mechanisms, the direction, and the outcome of political change in a particular country. Some nations could even resist and reject the global propensity toward regime change, but even they tended to liberalize more than they would have otherwise. The international environment offered opportunities to democratizers, but no guarantees. Ultimately, domestic forces had to take advantage of these openings to forge a winning coalition that could either defeat the tyrant or convince him that liberalization and even democratization were in his best interests. In many cases, they had to persuade the dictator that opening up the system would at least cost less than repression and minimize his losses if not maximize his gains.

As for domestic causes, no one could point to a convincing cultural theory of this sudden democratization, because Latin America's culture had not metamorphosed overnight. One possible internal explanation for the tsunami came from the level of socioeconomic development, as measured by per capita income, the share of the labor force in agriculture, and education. But those indicators had only a modest quantifiable effect on the presence of democracy in Latin American countries from 1945 to 1996. The overall level of development did not have as much of a statistical impact there as in the rest of the world, where it had been a reliable variable connected to democracy.

Instead, democracy flourished or floundered in Latin America almost regardless of the national level of socioeconomic wellbeing, except for the poorest countries. Indeed, the region as a whole reached a higher level of democracy compared to the rest of the world than its per capita income would have predicted. Compared to its level of development, Latin America contained both underachievers (e.g., Argentina and Mexico) and, perhaps more impressively, overachievers (e.g., Bolivia and Ecuador).

In general, it may be that a rising level of development over many decades had eventually made democracy more likely in Latin America. But it was hard to attribute the underlying cause of the recent democratization to striking gains in socioeconomic modernization because little in the fundamental structures had changed since the previous era, except perhaps in Central America. Moreover, neoliberal restructuring had not gone on long enough to account for the democratic trend.[20]

Along with economic developments, changing class structures, relations, and behaviors may have been factors in the tsunami. The upper and middle strata remained key players, and many of them now endorsed or accepted democracy as a safe alternative. Also important, the working class, after suffering more than other groups under many of the authoritarian regimes, helped promote democratization. Organized labor did so through its unions, political parties, and public demonstrations. It played a leading role in destabilizing the authoritarian regimes through strikes and protests and then pushing for democracy in Peru and Argentina. Workers played a secondary role in undermining the dictatorships and bringing about more ample democratization than the regimes had desired in Brazil, Uruguay, and Bolivia. Finally, laborers played a tertiary role as important disrupting and supporting actors in the élite-led democratization in Chile but virtually no role in the purely élite-engineered transition in Ecuador.[21]

Beyond these general explanations for the origins of these democracies, why did they prove to be exceptionally resilient? Nationally, many elites, politicians, and ordinary citizens decided that the unprecedented violations of human rights, economic mismanagement, and other egregious behavior by the outgoing military rulers meant that such regimes could never again be tolerated. The worst of the economic crisis in the early eighties was under control as most of these democracies settled in. They could blame the debt debacle on their predecessors. Inertia was on the side of these democracies, and most crises did not rise to the level of coup thresholds. At the same time, the economic disaster and restructuring undercut the very forces, such as organized labor, that previously had panicked the right and the military into making coups. In contrast with the radical threats from the 1930s to the 1970s, the left and populism declined and moderated, so that no comparable menace endangered the well-to-do in the new democracies.

Under the aegis of economic and political neoliberalism, protected democracies prevailed over popular democracies in terms of mass mobilization and benefits. These constrained democracies succeeded because international and national élites were more satisfied with their results. Since the privileged few and the armed forces had usually overthrown Latin American democracies, these political systems became stable in the 1980s and 1990s by catering to the interests of those dangerous groups.

The contingent voluntarism of the ruling classes seemed particularly important during the tsunami, when fundamental changes in economic, social, or cultural conditions, let alone irresistible pressures from the social underdogs, could not explain the gargantuan switch to democracy. The new regime's domination by élites, its receptiveness to foreign and domestic entrepreneurs, and its neglect of lower-class interests differed little from the performance of democracies in other parts of the capitalist world. However, the denial of popular democracy fueled the rise of mass discontent in societies plagued with so much poverty and inequality.[22]

More narrowly political factors also seemed of little utility for accounting for the democratic tsunami from the 1970s to the 1990s. While behavior and the international environment changed dramatically, culture, socioeconomic patterns, and institutions did not. The Latin Americans ignored widespread scholarly opinion that parliamentary systems were more likely to endure than presidential democracies. Attempts to counter presumptuous presidents with enhanced sub-national governments as well as national congresses and judiciaries made only a little headway. Claims that democracies could not last without firm civilian control over the military were gainsaid in Chile and Guatemala. Warnings that democracy could not survive without strong political parties and party systems fell on deaf ears in Brazil, Ecuador, Peru, and several other countries. Fears that democracies could not muddle through while neoliberal, free-market economics funneled resources to foreign lenders and denied social justice to the poor proved to be exaggerated. At least up to the 2000s, it seemed that so long as civilian and military élites agreed that protected democracies were desirable, almost regardless of other variables, those democracies could persevere, despite their shortcomings.[23]

Neoliberal versus New Left Democratic Ideas

The biggest change in thinking about democracy was the emphasis on its intrinsic value as a set of institutions and procedures rather than outcomes. Many Latin Americans moved away from popular democracy toward protected democracy, or at least closer to the U.S. view of democracy as essentially a way to organize governance. At a minimum, even most socialists welcomed stable electoral democracy as providing relief from the authoritarian past and as giving advocates of social reform an opportunity to bid for power. During and for a time after democratization, most leaders put notions of social justice on the back burner so as not to derail democratization. Once representative democracy became fairly well established in the region, three concepts about its functioning emerged: protected neoliberal democracies and two versions of new left democracies, one social democratic and the other popular democracies.[24]

Conservative politicians favored protected procedural democracies without mobilizing the masses or embracing welfare programs. They stressed the limitations of democratic institutions and the state. Opposed to extensive government interventions, they hailed neoliberal market mechanisms as the solutions to social problems, albeit sometimes aided by targeted programs for the poor. Examples of these rightwing proponents of protected democracies included presidents León Febres Cordero (1984–1988), Sixto Durán-Ballén (1992–1996), and Jamil Mahuad (1998–2000) in Ecuador, Julio María Sanguinetti (1985–1989) in Uruguay, Fernando Collor de Melo (1989–1992) in Brazil, Carlos Saúl Menem (1989–1995, 1995–1999) in Argentina, Alberto Fujimori (1990–1995 and 1995–2000) and Alejandro Toledo (2001–2006) in Peru, Gonzalo Sánchez de Losada (1993–1997 and 2001–2003) in Bolivia, Vicente Fox (2000–2006) and Felipe Calderón (2006–?) in Mexico, and Álvaro Uribe (2002–2006 and 2006–?) in Colombia.[25]

Dissatisfaction with neoliberal democracy grew around the turn of the century. Between the advocates of protected and popular democracy arose the social democratic new left in Latin America, mainly in the more developed economies and democracies. These presidents included Ricardo Lagos (2000–2006) and Michelle Bachelet (2006–?) in Chile, Tabaré Vázquez

(2004–?) in Uruguay, and above all, Luiz Inácio Lula da Silva (known as "Lula") (2002–2006 and 2006–?) in Brazil. These moderate reformers believed in democracy both as institutional procedures and as socioeconomic outcomes. They adhered to constitutional limitations on their power and the broad constraints of neoliberalism on their policies, but they promoted greater relief and equity for the impoverished. They did so within the framework of elected, representative democracy, eschewing the intense rallying of the poor against the national and international bourgeoisie practiced by Hugo Chávez, Evo Morales, and Rafael Correa.[26]

The new left champions of popular democracy railed against unsatisfactory socioeconomic performance under neoliberalism. They particularly complained about low levels of growth combined with high levels of poverty and inequality. This discontent dovetailed with protests against unresponsive, élitist, and corrupt political systems that denied the lower classes effective participation, representation, and benefits.

President Chávez (1998–2000, 2000–2006, 2006–?) of Venezuela embodied this countercurrent with his inchoate nationalistic vision of Bolivarian socialism. Although not articulated in any coherent ideology, his notion of *popular sovereignty* echoed the age-old dream in Latin America of *popular democracy*. As this charismatic strongman evoked past populist refrains, he placed more emphasis on majoritarian rule and social reform for the masses than on institutional checks and balances. Ruling a quasi-authoritarian democracy between tyranny and anarchy, "Chávez is not a dictator, but he's not a Thomas Jefferson either," observed one of his opponents after the president's re-election to a third term with 62 percent of the votes in 2006. Chávez wove bonds of solidarity with Castro (1959–?) in Cuba, elected presidents Morales (2005) in Bolivia and Correa (2006–?) in Ecuador, and others.[27]

Refining Political Institutions for Democratization

In broad terms, the historical institutional traditions of Latin America outshone any other factors in shaping the architecture of these new democracies. Almost regardless of international trends, lessons from abroad or the past, social science theories, authoritarian legacies, modes of transition, mild reforms, or the character of the new democratic governments, these countries stuck with their basic long-standing constitutional and electoral systems. In essence, they remained centralist and presidentialist, with a weak congress elected through proportional representation, a pallid judiciary, and unstable and undisciplined multiparty systems. Decentralization provided the most significant institutional reform. The only clear institutional difference between the most successful democracies—Costa Rica, Chile, and Uruguay—and the rest seemed to be sturdy systems of political parties, not governmental rules and regulations.[28]

DEMOCRATIZING CONSTITUTIONS

From the 1970s into the 2000s, constitutional stability outstripped all previous periods. The Latin Americans adopted fewer than twenty new charters, a lower number per country and per year than ever before. They did not feel the need to change constitutions frequently or to alter them fundamentally in order to enhance democracy. Instead, those documents held fast along with the new regimes.[29]

Before the tsunami, constitutional practices moved in an undemocratic direction. In Chile, Uruguay, Argentina, and Brazil, the bureaucratic authoritarian regimes circumvented previous democratic constitutions. They did so by suspending their application in full or in part, decreeing laws that made them either inoperable or perverted, or rewriting them altogether.

The military autocracies in Chile and Uruguay drafted new constitutions to constrain their successors. These charters envisioned a highly protected democracy shielded by extraordinary powers for the president and the armed forces. Alongside such authoritarian features, these documents still prescribed the basic outlines of an electoral democracy for the next regime. Even these extreme dictatorships saw no alternative to eventual restoration of some version of a constitutional democracy. These countries' constitutional and electoral traditions remained vibrant enough that even the heavy-handed military generally adhered to the laws they wrote, sought to be legitimized by voters, and stepped down when they lost the plebiscites they called.

In a plebiscite controlled by Pinochet in 1980, Chile adopted the most enduring authoritarian constitution. The dictatorship tailored it for a protected democracy to take over at the end of the 1980s. That document mandated another plebiscite in 1988 to choose the next president.

After voters failed to extend Pinochet's tenure in that election, the armed forces accepted the results, much to his surprise. They also tolerated mild constitutional reforms passed in 1989. Those amendments watered down prohibitions against ideologically leftist parties, eliminated the ban on union leaders being party members, weakened the militaristic National Security Council, and reduced the presidential term from eight to four years. After assuming office in 1990, Chile's democratic governments struggled to eliminate other authoritarian residues, principally the autonomy and oversight of the armed forces, non-elected senators, and an electoral system biased toward the rightwing minority.[30]

The Uruguayan military regime pretended to be governing under the 1966 Constitution. However, the despots suspended the congress, political parties, and elections, as well as numerous individual rights and liberties. Like Pinochet, they attempted to incorporate all their restrictions on freedom into a new constitution. The military designed a contradictory document maintaining most of the provisions of the 1966 charter while tacking on new national security powers for the president and the armed forces. They included a national security council similar to Pinochet's and guaranteed that the president's party would control a majority of the seats in the legislature.

To the Uruguayan dictatorship's surprise, its opponents voted that charter down in a plebiscite on November 30, 1980—just two months after Pinochet's undemocratic constitution had reputedly won approval in Chile. Showing the continuing significance of constitutions and elections, at least in Uruguay, that defeat began the breakdown of the authoritarian regime. After extensive negotiations with the opposition, the armed forces fully restored democratic rule under the 1966 constitution in 1984.[31]

Most of the transitions to democracy included reforming the old constitution or writing a new one, even though most provisions changed little from the past. While many countries kept their constitutions from the previous era or reformed them slightly, eleven (Ecuador, Peru, Chile, Honduras, El Salvador, Guatemala, Nicaragua, Haiti, Brazil, Colombia, and Paraguay, in chronological order) adopted new charters. Decentralization became the most novel institutional innovation. Also in accord with neoliberalism, a few constitutions enshrined a limited state. Lawmakers hoped these reforms would encourage democracy over dictatorship.[32]

Many new or revised constitutions also expanded social rights. Some stressed indigenous prerogatives: Guatemala in 1985, Colombia 1991, Mexico and Paraguay 1992, Peru 1993, Bolivia and Panama 1994, Nicaragua 1995, Ecuador 1998, and Venezuela 1999. As with many legal provisions, however, implementation left a lot to be desired.[33]

The first democratizer was historically one of the least successful. Using time-honored methods for regime change, Ecuador approved its new constitution of 1978 in a referendum. That document replaced its predecessor from 1945 and sixteen previous ones since 1830, which had lasted an average of nine years. It returned the country to democracy, which now held on longer than any prior attempt, including the previous record from 1948 to 1961.

Ecuadorean lawmakers tried to strengthen elected administrations by requiring a majority runoff for president and vice-president. The drafters also listed new economic, social and political rights, including referenda and popular initiatives. In 1998, Ecuador replaced this constitution with a similar one endorsing indigenous prerogatives.[34]

In like fashion, the 1979 constitution in Peru paved the way for an elected president in 1980. Following the typical Latin American procedure, an elected constituent assembly composed the new charter. It incorporated many of the social changes championed by the unusually reformist military governments from 1968 to 1980.

Like the Nicaraguan and Brazilian constitutions of the 1980s, this Peruvian blueprint set new standards for progressive principles, social guarantees, and declarations of human rights. For example, it prohibited *latifundia* and social discrimination. It promised "the creation of a just, free, and cultured society, without exploited or exploiters, exempt from all discrimination by reason of sex, race, creed or social condition, where the economy is at the service of man and not man at the service of the economy." The constitution vowed to eliminate "underdevelopment and injustice." It also proclaimed that: "The State rejects all forms of imperialism, colonialism, neocolonialism and racial discrimination. It is in solidarity with the oppressed peoples of the world." In 1993 President Fujimori replaced this document with another slightly modified constitution. Approved in a referendum, it followed neoliberal doctrines by shrinking the state and promoting decentralization.[35]

In four cases of democratization rather than re-democratization, the new Central American constitutions exhibited many features in common. These countries shared numerous historical and structural commonalities as well as small size. They influenced each other, enacted their constitutions in the same span of years in the 1980s, and imbibed some provisions from Costa Rica and the United States. Overall, their new charters reflected the usual outline in Latin America but with a few facets distinctly Central American.

Typically, constituent assemblies crafted these Central American constitutions. They usually created centralism with a nod to decentralization by allowing municipal elections. They also authorized presidents and vice presidents elected by a majority runoff, a unicameral legislature with appointive and investigative powers beyond those normally found on paper in South America, a constitutional court, electoral tribunals, referenda and popular initiatives, regulations for political parties to encourage larger and more durable organizations, and extensive socioeconomic rights normally honored in the breach. Outside constitutional arrangements, these governments remained under the thumb of rightwing forces, namely the concentrated socioeconomic interests, the military, and the United States.

As the bandwagon of constitutional democratization rolled through Central America, the Honduran constitution of 1982, its sixteenth, accorded great powers to a central government presided over by a president chosen by a simple plurality. For the first time in its history, El Salvador embarked on a sustained period of constitutional democracy, however limited and flawed. It consecrated the constitution of 1983 to establishing an electoral democracy that could bring peace out of a horrendous civil war. A conservative document, it envisioned a lean role for the state in the context of an economy driven by the private sector. Although it called for voters to elect municipal authorities, it designated the president to appoint governors. After the peace accords in 1992, El Salvador modified this constitution slightly to incorporate the agreements about human rights, elections, and the armed forces.

Guatemala's 1985 constitution founded a highly centralist and presidentialist democracy with extensive powers for the armed forces. It barred from the presidency anyone who had held that office unconstitutionally, a rebuke to former dictators. The democratization of Nicaragua commenced with the 1979 Sandinista revolution against Anastasio Somoza Debayle, heir to the dynastic familial dictatorship founded in 1936. After elections began in 1984, the revolutionary government codified the new democratic system in the 1987 constitution. It paid special attention to socioeconomic rights in the context of the Sandinista ideology.[36]

In 1988, Brazil constructed perhaps the most sweeping new, post-authoritarian constitution. Dubbed *the citizen's constitution*, it surpassed the Mexican document of 1917 in spelling out individual and social rights. After a prolonged period of authoritarian rule beginning in 1964, this democratizing manifesto heralded protecting the individual from the state and guaranteeing state services to underprivileged individuals and groups.[37]

In 1991, Colombia finally replaced the 1886 constitution through an elected national constituent assembly. The drafters sought to fortify democratic participation after the exclusionary National Front. This objective echoed other constitutional reforms throughout Latin America, but in this case within an existing democracy. The Colombian document bolstered decentralization and regional powers, required a majority runoff for president and vice-president, regulated the frequent states of exception, strengthened the legislature versus the chief executive, inaugurated new types of elections such as referenda, and defended political as well as socioeconomic rights.[38]

The Paraguayan Constitution of 1992 established a rare and flimsy democracy in a country with an elongated history of authoritarianism. In most respects, the charter replicated its counterparts in the rest of the region. It innovated by making the president and vice-president elected by a plurality and former democratic presidents senators for life.[39]

In 1999, Venezuela introduced its new constitution to supersede the one from 1961. An elected constituent assembly penned the fresh document and then a referendum approved it. That charter strengthened the central government and the presidency, with its term lengthened to six years and reelection permitted. It also created a weaker unicameral legislature, with guaranteed indigenous representation. Although hailed by the administration as a breakthrough for democracy, the new basic law of the land helped President Chávez take control of all branches of government.[40]

DEMOCRATIC DECENTRALIZATION AND MUNICIPALIZATION

Whereas centralization intensified in the 1930s to the 1970s, the global trend of decentralization coursed through Latin America in the 1980s to the 2000s. Hence democratization went unusually deep as well as broad. While federalism had mainly countered centralism in the nineteenth century, now municipalism asserted its claim. After *demunicipalization* from independence through the 1970s, *municipalization* took hold, even though most countries remained highly centralist.[41]

More than ever before in Latin America, many governors, state legislators, mayors, and city councilors obtained their positions through elections, wielded substantial authority, decided significant policies, and managed non-trivial fiscal revenues. Increasingly, these posts became rungs on the ladder to national offices. From 1980 to 1995, the direct election of mayors proliferated from three to seventeen countries. By the end of the 1990s, every country held municipal elections, while only six elected provincial governments with governors and legislatures. The latter comprised the four ongoing federalist countries of Mexico, Venezuela, Argentina, and Brazil, plus centralist Colombia and Ecuador.

The decentralizers advocated these innovations to increase both their own power and the legitimacy of wobbly democracies with low levels of public support. The impetus for decentralization normally came not from civil society but from national and sub-national political élites calculating their potential gains. Most decentralizations trickled down from the top, for example historically from competing national politicians in Chile and Uruguay. After the tsunami, political parties in power in the central government sometimes devolved electoral rights, governing authority, and financial resources to lower offices because they believed their future election prospects might be brighter below the national level. In the wake of the debt disaster, the fiscal crisis of the state also fostered the transfer of some taxes and services to local governments. Foreign agencies helped promote decentralization as complementary to the shrinkage of the central government prescribed by neoliberalism.

A few decentralizations percolated up from the bottom. Historically governors in Argentina and Brazil had promoted it, and now political parties and social movements with a stronger local than national base did so. Sometimes pressures for decentralization emanated from both the top and the bottom.

Especially in countries recovering from authoritarian rule but also in democracies losing support, reformers expected that decentralization would improve democracy. They believed it would enhance participation, representation, access, accountability, efficacy, efficiency, and legitimacy. Decentralizers also hoped it would invigorate a democratic civil society, energize new social and political movements at the grassroots, and render future centralist dictatorships less likely. However, they confronted the danger that decentralization would empower local bosses to expand their clientelistic and corrupt fiefdoms, to dominate the municipal councils as directly elected mayors, and to undermine the authority of feeble central governments.[42]

During the tsunami, no Latin American countries switched from centralism to federalism, but Argentina, Brazil, Mexico, and Venezuela fortified their existing federal systems. Contradictory crosscurrents promoted major decentralization in the 1980s and minor recentralization in the 1990s. From the 1930s into the 1970s, federalism had lost significance, both in Argentina and Brazil, as the central executive far overshadowed the provinces and the congress. Then in the 1980s, the new region-wide emphasis on decentralization breathed some life back into federalist institutions and even ceded greater autonomy to municipalities, always stronger in Brazil than in Argentina.

For example in Brazil, the 1988 constitution transferred more powers from the central to the provincial and municipal governments. The Brazilian states bargained effectively with the presidency and thwarted some of its initiatives. Even when presidents reclaimed some powers from sub-national units in the 1990s, Argentina and especially Brazil remained the most decentralized political systems in Latin America.[43]

In the six countries electing provincial officials, all picked their governors in direct elections. Only Brazil required an absolute majority. Mexico (the most consistently anti-reelectionist country in Latin America at every level), Colombia, and Ecuador prohibited reelection. For election to the state legislatures, all but Mexico used proportional representation, and all employed closed lists controlled by the political parties. In short, the provincial system tended to replicate the national system.

Historically, elected municipal councilors had selected most mayors who had been elected, as in the French system, which still prevailed in Mexico, Nicaragua, and Bolivia. Even when the president appointed mayors, voters almost always directly elected councilors, usually under a system of proportional representation, often the D'Hondt system. Typically voters marked a closed party list with candidates ranked by the party, which underscored party control and identification. Since they had to choose parties rather than individuals, voters still lacked complete control over picking the winners.

Now voters also directly elected most mayors, sometimes in imitation of the U.S. model. The central governments restrained their historic penchant for intervening in local elections to choose the mayor. Henceforth mayors needed just a plurality, except in Guatemala and Brazil, which required a runoff in the more populous municipalities if no one received 51 percent. Most mayors could be reelected, save in Mexico, Colombia, and Paraguay.[44]

Decentralization to the provinces and municipalities took big strides in the Andes, which broke with a long history of centralization. For example, the Peruvian Constitution of 1979 gave new powers to the provinces. Its neoliberal successor in 1993 promised that elected officials would run the regional and municipal governments, albeit still within a centralized system. Although President Fujimori recentralized some powers in the 1990s, President Toledo reinvigorated decentralization in the early 2000s.

Colombia added the direct election of mayors in 1988, which allowed smaller, newer parties to win some posts along with the traditional Conservatives and Liberals. Then the constitutional reforms of 1991 expanded administrative decentralization and installed popular election of governors. Ecuador also implemented administrative decentralization within a unitary system, establishing elected provincial and municipal authorities.

Venezuela inaugurated elections for governors and mayors in 1989, followed by fiscal and policy decentralization in the 1990s. That empowerment of federalism and municipalism weakened the central government and the two traditional political parties. After filling that void at the top in 1998, Chávez tried to carry out recentralization but backed off in the face of vigorous resistance from the states and municipalities. Even traditionally highly centralist Bolivia put through one of the most massive decentralizations in 1994. It launched the election of municipal councils and mayors and allocated to them substantial government revenues.[45]

Whereas in many countries national democratization spawned decentralization, in Mexico the opposite occurred. In the twentieth century, Mexico convened state and municipal elections with greater regularity than any other country in Latin America. One key reason was the absence of military coups. Another was the ruling party's ability to stage manage these elections through systematic chicanery. Indeed, the PRI was created partly to bring regional and local bosses under its control. Their inability to be reelected also deprived these officials of substantial autonomous power.

As their elections became more competitive in the 1980s, Mexico's provincial and municipal officials began to assert themselves. They became stepping stones from local to national democratization. This process illustrated that democratic institutions could make a difference over time, even when authoritarian rulers had turned them into a farce. Democratizers could capture those institutions and demand that the rulers live up to previously cynical claims about the democratic character of those offices.[46]

PERSISTENT PRESIDENTIALISM

Despite an academic chorus in favor of parliamentary democracies, all Latin Americans stuck with presidential systems. They did so out of habit, out of the hope that they would win the presidency, or out of a belief that the presidential arrangement was actually better for their democracies. Many still thought they needed a powerful president to spearhead national development, maintain order, and symbolize the nation at home and abroad.

Although presidentialism appeared in a few other Third World countries, it mainly took root in Latin America and the United States or in countries under heavy U.S. influence, such as South Korea and the Philippines. In the twentieth century, the historical record around the globe showed presidential democracies to be less durable than parliamentary ones. From 1945 to 1994, among stable democracies in the world lasting at least twenty-five years, twenty had parliamentary governments and only seven had presidential systems: Costa Rica, Venezuela, Colombia, Chile, Uruguay, the Philippines, and the United States. In that time span, all of the Latin American cases except Costa Rica endured authoritarian rule.

Among academics, some criticized presidentialism for excluding the losers from executive power, encouraging authoritarian behavior, making the chief executive hard to remove legally during a fixed term, and generating conflicts with the legislature. It also facilitated victories by personalistic, inexperienced candidates independent from established political parties as well as congress. All these problems provoked coups d'état.

Nevertheless, other scholars praised presidentialism for providing fixed terms in office as well as checks and balances with the legislature. A popularly elected president helped legitimize the new democracies, while neither legislatures nor political parties inspired the confidence necessary for a stable, effective parliamentary system. A directly elected president provided exceptional identifiability and accountability for the voters, while a proportionately elected legislature furnished exceptional representativeness for voters. Such a presidency could conceivably contribute to democratic consolidation, particularly if it was not too powerful vis-à-vis the congress and if it was based on a broad coalition. Despite the cautions of the partisans of parliamentary systems, most successful democracies of all types around the world developed strong chief executives.

Amidst the academic debate between parliamentary and presidential alternatives, Brazil held a referendum on the issue in 1993. First, voters selected a republic over a monarchy by 69 percent, and then a presidential over a parliamentary system by 59 percent.[47]

From the 1980s to the 2000s, Latin American presidencies stayed much the same as in the past, as did the requirements. Usually the candidates for president had to be citizens by birth. The minimum age for presidents and senators ranged from twenty-five to forty years of age, and for deputies from eighteen to thirty years of age. A few countries banned the clergy from the presidency. For example, the Argentine chief executive had to be a native or the son of a native, but the constitutional reform of 1994 eliminated the requirement of belonging to the Catholic faith.[48]

After Argentina jettisoned its electoral college in 1994, no Latin American country followed the U.S. example of indirect election of the president. Voters had more sway in the majority of countries (Mexico, Honduras, El Salvador, Nicaragua, Costa Rica, Panama, the Dominican Republic, Colombia, Chile, Argentina, Paraguay, and Uruguay) that used national primary elections for presidential candidates at least once from 1990 to 2001. A minority still did not hold presidential elections at the same time as those for congress. Thus chief executives frequently locked horns with legislators. However, Mexico, all of Central America (except El Salvador), Venezuela, Ecuador, Peru, Bolivia, Paraguay, and Uruguay (which required voters to choose the same party for the presidency and congress) normally scheduled presidential and congressional elections together. By the mid-1990s, the presidential terms varied from four to six years, for an average of 4.72 years in length. Reducing the presidential term to four years became the trend in the era.[49]

As in the past, most Latin American presidential systems did not allow for immediate reelection. By the 1990s, some countries, especially those with long histories of authoritarian rule, disallowed any reelection of the president ever (Mexico, Guatemala, Honduras, Nicaragua until 1995, Costa Rica, Colombia from 1991 until 2006, and Paraguay), some until two terms out of office (Panama and Venezuela until 2000), and some until one term out of office (El Salvador, the Dominican Republic, Colombia before 1991, Ecuador, Peru before Fujimori's change in 1995, Bolivia, Chile, Argentina before Menem, and Uruguay). Under pressure from popular chief executives, some South American countries switched to permit reelection for two consecutive terms (Venezuela under Chávez, Colombia under Uribe, Peru under Fujimori, Argentina under Menem, and Brazil under Cardoso). No country authorized unlimited reelection, although Nicaragua, the Dominican Republic, and Paraguay had done so at the start of the decade.

Despite some relaxation of the prohibition against reelection, feelings still ran strong against perpetuation in office. According to the Honduran constitution, "Alternation in the exercise of the presidency of the Republic is obligatory" and to be defended by the armed forces. The declaration in the 1983 constitution of El Salvador showed the continuing salience of the reelection issue: "Alternation in the exercise of the presidency of the republic is indispensable for the maintenance of the established form of government and political system. The violation of this norm requires insurrection."

The restrictions on reelection inhibited *continuismo*. However, they also reduced presidential accountability to the electorate, unless the chief executives cared about the future chances of their party. Furthermore, these rules disclined legislators to cooperate with a president who could not continue in power. Proponents of allowing reelection also pointed out that it constituted less of a threat to democracy now that elections were clean. When countries instituted reelection, they sometimes reduced the presidential term, for example from six to four years in Argentina and from five to four in Brazil.[50]

Most countries changed their presidential elections from simple plurality contests to require a second round in the absence of a majority winner. They mandated runoffs only if the leading candidate fell below a particular percentage in Costa Rica (40%), Argentina (45%), and Nicaragua (45%). Meanwhile Guatemala, El Salvador, Haiti, the Dominican Republic, Colombia, Ecuador, Peru, Bolivia, Chile, Paraguay, Uruguay, and Brazil adopted strict majoritarian runoffs.

Reformers promoted runoffs to give presidents a bigger popular base, more legitimacy, and a centrist orientation. The specter of Allende's minority leftist government in Chile motivated some advocates. They also hoped to transform a fragmented multiparty system into, in effect, a stable two-party system.

Contrary to some expectations, runoff systems actually encouraged the proliferation of parties and candidates. Many contenders had a long shot in the first round, even though they often forged alliances for the second round. In fact, plurality presidential elections were more likely to induce contests with fewer parties and even two-party systems. Runoffs were more prone to generate divided government by producing different results for political parties in the non-concurrent presidential and legislative elections, by denying the president a majority in congress, and by opening the door to outsider presidents without strong parties. In terms of tradeoffs, plurality elections risked producing a president with a small winning percentage, while absolute majority elections risked producing a president with an even smaller base in congress.[51]

The power of presidents varied depending on the authority prescribed in the constitution, the strength of other governmental institutions, the size and discipline of their party and its representation in the legislature, the extent of their support among voters and élite actors, and historical traditions. Chile, Colombia, Peru, Ecuador, and Brazil hosted unusually strong presidents based solely on their constitutional endowments. But the last four possessed rather ineffectual ones based on the representation of their parties in congress. Weaker constitutional presidential powers were associated with longer lasting democracies in the United States, Costa Rica, the Dominican Republic, Venezuela (even after Chávez bolstered the legal leverage of that office), and Uruguay. However, Mexico, Honduras, El Salvador, Nicaragua, Bolivia, and Paraguay also gave their presidents lesser legal authority, without noticeably improving democracy.[52]

In expectation that Pinochet would succeed himself, Chile's quasi-authoritarian constitution of 1980 created one of Latin America's most formidable presidencies. The new charter granted that officeholder exceptional capacity to name government officials and to cow the legislature. This potentate also possessed ample abilities to suspend constitutional guarantees during external or internal emergencies. However, the constitution checked the chief executive by ceding extraordinary authority to the military. Although extremely powerful, presidents could not leave Chile for more than thirty days or during the last ninety days of their term without senate approval.[53]

Regardless of comparisons within Latin America, all the countries retained strong presidents, much more awesome in law and practice than in the United States. After the tsunami, many presidents actually became more powerful, particularly where they had to be elected by majorities and could be reelected. They continued to browbeat the legislature, the judiciary, and the provinces and municipalities. Even as those subordinate institutions gained strength, the chief executives expanded their arsenals to maintain their preeminence. Presidents maintained wholesale appointment powers, with only a few offices subject to congressional approval. Furthermore, they preserved the constitutional right to impose regimes of exception, although now less frequently and with more restrictions in some countries, including Colombia and Ecuador. However, a few countries, including Venezuela, bolstered presidential regime of exception authority.

Presidents presided as commander-in-chief over the armed forces, which also maintained significant perquisites and prerogatives but fewer than in the past. Many chief executives exerted greater influence over military budgets, personnel, and behavior. They no longer governed with much fear of military ouster. Although the armed forces remained powerful behind the scenes and retained the capacity to intervene, they rarely removed any administrations with a coup d'état, let alone a sustained takeover. From 1978 to 2000, fifteen successful coups occurred before the restoration of democracy (two in Guatemala, one in Honduras, one in El Salvador, one in Panama, four in Haiti, five in Bolivia, and one in Paraguay) but only two short-lived affairs thereafter (one each in Ecuador and Haiti); all of them took place in countries historically exceptionally prone to dictatorships.[54]

Presidents still lorded over congress in many ways. They had more control over the legislative agenda and usually much higher success rates for their legislation than did their U.S. counterparts. Unlike the U.S. president, most could propose legislation. They usually possessed the exclusive right to introduce certain types of bills, including budgets. Many also enjoyed the authority to insist on urgent action on their proposals. Except in Mexico, Honduras, Nicaragua, Costa Rica, Venezuela, and Paraguay, presidents also wielded strong vetoes, which normally required a two-thirds vote of the legislature to override.

Numerous chief executives could also make laws by decree in lieu of action by the congress, notably in Argentina, Brazil, Colombia, Venezuela, Chile, Guatemala, Bolivia, Ecuador, and Peru. Moreover, some chief executives expanded their decree authority, both under normal conditions and under states of exception, although the legislature frequently authorized and circumscribed their decree power. For example, Argentina reformed its constitution in 1994, particularly to permit decree legislation and popular initiative, as well as to shorten the presidential term to four years, to allow for one immediate reelection, and to establish a two-round system.[55]

Weighing legal presidential powers over legislation required assessing four attributes: package veto, item veto, decree authority, and exclusive powers to introduce certain key legislation (the first two being *reactive* powers and the second two being *proactive* powers). By these constitutional measures, the highest presidential leverage in the late 1990s, in descending order, existed in Argentina, Chile, Colombia, Peru, Brazil, and Ecuador, the lowest in Costa Rica, Honduras, Mexico, Nicaragua, Paraguay, and Venezuela. This ranking suggested that some strong presidencies, as historically in Mexico, rested on non-constitutional factors, such as domination by the president's political party and intimidation by custom, tradition, and other means not spelled out in the law.[56]

Like the caudillos of yesteryear, some Latin American presidents still turned their political systems into *delegative democracies*. Once delegated power by the voters, they governed as though they stood above the law, constitution, and other institutions, largely only constrained by their term in office. They tolerated minimal accountability. Above all, presidents continued to seek ways to master or skirt the legislature. They charged that it was cantankerous, corrupt, and counterproductive. Divided government made it particularly tempting for presidents to engage in authoritarian behavior in order to bypass the legislature. For example they ruled by decree, stretched their powers beyond legal limits, or, in rare cases, dissolved the congress.

Presidents Collor—in Brazil during 1989 to 1992—and Menem—in Argentina from 1989 to 1999—tried repeatedly to circumvent the legislature. Most egregiously, Fujimori in Peru simply closed the congress with a self-coup in 1992. He followed up in 1993 with a new constitution that beefed up his powers, allowed immediate presidential reelection, and shrank the legislature into a unicameral body. Since the legislators remained recalcitrant thereafter, Fujimori resorted to bribes. In 1993, President Jorge Serrano Elias of Guatemala tried a similar shutdown of congress but was blocked by the United States, the business sector, and the armed forces.

Chávez in Venezuela used legal democratic institutions, particularly elections and constitutional reforms, to fortify an increasingly authoritarian presidency. In 1999 to 2000, he convened a national constituent assembly that rammed through a new constitution. It expanded the powers of the president to call referenda, to control promotions in the armed forces, to subordinate the legislature, to utilize vetoes and decrees, and to serve for two consecutive six-year terms. After his reelection in 2006, Chávez arrogated even more authority to the presidency.[57]

The one attempt to eliminate presidentialism failed. After the fall of the Duvalier dynasty in 1986, the Haitian constitution of 1987 created a semi-presidential government with both a president and a prime minister. But the system suffered from a lack of legitimacy, chronic instability, authoritarianism, and dysfunctionality amidst grinding poverty.[58]

The existence of multiparty systems in most of Latin America frustrated presidents trying to secure legislative majorities. A high number of parties and a low level of party discipline spelled problems for presidential governance. Normally, the opposition controlled the congress, even though a majority of the countries slated their presidential and legislative elections concurrently. Standoffs between the executive and legislative branches were dangerous because they had led historically to presidential ineffectiveness and even regime breakdown.

Whether or not presidents could succeed themselves, their party found it very difficult to continue in office. They lost the presidency 68 percent of the time, over twice the rate in developed countries. On the positive side, this turnover meant that continuism by the ruling group was unlikely. It also signified that voters were expressing their dissatisfaction with incumbents by removing them rather than the regime.[59]

Civil liberties also constrained presidents, although governments often abridged those rights, especially in Central America outside Costa Rica. Surprisingly, the protection of civil liberties under democracies in Latin America declined from the 1970s through the 1990s. Not surprisingly, throughout the 1990s, Costa Rica, Uruguay, and Chile boasted the best records, as they had historically. In most countries, government pressures and anti-defamation laws still infringed on freedom of the press, with little sign of improvement. The rule of law remained at best uneven, often farcical, especially for the lower classes.

As a result, Latin America suffered from numerous *illiberal democracies* that often oppressed their citizens and served them poorly. Presidents applied traditional constitutional restraints on freedom of the press, association, and assembly. In much of the region, violations of civil liberties increased partly because governments relied on repression to prop up democratic institutions that denied the impoverished multitudes effective participation, representation, and satisfaction of socioeconomic demands. Protected democracies resorted to constitutional and unconstitutional authoritarian practices to forestall popular democracies.[60]

Military depositions of presidents became rare. The few attempts usually failed or quickly gave way to constitutional or semi-constitutional civilian governments. The most controversial coup occurred against Chávez in Venezuela in 2002, but he swiftly defeated it, despite U.S. sympathy for his ouster. Without full-scale military takeovers, other methods now toppled some presidents. Congressional impeachment proceedings brought down the chief executives in Brazil in 1992, Venezuela and Guatemala in 1993, Ecuador in 1997, and Paraguay in 1999; these removals represented impressive constitutional accountability by any standard in the world. Informally, social movements and popular protests also sometimes held presidents accountable and drove them from office, especially in the frail states of Peru (2000), Ecuador (2000, with the assistance of the armed forces, and again in 2005), and Bolivia (2003 and 2005).

In the Central Andes, mass movements still dared to risk repression by challenging and destabilizing elected governments. Whereas lower-class unrest might have sparked military reprisals in the past, now they convinced the armed forces to usher out the chief executives and to cobble together a constitutional formula for their replacement. These uprisings reflected growing dissatisfaction with corrupt and elitist democracies that imposed neoliberal economic policies and slighted social justice. Many of the unprivileged still preferred popular to protected democracies.[61]

In the early 2000s, popular agitation capsized one Bolivian government after another. "During the twentieth century Bolivia lived between the polling stations and rifles, which is to say between democracy and dictatorship. But since 2000, policies are formed between parliament and the streets, with strikes, blockades, and marches." The 2005 election to the presidency of the protestors' indigenous leader, Morales, offered a new formula for sustaining democracy between tyranny and anarchy.[62]

MINOR GAINS BY LEGISLATURES

As the new democracies stabilized, legislatures became more effective, and presidents made more of an effort to work with them. The executive branch still usually subjugated the assemblies. Most of them remained deficient in discipline and cohesion, as well as experience, staff and resources. Primarily reactive, they still lacked the leverage of their proactive U.S. counterpart. For U.S. congresspersons, reelection rates continued much higher than in Latin America and increased their clout vis-à-vis the executive. For example in the mid-1990s, the percentage of legislators returning to office ranged from 0 percent in Mexico (which prohibited reelection) to 17 percent in Argentina to 43 percent in Brazil to 59 percent in Chile to 83 percent in the United States.

Despite their debilities, Latin American legislators increasingly influenced policy outcomes, still mainly by interfering with legislation introduced by the president. They reacted primarily by approving, stalling, amending, or rejecting administration proposals. Even the long submissive Mexican congress played a bigger role in shaping legislation from 1997 onward.[63]

In South America, Ecuador, Venezuela, and Peru established unicameral legislatures, which blanketed Central America, partly because of the small

size of the countries. Ceteris paribus, unicameral assemblies provided less of
an obstacle to presidential domination. In both unicameral and bicameral
systems, the congresspersons typically had to be born in the nation and to
have reached a minimum age, usually higher for senators than deputies. Only
a handful of countries required them to be born or reside in their district.
Only a couple still demanded some level of education or economic means.
A few still barred clergy. Ecuador eliminated the functional representatives
initiated in 1929. Throughout Latin America, deputies served from two to
five years, senators from four to eight.

After Paraguay joined the field in 1990, standard proportional representation prevailed in all congressional elections except those in Mexico, Haiti,
and Chile. It facilitated the development of small parties and multiparty systems. In almost every country, voters had to choose a political party, which
drew up the closed list of candidates in order of preference, although a few
systems allowed voters to switch the order. This party control limited the
democratic expression of voter preferences for the legislature, as did malapportionment. Except for Mexico and Costa Rica, all Latin American legislatures permitted reelection. Some congresses scaled new heights of power
by successfully impeaching presidents.[64]

Despite constitutional guarantees of equal votes for all citizens, many
voters selected deputies as well as senators in malapportioned districts.
This distortion characterized Latin America throughout most of its history.
Thanks to manipulation by rightwing élites, the region led the world in the
malapportionment of its upper and lower chambers at the end of the 1990s.
The most egregious levels of bias in the chamber of deputies existed in Colombia, Ecuador, Bolivia, Chile, Argentina, and Brazil.

This congressional misrepresentation typically favored rural and conservative forces, as in some countries outside Latin America. This imbalance
contributed to deadlock between a congress more attuned to rural interests and a president more beholden to the burgeoning cities. It forced progressive presidents to compromise or clash with rightist legislatures, which
sometimes caused the chief executive to be much less reformist in office
than on the campaign trail. This situation also motivated some presidents to
sidetrack the congress by ruling by decree. It also cast in doubt the wisdom
of strengthening legislatures exhibiting severe malapportionment. In this as-
pect as well as others, Latin American democracies were undermined not
only by informal behavior that defied the formal rules but also by formal
rules that were unfair.[65]

Under Pinochet's constitution, Chile became one of the few countries
to weaken the legislature. It even moved it from the capital of Santiago to

the port city of Valparaiso, supposedly in the cause of decentralization. The dictatorship also created a congress with a few non-elected members and many others elected in a biased way, all intended to fortify the right, since that sector was unlikely to command majority support.

According to the 1980 Constitution, deputies, elected for four-year terms, had to be citizens with twenty-one years of age, educated at least through middle school, and residents of their electoral district. All senators faced the same requirements as deputies except they had to be forty years old. Senators were elected for eight years or were ex-presidents (senators for life) or designees (for eight years). Those designated included two ex-Supreme Court justices chosen by the supreme court, one ex-comptroller general chosen by the supreme court, one ex-commander of each of the four branches of the armed services chosen by the National Security Council, one ex-university rector chosen by the president, and one ex-cabinet minister chosen by the president.[66]

In addition to the nine designated representatives in the senate, Pinochet favored the right with the binomial electoral system. For both houses of congress, each district received two representatives. Parties formed coalitions to present two candidates in each race, but they had to garner over two-thirds of the votes to capture both seats in a chamber. If they did not snare over twice as many votes as the next most popular list, then the runner-up took one of the seats with anywhere above one-third of the votes. Thanks to this system, the rightwing minority usually took one of the two seats, even if its top candidate ran behind both those for the center-left Concertation. As a result, the conservative parties obtained greater representation than justified by their percentages of votes. Parties excluded from the two big coalitions, most significantly the Communists, had virtually no chance of winning seats.[67]

In contrast with authoritarian Chile under Pinochet, several democratic countries attempted to empower legislatures. For example, some constitutions allowed congress to censure cabinet ministers. Since wrangles between the legislative and executive branches have frequently caused coups in Latin America, perhaps fortifying the congress to collide with the president might be unhealthy for democratic stability. However, many regimes in the region have survived despite divided government and confrontations between the two branches, especially in the current wave of democracies. In the few recent instances when those standoffs escalated into a constitutional crisis, the legislature usually outlasted the chief executive. Although normally subordinate to the president, congress should not be underestimated.[68]

As legislatures gained stature, they also normally fell under the control of parties opposed to the executive, not uncommon in multiparty systems.

From the 1980s through the 1990s, only presidents in Honduras, Nicaragua, Colombia, Chile, and Paraguay encountered majorities of their own in the chamber of deputies. The other chief executives confronted hostile assemblies and frequent stalemates. However, those legislative majorities opposed to the president were mainly fractious and obstructionist, not cohesive and disciplined enough to present a proactive programmatic alternative. From the 1980s to the 1990s, the number of elections producing a congressional majority held by one party or an alliance of parties declined to a small minority of cases.[69]

In one noteworthy change from 1990 to 2000, Latin American women rose from 5 percent to 13 percent among senators and from 9 percent to 15 percent among deputies, about the same as in the United States. In 2000, the percentage among deputies ranged from a high of 27 percent in Argentina to a low of 3 percent in Paraguay. In eleven of the countries, one cause for gains was quota laws requiring parties to nominate 20 percent to 40 percent women as legislative candidates. More women also became cabinet ministers and even presidents, but in 2000 they only accounted for 6 percent of mayors. Overall, the low percentage of women in high government posts registered about the same as in Asia and most of Europe.[70]

The number of indigenous peoples in the lower or single chamber of the legislature also made small gains but lagged far behind their percentage in the population. By 2001 to 2002, those percentages in the legislature and in the population stood at 12 percent and 60 percent in Guatemala, 1 percent and 43 percent in Peru, 3 percent and 34 percent in Ecuador, and 26 percent and 61 percent in Bolivia, where a Native American also captured the presidency in 2005. By 1995 to 1999, people of African descent represented 3 percent of the seats and approximately 44 percent of the population in Brazil.[71]

INCOMPLETE DEMOCRATIZATION OF JUDICIARIES

From the 1980s to the 2000s, changes in the judiciary went farther than ever before. Nearly all countries initiated significant reforms with two central emphases. First, they sought to modernize the administration of justice, partly to facilitate judicial support for the neoliberal economic model. Second, they tried to enhance judicial contributions to democracy, partly by encouraging relief for human rights abuses. Reformers also attempted to improve legal education, the rule of law, access to justice, and judicial conduct, but huge problems remained, especially for the poor.[72]

Concurrent with democratization efforts, some countries stiffened judicial independence. The formal autonomy and authority of the judiciary grew, although the reality still left much to be desired. Increasingly, the supreme court or an independent council nominated judges to be approved by the congress. By 2002, every country included the legislature directly in the appointment process, and only five the president.[73]

To buffer judges from their colleagues as well as politicians, several governments took the management of the courts, including the appointment and discipline of lower court justices, out of the hands of both the supreme court and elected officials. They placed that authority in an independent entity, typically termed a judicial council. Many nations also joined the trend in continental civil law countries toward the establishment of constitutional courts to centralize constitutional adjudication in a separate body.[74]

Particularly in the Southern Cone and Central America, the democratic transitions highlighted the need to address human rights violations by the former authoritarian regimes. Elected governments tackled the question of retributive justice in various ways. These efforts ranged from noble but fairly toothless truth commissions to a few courageous trials and convictions of military personnel. Several countries amended their constitutions to integrate the spirit if not always the letter of international human rights treaties. Those treaties often became equal or superior to ordinary laws and even constitutions. Furthermore, all the countries ratified the American Convention on Human Rights, and seventeen of them recognized the contentious jurisdiction of the Inter-American Court of Human Rights.[75]

Many judges remained reluctant to shield human and civil rights, counter executive and legislative misbehavior, and uphold the constitution. Therefore numerous countries by the late 1990s created an independent ombudsperson for the defense of human rights. Both accounting for past violations and preventing future ones remained a work in progress. So did the establishment of judiciaries dedicated to constitutional democracy.[76]

DEMOCRATIZING ELECTIONS

In the 1980s, Latin America experienced some of the most significant elections in its history. Quantitatively, more Latin Americans cast more votes in more elections in more countries than in any previous decade. Qualitatively, many of these elections became watersheds, inaugurating democratization in the wake of military rule and/or civil war. Whereas approximately 66 percent of Latin Americans lived under military rule in 1979, nearly 90 percent enjoyed more democratic governments by the mid-eighties. However, programmatically, most of those elections postponed burning socioeconomic and human rights issues until democracy and peace could be firmly established.[77]

More and more countries held competitive and honest elections, even in Central America and Mexico. The inclusiveness and fairness of elections no longer presented significant problems. All countries recognized universal suffrage, albeit with some restrictions on voting by military, police, clergy, foreign residents, and expatriate nationals. Elections became cleaner, with almost none—except the Dominican Republic in 1994 and Peru in 2000—containing flaws sufficient to discredit the outcome. Out of thirty-five elections from 1990 to 1996, only ten exhibited significant irregularities, while out of thirty-five elections from 1997 to 2002, only two did so. In the same two periods, restrictions on free competition by all parties and candidates dropped from eight to two. By the end of the 1990s, all the countries had created national electoral commissions to supervise free and fair elections.[78]

Foreign observers and advisors also improved the management and integrity of elections. These agents included ad hoc, NGO, political party, and governmental missions from Europe and the United States, the United Nations, the Carter Center, the Inter-American Institute for Human Rights and its Center for Electoral Assistance and Training in Costa Rica, and, most actively, the Organization of American States. Very few elections were judged to be fakes in this wave of democratization. Nevertheless, polls showed that many Latin Americans thought they were fraudulent because local bosses sometimes still cheated and mainly because candidates failed to keep their campaign pledges. In a 2002 survey, only 2 percent of Latin Americans opined that winners lived up to their electoral promises, while 65 percent concluded that politicians lied in order to get elected, a phenomenon scarcely unique to Latin America.[79]

The new democracies became more participatory. They increasingly used voting for governors and mayors, plebiscites, referenda, recall elections, and intra-party primaries. Many countries legalized popular consultations, some initiated by the government and some by the citizenry. By the early 2000s, only Mexico and the Dominican Republic authorized no mechanisms of direct democracy. By 2002, nine countries had actually employed instruments of direct democracy, all initiated by the national governments.[80]

The franchise broadened more than ever. Suffrage for 18-year-olds had become the norm by the 1970s, and then Cuba (1976), Nicaragua (1984), and Brazil (1988) lowered the age to sixteen. Ecuador in 1978, Peru in 1979, and Brazil in 1988 became the last stragglers to give the vote to illiterates. By 2006, only Guatemala, Honduras, Cuba, Colombia, and Ecuador still banned military on active duty. All countries awarded the vote to citizens, and Colombia, Venezuela, Bolivia, Chile, Uruguay, and Paraguay also accorded it to resident foreigners for particular elections, usually municipal contests. All but Colombia made voting mandatory for the overwhelming majority of voters, except some excused illiterates, women, and very young or old voters. However, fewer than half the countries levied fines for not voting.[81]

For example, Brazil adopted a new constitution and electoral rules at the end of the 1980s. They authorized plebiscites, referenda, and popular initiatives. Whether in a first or second round, presidents, governors, and mayors had to be elected by a majority, but senators needed only a plurality. Voters elected deputies through a system of proportional representation using the d'Hondt quota. Voters chose candidates from party lists, and their choices, not the party's, determined who got elected. This system encouraged factionalism, clientelism, and personalism. It discouraged strong parties and programs, with politicians frequently changing parties. Voters flocked to the polls in high percentages, partly because it was compulsory for those between eighteen and seventy years old and because elections were holidays.[82]

In 1988 to 1990, registered voters as a percentage of the population averaged around 50 percent in Latin America. Registration reached the highest level in five of the most developed and historically most democratic countries, ranging from 56 percent to 79 percent of the population in Costa Rica, Chile, Argentina, Uruguay, and Brazil. It fell lowest in Bolivia, El Salvador, and Guatemala, hovering between 30 percent to 35 percent.

In presidential elections throughout the region, the turnout of registered voters generally rose highest, averaging around 75 percent. It peaked between 82 percent and 95 percent in Nicaragua, Costa Rica, Venezuela, Chile, Argentina, Uruguay, and Brazil. It plunged to between 44 percent and 59 percent in Mexico, Guatemala, El Salvador, the Dominican Republic, Colombia, and Paraguay, about as low as the United States at 55 percent. The percentage of the population casting ballots averaged almost 40 percent, varying from 19 percent in Guatemala and El Salvador, where fear and apathy reigned after their devastating civil wars, to 70 percent in Uruguay. In South America, voters as a percentage of those registered had been about as high from 1940 to 1977 as from 1978 to 2000.

Measuring electoral participation from 1990 through 2002 as a percentage of the population eligible to vote, those registered averaged 89 percent and those casting ballots averaged 63 percent (the highest average turnout being Uruguay at 95 percent and the lowest being Colombia at 33 percent). The comparable general figures for Western Europe were higher at 96 percent registration and 74 percent turnout and for the United States lower at 70 percent and 43 percent. In Latin America, valid votes as a percentage of the population eligible to vote averaged 56 percent, ranging again from a high of 92 percent in Uruguay to a low of 30 percent in Colombia. In general, these Latin American percentages were fairly high and stable.[83]

Overall high turnout in Latin America may have been partly due to obligatory voting, even though enforcement was patchy, but it was impossible to measure the precise impact of these laws. A third of the countries made registration automatic. Higher levels of prosperity, urbanization, and education correlated with higher voter turnout. In the tsunami years, voter participation soared in founding elections that inaugurated new democracies. In a few countries, declining turnout after the euphoria of the first return to the polls suggested a restoration of normal expectations or disenchantment with the socioeconomic results of the new regimes.[84]

Especially dramatic founding and democratizing elections took place in Chile in 1988 to 1989 and Mexico in 2000. Rather than following the exit of an authoritarian regime, these contests brought about its downfall. In both cases, foreign observers ratified the victory of the democratic opposition. Chile's 1988 plebiscite to continue Pinochet as president for 8 more years captured world attention. Overcoming fear, a record 92 percent of the eligible voters registered. Voters jammed the polls in another record 96 percent of those registered (90 percent of those eligible to vote), duplicated the next year in the election to replace the dictator after his loss. In the 1988 plebiscite, the democratic Concertation defeated Pinochet by 55 percent to 43 percent, and thereafter continued to win all the presidential elections through 2006 by similar percentages.[85]

In Mexico in 2000, the PRI finally allowed voters to run them out of the presidency after 72 years in power. Vicente Fox of the Party of National Action (PAN) won that office with 44 percent to 38 percent for the PRI after two decades of gradual opposition victories at the municipal, state, and congressional levels. From the late 1970s until the eve of Fox's victory, the PRI had declined from 99 percent to less than 50 percent of the mayors, from 100 percent to 69 percent of the governors, from 100 percent to 60 percent of the senators, and from a vast majority to a minority of the deputies.[86]

In the first stage of democratization in many countries, politicians and voters behaved cautiously. They evinced more concern about reinstating a sustainable democracy than advancing social reforms. After the new democracies stabilized, sometimes more reformist candidates broke through in the second stage.

By the turn of the century, a diverse new left captured many presidencies. That swing began with Hugo Chávez in Venezuela (1998), followed

by Ricardo Lagos (2000) and Michelle Bachelet (2006) in Chile, Luiz Inácio Lula da Silva ("Lula") in Brazil (2002), Nestor Kirchner in Argentina
(2003), Tabaré Vázquez in Uruguay (2004), Evo Morales in Bolivia (2005),
and Daniel Ortega in Nicaragua and Rafael Correa in Ecuador (both 2006).
They attracted voters chafing at the constraints of neoliberal economics
amidst persistent poverty and inequality.

The new left's supporters believed that their democracies should do
more about social inequities and their own well-being. Indeed, many Latin
Americans still defined democracy in terms of performance rather than just
procedure. At the ballot box, they increasingly expressed a preference for
popular rather than protected democracies.[87]

MULTIPLICATION AND MODERATION OF POLITICAL PARTIES

Political party systems varied according to the number of dominant parties. When counting the parties in a system, the key was the number
of relevant or effective parties, those winning enough votes and seats to
be significant contenders in congressional races. In lower-house elections
from the 1970s to the early 1990s, the mean number of effective parties
was lowest or closest to two in Colombia, Paraguay, Mexico, and Costa
Rica, and highest or between five and nine in Peru, Bolivia, Chile, Brazil,
and Ecuador, all in ascending numbers of parties. The systems with the
highest number of effective parties, the largest ideological distance among
those parties, and the strongest anti-democratic parties tended to be the
most ungovernable and unstable. The party lineup derived from rules for
party existence, operation, and interaction. It also reflected national social
and historical characteristics.[88]

Latin American party systems and parties also varied in their degree
of institutionalization. Strong versus weak systems differed partly on the
amount of electoral volatility (low versus high) and the gap between votes
cast for president and for legislators (small versus large) by party. One of
the more reliable correlations in the region was still between sturdy party
systems and hardy democracies. In terms of stable patterns of parties and
electoral outcomes, Costa Rica, Colombia, Chile, and Uruguay continued
to outshine their neighbors, although even these cases witnessed new party
contenders and configurations. The least institutionalized systems reigned
in Central America, the Central Andes, and Brazil, far surpassing levels of
volatility in Europe.

Polling data showed lower public attachment to political parties in Latin
America than Europe. For most Latin Americans, redemocratization ushered in high levels of voter participation but not party identification, which

actually shrank. Voters often attached themselves to personalities or movements, not political parties.

In the context of neoliberal market reforms favoring individual rather than collective action, parties became more heterogeneous and less class-based. Both programmatic and clientelistic parties saw state resources for initiatives, patronage and pork dwindle under neoliberalism. Many Latin Americans complained that parties remained authoritarian internally, patron-client machines for distributing pork, corrupt and opportunistic, unrepresentative of the citizenry, and untrustworthy programmatically.[89]

A majority of administrations coped with this multiparty potpourri by forging coalition governments, either before or after their election. They also passed laws intended to foment larger, longer-lasting parties. From 1990 to 2001, eleven of the countries favored political parties by giving them a monopoly on selecting candidates, while seven allowed independent candidacies. Almost all governments established regulations for political parties, both in the constitution and in separate legislation. By 2002, most of the laws on forming national parties imposed moderate restrictions on their organization, size, and behavior. A majority of the republics also introduced rules on party finances and started public subventions for parties, especially their electoral activities. But the bulk of the private financing of parties and candidates still escaped public knowledge, scrutiny, and control.[90]

As most rightwing and leftwing authoritarians—both armed reactionaries and revolutionaries—exited the stage, political parties became increasingly important, as well as less ideological and more pragmatic. However, they failed to take charge effectively. The party panorama changed dramatically from the previous era, particularly with the decline of two-party systems. While some traditional parties eroded, they were not replaced by comparably large and stable newcomers. More often a plethora of smaller, flighty, personalistic, social movement, or ideological parties took their place. Despite proliferating problems with multiple parties and their factions, some parties became more unified and effective in the legislatures in this period, particularly in the Southern Cone (Chile, Argentina, and Uruguay). This made their positions more identifiable and thus accountable to voters.

The fate of political parties in the various countries largely reflected their historical experience. For example in Chile, despite Pinochet's repression and electoral rigging, as well as some changes in party nomenclature, the broad outlines of the party system remained remarkably durable from the pre- to the post-authoritarian period. Through the 1990s, Colombia retained a political system dominated by the two traditional parties, albeit with voters choosing among competing lists within the factionalized two parties, not dissimilar to the process in Uruguay. Then in the 2000s, the two historic parties lost support in both Colombia and Uruguay.[91]

Despite Draconian efforts by some of the military governments to get rid of the existing political parties, particularly on the left, most of those organizations survived the dictatorships. Even when their names and supporters endured, however, their aspirations became more modest. Laborite and leftist political parties changed their programs to accommodate the trends toward neoliberalism, centrist moderation, and social democratic positions. To varying degrees, this pattern held for the Peronists in Argentina, the Socialists in Chile, the Workers' Party (PT) in Brazil, the Broad Front in Uruguay, and the APRA in Peru, especially once they occupied the presidency.

Leftwing and pro-labor parties moderated and thus made low-intensity, protected democracy more acceptable to domestic and foreign élites for several reasons: (1) fear and trauma from the dictatorships; (2) debilitation under economic neoliberalism and globalization; (3) weakening of trade unions; (4) the end of the Cold War and the waning of socialist, populist, and social democratic options; and (5) determination to preserve liberal democracy as a precious value in and of itself. The tradeoff was that by exercising restraint to solidify democracy the labor parties and movements gained very little in the distribution of socioeconomic power or concrete benefits.

After discarding most of their radical programs, some of the older working-class parties in South America took power soon after redemocratization. Their counterparts in Mexico and Central America did not enjoy as much success, although they all won their political freedom. In Argentina, Brazil, and Uruguay, the parties representing labor lost the first democratizing elections to more conservative groups but then won subsequently. However, once in office, they disappointed workers by adhering to many neoliberal policies, illustrating the programmatic limits of the new democracies. The Socialists in Chile and the APRA in Peru also returned to power but now in a much more temperate mode.[92]

The multiplication of political parties became the dominant trend. This growth occurred even in countries like Colombia, Venezuela, and Uruguay where two-party systems had long prevailed. It also appeared in Mexico, where the formerly omnipotent PRI plummeted. This pattern reflected dissatisfaction with the traditional and new parties, as voter support for these organizations oscillated. In many countries, voters punished parties that failed to deliver on issues of social injustice, unsatisfactory economic growth and distribution, corruption, and insecurity.

On the right, new, usually more moderate parties arose, for example in Chile. Some older rightist parties became more democratic and made gains, notably in Central America and Mexico. The latter developed a three-party system wherein the conservative PAN won the first two free presidential elections in 2000 and 2006. The rise of neoliberalism facilitated the upsurge of rightwing parties. Some served as personal vehicles, as with Fujimori in Peru and Uribe in Colombia. In many countries, the right's stronghold existed among rural dwellers, élites, and conservative Catholics, as it had for centuries. By including upper-class groups in the electoral system, these conservative parties may have dissuaded them from knocking on the doors of the barracks.

Among leftist parties, former guerrilla movements in Venezuela, Colombia, Guatemala, Nicaragua, and El Salvador launched some toned-down newcomers. The last three countries switched from catastrophic civil wars to peaceful electoral competition, normally won by conservative parties rather than former revolutionaries. Social movements spawned the most innovative, more militant new parties. At first, it looked as though they could become major players but not take power. However, for some, their tireless struggles soon reached the top. The most famous was the Workers' Party in Brazil, begun by laborers and eventually capable of propelling their working-class leader, Lula, to the presidency. Indigenous groups also gave birth to socialistic parties in Ecuador and Bolivia, with the latter capturing the presidential palace for Morales. Other new leftist parties thrived as creatures of their personalistic leaders, notably Chávez in Venezuela.[93]

Conclusion

From the 1970s to the 2000s, Latin America achieved its greatest success ever with democracy, despite lingering and sometimes severe deficiencies. It converted from one of the most dictatorial to one of the most democratic regions on the planet. Within the region, continuity prevailed in the historical pattern of the most and least democratic countries.

Under the constraints of neoliberal economics, protected rather than popular democracies dominated, restricting mass mobilization and benefits. Consequently, the unprivileged expressed rising discontent with the quality and content of neoliberal democracies, especially their inability to address poverty and inequality. Propelling the new left, the marginalized majority struggled to turn protected into popular democracies or the intermediate model of social democracies.

While maintaining most of their historical features, political institutions became increasingly democratic and stable. More durable constitutions inscribed additional social rights. Centralism held fast, but unprecedented decentralization took place, expanding municipal elections, responsibilities, and resources.

Still outclassing the other branches of government, presidents accrued more powers, partly through direct majoritarian elections. A few obtained the right to reelection. Almost none faced viable threats of military overthrows. They frequently slighted accountability and civil liberties.

Malapportionment kept many legislatures conservative and obstructionist. They remained essentially reactive. However, assemblies became more assertive, notably by impeaching presidents.

Reformers sought to improve the administration of justice and its attention to human rights abuses. They also attempted to instill democratic practices in legal education, the rule of law, access to justice, and judicial conduct. However, the courts still did little to serve the poor or constitutional democracy.

Elections became increasingly regular, inclusive, participatory, competitive, and honest. They expanded to allow direct democracy. At the beginning of this period, they inaugurated new democracies. At the end, they permitted the rise of the new left.

Political parties and multiparty systems proliferated and gained importance, yet remained fragile in most cases. New vehicles replaced many older ones. Several countries enacted regulations to foster larger and longer-lasting parties. The strongest parties and party systems still undergirded some of the healthiest democracies.

In the wake of the tsunami, Latin America had come a long way across two hundred years of struggles for democracy. At the start of the nineteenth century, the liberators would never have dreamed of such positive results, despite the remaining shortcomings. Whether these latest democracies would deepen and endure was as hard to predict as their arrival.

Chapter 8

Two Centuries of Building Democracy in Latin America, 1800–2006

As often happens with complicated construction projects, the developers took an unexpectedly long time to build democracies in Latin America. They encountered enormous obstacles and setbacks, compounded by an inhospitable environment and severely divided societies. Even from the 1970s to the 2000s, when they at long last managed to erect most of the edifices, many features remained incomplete.

At the beginning of the nineteenth century, the initiators of this project bulldozed the landscape and removed the previous authoritarian occupants. They quarreled over whether to replace them with dictatorships, constitutional monarchies, or democratic republics. Many of the founders drew up blueprints for either protected—or, much less commonly—popular democracies. Most recommended centralized, representative, elected governments presided over by powerful presidents and weak legislatures and judiciaries. However, other early leaders deviated from those plans or even tore them to shreds. Although the original buildings did not survive, many of the blueprints did. By the 1820s, the liberators left to their descendants the task of following their rough drafts to construct democratic systems that could withstand the winds of tyranny and anarchy.

From the 1820s to the 1870s, marauders and despots seized most of the neighborhood and razed most of the early dwellings. The original project lacked funds, backers, and buyers. Only a couple of architects managed to adhere to the inherited designs and hammer together stable, constitutional, oligarchic republics. Even in the few successful ventures, those structures only housed a handful of people. The landlords turned back a temporary surge of popular participation. As finances improved from mid-century onward, however, leaders succeeded in putting up a few more republican villages.

From the 1880s to the 1920s, increased prosperity allowed developers to raise up a few more sturdy oligarchic republics. They labored in a very dangerous neighborhood still dominated by slums and authoritarian predators. Nevertheless, the aristocratic republicans' partial and protected democracies laid the foundations for stronger, bigger houses to be built in the future. Then the Great Depression of the 1930s and a band of dictators laid waste to most of their residences.

From the 1930s to the 1970s, developers replaced those Victorian mansions with more spacious accommodations fit for popular democracy. Multitudes of poor citizens entered the project, as it expanded to encompass more plots in the neighborhood. Their appropriation of numerous sites disturbed the well-to-do. In reaction, the richer inhabitants and their armed enforcers evicted the common people and suspended the construction of democracy once more.

From the 1970s to the 2000s, the building of democracies recommenced and filled almost the entire neighborhood. Those constructs lasted longer than the previous ones because the unprivileged generally stayed in their segregated districts. The disadvantaged groups and their leaders wanted to avoid setting off alarms among the wealthy and their security forces. Although still using the outlines of the ancient blueprints, now the ruling élites installed gated communities to keep out leftist firebrands, ideas, and movements. Once again, a few troublemakers broke into protected parts of the neighborhood, but most areas remained off limits. The longest-standing houses retained the most value. By 2006, the poorer inhabitants celebrated the reconstruction of democratic lodgings but longed for better accommodations. Those in charge promised to correct remaining defects, now that they had finally nearly completed the full project. Over time, the developers preserved most of the foundational infrastructure, but they remodeled some features, especially in the electoral arena. As in all democracies, the work was never really done. Table 8.1 lists which institutional facets held fast to the original architectural drawings and which ones changed, from the nineteenth to the twenty-first century.

TABLE 8.1
Major institutional trends, nineteenth to twenty-first century

	Nineteenth century	Twenty-first century
Constitutions		
Origins	Decree	Assembly, congress, or plebiscite
Durability	Short	Longer
Civil liberties	Weak	Stronger
Socioeconomic rights	Weak	Stronger
Organization	Centralist	Centralist
Local government	Appointed and weak	Elected and weak
Presidents		
Election	Indirect	Direct
	Plurality	Majority
Reelection	No	No
Eligibility	Narrow	Broad
Powers	Broad	Broad
Decrees	Frequent	Less frequent
Regimes of exception	Easy and frequent	Less easy and less frequent
Cabinet accountability	President	President
Control of military	Weak	Stronger
Legislatures		
Election	Indirect	Direct
Reelection	Yes	Yes
Apportionment	Disproportional	Disproportional
Eligibility	Narrow	Broad
Powers	Narrow	Narrow
Organization	Weak	Weak
	Bicameral	Bicameral
Judiciaries		
Appointment	President	Congress
Independence	Weak	Weak
Powers	Weak	Weak
Judicial review	Weak	Weak
Defense of constitutional democracy	Weak	Weak
Defense of individual, social, and human rights	Weak	Weak
Organization	Weak	Weak
Accessibility	Narrow	Narrow
Elections		
Suffrage	Narrow	Broad
Scheduling	Irregular	Regular
	Staggered	Concurrent
Procedures	Unfree, unfair, dishonest, and disrespected	Free, fair, honest, and respected
Voting	Public	Secret
Plebiscites/referenda	No	Yes
Parties		
Number	None, one, two or more	Multiple
Organization	Weak	Stronger
	Authoritarian	More democratic
Finances	Private	Private
Primaries	No	Yes
Durability	Short	Longer

Across two centuries, the builders of Latin American democracy succeeded most when a benign climate from offshore enveloped the neighborhood. Within the region, the more durable democracies arose in the more prosperous communities, with larger middle and working classes and more homogeneous populations. The houses with the oldest, most solid foundations weathered storms better than the newer dwellings. Stability reigned when the few residents with most of the wealth and weapons reached agreement on the zoning, covenants, and rules. As a result, protected democracies outlasted popular ones.

By the early 2000s, all of Latin America's democratic communities and their institutional underpinnings still needed major upgrading. The latecomers faced the most daunting remaining tasks. Above all, the region's humbler inhabitants clamored for drastic improvements. As history suggests, it remained too soon to tell whether the most recent buildings would stand the test of time or tumble once more to anarchy or tyranny.

Notes to Preface

1. Albert O. Hirschman, *Journeys toward Progress: Studies in Economic Policy-Making in Latin America* (Boulder: Westview Press, 1993).

2. Another reason for minimizing tables on the pre-1930s periods is that many of the sources disagree somewhat with each other, even on tabulations of precedents for current electoral rules; one problem is distinguishing between when laws were enacted and when they actually took effect. This book also includes very few tables for the post-1970s era, because many have already been published in several convenient sources; consequently, this study usually just summarizes their findings in the narrative and refers readers to the originals.

Notes to Chapter 1

1. Gerald E. Fitzgerald, ed., *The Political Thought of Bolívar: Selected Writings* (The Hague: Martinus Nijhoff, 1971), 96. "Every democracy, whether parliamentary or presidential, federal or unitary, treads this space between tyranny and anarchy." Stephan Haggard and Mathew D. McCubbins, "Introduction: Political Institutions and the Determinants of Public Policy," in Stephan Haggard and Mathew D. Mc-Cubbins, eds., *Presidents, Parliaments, and Policy* (New York: Cambridge University Press, 2001), 1–17, quote from 2. ". . . democracy is neither chaos nor anarchy . . . democracy is a system of organized uncertainty." Adam Przeworski, *Democracy and the Market: Political and Economic Reforms in Eastern Europe and Latin America* (Cambridge: Cambridge University Press, 1991), 12–13. Robert A. Dahl, *Dilemmas of Pluralist Democracy: Autonomy vs. Control* (New Haven: Yale University Press, 1982).

2. Jonathan Hartlyn and Arturo Valenzuela, "Democracy in Latin America since 1930," in Leslie Bethell, ed., *Latin America: Politics and Society since 1930* (Cambridge: Cambridge University Press, 1998), 3–66, quote from 63.

3. Jacques Lambert, *Latin America: Social Structures and Political Institutions* (Berkeley: University of California Press, 1967), 15.

4. David Collier and Robert Adcock, "Democracy and Dichotomies: A Pragmatic Approach to Choices and Concepts," *Annual Review of Political Science*, vol. 2 (1999), 537–565. Giovanni Sartori, *The Theory of Democracy Revisited*, 2 vols. (Chatham, New

Jersey: Chatham House, 1987). Fernando Limongi and Adam Przeworski, "Democracy and Development in South America, 1946–1988," *Estudios/Working Papers* (Instituto Juan March de Estudios e Investigaciones, February, 1994), 1–32. Adam Przeworski, Michael E. Alvarez, Jose Antonio Cheibub, and Fernando Limongi, *Democracy and Development: Political Institutions and Well-Being in the World 1950–1990* (Cambridge: Cambridge University Press, 2000). Juan J. Linz, "An Authoritarian Regime: Spain," in Erik Allardt and Yrjo Littunen, eds., *Cleavages, Ideologies and Party Systems: Contributions to Comparative Political Sociology* (Finland: Abo Tidnings, 1964), 291–342. H. E. Chehabi and Juan J. Linz, "A Theory of Sultanism: A Type of Nondemocratic Rule," in H. E. Chehabi and Juan J. Linz, eds., *Sultanistic Regimes* (Baltimore: The Johns Hopkins University Press, 1998), 3–25, especially 7, 10, 23–25.

5. Paul W. Drake, "Debt and Democracy in Latin America, 1920s–1980s," in Barbara Stallings and Robert Kaufman, eds., *Debt and Democracy in Latin America* (Boulder, CO: Westview Press, 1989), 39–58. J. Samuel Valenzuela, "Class Relations and Democratization: A Reassessment of Barrington Moore's Model," in Miguel Angel Centeno and Fernando Lopez-Alves, eds., *The Other Mirror: Grand Theory through the Lens of Latin America* (Princteon: Princeton University Press, 2001), 240–286.

6. Samuel P. Huntington, *The Third Wave: Democratization in the Late Twentieth Century* (Norman: University of Oklahoma Press, 1991), 7–13, quote from 7. Peter H. Smith, *Democracy in Latin America: Political Change in Comparative Perspective* (New York: Oxford University Press, 2005), 8–14. Larry Diamond, Juan J. Linz, Seymour Martin Lipset, "Preface," in Larry Diamond, Juan J. Linz, and Seymour Martin Lipset, eds., *Democracy in Developing Countries: Latin America* (Boulder, CO: Lynne Rienner, 1989), ix–xxviii. Przeworski, Alvarez, Cheibub, Limongi, *Democracy*, especially 14–22. Adam Przeworski, Susan C. Stokes, and Bernard Manin, eds., *Democracy, Accountability, and Representation* (Cambridge: Cambridge University Press, 1999). Joseph A. Schumpeter, *Capitalism, Socialism, and Democracy* (New York: Harper & Brothers Publishers, 1942). Dietrich Rueschemeyer, Evelyne Huber Stephens, and John D. Stephens, *Capitalist Development and Democracy* (Chicago: University of Chicago Press, 1992), 41–44. Giuseppe Di Palma, *To Craft Democracies: An Essay on Democratic Transitions* (Berkeley: University of California Press, 1990). Sanford Lakoff, *Democracy: History, Theory, Practice* (Boulder, CO: Westview Press, 1996). Hartlyn and Valenzeula, "Democracy," 4–5.

7. Shannan Mattiace and Roderic Ai Camp, "Democracy and Development: An Overview," in Roderic Ai Camp, ed., *Democracy in Latin America: Patterns and Cycles* (Wilmington: Scholarly Resources, Inc., 1996), 3–19. Anthony Downs, *An Economic Theory of Democracy* (New York: Harper and Row, 1957), 23–24. Robert A. Dahl, *Polyarchy: Participation and Opposition* (New Haven: Yale University Press, 1971), 2–3; *Dilemmas*. Arend Lijphart, *Democracies: Patterns of Majoritarian and Consensus Government in Twenty-One Countries* (New Haven: Yale University Press, 1984). G. Bingham

Powell, Jr., *Contemporary Democracies: Participation, Stability, and Violence* (Cambridge, MA: Harvard University Press, 1982). David Collier and Steven Levitsky, "Democracy with Adjectives: Conceptual Innovation in Comparative Research," *World Politics*, 49:3 (1997), 430–451. Terry Lynn Karl, "Dilemmas of Democratization in Latin America," in Camp, *Democracy*, 21–46. Philippe C. Schmitter and Terry Lynn Karl, "What Democracy Is . . . and Is Not," *Journal of Democracy*, 2:3 (Summer, 1991), 75–88. Paul W. Drake and Eduardo Silva, "Introduction: Elections and Democratization in Latin America, 1980–1985," in Paul W. Drake and Eduardo Silva, eds., *Elections and Democratization in Latin America, 1980–1985* (La Jolla, California: Center for Iberian and Latin American Studies, 1986), 1–8.

8. Rueschemeyer, Stephens, and Stephens, *Capitalist*, 43–44, 160–162, 170–171, 205–206, 303–308. Smith, *Democracy*, 348–353. Brian Loveman, *The Constitution of Tyranny: Regimes of Exception in Spanish America* (Pittsburgh: University of Pittsburgh Press, 1993). Keith S. Rosenn, "The Success of Constitutionalism in the United States and Its Failure in Latin America: An Explanation," in Kenneth W. Thompson, ed., *The U.S. Constitution and the Constitutions of Latin America* (Lanham: University Press of America, 1991), 53–96. Seymour Martin Lipset and Jason M. Lakin, *The Democratic Century* (Norman: University of Oklahoma Press, 2004), 270. Scott Mainwaring and Francis Hagopian, "Introduction: The Third Wave of Democratization in Latin America," in Francis Hagopian and Scott P. Mainwaring, eds., *The Third Wave of Democratization in Latin America: Advances and Setbacks* (New York: Cambridge University Press, 2005), 1–13.

9. Table 1.1 represents an amalgamation and adaptation from the following sources: Rueschemeyer, Stephens, and Stephens, *Capitalist*, 43–44, 160–162, 170–171, 205–206, 303–308. Smith, *Democracy*, 348–353. Brian Loveman, *The Constitution of Tyranny: Regimes of Exception in Spanish America* (Pittsburgh: University of Pittsburgh Press, 1993). Keith S. Rosenn, "The Success of Constitutionalism in the United States and Its Failure in Latin America: An Explanation," in Kenneth W. Thompson, ed., *The U.S. Constitution and the Constitutions of Latin America* (Lanham: University Press of America, 1991), 53–96. Seymour Martin Lipset and Jason M. Lakin, *The Democratic Century* (Norman: University of Oklahoma Press, 2004), 270. Scott Mainwaring and Francis Hagopian, "Introduction: The Third Wave of Democratization in Latin America," in Francis Hagopian and Scott P. Mainwaring, eds., *The Third Wave of Democratization in Latin America: Advances and Setbacks* (New York: Cambridge University Press, 2005), 1–13, here 3.

10. Huntington, *The Third*, 15–26, quote from 15.

11. Di Palma, *To Craft*, quote from 15. Paul W. Drake, "The International Causes of Democratization, 1974–1990," in Paul W. Drake and Mathew D. McCubbins, eds., *The Origins of Liberty: Political and Economic Liberalization in the Modern World* (Princeton: Princeton University Press, 1997), 70–91.

12. Paul W. Drake, "Latin America in the Changing World Order, 1492–1992" in Roberto G. Rabel, ed., *Latin America in a Changing World Order* (Dunedin, New Zealand: University of Otago, 1992), 18–36. Abraham F. Lowenthal, ed., *Exporting Democracy: The United States and Latin America* (Baltimore: The Johns Hopkins University Press, 1991). For an analysis that gives international currents less credence, particularly as catalysts for democratization, see Smith, *Democracy*, 107–133.

13. Rueschemeyer, Stephens, and Stephens, *Capitalist*, 210–222. Huntington, *The Third*, 59–72. Paul W. Drake, "From Good Men to Good Neighbors," in Lowenthal, *Exporting*, 3–40; "Debt"; "The International." Przeworski, *Democracy and the Market*, 188–189. Przeworski, Alvarez, Cheibub, and Limongi, *Democracy*.

14. Karl, "Dilemmas," 24–27. Dahl, *Polyarchy*, 63–80. J. Samuel Valenzuela, *Democratización via reforma: La expansión del sufragio en Chile* (Buenos Aires: IDIS, 1985); "Class." James M. Malloy and Mitchell A. Seligson, eds., *Authoritarians and Democrats: Regime Transition in Latin America* (Pittsburgh: University of Pittsburgh Press, 1987). Howard J. Wiarda, ed. *Politics and Social Change in Latin America: The Distinct Tradition* (Amherst: The University of Massachusetts Press, 1974). Martin C. Needler, "Ideas and Interests in the Struggle for Democracy in Latin America," in Kenneth W. Thompson, ed., *The U.S. Constitution and the Constitutions of Latin America* (Lanham, Maryland: University Press of America, Inc., 1991), 127–148. Barrington Moore, Jr., *Social Origins of Dictatorship and Democracy: Lord and Peasant in the Making of the Modern World* (Boston: Beacon Press, 1966), 55–61. Evelyne Huber and Frank Safford, eds., *Agrarian Structure and Political Power: Landlord and Peasant in the Making of Latin America* (Pittsburgh: University of Pittsburgh Press, 1995). Charles Tilly, "Democracy is a Lake," in George Reid Andrews and Herrick Chapman, eds., *The Social Construction of Democracy, 1870–1990* (New York: New York University Press, 1995), 365–387. Deborah Yashar, *Demanding Democracy: Reform and Reaction in Costa Rica and Guatemala, 1870s–1950s* (Stanford: Stanford University Press, 1997), 11. Carlos Forment, *Democracy in Latin America, 1760–1900: Civic Selfhood and Public Life. Mexico and Peru* (Chicago: University of Chicago Press, 2003). Fernando Henrique Cardoso and Enzo Faletto, *Dependency and Development in Latin America* (Berkeley: University of California Press, 1979). Hartlyn and Valenzuela, "Democracy," 3–10, 17–18.

15. Seymour Martin Lipset, "Some Social Requisites of Democracy: Economic Development and Political Legitimacy," *American Political Science Review*, 53 (March, 1959), 69–105; *Political Man: The Social Bases of Politics*, revised ed. (Baltimore: Johns Hopkins University Press, 1981), 31–58. Larry Diamond, "Economic Development and Democracy Reconsidered," *American Behavioral Scientist* 35:4/5 (March/June, 1992), 450–499. Carles Boix and Susan Stokes, "Endogenous Democratization," *World Politics*, 53:4 (2003), 517–549. David L. Epstein, Robert Bates, Jack Goldstone, Ida Kristensen, and Sharyn O'Halloran, "Democratic Transitions," *American Journal*

of Poitical Science, 50:3 (July, 2006), 551–569. Scott Mainwaring and Anibal Perez-Linan, "Level of Development and Democracy: Latin American Exceptionalism, 1945–1996," *Comparative Political Studies*, 36:9 (November, 2003), 1031–1067. Mitchell A. Seligson, "Political Culture and Democratization in Latin America," in Camp, *Democracy*, 67–90. Przeworski, Alvarez, Cheibub, and Limongi, *Democracy*, especially 98–137. Smith, *Democracy*, 48–53. Hartlyn and Valenzuela, "Democracy," 3 10. Lijphaiʟ, *Democracies*, 40–41. Huntington, *The Third*, 59–72.

16. For the entire discussion of social classes in this section, see Rueschemeyer, Stephens, and Stephens, *Capitalist*, 1–8, 181–186. Ruth Berins Collier, *Paths toward Democracy: The Working Class and Elites in Western Europe and South America* (New York: Cambridge University Press, 1999). T. H. Marshall, *Citizenship and Social Class* (Cambridge: Cambridge University Press, 1950).

17. J. Samuel Valenzuela, *Democratización*. Charles W. Bergquist, *Coffee and Conflict in Colombia, 1866–1910* (Durham: Duke University Press, 1978). Rafael Quintero Lopez, *El mito del populismo en el Ecuador: Analisis de los fundamentos del estado ecuatoriano moderno (1895–1934)*, 3rd ed. (Quito: Ediciones Abya-Yala, 1997).

18. Maurice Zeitlin, *The Civil Wars in Chile (or the Bourgeois Revolutions that Never Were)* (Princeton: Princeton University Press, 1984). Maurice Zeitlin and Richard Ratcliff, *Landlords and Capitalists: The Dominant Class of Chile* (Princeton: Princeton University Press, 1988). John J. Johnson, *Political Change in Latin America: The Emergence of the Middle Sectors* (Stanford: Stanford University Press, 1958). Jose Nun, "The Middle-Class Military Coup," in Claudio Veliz, ed., *The Politics of Conformity in Latin America* (New York: Oxford University Press, 1967), 66–118.

19. From the point of view of the ruling élites, "the more the costs of suppression exceed the costs of toleration, the greater the chance for a competitive regime." Dahl, *Polyarchy*, 4–5, 14–16. Smith, *Democracy*, 8–14. Diamond, Linz, and Lipset, "Preface," in Diamond, Linz, and Lipset, *Democracy*, IV, ix–xxviii. Lipset, *Political Man*, 64–67. Przeworski, *Democracy and the Market*, x. Paul W. Drake and Mathew D. McCubbins, "The Origins of Liberty," in Drake and McCubbins, *The Origins*, 3–12. Peter Gourevitch, "Politics, Institutions, and Society: Seeking Better Results," Ms. (2006).

20. Rueschemeyer, Stephens, and Stephens, *Capitalist*, 155–157, 171, quote from 269. Karl, "Dilemmas," 31–38. Smith, *Democracy*. Drake and Silva, "Introduction."

21. Smith, *Democracy*, 77–80. Warren Dean, "Latin American Golpes and Economic Fluctuations, 1823–1966," *Social Science Quarterly* (June, 1970), 70–80. Brian Loveman, "When You Wish upon the Stars: Why the Generals (and Admirals) Say Yes to Latin American 'Transitions' to Civilian Government," in Drake and McCubbins, *The Origins*, 115–145; *For La Patria: Politics and the Armed Forces in Latin America* (Wilmington: Scholarly Resources, 1999). Przeworski, *Democracy and the Market*, quote from 51.

22. Rueschemeyer, Stephens, and Stephens, *Capitalist*, 275.

23. Collier, *Paths*. Ruth Berins Collier and David Collier, *Shaping the Political Arena: Critical Junctures, the Labor Movement, and Regime Dynamics in Latin America* (Princeton: Princeton University Press, 1991). Smith, *Democracy*, 53–62. Paul W. Drake, *Labor Movements and Dictatorships: The Southern Cone in Comparative Perspective* (Baltimore: The Johns Hopkins University Press, 1996). Charles W. Bergquist, *Labor in Latin America: Comparative Essays on Chile, Argentina, Venezuela, and Colombia* (Stanford: Stanford University Press, 1986). Steven Levitsky and Scott Mainwaring, "Organized Labor and Democracy in Latin America," *Comparative Politics* (October, 2006), 21–42.

24. Smith, *Democracy*, 313–326.

25. Hartlyn and Valenzuela, "Democracy." Dahl, *Polyarchy*, 4–5, 14–16. Smith, *Democracy*, 313–326.

26. Dahl, *Polyarchy*, 81–123. Arend Lijphart, *Democracy in Plural Societies: A Comparative Exploration*, (New Haven: Yale University Press, 1977), 65–70; *Democracies*, 42–43. Robert A. Dahl and Edward A. Tufte, *Size and Democracy* (Stanford: Stanford University Press, 1973). Charles C. Cumberland, "Political Implications of Cultural Heterogeneity in Latin America," in Fredrick B. Pike, ed., *Freedom and Reform in Latin America* (Notre Dame: University of Notre Dame Press, 1959), 59–80. Donna Lee Van Cott, *From Movements to Parties in Latin America: The Evolution of Ethnic Politics* (New York: Cambridge University Press, 2005).

27. Statistical evidence for these long-term trends is provided by Smith, *Democracy*, 39–41.

28. Cecil Jane, *Liberty and Despotism in Spanish America* (New York: Cooper Square Publishers, Inc., 1966), 1–12, quote from 12. Richard M. Morse, "The Heritage of Latin America," in Wiarda, *Politics*, 25–69; "Toward a Theory of Spanish American Government," in Wiarda, *Politics*, 105–128. Glenn Dealy, "The Tradition of Monistic Democracy in Latin America," in Wiarda, *Politics*, 71–104. Louis Hartz, ed., *The Founding of New Societies* (New York: Harcourt Brace Jovanovich, Inc., 1964). Javier Alcalde, "Differential Impact of American Political and Economic Institutions on Latin America," in Thompson, *The U.S.,* 97–126.

29. Hartlyn and Valenzuela, "Democracy," 3–10. Collier, *Paths*. Collier and Collier, *Shaping*. Leonard Binder, et al., eds., *Crises and Sequences in Political Development* (Princeton: Princeton University Press, 1971). Steve Steimo, Kathleen Thelen, and Frank Longstreth, eds., *Structuring Politics: Historical Institutionalism in Comparative Analysis* (Cambridge: Cambridge University Press, 1992).

30. Dahl, *Polyarchy*, 33–49. Hartlyn and Valenzuela, "Democracy," 3–10.

31. Reuschemeyer, Stephens, and Stephens, *Capitalist*, 204–213. Smith, *Democracy*, 23–31. Guillermo O'Donnell, *Modernization and Bureaucratic Authoritarianism: Studies in South American Politics* (Berkeley: Institute of International Studies, 1973). Charles W. Anderson, *Politics and Economic Change in Latin America: The Governing of Restless Nations* (Princeton: D. Van Nostrand Company, Inc., 1967).

32. Smith, *Democracy*, 19–43, 313–326.

33. During the wars for independence, monarchists like José de San Martín in Argentina occupied an even farther right position. Miguel Jorrin and John D. Martz, *Latin American Political Thought and Ideology* (Chapel Hill: The University of North Carolina Press, 1970), 199–206. W. Rex Crawford, "The Concept of Freedom in Latin America," in Pike, ed., *Freedom*, 16–27. Cumberland, "Political," 59–60. Leonardo Avritzer, *Democracy and the Public Space in Latin America* (Princeton: Princeton University Press, 2002). William R. Nylen, *Participatory Democracy versus Elitist Democracy: Lessons from Brazil* (New York: Palgrave Macmillan, 2003).

34. Manuel Antonio Garretón, *Incomplete Democracy: Political Democratization in Chile and Latin America* (Chapel Hill: The University of North Carolina Press, 2003), 60.

35. E. Bradford Burns, *Latin America: A Concise Interpretive History*, 3rd ed. (Englewood Cliffs, New Jersey: Prentice-Hall, Inc., 1982).

36. Arthur P. Whitaker, "The Pathology of Democracy in Latin America: A Historian's Point of View," in Asher N. Christensen, ed., *The Evolution of Latin American Government* (New York: Henry Holt and Company, 1951), 247–269, especially 248–259.

37. Paul W. Drake, "Requiem for Populism?" in Michael Conniff, ed., *Latin American Populism in Comparative Perspective* (Albuquerque: University of New Mexico Press, 1982), 217–245; and Eric Hershberg, eds., *State and Society in Conflict: Comparative Perspectives on Andean Crises* (Pittsburgh: University of Pittsburgh Press, 2006).

38. Gerardo L. Munck, "Democratic Politics in Latin America: New Debates and Research Frontiers," *Annual Review of Political Science*, 7 (2004), 437–462; "Democracy Studies: Agendas, Findings, Challenges," in Dirk Berg-Schlosser, ed., *Democratization: The State of the Art* (Wiesbaden, Germany: VS Verlag fur Sozialwissenschaften, 2004), 65–97; ed., *Regimes and Democracy in Latin America: Theories and Methods* (New York: Oxford University Press, 2007).

Notes to Chapter 2

1. Jonathan Hartlyn and Arturo Valenzuela, "Democracy in Latin America since 1930," in Leslie Bethell, ed., *Latin America: Politics and Society since 1930* (Cambridge: Cambridge University Press, 1998), 3–66, especially 3–10. Adam Przeworski, *Democracy and the Market: Political and Economic Reforms in Eastern Europe and Latin America* (Cambridge: Cambridge University Press, 1991), quote from x.

2. Terry Lynn Karl, "Dilemmas of Democratization in Latin America," in Roderic Ai Camp, ed., *Democracy in Latin America: Patterns and Cycles* (Wilmington: Scholarly Resources, Inc., 1996), 21–46, especially 30. Przeworski, *Democracy and the Market*, 35–37. Arend Lijphart, *Democracies: Patterns of Majoritarian and Consensus Government in Twenty-One Countries* (New Haven: Yale University Press, 1984), 6–9,

23–36. Seymour Martin Lipset, *Political Man: The Social Bases of Politics*, revised ed. (Baltimore: Johns Hopkins University Press, 1981), 71, 80–86. Anthony Downs, *An Economic Theory of Democracy* (New York: Harper and Row, 1957), 23–24. Robert A. Dahl, *Polyarchy: Participation and Opposition* (New Haven: Yale University Press, 1971), 2–3, 227.

3. The "conventional wisdom" displayed in this table is culled from numerous authors, including Terry Lynn Karl, "Dilemmas of Democratization in Latin America," in Roderic Ai Camp, ed., *Democracy in Latin America: Patterns and Cycles* (Wilmington: Scholarly Resources, Inc., 1996), 21–46, especially 30. Przeworski, *Democracy and the Market*, 35–37. Arend Lijphart, *Democracies: Patterns of Majoritarian and Consensus Government in Twenty-One Countries* (New Haven: Yale University Press, 1984), 6–9, 23–36. Seymour Martin Lipset, *Political Man: The Social Bases of Politics*, revised ed. (Baltimore: Johns Hopkins University Press, 1981), 71, 80–86. Anthony Downs, *An Economic Theory of Democracy* (New York: Harper and Row, 1957), 23–24. Robert A. Dahl, *Polyarchy: Participation and Opposition* (New Haven: Yale University Press, 1971), 2–3, 227.

4. William W. Pierson and Federico G. Gil, *Government and Politics of Latin America* (New York: McGraw-Hill Book Company, Inc., 1955), 188–190. Austin F. Macdonald, *Latin American Politics and Government* (New York: Thomas Y. Crowell Company, 1949). Rosendo A. Gomez, *Latin American Politics and Government* (New York: Random House, 1960), 26–27.

5. William S. Stokes, *Latin American Politics* (New York: Thomas Y. Crowell Company, 1959), 459.

6. Most tabulations of the awesome numbers of Latin American constitutions usually disagree slightly with each other. They also sometimes give different dates, depending on whether they are referring to when countries approved or implemented these documents. The analyses in this book rely most on the following constitutions: Mexico (1824, 1857, 1917), Guatemala (1945, 1985), Honduras (1982), El Salvador (1886, 1962, 1983), Nicaragua (1939, 1987), Costa Rica (1871, 1949), Cuba (1940), Haiti (1987), the Dominican Republic (1947), Venezuela (1811, 1947, 1961, 1999), Colombia (1811, 1821, 1830, 1832, 1843, 1853, 1858, 1861, 1863, 1886, 1991), Ecuador (1946, 1978, 1998), Peru (1823, 1828, 1856, 1860, 1920, 1933, 1979, 1993), Bolivia (1826, 1938, 1945), Chile (1818, 1833, 1925, 1980), Argentina (1853, 1949), Uruguay (1830, 1918, 1934, 1966), Paraguay (1940, 1992), and Brazil (1821, 1824, 1891, 1946, 1988). Keith S. Rosenn, "The Success of Constitutionalism in the United States and Its Failure in Latin America: An Explanation," in Kenneth W. Thompson, ed., *The U.S. Constitution and the Constitutions of Latin America* (Lanham: University Press of America, 1991), 53–96, especially 57, 87–92. Brian Loveman, *The Constitution of Tyranny: Regimes of Exception in Spanish America* (Pittsburgh: University of Pittsburgh Press, 1993), 370. Alexander T. Edelmann, *Latin American Government and*

Politics: The Dynamics of a Revolutionary Society, revised ed. (Homewood, Illinois: The Dorsey Press, 1969), 383–387.

7. Jacques Lambert, *Latin America: Social Structures and Political Institutions* (Berkeley: University of California Press, 1967), 107–109, 257–262.

8. Rosenn, "The Success." Lambert, *Latin*, 257–260.

9. George I. Blanksten, "Constitutions and the Structure of Power," in Harold Eugene Davis, *Government and Politics in Latin America* (New York: The Ronald Press Company, 1958), 225–251, especially 226–227. Antonio Colomer Viadel, *Introducción al constitucionalismo iberoamericano* (Madrid: Ediciones de Cultura Hispanica, 1990), 83. Gerald E. Fitzgerald, *The Constitutions of Latin America* (Chicago: Henry Regnery Company, 1968), vii–xiii. Luis Sánchez Agesta, *La democracia en Hispanoamérica: Un balance histórico* (Madrid: Ediciones RIALP, S. A., 1987), 10–12.

10. Thomas Buergenthal, et al., *La constitución norteamericana y su influencia en Latinoamérica: 200 años, 1787–1987* (San José, Costa Rica: IIDH, 1987). Rosenn, "The Success," 70–71. Blanksten, "Constitutions," 228. Stokes, *Latin*, 460–464. Colomer, *Introduccion*, 104–105. Sánchez Agesta, *La democracia*, 10–12. Javier Alcalde, "Differential Impact of American Political and Economic Institutions on Latin America," in Kenneth W. Thompson, ed., *The U.S. Constitution and the Constitutions of Latin America* (Lanham, Maryland: University Press of America, Inc., 1991), 97–126. Rafael Altamira, *El derecho constitucional americano* (Buenos Aires: COM, 1928).

11. Roberto Gargarella, "Towards a Typology of Latin American Constitutionalism, 1810–1860," *Latin American Research Review*, 39:2 (2004), 141–153. Brian Loveman, "When You Wish Upon the Stars," in Paul W. Drake and Matthew D. McCubbins, eds., *The Origins of Liberty: Political and Economic Liberalization in the Modern World* (Princeton: Princeton University Press, 1998), 134–139; *The Constitution*.

12. Macdonald, *Latin*. Gomez, *Latin*, 25–26. Rosenn, "The Success," 59–75.

13. J. Lloyd Mecham, "Latin American Constitutions," in Peter G. Snow, ed., *Government and Politics in Latin America* (New York: Holt, Rinehart and Winston, Inc., 1967), 144–157.

14. Gomez, *Latin*, 28–31. Hartlyn and Valenzuela, "Democracy," 3–10. Loveman, "When." Gargarella, "Towards," 141–142. Charles O. Porter and Robert J. Alexander, *The Struggle for Democracy in Latin America* (New York: The Macmillan Company, 1961), 14–15. George I. Blanksten, *Ecuador: Constitutions and Caudillos* (New York: Russell and Russell, Inc., 1964), 169–171; "Constitutions," 228. T. H. Marshall, *Class, Citizenship, and Social Development* (Chicago: The University of Chicago Press, 1977), 78–79, 86. Carl J. Friedrich, *Constitutional Government and Democracy: Theory and Practice in Europe and America*, 4th ed. (Waltham, MA: Blaisdell Publishing Company, 1968).

15. Alexis de Tocqueville, *Democracy in America* (New York: New American Library, 1956). Carlos Forment, *Democracy in Latin America, 1760–1900: Civic Selfhood*

and Public Life. Mexico and Peru (Chicago: University of Chicago Press, 2003). William H. Riker, *Federalism: Origin, Operation, Significance* (Boston: Little Brown, 1964).

16. Aspasia Camargo, "La federación sometida. Nacionalismo desarrollista e inestabilidad democrática," in Marcello Carmagnani, ed., *Federalismos latinoamericanos: Mexico/Brasil/Argentina* (Mexico: Fondo de Cultura Economica, 1993), 300–362, especially 348.

17. William S. Stokes, "Latin American Federalism," in Snow, *Government*, 158–173. Mecham, "Latin," 147–149. C. H. Haring, "Federalism in Latin America," in Asher N. Christensen, ed., *The Evolution of Latin American Government* (New York: Henry Holt and Company, 1951), 335–342. Lambert, *Latin*, 296–307, 312–319.

18. Stokes, "Latin American Federalism." Mecham, "Latin," 147–149. Pierson and Gil, *Government*, 296–312.

19. Carlos Mouchet, "Municipal Government," in Harold E. Davis, ed., *Government and Politics of Latin America* (New York: Ronald, 1956), 368–392. Lambert, *Latin*, 307–312.

20. The U.S. vice presidency did not work out well in Latin America, partly because that office and the president frequently came into conflict, particularly when the vice president conspired to overthrow the president. By contrast, some people feared that vice-presidents would be pawns of presidents and could carry on their authority by succeeding them. Instead of providing a vice-president, some of the constitutions came to designate another official, such as the chief justice of the supreme court, to succeed a president briefly until the congress or the general electorate could choose a new one. When Mexican novelist Carlos Fuentes was asked why his country did not have a vice president, he replied, "Because immediately he would plot against the president and have him unseated and probably killed, which is what happened when the vice-presidential function existed in Mexico in the nineteenth century," in "Novel Politics," *The New York Times Magazine* (April 30, 2006), 19. Harold E. Davis, "The Presidency," in Davis, *Government*, 252–289, especially 256–262. Lambert, *Latin*, 328–323. Salvador Valencia Carmona, *El poder ejecutivo latinoamericano* (Mexico: Universidad Nacional Autonoma de Mexico, 1979), 94–97.

21. Sánchez Agesta, *La democracia*, 211–222. Pierson and Gil, *Government*, 221, 236–239. Colomer, *Introducción*, 120–124. Lambert, *Latin*, 16–20, 320–326, 333–344. Matthew Soberg Shugart and John M. Carey, *Presidents and Assemblies: Constitutional Design and Electoral Dynamics* (Cambridge: Cambridge University Press, 1992), especially 28–54, 110–117.

22. Loveman, *The Constitution*. Colomer, *Introducción*, 87, 93–96.

23. Shugart and Carey, *Presidents*, 28–54.

24. The right of "amparo" began with the Brazilian penal code of 1830. Colomer, *Introducción*, 105–110. Helen L. Clagett, "Law and Court Systems," in Davis, *Government*, 333–367, especially 348–351.

25. The Latin Americans never installed a true parliamentary system in which the legislature picked the chief executive. When they referred to parliamentary or semi-parliamentary systems, they were alluding to rare ones where the congress exerted unusual power over the president. In those cases, the legislators could hold the cabinet ministers to account and sometimes remove them. Granting congress leverage over the cabinet was rarely effective in undermining the authority of the president, except in Chile under the so-called Parliamentary Republic. In the few other instances where congress could actually force ministers to resign, presidents, like Allende later in Chile, usually just switched them to another post and/or replaced them with someone equally unpalatable to the legislature. Latin Americans often used the word "parliament" simply as a synonym for "congress." Stokes, *Latin*, 421–422. Colomer, *Introducción*, 126–137. Gargarella, "Towards," 144–146. Harry Kantor, "Efforts Made by Various Latin American Countries to Limit the Power of the President," in Thomas V. DiBacco, ed., *Presidential Power in Latin American Politics* (New York: Praeger Publishers, 1977), 21–32.

26. Robert H. Dix, "The Colombian Presidency: Continuities and Changes," in DiBacco, *Presidential*, 72–95. Guillermo O'Donnell, *Counterpoints: Selected Essays on Authoritarianism and Democratization* (Notre Dame: University of Notre Dame Press, 1999), 133–158.

27. David Samuels, "Legislative Lilliputians: Towards a Theory of Party Cohesion in the Brazilian Chamber of Deputies," Ms. (Latin American Studies Association, 1997). Gary W. Cox and Mathew D. McCubbins, *Legislative Leviathan: Party Government in the House* (Berkeley: University of California Press, 1993).

28. For this entire section on legislatures, see Edelmann, *Latin*, especially 443–464; and Mecham, "Latin," 146–148.

29. Sánchez Agesta, *La democracia*, 59––61. David Bushnell, *The Santander Regime in Gran Colombia* (Newark, Delaware: University of Delaware Press, 1954), 50–57. Colomer, *Introducción*, 167–170.

30. Weston H. Agor, "Introduction," in Weston H. Agor, ed., *Latin American Legislatures: Their Role and Influence* (New York: Praeger Publishers, 1971), xxiii–xlviii, esp. xxiv–xxvi, xlii–xliii. Robert E. Scott, "Legislatures and Legislation," in Davis, *Government*, 290–332. Pierson and Gil, *Government*, 260–261.

31. Snow, *Government*, 141. Stokes, *Latin*, 412–414. Lambert, *Latin*, 345–358. Richard Snyder and David J. Samuels, "Legislative Malapportionment in Latin America: Historical and Comparative Perspectives," in Edward L. Gibson, ed., *Federalism and Democracy in Latin America* (Baltimore: The Johns Hopkins University Press, 2004), 131–172.

32. Edelmann, *Latin*, 458.

33. Most civil law judges did not engage in successful democratic judicial review because of their formation through the strict legalism and adherence to positivism

traditionally central to civil law education and jurisprudence. John Henry Merry-man, *The Civil Law Tradition*, 2nd ed. (Stanford: Stanford University Press, 1985). John Leddy Phelan, "Authority and Flexibility in the Spanish Imperial Bureaucracy," *Administrative Science Quarterly*, 5 (June, 1960), 47–65. Asher N. Christensen, "Strong Governments and Weak Courts," in Christensen, *The Evolution*, 468–475. Kenneth L. Karst and Keith S. Rosenn, *Law and Development in Latin America: A Case Book* (Berkeley: University of California Press, 1975). Clagett, "Law," 333–367. Edelmann, *Latin*, 465–487. Pierson and Gil, *Government*, 266–294. Loveman, *The Constitution*.

34. This entire section on elections relies on Rolando Franco, *Los sistemas electorales y su impacto político* (San José: CAPEL, 1987), especially 18–19, 20–30; and Dieter Nohlen, "Elections and Electoral Systems in the Americas," in Dieter Nohlen, ed., *Elections in the Americas: A Data Handbook*, 2 vols. (New York: Oxford University Press, 2005), I, 1–60; II, 1–58. Loveman, "When," 131–132.

35. Carlos Malamud, "Introducción," in Carlos Malamud, ed., *Legitimidad, representación, y alternancia en España y América Latina: Las reformas electorales (1880–1930)* (Mexico: Fonda de Cultura Economica, 2000), 7–16.

36. J. Samuel Valenzuela, *Democratización via reforma: La expansión del sufragio en Chile* (Buenos Aires: IDIS, 1985), 15–19, 22–35. In the United States, in the early nineteenth century non-property owners and, on into the twentieth century, paupers and illiterates were often legally banned from voting. By the middle of the nineteenth century, the United States led the world in removing property requirements but not in lowering other restrictions, which tightened thereafter. It was far ahead of Latin America in allowing women to vote. The U.S. experience with voting rights was always complicated by widespread diversity among the states. Alexander Keyssar, *The Right to Vote: the Contested History of Democracy in the United States* (New York: Basic Books, 2000), xvi–xxiv, 316–324.

37. Antonio Annino, "Introducción," in Antonio Annino, ed., *Historia de las elecciones en Iberoamérica, siglo xix de la formación del espacio político nacional* (Buenos Aires: Fondo de Cultura Economica de Argentina, 1995), 7–18, especially 10–14.

38. Universal suffrage refers to voting rights for all adults without restrictions based on property or race. However, many countries only subsequently removed other economic, educational, and status limitations. Sometimes a distinction needs to be made between when these laws were passed and when they were implemented. Benchmarks for universal male suffrage, sometimes adopted more than once, included France and Switzerland in 1848, England in 1866 and 1918, Germany and Spain in 1869 and 1907, Norway in 1898, Sweden in 1909, Portugal in 1911, Italy in 1912, Denmark in 1915, Holland in 1917, Belgium and Luxembourg in 1919, and Canada in 1920. Universal female suffrage achieved victory in New Zealand in 1893, Germany in 1919, Canada in 1920, Great Britain in 1928, Spain in 1931, France and Italy in 1946, and Japan in 1947. Only in a few cases was universal suffrage granted to men

and women simultaneously. In Europe the earliest countries were Germany and Spain (1869). Like Latin America, others also took their time between men and women, such as Greece (1877 and 1952), Belgium (1893 and 1948), Portugal (1911 and 1974), Italy (1912 and 1946), and Switzerland (1919 and 1971). On through the beginning of the 2000s, places like Saudi Arabia and Yemen never extended the franchise to women. Dieter Nohlen, *Elecciones y sistemas electorales*, 3rd ed (Caracas: Editorial Nueva Sociedad, 1995), 22–25. Natalio Botana, *El orden conservador: La política argentina entre 1880 y 1916*, 4th ed. (Buenos Aires: Editorial Sudamericana, 1994), 43, 254–258.

39. Latin Americans often granted lower voting ages to those married. In 1988, Brazil also gave the vote to 16-year-olds, but it remained voluntary up to age 18 and mandatory from then until 70.

40. Lambert, *Latin*, 175–177. In 1988, Brazil also exempted illiterates from the obligatory requirement to vote.

41. Nohlen, "Elections" in Nohlen, *Elections*, I, 1–60; II, 1–58, table mainly adapted from 12, with some amendments from individual country studies cited later in my book's chronological chapters, and from Loveman, "When," 133–134.

42. Patricia Pinzon de Lewin, *El ejército y las elecciones: Ensayo histórico* (Bogotá: CEREC, 1994), 10–13.

43. The secret ballot gained acceptance in many U.S. states, Belgium, Switzerland, and Sweden early in the nineteenth century, then in England in 1872, Denmark in 1901, and thereafter other parts of Europe, including France in 1913. As with other landmarks for suffrage improvements, scholars sometimes disagree about the legal and effective dates. For example, various authors credit Chile with secret voting beginning in 1890, 1925, or 1958. Botana, *El orden*, 43, 254–258. Hartlyn and Valenzuela, "Democracy," 33–35.

44. Rein Taagepera and Matthew Soberg Shugart, *Seats and Votes: The Effects and Determinants of Electoral Systems* (New Haven: Yale University Press, 1989), 17. G. Bingham Powell, Jr., *Contemporary Democracies: Participation, Stability, and Violence* (Cambridge: Harvard University Press, 1982), 113–122.

45. Proportional representation first appeared in Europe in 1899 in Belgium and 1909 in Sweden. Botana, *El orden*, 254–258. Bernard Grofman and Arend Lijphart, *Electoral Laws and Their Political Consequences*, New York: Agathon Press, Inc., 1986. Arend Lijphart and Bernard Grofman, "Choosing an Electoral System," in Arend Lijphart and Bernard Grofman, eds., *Choosing an Electoral System: Issues and Alternatives* (New York: Praeger, 1984), 3–14. Ferdinand A. Hermens, "Representation and Proportional Representation," in Lijphart and Grofman, *Choosing*, 15–30. Maurice Duverger, "Which is the Best Electoral System?" in Lijphart and Grofman, *Choosing*, 31–40. Giovanni Sartori, *Comparative Constitutional Engineering: An Inquiry into Structures, Incentives, and Outcomes* (New York: New York University Press, 1994). Taagepera and Shugart, *Seats*.

46. This discussion of two basic types of lists oversimplifies a complex variety that includes mixed systems and produces differing effects. Lijphart, *Democracies*, 152–156. Taagepera and Shugart, *Seats*, 12–37. Duverger, "Which," 38–39.

47. Culumer, *Introducción,* 165–167.

48. Nohlen, "Elections" in Nohlen, *Elections*, I, 1–60; II, 1–58, especially 12, 49. Botana, *El orden*, 43, 254–258. Mario Fernández Baeza, "El voto obligatorio," in Dieter Nohlen, Sonia Picado, and Daniel Zovatto, eds., *Tratado de derecho electoral comparado de América Latina* (Mexico: Fondo de Cultura Economica, 1998), 123–139, especially 128–134. Bernhard Thibaut, "Instituciones de democracia directa," in Nohlen, Picado, and Zovatto, *Tratado*, 65–88, especially 70. Loveman, "When," 134.

49. Powell, *Contemporary*, 170–174.

50. Leon D. Epstein, *Political Parties in Western Democracies* (New York: Frederick A. Praeger, 1967), quote from 9. Giovanni Sartori, *Parties and Party Systems: A Framework for Analysis* (Cambridge: Cambridge University Press, 1976). Maurice Duverger, *Political Parties: Their Organization and Activity in the Modern State* (New York: John Wiley & Sons, Inc., 1963). Joseph LaPalombara and Myron Weiner, "The Origin and Development of Political Parties," in Joseph LaPalombara and Myron Weiner, eds., *Political Parties and Political Development* (Princeton: Princeton University Press, 1966), 3–42, especially 6–15. Robert E. Scott, "Political Parties and Policy-Making in Latin America," in LaPalombara and Weiner, *Political Parties*, 331–368. Scott Mainwaring and Timothy R. Scully, eds., *Building Democratic Institutions: Party Systems in Latin America* (Stanford: Stanford University Press, 1995). Ulrich Muecke, *Political Culture in Nineteenth-Century Peru: The Rise of the Partido Civil* (Pittsburgh: University of Pittsburgh Press, 2004), 8–13. Edelmann, *Latin*, 350–380. Powell, *Contemporary*, 152–153.

51. Lijphart, *Democracies*, 128–129. Erik Allardt and Yrjo Littunen, eds., *Cleavages, Ideologies and Party Systems: Contributions to Comparative Political Sociology* (Finland: Abo Tidnings, 1964). Seymour Martin Lipset and Stein Rokkan, "Cleavage Structures, Party Systems, and Voter Alignments: An Introduction," in Seymour M. Lipset and Stein Rokkan, eds., *Party Systems and Voter Alignments: Cross-National Perspectives* (New York: The Free Press, 1967), 1–64, especially 47. Douglas W. Rae, *The Political Consequences of Electoral Laws*, revised edition (New Haven: Yale University Press, 1971), especially 47–70, 87–88, 92–103, 148–149.

52. Lipset and Rokkan, "Cleavage." Ruth Berins Collier and David Collier, *Shaping the Political Arena: Critical Junctures, the Labor Movement, and Regime Dynamics in Latin America* (Princeton: Princeton University Press, 1991).

53. Ronald H. McDonald and J. Mark Ruhl, *Party Politics and Elections in Latin America* (Boulder: Westview Press, 1989).

54. Rae, *The Political*, 49–55. McDonald and Ruhl, *Party*. Taagepera and Shugart, *Seats*, 77–83. Scott Mainwaring and Timothy R. Scully, "Introduction: Party Systems in Latin America," in Mainwaring and Scully, *Building*, 1–36, especially 28–33.

55. Downs, *An Economic*, 297. Lijphart, *Democracy*, 12–13, 62–65. Dahl, *Polyarchy*, 122–123, 223. Epstein, *Political*, 59. Sartori, *Parties*, 188. Duverger, *Political*, 206–280.

Notes to Chapter 3

1. Cuba became independent from Spain in 1898 and Panama from Colombia in 1903, for a total of twenty countries.

2. Jaime E. Rodriguez O., *The Independence of Spanish America* (Cambridge: Cambridge University Press, 1998), 2–6, 75. Jorge I. Dominguez, *Insurrection or Loyalty: The Breakdown of the Spanish American Empire* (Cambridge: Harvard University Press, 1980). R. A. Humphreys and John Lynch, eds., *The Origins of the Latin American Revolutions, 1808–1826* (New York: Alfred A. Knopf, 1965).

3. Jay Kinsbruner, *Independence in Spanish America: Civil Wars, Revolutions, and Underdevelopment*, 2nd revised ed. (Albuquerque: University of New Mexico Press, 2000), 43–57.

4. Rodriguez O., *The Independence*, 194–197. Kinsbruner, *Independence*, 72–107. Leslie Bethell, ed., *The Independence of Latin America* (Cambridge: Cambridge University Press, 1987).

5. John Thomas Vance, *The Background of Hispanic-American Law: Legal Sources and Juridical Literature of Spain* (New York: Central Book Company, 1943), 184–202. Leslie Bethell, ed., *Colonial Spanish America* (Cambridge: Cambridge University Press, 1987).

6. Larry Diamond and Juan J. Linz, "Introduction: Politics, Society, and Democracy in Latin America," in Larry Diamond, Juan J. Linz, and Seymour Martin Lipset, eds., *Democracy in Developing Countries: Latin America,* Vol. IV (Boulder, 1989), 1–58. Seymour Martin Lipset and Jason M. Lakin, *The Democratic Century* (Norman: University of Oklahoma Press, 2004), 241–415.

7. Paul H. Lewis, *Authoritarian Regimes in Latin America: Dictators, Despots, and Tyrants* (Lanham, Maryland: Rowman & Littlefield Publishers, Inc., 2006), 7–17. Hugh M. Hamill, Jr., ed. *Dictatorship in Spanish America* (New York: Alfred A. Knopf, 1965).

8. Because stabilization of the state and its authority took so long in some countries (for example, the Central Andes), it remained incomplete and fragile in the twentieth century when lower-class demands for inclusion escalated. Dietrich Rueschemeyer, Evelyne Huber Stephens, and John D. Stephens, *Capitalist Development and Democracy* (Chicago: University of Chicago Press, 1992), 172–173. Kinsbruner, *Independence*, 130–157.

9. Arthur P. Whitaker, *The United States and the Independence of Latin America, 1800–1830* (New York: Russell and Russell, Inc., 1962).

10. John Lynch, "Introduction," in John Lynch, ed., *Latin American Revolutions, 1808–1826* (Norman: University of Oklahoma Press, 1994), 5–40, quote from 28.

Arthur P. Whitaker, ed., *Latin America and the Enlightenment*, 2nd ed. (Ithaca: Cornell University Press, 1961). Bernard Moses, *The Intellectual Background of the Revolution in South America, 1810–1824* (New York: Russell and Russell, 1966). Jose Luis Romero, *A History of Argentine Political Thought* (Stanford: Stanford University Press, 1963), 2–58. Simon Collier, *Ideas and Politics of Chilean Independence, 1808–1833* (Cambridge: Cambridge University Press, 1967), 35–43. Mario Aguilera Peña and Renan Vega Cantor, *Ideal democrático y revuelta popular: Bosquejo histórico de la mentalidad política popular en Colombia, 1781–1948* (Bogotá: Instituto Maria Cano, 1991).

11. Arthur P. Whitaker, *The Western Hemisphere Idea: Its Rise and Decline* (Ithaca: Cornell University Press, 1954), 2.

12. Time and again, the United States and Latin America have also been severely divided by heritage, language, culture, religion, race, ethnicity, economics, power, ideology, politics, geopolitics, and numerous other factors that have caused people in both areas to reject any notion of a community of nations. Whitaker, *The Western*. Abraham F. Lowenthal, ed., *Exporting Democracy* (Baltimore: John Hopkins University Press, 1991).

13. Silvio Zavala, *La defensa de los derechos del hombre en América Latina (Siglos XVI–XVII)* (Mexico: Comisión Nacional de Derechos Humanos, 1963).

14. Bethell, *Colonial*. Mark A. Burkholder and Lyman L. Johnson, *Colonial Latin America*, 3rd ed. (New York: Oxford University Press, 1998). C. H. Haring, *The Spanish Empire in America* (New York: Harcourt, Brace and World, Inc., 1952).

15. O. Carlos Stoetzer, "The Hispanic Tradition," in Lynch, Latin, 241–246; *The Scholastic Roots of the Spanish American Revolution* (New York: Fordham University Press, 1979); *El pensamiento político en la América Española durante el período de la emancipación (1789–1825)*, 2 vols. (Madrid: Instituto de Estudios Políticos, 1966). Luis Sánchez Agesta, *La democracia en Hispanoamérica: Un balance histórico* (Madrid: Ediciones RIALP, S. A., 1987) 9, 20–39.

16. Collier, *Ideas*, 64–72, 129–142. Alfredo Jocelyn-Holt Letelier, *La independencia de Chile: Tradición, modernización y mito* (Madrid: Editorial MAPFRE, 1992), 181–221.

17. David Bushnell and Neill Macaulay, *The Emergence of Latin America in the Nineteenth Century*, 2nd ed. (New York: Oxford University Press, 1994), 12, 31–34.

18. Javier Malagon and Charles C. Griffin, *Las actas de independencia de América* (Washington, D.C.: PanAmerican Union, 1954).

19. D. A. Brading, *The First America: The Spanish Monarchy, Creole Patriots, and the Liberal State, 1492–1867* (Cambridge: Cambridge University Press, 1991). William Spence Robertson, *Rise of the Spanish-American Republics as Told in the Lives of Their Liberators* (New York: The Free Press, 1965). Miguel Jorrín and John D. Martz, *Latin-American Political Thought and Ideology* (Chapel Hill: The University of North Carolina Press, 1970), 77–79. Victor Andres Belaunde, *Bolívar and the Political Thought of the*

Spanish American Revolution (New York: Octagon Books, Inc., 1967), 189–194. Another proponent of a constitutional monarchy was the eminent Venezuelan intellectual Andrés Bello. He evolved into an advocate of conservative republicanism and helped construct the 1833 constitution in Portalian Chile. Ivan Jaksic, *Andrés Bello: Scholarship and Nation-Building in Nineteenth-Century Latin America* (Cambridge: Cambridge University Press, 2001), 41–47, 99–104. Rodriguez O., *The Independence*, 174–175.

20. Jorrin and Martz, *Latin*, 57–59. Harold E. Davis, *Makers of Democracy in Latin America* (New York: Cooper Square Publishers, Inc., 1968), 21–24. At one time Miranda suggested giving women the vote on issues pertaining to them, including marriage, divorce, and education. Belaunde, *Bolívar*, 77.

21. Jorrin and Martz, *Latin*, 60–68. Rodriguez O., *The Independence*, 59–106. Brading, *The First*, 540–544.

22. Rodriguez O., *The Independence*, 91–103, 246.

23. Timothy E. Anna, "Iturbide, Congress, and Constitutional Monarchy in Mexico," in Kenneth J. Andrien and Lyman L. Johnson, eds., *The Political Economy of Spanish America in the Age of Revolution, 1750–1850* (Albuquerque: University of New Mexico Press, 1994), 17–38. William Spence Robertson, *History of the Latin American Nations*, 3rd ed. (New York: D. Appleton-Century Co., 1943), 451–454.

24. Leslie Bethell, "The Independence of Brazil," in Bethell, *The Independence*, 155–194. C. H. Haring, *Empire in Brazil: A New World Experiment with Monarchy* (Cambridge: Harvard University Press, 1958).

25. Sánchez Agesta, *La democracia*, 39–45.

26. The Creoles sometimes used the words republic and democracy interchangeably for elected representative governments, although the latter implied broader participation. Collier, *Ideas*, 142–150, 177–178. Kinsbruner, 109–112. Vincent C. Peloso and Barbara A. Tenenbaum, eds., *Liberals, Politics, and Power: State Formation in Nineteenth-Century Latin America* (Athens: The University of Georgia Press, 1996), 2. Hector Gros Espiell, *Las constituciones del Uruguay (exposición, crítica y textos)* (Madrid: Ediciones Cultura Hispanica, 1956), 18.

27. Charles C. Griffin, "Enlightenment and Independence," in Lynch, *Latin*, 247–257.

28. Cecil Jane, *Liberty and Despotism in Spanish America* (New York: Cooper Square Publishers, Inc., 1966), 164–165. Bushnell and Macaulay, *The Emergence*, 34–36. Lynch, "Introduction," in Lynch, *Latin*, 28–29. Dominguez, *Insurrection*, 238. Charles A. Hale, *Mexican Liberalism in the Age of Mora, 1821–1853* (New Haven: Yale University Press, 1968).

29. Jorrin and Martz, *Latin*, 59–64.

30. Lynch, "Introduction," in Lynch, *Latin*, 21–24. Jorrin and Martz, *Latin*, 68–69. Steve J. Stern, ed., *Resistance, Rebellion, and Consciousness in the Andean Peasant World, 18th to 20th Centuries* (Madison: University of Wisconsin Press, 1987). John

Leddy Phelan, *The People and the King: The Comunero Revolution in Colombia, 1781* (Madison: University of Wisconsin Press, 1978). Apparently L'Ouverture planned to become a lifetime constitutional dictator. Madison Smartt Bell, *Toussaint Louverture: A Biography* (New York: Pantheon, 2007).

31. Hugh M. Hamill, Jr., *The Hidalgo Revolt: Prelude to Mexican Independence* (Gainesville: University of Florida Press, 1966). Eric Van Young, *The Other Rebellion: Popular Violence, Ideology, and the Mexican Struggle for Independence, 1810–1821* (Stanford: Stanford University Press, 2001).

32. Jorrin and Martz, *Latin*, 64–67.

33. This conservative vision bore some similarity to the contemporary notion of "delegative democracy," in which mass elections confer on a narrow elite the right to run the government with little accountability to the citizens. Guillermo O'Donnell, *Counterpoints: Selected Essays on Authoritarianism and Democratization* (Notre Dame: University of Notre Dame Press, 1999), 159–174.

34. Jane, *Liberty*, 128–131, quote from 131. To an extent, this rightwing attitude presaged General Augusto Pinochet's argument in the late twentieth century that Chileans had economic and social but not political liberty under his dictatorship.

35. The independence movements in Mexico, Central America, and Peru, not to mention Brazil, tended toward more conservatism than those in Venezuela, Colombia, Chile, Argentina, and Uruguay. Jane, *Liberty*, quote from 144.

36. Collier, *Ideas*, 287–360, quote from 339. Bernardino Bravo Lira, *Historia de las instituciones políticas de Chile e Hispanoamérica* (Santiago: Editorial Andrés Bello, 1986), 180–181.

37. Gerald E. Fitzgerald, ed., *The Political Thought of Bolívar: Selected Writings* (The Hague: Martinus Nijhoff, 1971), 4–6; for slightly different but compatible translations of Bolívar's writings, see David Bushnell, ed., *El Libertador: Writings of Simón Bolívar* (New York: Oxford University Press, 2003). Belaunde, *Bolívar*, especially x–xii. John J. Johnson, with the collaboration of Doris M. Ladd, *Simón Bolívar and Spanish American Independence, 1783–1830* (Princeton: D. Van Nostrand Company, Inc., 1968). John Lynch, *Simón Bolívar: A Life* (New Haven: Yale University Press, 2006).

38. Jorrin and Martz, *Latin*, 70–76. William W. Pierson and Federico G. Gil, *Government and Politics of Latin America* (New York: McGraw-Hill Book Company, Inc., 1957), 124–131. Brading, *The First*, 605–619. Belaunde, *Bolívar*, 169–187. Lynch, *Simón*.

39. Simón Bolívar, "An American's Convictions," in Lynch, *Latin*, 308–320; quote from 317.

40. R. A. Humphreys, "Democracy and Dictatorship," in Asher N. Christensen, ed., *The Evolution of Latin American Government* (New York: Henry Holt and Company, 1951), 318–332, quotes from 319 and 320.

41. Fitzgerald, *The Political*, 54, 62.

42. Fitzgerald, *The Political*, 45–68. Brading, *The First*, 613–614.

43. Fitzgerald, *The Political*, 95–105, quote from 96. Brading, *The First*, 615.

44. Torcuato S. Di Tella, *Latin American Politics: A Theoretical Framework* (Austin: University of Texas Press, 1990), 53–54. Jorrin and Martz, *Latin*, 68. Davis, *Makers*, 17–18. Johnson, *Simón*. Lynch, *Simón*. At its most extreme, Bolívar's model sounded almost like the 1980s advocacy by Chilean dictator Pinochet of an "authoritarian democracy" or a "protected democracy."

45. Brading, *The First*, 618. Humphreys, "Democracy," 321. Fitzgerald, *The Political*. Belaunde, *Bolívar*.

46. Sánchez Agesta, *La democracia*, 9–10, 20–39. George I. Blanksten, *Ecuador: Constitutions and Caudillos* (New York: Russell and Russell, Inc., 1964).

47. Jane, *Liberty*, 110–114.

48. Humphreys, "Democracy," 318.

49. Sánchez Agesta, *La democracia*, 9, 20–39. Collier, *Ideas*, 150–155. Russell H. Fitzgibbon, "Constitutional Development in Latin America: A Synthesis," in Christensen, *The Evolution*, 209–223, *especially* 214–217. George I. Blanksten, "Constitutions and the Structure of Power," in Harold Eugene Davis, ed., *Government and Politics in Latin America* (New York: The Ronald Press Company, 1958), 225–251. Thomas Buergenthal, Jorge Mario García Laguardia, and Rodolfo Piza Rocafort, *La constitución norteamericana y su influencia en Latinoamérica (200 años 1787–1987)* (San José: CAPEL, 1987). Alexander T. Edelman, *Latin American Government and Politics: The Dynamics of a Revolutionary Society*, revd. ed., (Homewood: The Dorsey Press, 1969), 389–397. Brian Loveman, *The Constitution of Tyranny: Regimes of Exception in Spanish America* (Pittsburgh: University of Pittsburgh Press, 1993). Claudio Grossman, "States of Emergency: Latin America and the United States," in Louis Henkin and Albert J. Rosenthal, eds., *Constitutionalism and Rights: The Influence of the United States Constitution Abroad* (New York: Columbia University Press, 1990), 176–198. Ariosto D. González, *Las primeras fórmulas constitucionales en los países del plata, 1810–1814* (Montevideo: Claudio García & Cia., 1962).

50. David Bushnell, *The Santander Regime in Gran Colombia* (Newark, Delaware: University of Delaware Press, 1954), 19. Di Tella, *Latin*, 29. Sánchez Agesta, *La democracia*, 9, 20–39. Jorge Mario García Laguardia, Carlos Meléndez Chaverii, and Marina Volio, *La constitución de Cádiz y su influencia en América (175 años 1812–1987)* (San José: CAPEL (Centro Interamericano de Asesoría y Promoción Electoral), 1987), 13–16. Pierson and Gil, *Government*, 111–112.

51. Frank Safford, "Politics, Ideology and Society," in Leslie Bethell, ed., *Spanish America after Independence, c. 1820–c. 1870* (Cambridge: Cambridge University Press, 1987), 48–122, especially 62–68. Edelman, *Latin*, 384.

52. Sánchez Agesta, *La democracia*, 66–73. Edelmann, *Latin*, 392–396. Kinsbruner, *Independence*, 124–129. Bushnell, *The Santander*, 15. Russell H. Fitzgibbon, ed., *The*

Constitutions of the Americas (Chicago: The University of Chicago Press, 1948), 137–138, 164–165. Miron Burgin, *The Economic Aspects of Argentine Federalism, 1820–1852* (New York: Russell and Russell, 1971).

53. Lynch, *Simón*, quote from 261.

54. Burkholder and Johnson, *Colonial*, 80–92. Claudio Veliz, *The Centralist Tradition of Latin America* (Princeton: Princeton University Press, 1980). James Lockhart and Stuart B. Schwartz, *Early Latin America: A History of Colonial Spanish America and Brazil* (New York: Cambridge University Press, 1983), 425.

55. Jane, *Liberty*, 112, 116–122. Sánchez Agesta, *La democracia*, 66–73. Marcello Carmagnani, ed., *Federalismos latinoamericanos: Mexico/Brasil/Argentina* (Mexico: Fondo de Cultura Economica, 1993).

56. William Marion Gibson, *The Constitutions of Colombia* (Durham: Duke University Press, 1948), vii–viii, 5–31, 35–67, quote from 41. Javier Ocampo López, *La independencia de los Estados Unidos de América y su proyección en hispanoamérica: El modelo norteamericano y su repercusión en la independencia de Colombia: Un estudio a través de la folletería de la independencia de Colombia* (Caracas: Instituto PanAmericano de Geografía e Historia, 1979). Bushnell, *The Santander*.

57. Austin F. Macdonald, *Government of the Argentine Republic* (New York: Thomas Y. Crowell Company, 1942), 46–78. Pierson and Gil, *Government*, 115–116. Robertson, *History*, 213.

58. Julio Heise González, *Años de formación y aprendizaje políticos, 1810–1833* (Santiago: Editorial Universitaria, 1978). Bravo Lira, *Historia*, 176–180, 184–186. Robertson, *History*, 268–271. Pierson and Gil, *Government*, 116–120. Collier, *Ideas*, 150–155.

59. Burkholder and Johnson, *Colonial*, 88–92.

60. Carlos Mouchet, "Municipal Government," in Davis, *Government*, 368–392, especially 368–374. Pierson and Gil, *Government*, 296–312. Burkholder and Johnson, *Colonial*, 85. Haring, *The Spanish*, 147–165.

61. Bushnell, *The Santander*, 17–18, 30–31, 43–44.

62. Salvador Valencia Carmona, *El poder ejecutivo latinoamericano* (Mexico: Universidad Nacional Autonoma de Mexico, 1979), 15–32. Charles C. Cumberland, "Political Implications of Cultural Heterogeneity in Latin America," in Fredrick B. Pike, ed., *Freedom and Reform in Latin America* (Notre Dame: University of Notre Dame Press, 1959), 59–80. J. H. Parry, *The Spanish Seaborne Empire* (New York: Alfred A. Knopf, 1966), 373–374.

63. C. H. Haring, *The Spanish*. Valencia Carmona, *El poder*, 22–23.

64. Valencia Carmona, *El poder*, 23–25. John Leddy Phelan, "Authority and Flexibility in the Spanish Imperial Bureaucracy," *Administrative Science Quarterly*, 5 (June, 1960), 47–65. Harold E. Davis, "The Presidency," in Davis, *Government*, 252–289, especially 256–261.

65. Blanksten, *Ecuador*, quote from 169. Valencia Carmona, *El poder*, 33–47.

66. Sánchez Agesta, *La democracia*, 44–45. Víctor Andrés Belaúnde, "The Political Ideas of Bolívar," in Christensen, ed., *The Evolution*, 81–102.

67. Sánchez Agesta, *La democracia*, 40. Davis, "The Presidency," 257–258. Valencia Carmona, *El poder*, 40.

68. Sánchez Agesta, *La democracia*, 54–59. Bushnell, *The Santander*, 17–18. Eduardo Aleman and George Tsebelis, "The Origins of Presidential Conditional Agenda-Setting Power in Latin America," *Latin American Research Review*, 40:2 (June, 2005), 3–26. In similar fashion, Brazil's emperor, Pedro I, appointed the presidents of provinces, although municipalities had elected councils. Robertson, *History*, 172–173, 179–186.

69. In an attempt to limit the influence of Roman Catholicism, the 1825 Constitution of Guatemala recognized it as the official national religion but said that of the two senators elected from each state, only one could be a member of the clergy. Ralph Lee Woodward, Jr., "The Liberal-Conservative Debate in the Central American Federation, 1823–1840," in Peloso and Tenenbaum, *Liberals*, 59–89. Sánchez Agesta, *La democracia*, 53–59. Bushnell, *The Santander*, 18, 31–33. Loveman, *The Constitution*. Grossman, "States."

70. Sánchez Agesta, *La democracia*, 54–59. Hamill, *Dictatorship*.

71. Collier, *Ideas*, 239–259, quote from 258. Robertson, *History*, 268–271. Pierson and Gil, *Government*, 116–120.

72. Robertson, *History*, 313–314. Sánchez Agesta, *La democracia*, 42.

73. Bushnell, *The Santander*. Gibson, *The Constitutions*, 35–67.

74. Sánchez Agesta, *La democracia*, 26–39, 51–52. Pierson and Gil, *Government*, 107–133.

75. Belaunde, "The Political," 88–89. Fitzgerald, *The Political*, 58–61. Pierson and Gil, *Government*, 113–115.

76. Safford, "Politics," 62–68. Collier, *Ideas*, 155–164.

77. Bushnell and Macaulay, *The Emergence*, 65. Kinsbruner, *Independence*, quote from 112.

78. Bravo Lira, *Historia de las instituciones*, 166–168.

79. Sánchez Agesta, *La democracia*, 50–51, 59–61. Jane, *Liberty*, 131–135.

80. Kinsbruner, *Independence*, 124.

81. Sánchez Agesta, *La democracia*, 59–61. Bushnell, *The Santander*, 50–57.

82. Sánchez Agesta, *La democracia*, 186. Belaunde, "The Political," 88–90. Fitzgerald, *The Political*, 57–58. Pinochet later echoed Bolívar's recommendation for military influence in the senate.

83. Robertson, *History*, 292–294. Belaúnde, "The Political," 93–96. Fitzgerald, *The Political*, 97–98.

84. Robertson, *History*, 172–173, 179–186.

85. Parry, *The Spanish*. Eduardo Zimmerman, ed., *Judicial Institutions in Nineteenth-Century Latin America* (London: Institute of Latin American studies, 1999).

86. Kenneth L. Clark and Keith S. Rosenn, *Law and Development in Latin America: A Case Book* (Berkeley: University of California Press, 1975). Kenneth W. Thompson, *The U.S. Constitution and the Constitutions of Latin America*. (Lanham, Maryland: University Press of America, 1991). David S. Clark, "Judicial Protection of the Constitution in Latin America," *Hastings Constitutional Law Quarterly* 2 (Spring, 1975), 405–442. Felipe Saez Garcia, "The Nature of Judicial Reform in Latin America and Some Strategic Considerations." *American University International Law Review* 13 (1998), 1267. Francisco J. Moreno, *Legitimacy and Stability in Latin America: A Study of Chilean Political Culture* (New York, New York University Press, 1969). Louis G. Kahle, "The Spanish Colonial Judiciary," *The Southwestern Social Science Quarterly* 32:1 (1951), 26–37. Mark A. Burkholder, *The Politics of a Colonial Career: José Basquíjano and the Audiencia of Lima* (Albuquerque: University of New Mexico Press, 1980). Mark A. Burkholder and D.S. Chandler, *From Impotence to Authority: The Spanish Crown and the American Audiencias, 1687–1808* (Columbia: University of Missouri Press, 1977). John Lynch, *Spanish Colonial Administration, 1782–1810: The Intendant System in the Viceroyalty of the Río de la Plata*.(London: University of London, Athlone Press, 1958). Teresa Beatriz Cauzzi, *Historia de la primera audiencia de Buenos Aires, 1661–1672* (Buenos Aires: Universidad Catolica Argentina, 1984). Phelan, "Authority." Haring, *The Spanish*, 124–127, 141.

87. Karst and Rosenn, *Law*. Bravo Lira, *Historia de las instituciones*, 166. Zimmerman, *Judicial*. Bushnell, *The Santander*, 45–50. Fitzgerald, *The Political*, 52, 64. Hale, *Mexican Liberalism*, 94–95, 112.

88. Antonio Annino, "Introducción," in Antonio Annino, ed., *Historia de las elecciones en Iberoamérica, siglo xix de la formación del espacio político nacional* (Buenos Aires: Fondo de Cultura Economica de Argentina, 1995), 7–18. Hilda Sabato, "On Political Citizenship in Nineteenth-Century Latin America," *The American Historical Review*, 106:4 (October, 2001), 1290–1315.

89. Eduardo Posada-Carbo, "Introduction: Elections before Democracy: Some Considerations on Electoral History from a Comparative Approach," in Eduardo Posada-Carbo, ed., *Elections before Democracy: The History of Elections in Europe and Latin America* (London: Institute of Latin American Studies, 1996), 1–16.

90. José Carlos Chiaramonte, "Vieja y nueva representación: los procesos electorales en Buenos Aires, 1810–1820," in Annino, *Historia*, 19–64.

91. Chiaramonte, "Vieja," 20–40.

92. Rodriguez O., *The Independence*, 112–113, 121. Sánchez Agesta, *La democracia*, 26–27. Fitzgerald, *The Political*, 14.

93. Fernando Campos Harriet, *Historia constitucional de Chile: Las instituciones políticas y sociales*, 4th ed. (Santiago: Editorial Juridica de Chile, 1969), 349–350. Julio Heise González, *El período parlamentario, 1861–1925: democracia y gobierno representativo*

en el período parlamentario (Historia del poder electoral), 2 vols. (Santiago: Editorial Universitaria, 1982), II, 12–14.

94. Marie-Danielle Demelas-Bohy, "Modalidades y significación de elecciones generales en los pueblos andinos, 1813–1814," in Annino, *Historia*, 291–314.

95. Annino, "Introducción," 10–12.

96. Rodriguez O., *The Independence*, 92–103.

97. Richard Warren, "Elections and Popular Political Participation in Mexico, 1808–1836," in Peloso and Tenenbaum, *Liberals*, 30–58; *Vagrants and Citizens: Politics and the Masses in Mexico City from Colony to Republic* (Wilmington: Scholarly Resources, Inc., 2001). Antonio Annino, "The Ballot, Land and Sovereignty: Cadiz and the Origins of Mexican Local Government, 1812–1820," in Posada-Carbo, *Elections*, 61–86. Electoral fraud was so widespread that one wag recommended that the only remedy was to shoot the perpetrators immediately on polling day. Torcuato S. Di Tella, *National Popular Politics in Early Independent Mexico, 1820–1847* (Albuquerque: University of New Mexico Press, 1996), 92–104.

98. Demelas-Bohy, "Modalidades," 294–298.

99. Campos Harriet, *Historia*, 350. Heise González, *El período*, 14–18.

100. Richard Graham, *Patronage and Politics in Nineteenth-Century Brazil* (Stanford: Stanford University Press, 1990), 101–103. Lucía María Bastos P. Neves, "Las elecciones en la construcción del imperio brasileño: Los límites de una nueva practica de la cultura política lusobrasileña, 1820–1823," in Annino, *Historia*, 381–408.

101. Posada-Carbo, "Introduction," 1–16.

102. Peloso and Tenenbaum, *Liberals*, 11.

103. Di Tella, *Latin*, 29. Kinsbruner, *Independence*, 109–112. Pierson and Gil, *Government*, 111–112. Davis, "The Presidency," 261.

104. Sánchez Agesta, *La democracia*, 47–48.

105. Kinsbruner, *Independence*, 110–111. Rodriguez O., *The Independence*, 115–116, 183–184. Bushnell, *The Santander*, 18–19. Bushnell and Macaulay, *The Emergence*, 27–28. González, *Las primeras*, 50–53.

106. Bushnell, *The Santander*, 13–41; quote from 18–19. Gibson, *The Constitutions*, 35–67. Sánchez Agesta, *La democracia*, 46–47.

107. Annino, "Introducción," 14–18. Fitzgerald, *The Political*, 96–97. Belaunde, *Bolívar*, 235–237.

108. Annino, "Introducción," 14–18. González, *Las primeras*, 13–38.

Notes to Chapter 4

1. I am indebted to Ivan Jaksic for the phrase "archaeology of democracy."

2. Frank Safford, "Politics, Ideology and Society," in Leslie Bethell, ed., *Spanish America after Independence, c. 1820-c. 1870* (Cambridge: Cambridge University Press, 1987), 48–122, especially 56–57.

3. David Bushnell and Neill Macaulay, *The Emergence of Latin America in the Nineteenth Century*, 2nd ed. (New York: Oxford University Press, 1994), 180–191. Safford, "Politics," 54–55

4. Larry Diamond and Juan J. Linz, "Introduction: Politics, Society, and Democracy in Latin America," in Larry Diamond, Juan J. Linz, and Seymour Martin Lipset, eds., *Democracy in Developing Countries: Latin America* (Boulder: Lynne Rienner, 1989), 1–58. R. A. Humphreys, "Democracy and Dictatorship," in Asher N. Christensen, ed., *The Evolution of Latin American Government* (New York: Henry Holt and Company, 1951), 317–332, especially 325.

5. Alexis de Tocqueville, *Democracy in America* (New York: New American Library, 1956), 133.

6. Safford, "Politics," 48. Leopoldo Zea, *The Latin-American Mind* (Norman: University of Oklahoma Press, 1963), 83–86. Torcuato S. Di Tella, *National Popular Politics in Early Independent Mexico, 1820–1847* (Albuquerque: University of New Mexico Press, 1996), 2–5.

7. John Lynch, *Caudillos in Spanish America, 1800–1850* (Oxford: Clarendon Press, 1992), 205–206, 406–411. Tulio Halperin-Donghi, *The Aftermath of Revolution in Latin America* (New York: Harper and Row, 1973), 1–43.

8. Jose Luis Romero, *A History of Argentine Political Thought* (Stanford: Stanford University Press, 1963). E. Bradford Burns, *The Poverty of Progress: Latin America in the Nineteenth Century* (Berkeley: University of California Press, 1980), 86–92, 111.

9. Zea, *The Latin*, 49–51. Miguel Jorrin and John D. Martz, *Latin-American Political Thought and Ideology* (Chapel Hill: The University of North Carolina Press, 1970), 100–102.

10. Halperin, *The Aftermath*, 111–115. Hilda Sabato, "Introducción," in Hilda Sabato, ed., *Ciudadanía política y formación de las naciones: Perspectivas históricas de América Latina* (Mexico: Fondo de Cultura Economica, 1997), 11–32.

11. Safford, "Politics," 67–70. Charles A. Hale, *Mexican Liberalism in the Age of Mora, 1821–1853* (New Haven: Yale University Press, 1968), 188–214.

12. Halperin, *The Aftermath*, 129–140.

13. Guy Thomson, ed., *The European Revolutions of 1848 and the Americas* (London: Institute of Latin American Studies, 2002). Helen Delpar, *Red Against Blue: The Liberal Party in Colombian Politics, 1863–1899* (University, Alabama: The University of Alabama Press, 1981). Cristián Gazmuri Riveros, *El "48" chileno: Igualitarios, reformistas, radicals, masones y bomberos* (Santiago: Editorial Universitaria, 1992). Bushnell and Macaulay, *The Emergence*, 186–192. Safford, "Politics," 93–99.

14. Hale, *Mexican*, 39.

15. Hale, *Mexican*, 72–107, 124, 215–247.

16. Bushnell and Macaulay, *The Emergence*, 193–209. Richard N. Sinkin, *The Mexican Reform, 1855–1876: A Study in Liberal Nation-Building* (Austin: University of

Texas Press, 1979). Charles A. Hale, *The Transformation of Liberalism in Late Nineteenth-Century Mexico* (Princeton: Princeton University Press, 1989).

17. Jorrin and Martz, *Latin*, 110–113. Natalio R. Botana, *La tradición republicana: Alberdi, Sarmiento y las ideas políticas de su tiempo* (Buenos Aires: Editorial Sudamericana, 1984), especially 263–308 and 465–466, quote from 310. Tulio Halperin Donghi, Ivan Jaksic, Gwen Kirkpatrick, and Francine Masiello, eds., *Sarmiento: Author of a Nation* (Berkeley: University of California Press, 1994).

18. Botana, *La tradición*, 310–311, 344–352, 472–493; *El orden conservador: La política argentina entre 1880 y 1916*, 4th ed. (Buenos Aires: Editorial Sudamericana, 1994), quote from 65–66. Romero, *A History*, 126–164. Jeremy Adelman, *Republic of Capital: Buenos Aires and the Legal Transformation of the Atlantic World* (Stanford: Stanford University Press, 1999), 165–190.

19. Florencia E. Mallon, *Peasant and Nation: The Making of Postcolonial Mexico and Peru* (Berkeley: University of California Press, 1995), 9–19, 155–160. Burns, *The Poverty*.

20. Safford, "Politics," 58–59. Russell H. Fitzgibbon, ed., *The Constitutions of the Americas* (Chicago: The University of Chicago Press, 1948).

21. Loveman, *The Constitution*, 370. Keith S. Rosenn, "The Success of Constitutionalism in the United States and its Failure in Latin America," in Kenneth W. Thompson, ed., *The U.S. Constitution and the Constitutions of Latin America* (Lanham: University Press of America, 1991), 53–96, especially 87–94.

22. Although the Chilean constitution provided for some civil liberties, governments often suspended them to cope with alleged "emergencies." Brian Loveman, *Chile: The Legacy of Hispanic Capitalism*, 2nd ed. (New York: Oxford University Press, 1988), 123–126, quote from 124. Arturo Valenzuela, *Political Brokers in Chile: Local Government in a Centralized Polity* (Durham: Duke University Press, 1977), 172–190. Bernardino Bravo Lira, *Historia de las instituciones políticas de Chile e Hispanoamérica* (Santiago: Editorial Andrés Bello, 1986). Karen L. Remmer, *Party Competition in Argentina and Chile: Political Recruitment and Public Policy, 1890–1930* (Lincoln: University of Nebraska Press, 1984), 10–14. Maurice Zeitlin, "The Social Determinants of Political Democracy in Chile," in James Petras and Maurice Zeitlin, eds., *Reform or Revolution in Latin America?* (New York: Fawcett World Library, 1968), 220–234.

23. Austin F. Macdonald, *Government of the Argentina Republic* (New York: Thomas Y. Crowell Company, 1942), quote from 128. Carlos H. Waisman, "Argentina: Autarkic Industrialization and Illegitimacy," in Diamond, Linz, and Lipset, *Democracy*, 59–110.

24. Macdonald, *Government*, 126–146. Adelman, *Republic*, 194–223. William Columbus Davis, *Warnings from the Far South: Democracy versus Dictatorship in Uruguay, Argentina, and Chile* (Westport, Connecticut: Praeger, 1995), 74–75. Edward L. Gibson and Tulia G. Falleti, "Unity by the Stick: Regional Conflict and the Origins of

Argentine Federalism," in Edward L. Gibson, ed., *Federalism and Democracy in Latin America* (Baltimore: The John Hopkins University Press, 2004), 226–254. Eduardo Aleman and George Tsebelis, "The Origins of Presidential Conditional Agenda-Setting Power in Latin America," *Latin American Research Review*, 40:2 (June, 2005), 3–26, Alberdi, quote from 20.

25. William W. Pierson and Federico G. Gil, *Government and Politics of Latin America* (New York: McGraw-Hill Book Campany, Inc., 1957), 123–124, 160–164. George I. Blanksten, *Ecuador: Constitutions and Caudillos* (New York: Russell and Russell, Inc., 1964), 169–171. Graham H. Stuart, *The Governmental System of Peru*, (Washington, D.C.: The Carnegie Institution of Washington, 1925), 3–18.

26. William Spence Robertson, *History of the Latin American Nations*, 3rd ed. (New York: D. Appleton-Century Co., 1943), 238–239. Hector Gros Espiell, *Las constituciones del Uruguay*, 2nd ed (Madrid: Centro Ibero Americano de Cooperacion, 1978), 37–57, 130–177.

27. Manuel Alcántara Saez, *Sistemas políticos de América Latina*, 2nd ed., 2 vols. (Madrid: Tecnos, 1999), II, 91–92.

28. Fitzgibbon, *The Constitutions*, 666–667. Stuart, *The Governmental*, 3–18.

29. Safford, "Politics," 84–85. Fitzgibbon, *The Constitutions*, 137–138, 164–165. Robertson, *History*, 338–343. For example, Peru in the 1870s preserved centralism while also placating regional elites by devolving to departmental and municipal governments a few responsibilities and taxes. Ulrich Muecke, *Political Culture in Nineteenth-Century Peru: The Rise of the Partido Civil* (Pittsburgh: University of Pittsburgh Press, 2004), 38–39.

30. Pierson and Gil, *Government*, 170–179. Marcello Carmagnani, ed., *Federalismos latinoamericanos: Mexico/Brasil/Argentina* (Mexico: Fondo de Cultura Economica, 1993). Kent Eaton, *Politics Beyond the Capital: The Design of Subnational Institutions in South America* (Stanford: Stanford University Press, 2004), 36–44. Miron Burgin, *The Economic Aspects of Argentine Federalism, 1820–1852* (New York: Russell and Russell, 1946).

31. Matthew Soberg Shugart and John M. Carey, *Presidents and Assemblies: Constitutional Design and Electoral Dynamics* (Cambridge: Cambridge University Press, 1992), 5–9.

32. Fitzgibbon, *The Constitutions*, 217–218.

33. Pierson and Gil, *Government*, 164–167. Brian Loveman, *The Constitution of Tyranny: Regimes of Exception in Spanish America* (Pittsburgh: University of Pittsburgh Press, 1993).

34. Ivan Jaksic, ed., *The Political Power of the Word: Press and Oratory in Nineteenth-Century Latin America* (London: Institute of Latin American Studies, 2002). Stuart, *The Governmental*, 5–7.

35. Loveman, *Chile*, 123–126. Arturo Valenzuela, *Political Brokers*, 185–186. Bravo Lira, *Historia de las instituciones*, 181–184, 188–195, 229–264. Fitzgibbon, *The Constitutions*, 138. Robertson, *History*, 271–275. William S. Stokes, "Parliamentary Government in Latin America," in Christensen, *The Evolution*, 454–467, especially 456–457.

36. The provision freezing salaries appeared in some other Latin American constitutions. The authors intended it to prevent personal aggrandizement by the president or influence over the president by the legislature raising or lowering his salary. Fitzgibbon, *The Constitutions*, 25–28. Macdonald, *Government*, 126–146, 190–230. Botana, *El orden*, quote from 48–49.

37. Macdonald, *Government*, quote from 129.

38. Richard Warren, *Vagrants and Citizens: Politics and the Masses in Mexico City from Colony to Republic* (Wilmington: Scholarly Resources, Inc., 2001), 169.

39. Fitzgibbon, *The Constitutions*, 211.

40. Bravo Lira, *Historia de las instituciones*, 192–193. Pierson and Gil, *Governments*, 118–120. Landowner congressional data comes from Arnold J. Bauer," Landlord and Campesino in the Chilean Road to Democracy," in Evelyne Huber and Frank Safford, eds., *Agrarian Structure and Political Power: Landlord and Peasant in the Making of Latin America* (Pittsburgh: University of Pittsburgh Press, 1995), 21–38, especially 33. Germán Urzúa Valenzuela, *Historia política de Chile y su evolución electoral (Desde 1810 a 1992)* (Santiago: Editorial Juridica de Chile, 1992), 79, 103.

41. Fitzgibbon, *The Constitutions*, 18–24.

42. Josefina Zoraida Vazquez, "El federalismo mexicano, 1823–1847," in Carmagnani, *Federalismos*, 15–50, especially 45–46.

43. Robert Packenham, "Functions of the Brazilian National Congress," in H. Weston Agor, ed., *Latin American Legislatures: Their Role and Influence* (New York: Praeger, 1971), 259–292, especially 260–263.

44. Helen L. Clagett, "Law and Court Systems," in Davis, *Government*, 333–367. Edelmann, *Latin*, 465–487. Lambert, *Latin*, 287–295.

45. Loveman, *The Constitution*. Bravo Lira, *Historia de las instituciones*. Helen L. Clagett, *The Administration of Justice in Latin America* (New York: Oceana Publications, 1952). Alberto David Leiva, *Fuentes para el estudio de la historia institucional argentina* (Buenos Aires: Editorial Universitaria de Buenos Aires, 1982). Miguel Jorrin, *Governments of Latin America* (New York: D. Van Nostrand Company, Inc., 1953). The judiciary in Spanish America was not the object of high stakes political battles during the independence and early nation-building periods. In Brazil, however, the judiciary became the terrain upon which liberal reformism and decentralization battled against conservative centralization under the constitutional monarch. Control of the judiciary became a hot political question, and transfer of justices the main means to achieve

it. Thomas *Flory, Judge and Jury in Imperial Brazil, 1808–1871: Social Control and Political Stability in the New State* (Austin: University of Texas Press, 1981).

46. Jonathan M. Miller, "Courts and the Creation of a 'Spirit of Moderation:' Judicial Protection of Revolutionaries in Argentina, 1863–1929," *Hastings International and Comparative Law Review* 20 (1997), 231–329. By contrast, the Chilean Constitution of 1833 did not recognize a judicial role in constitutional adjudication. Instead, the Chileans placed the preservation of the constitution in the hands of the "comisión conservadora" named by the senate to watch over the constitution and the laws and make recommendations to the president concerning such matters during periods of legislative recess. Chile vested the power to interpret and construe the constitution solely in congress until the constitution of 1925. Pierson and Gil, *Government*. Kenneth L. Clark and Keith S. Rosenn, *Law and Development in Latin America: A Case Book* (Berkeley: University of California Press, 1975).

47. Felipe Saez Garcia, "The Nature of Judicial Reform in Latin America and Some Strategic Considerations." *American University International Law Review* 13 (1998), 1267.

48. Governments decreased judicial arbitrariness and the potential for judicial dictatorship by insisting that judicial decisions could not be a source of law, that the judiciary must not assume legislative functions, and that judges must decide cases according to the law and the decisions of other judges. John Henry Merryman, *The Civil Law Tradition*, 2nd ed. (Stanford: Stanford University Press, 1985). Juan E. Vargas Viancos and Jorge Correa Sutil, *Diagnóstico del sistema judicial chileno* (Santiago: Corporación de Promoción Universitaria, 1995).

49. David S. Clark, "Judicial Protection of the Constitution in Latin America," *Hastings Constitutional Law Quarterly* 2 (Spring, 1975), 405–442. Keith S. Rosenn, "Judicial Review in Latin America," *Ohio State Law Journal* 35 (1974), 785–819. Phanor James Eder, *A Comparative Survey of Anglo-American and Latin American Law* (New York: New York University Press, 1950).

50. Hilda Sabato, "On Political Citizenship in Nineteenth-Century Latin America," *The American Historical Review*, 106:4 (October, 2001), 1290–1315; *The Many and the Few: Political Participation in Republican Buenos Aires* (Stanford: Stanford University Press, 2001). James E. Sanders, *Contentious Republicans: Popular Politics, Race, and Class in Nineteenth-Century Colombia* (Durham: Duke University Press, 2004), 3–5. Marta Irurozqui, "Sobre leyes y transgresiones: Reformas electorales en Bolivia, 1826–1952," in Carlos Malamud, ed., *Legitimidad, representación y alternancia en España y América Latina: Las reformas electorales (1880–1930)* (Mexico: Fondo de Cultura Economica, 2000), 262–291.

51. Sources disagee on the precise dates for the legal introduction of universal male suffrage. Some would delay Chile until 1925, others Argentina until 1912. Sabato, "Introducción," in Sabato, ed., *Ciudadanía*, 19–20. T. H. Marshall, *Class, Citizen-*

ship, and Social Development (Chicago: University of Chicago Press, 1977). The term "cowboyocracy" comes from Charles E. Chapman, "The Age of the Caudillos: A Chapter in Hispanic American History," in Christensen, *The Evolution*, 65–80, especially 75–76. Russell H Fitzgibbon, "The Pathology of Democracy in Latin America: A Political Scientist's Point of View," in Christensen, *The Evolution*, 270–284. Arthur P. Whitaker, "The Pathology of Democracy in Latin America: A Historian's Point of View," in Christensen, *The Evolution*, 247–269, especially 251–253. Dieter Nohlen, "Elections and Electoral Systems in the Americas," in Dieter Nohlen, ed., *Elections in the Americas: A Data Handbook*, 2 vols. (New York: Oxford University Press, 2005), I, 28; II, 1–58, especially 12. Torcuato S. Di Tella, *Latin American Politics: A Theoretical Approach* (Austin: University of Texas, 1990), 1–2.

52. Botana, *La tradición*. Sabato, "Introducción," 20–24.

53. In Bolivia, fraud was punishable by loss of citizenship. Irurozqui, "Sobre," in Malamud, ed., *Legitimidad*, 262–291.

54. Safford, "Politics," 103–104.

55. Vincent C. Peloso, "Liberals, Electoral Reform, and the Popular Vote in Mid-Nineteenth-Century Peru," in Peloso and Tenenbaum, *Liberals*, 186–211, especially 186–188.

56. Rolando Franco, *Los sistemas electorales y su impacto político* (San José: CAPEL, 1987), 26–28. From the 1850s to the 1870s, Colombia, Mexico, Ecuador, the Dominican Republic, and Chile became the first Latin American countries to legally promise secret voting, but that may have meant little in practice. Nohlen, "Elections," I, 12.

57. Halperin, *The Aftermath*, 115–118.

58. Lynch, *Caudillos*, 205–206. Kevin Kelly, "Rosas and the Restoration of Order through Populism," in Mark D. Szuchman and Jonathan C. Brown, eds., *Revolution and Restoration: the Rearrangement of Power in Argentina, 1776–1860* (Lincoln: University of Nebraska Press, 1994), 208–239. Marcela Ternavasio, "Hacia un regimen de unanimidad. Política y elecciones en Buenos Aires, 1828–1850," in Sabato, *Ciudadanía*, 119–141.

59. William Marion Gibson, *The Constitutions of Colombia* (Durham: Duke University Press, 1948).

60. Fitzgibbon, *The Constitutions*, 210.

61. Richard Graham, *Patronage and Politics in Nineteenth-Century Brazil*, (Stanford: Stanford University Press, 1990), 2–3, 71–145, 265–272. C. H. Haring, *Empire in Brazil: A New World Experiment with Monarchy* (Cambridge: Harvard University Press, 1966).

62. Halperin, *The Aftermath*, 115–118. J. Samuel Valenzuela, *Democratización via reforma: La expansión del sufragio en Chile*, (Buenos Aires: Ediciones del IDES, 1985); "Building Aspects of Democracy Before Democracy: Electoral Practices in

Nineteenth-Century Chile," in Eduardo Posada-Carbo, ed., *Elections before Democ racy: The History of Elections in Europe and Latin America* (London: Institute of Latin American Studies, 1996), 223–258.

63. Halperin, *The Aftermath*, 117–127. Sanders, *Contentious*.

64. Marcela Ternavasio, "Nuevo régimen representativo y expansión de la frontera política. Las elecciones en el estado de Buenos Aires: 1820–1840," in Antonio Annino, ed., *Historia de las elecciones en Iberoamérica, siglo xix de la formación del espacio político nacional* (Buenos Aires: Fondo de Cultura Economica de Argentina, 1995), 65–106. Paula Alonso, "Voting in Buenos Aires, Argentina, before 1912," in Posada-Carbo, *Elections*, 181–200.

65. Hilda Sabato, "Elecciones y prácticas electorales en Buenos Aires, 1860–1880. Sufragio universal sin ciudadanía política?" in Annino, *Historia* 107–142; *The Many*. Luis Sánchez Agesta, *La democracia en Hispanoamérica: Un balance histórico* (Madrid: Ediciones RIALP, S.A., 1987), 48–49. Macdonald, *Government*, 68–88. Alonso, "Voting," 190–191.

66. Robert A. Dahl, *Polyarchy: Participation and Opposition* (New Haven: Yale University Press, 1971), 133.

67. Alonso, "Voting," 181–189. Darío Cantón, *Elecciones y partidos políticos en la Argentina: Historia, interpretación y balance: 1910–1966* (Buenos Aires: Siglo Veintiuno Argentina Editores, SA, 1973), 20. Sabato, *The Many*, newspaper quote from 60. Bushnell and Macaulay, *The Emergence*, 223–224.

68. Valenzuela, "Building;" *Democratización*. For example, the 1823 competitive elections required voters to be free male residents with 23 years, literacy, and sufficient property, income, professional degrees, or military or ecclesiastical positions, although many voters broke the rules. Urzúa Valenzuela, *Historia*, 13–288, especially 18–38.

69. Julio Heise González, *El período parlamentario, 1861–1925: Democracia y gobierno representativo en el período parlamentario (Historia del poder electoral)*, 2 vols. (Santiago: Editorial Universitaria, 1982), II, 18–22.

70. The category of agricultural workers among registered voters may well have included some landowners. Samuel Valenzuela, *Democratización*, especially 11–41, 117–121, 150; "Building," 234–250. Bravo Lira, *Historia de las instituciones*, 190–195, 260–264. Arturo Valenzuela, *Political Brokers*, 189–190. Bauer, "Landlord," 32–33. Remmer, *Party*, 84. Dahl, *Polyarchy*, 33–49. Despite similarities, the reformist path opened up in Argentina by the electoral liberalization of 1912 did not lead to a stable democracy buttressed by democratic rightwing parties.

71. Graham, *Patronage*, 101–121. Herbert S. Klein, "Participación política en Brasil en el siglo xix: Los votantes de San Pablo en 1880," in Annino, *Historia*, 453–468.

72. Peloso, "Liberals," 188–205. Muecke, *Political*, 14–17, 36–39, 82–83. Carmen McEvoy, *La utopía republicana: Ideales y realidades en la formación de la cultura política*

peruana (1871–1919) (Lima: Fondo Editorial de la Pontifica Universidad Catolica del Peru, 1997), 1–120; *Forjando la nación: Ensayos sobre historia republicana* (Lima: La Pontifica Universidad Catolica del Peru, 1999), 169–188, quotes from 178; *Un proyecto nacional en el siglo xix. Manuel Pardo y su visión del Peru* (Lima: Fondo Editorial de la Pontifica Universidad Catolica del Peru, 1994); *Humo Politicus: Manuel Pardo, la política peruana y sus dilemmas, 1871–1878* (Lima: Instituto de Estudios Peruanos, 2007). Jorge Basadre, *Historia de la República del Perú, 1822–1933*, Vols. III–V (Lima: Editorial Universitaria, 1968–1970), V, 261–270.

73. Gibson, *The Constitutions*, 109–187, quotes on government and voters from 120, on military from 145. Malcolm Deas, "The Role of the Church, the Army and the Police in Colombian Elections, c. 1850–1930," in Posada-Carbo, *Elections*, 163–180. All the paragraphs here on Colombia rely partially on Sanders, *Contentious*, especially 126–129, 187–192.

74. Eduardo Posada-Carbo, "New Granada and the European Revolutions of 1848," in Thomson, ed., *The European*, 217–240; "Alternancia y república: Elecciones en la Nueva Granada y Venezuela, 1835–1837," in Sabato, ed., *Ciudadanía*, 162–180.

75. Deas, "The Role." Gibson, *The Constitutions*, 191–214. In the province of Velez, the Liberals also established female suffrage, a first in Latin America, but it was nullified by the Supreme Court before it could be implemented. Bushnell and Macaulay, *The Emergence*, 212.

76. Delpar, *Red*, 15–16, 68, 84–109. Eduardo Posada-Carbo, "Elections and Civil Wars in Nineteenth-Century Colombia: The 1875 Presidential Campaign," *Journal of Latin American Studies*, 26 (1994), 621–649; "Civilizar las urnas: Conflicto y control en las elecciones colombianas, 1830–1930," in Carlos Malamud, ed., "Partidos políticos y elecciones en América Latina y la Peninsula Ibérica, 1830–1930," Manuscript, 2 vols. (Madrid: Instituto Universitario Ortega y Gasset, 1995), I, 145–166.

77. Juan Maiguascha, "The Electoral Reforms of 1861 in Ecuador and the Rise of a New Political Order," in Posada-Carbo, *Elections*, 87–116.

78. Maiguascha, "The Electoral," 89–111.

79. Richard Warren, "Elections and Popular Political Participation in Mexico, 1808–1836," in Peloso and Tenenbaum, *Liberals*, 30–58; *Vagrants and Citizens: Politics and the Masses in Mexico City from Colony to Republic* (Wilmington: Scholarly Resources, Inc., 2001), 75–171.

80. Gibson, *The Constitutions*, 247–297. Bushnell and Macaulay, *The Emergence*, 209–220.

81. Peloso, "Liberals," especially 192–205.

82. Graham, *Patronage*, 182–206.

83. Muecke, *Political Culture*, 1–17.

84. Di Tella, *Latin*, 60–62. Sabato, "Introducción," 21–23; *The Many*. Pilar González Bernaldo, "Los clubes electorales durante la secessión del Estado de Buenos

Aires (1852–1861): La articulación de dos lógicas de representación política en el seno de la esfera pública porteña," in Sabato, *Ciudadanía*, 142–161.

85. Diamond and Linz, "Introduction," 20–24. Alonso, "Voting," 190–193. J. Samuel Valenzuela, "Building," 248–250. Safford, "Politics," 104–113.

86. Bravo Lira, *Historia de las instituciones*, 229–243. Remmer, *Party*, 14–24.

87. Delpar, *Red*, x–xii, 15. Sanders, *Contentious*.

88. McEvoy, *La utopía; Un proyecto*. Muecke, *Political*.

89. Graham, *Patronage*, 146–181.

Notes to Chapter 5

1. On the role of the United States, see Paul W. Drake, "From Good Men to Good Neighbors," in Abraham F. Lowenthal, ed., *Exporting Democracy* (Baltimore: John Hopkins University Press, 1991), 3–40; "The Hegemony of U.S. Economic Doctrines in Latin America," in Valpy Fitzgerald and Rosemary Thorp, eds., *Economic Doctrines in Latin America: Origins, Embedding and Evolution* (London: Palgrave Mac-Millan, 2005), 72–96.

2. Jonathan Hartlyn and Arturo Valenzuela, "Democracy in Latin America since 1930," in Leslie Bethell, ed., *Latin America: Politics and Society since 1930* (Cambridge: Cambridge University Press, 1998), 3–66, quote from 3–4. Peter H. Smith, *Democracy in Latin America: Political Change in Comparative Perspective* (New York: Oxford University Press, 2005), especially 19–58.

3. Although most of these rough time periods are generally accepted, even the dates for the more successful oligarchic republics are subject to debate. For example, some scholars would set the starting date for Argentina in 1853, when it adopted its enduring constitution, or in 1880, when it consolidated the power of its national central government and presidency. Others might place the commencement of Colombia's episode in 1863 or 1867. A case could be made that Uruguay launched its oligarchic republic in 1872 or 1897. Since these cut-off points are not sharply defined, the chronology for the more limited and unstable regimes is even more disputable because of the slender historiography. For example, some experts would start Costa Rica with the constitution of 1871, while others would prefer the beginning of regular electoral turnover in a constitutional regime in 1889. In similar fashion, Peru could be dated from 1867 or 1886, Ecuador from 1895, 1906, or 1913, Honduras from 1880, 1904, or 1916, and El Salvador from 1919. Regardless of precise dates and some severe disruptions, these regimes predominated in these countries in this approximate time period. Scholarly disagreements about these dates do not affect this book's uncontroversial argument about the general political trends in the era. Dietrich Rueschemeyer, Evelyne Huber Stephens, and John D. Stephens, *Capitalist Development and Democracy* (Chicago: University of Chicago Press, 1992), 160–161. Smith, *Democracy*, 348–353. Brian Loveman, *The Constitution of Tyranny: Regimes of Exception in Spanish America*

(Pittsburgh: University of Pittsburgh Press, 1993). Keith S. Rosenn, "The Success of Constitutionalism in the United States and Its Failure in Latin America: An Explanation," in Kenneth W. Thompson, ed., *The U.S. Constitution and the Constitutions of Latin America* (Lanham: University Press of America, 1991), 53–96.

4. Natalio Botana, *El orden conservador: La política argentina entre 1880 y 1916*, 4th ed. (Buenos Aires: Editorial Sudamericana, 1994), 43, 254–258. Carlos Forment, *Democracy in Latin America, 1760–1900: Civic Selfhood and Public Life. Mexico and Peru* (Chicago: University of Chicago Press, 2003).

5. Marcello Carmagnani, *Estado y sociedad en América Latina, 1850–1930* (Barcelona: Editorial Critica, 1984).

6. James Bryce, *South America: Observations and Impressions* (New York: The Macmillan Company, 1912), 543.

7. Arthur P. Whitaker, "The Pathology of Democracy in Latin America: A Historian's Point of View," in Asher N. Christensen, ed., *The Evolution of Latin American Government* (New York: Henry Holt and Company, 1951), 247–269, especially 264. R. A. Humphreys, "Democracy and Dictatorship," in Christensen, *The Evolution*, 318–332, especially 325–328. Paul W. Drake, "Debt and Democracy in Latin America, 1920s–80s," in Barbara Stallings and Robert Kaufman, eds., *Debt and Democracy in Latin America* (Boulder: Westview Press, 1988), 39–58. H. E. Chehabi and Juan J. Linz, *Sultanistic Regimes* (Baltimore: Johns Hopkins University Press, 1998). Smith, *Democracy*, 27.

8. Smith, *Democracy*, 354–355.

9. Ruth Berins Collier and David Collier, *Shaping the Political Arena: Critical Junctures, the Labor Movement, and Regime Dynamics in Latin America* (Princeton: Princeton University Press, 1991). Paul W. Drake and Matthew D. McCubbins, eds., *The Origins of Liberty: Political and Economic Liberalization in the Modern World* (Princeton: Princeton University Press, 1998).

10. Paul W. Drake, "Requiem for Populism," in Michael L. Conniff, ed., *Latin American Populism in Comparative Perspective* (Albuquerque, University of New Mexico Press, 1982), 217–245. Michael L. Conniff, "Introduction," in Michael L. Conniff, ed., *Populism in Latin America* (Tuscaloosa: The University of Alabama Press, 1999), 1–21. Michael L. Conniff, *Urban Politics in Brazil: The Rise of Populism, 1925–1945* (Pittsburgh: University of Pittsburgh Press, 1981).

11. According to Bryce, the Indians remained the group most excluded from political life: "They have nothing to do with the white people, except in so far as they pay rent or work for employers. By the constitution they are, in many states, citizens and have votes. But they have never heard of the constitution and they never think of voting, having, although free, no more to do with the government than the slaves had in the southern United States before the Civil War." Bryce, *South*, 527–551, quote from 529. Whitaker, "The Pathology," 259–270.

12. Bryce, *South*, 537.

13. Peter H. Smith, *Argentina and the Failure of Democracy: Conflict among Political Elites, 1904–1955* (Madison: University of Wisconsin Press, 1974), xv.

14. President Woodrow Wilson's Ambassador to England explained to the British that Washington would continue to use force to impose electoral democracy in Latin America: "The United States will be here for two hundred years and it can continue to shoot men for that little space till they learn to vote and rule themselves." Drake, "From Good Men," quote from note 14. The last point is made statistically by Smith, *Democracy*, 36–39, 108–111.

15. David F. Schmitz, *Thank God They're on Our Side: The United States and Right-Wing Dictatorships, 1921–1965* (Chapel Hill: The University of North Carolina Press, 1999).

16. Miguel Jorrín and John D. Martz, *Latin-American Political Thought and Ideology* (Chapel Hill: The University of North Carolina Press, 1970), 126–144. Charles A. Hale, *The Transformation of Liberalism in Late Nineteenth-Century Mexico* (Princeton: Princeton University Press, 1989). Sandra McGee Deutsch, *Las Derechas: The Extreme Right in Argentina, Brazil, and Chile, 1890–1939* (Stanford: Stanford University Press, 1999), 1–141.

17. Jorrin and Martz, *Latin*, 199–385.

18. Jorrin and Martz, *Latin*, 164–167.

19. Whitaker, "The Pathology," 255–259.

20. David Rock, *Politics in Argentina, 1890–1930: The Rise and Fall of Radicalism* (London: Cambridge University Press, 1975), 116–117.

21. By the early decades of the twentieth century, another current promoting social reforms arrived from abroad in the form of social Catholicism, which later blossomed into social Christianity and Christian Democracy. Jorrin and Martz, *Latin*, 181–196, 270–315.

22. Bryce, *South*, quote from 539. Rosenn, "The Success," especially 87–94.

23. William S. Stokes, "Parliamentary Government in Latin America," in Christensen, *The Evolution*, 454–467, especially 460–461. William Spence Robertson, *History of the Latin American Nations*, 3rd ed. (New York: D. Appleton-Century Co., 1943), 328. Graham H. Stuart, *The Governmental System of Peru* (Washington, D.C.: The Carnegie Institution of Washington, 1925), 19–35, 129–132. Alexander T. Edelmann, *Latin American Government and Politics: The Dynamics of a Revolutionary Society*, revd. ed. (Homewood: The Dorsey Press, 1969), 383.

24. Edelmann, *Latin*, 383.

25. Russell H. Fitzgibbon, ed., *The Constitutions of the Americas* (Chicago: University of Chicago Press, 1948), 498.

26. According to the 1917 Constitution, "Any citizen who has discharged the office of President of the Republic, popularly elected or in the character of interim, provision-

al, or substitute, may in no case and for no reason again hold this office." Thereafter the only president who tried to return following an intervening term was Alvaro Obregón (1920–24) in his reelection in 1928, but he was assassinated before donning the sash a second time. Harold E. Davis, "The Presidency," in Harold Eugene Davis, ed., *Government and Politics in Latin America* (New York: The Ronald Press Company, 1958), 252–289, quote from 269. James L. Busey, *Latin America: Political Institutions and Processes* (New York: Random House, 1964), 18–21. Fitzgibbon, *The Constitutions*, 496–553.

27. Jorrin and Martz, *Latin*, 208.

28. William Columbus Davis, *Warnings from the Far South: Democracy versus Dictatorship in Uruguay, Argentina, and Chile* (Westport, Connecticut: Praeger, 1995), 19–22. Milton I. Vanger, *José Batlle y Ordóñez of Uruguay: The Creator of His Times, 1902–1907* (Cambridge: Harvard University Press, 1963); *The Model Country: José Batlle y Ordóñez of Uruguay, 1907–1915* (Hanover, New Hampshire: Brandeis University Press, 1980), 99–103.

29. Hector Gros Espiell, *Las constituciones del Uruguay (Exposición, crítica y textos)*, (Madrid: Ediciones Cultura Hispanica, 1956), 59–74, 179–215. Davis, *Warnings*, 22–24. Jorrin and Martz, *Latin*, 227–237. Robertson, *History*, 244–248.

30. Robertson, *History*, 286–287. Bernardo Bravo Lira, *Historia de las instituciones políticas de Chile e Hispanoamérica* (Santiago: Editorial Andrés Bello, 1986), 322–324. Fitzgibbon, *The Constitutions*, 139–144, quotes from 144.

31. William Marion Gibson, *The Constitutions of Colombia* (Durham: Duke University Press, 1948), 229–230, 306–310, quotes from 306–307. Fitzgibbon, *The Constitutions*, 167, 194–198. Robertson, *History*, 343–344. Helen Delpar, *Red Against Blue: The Liberal Party in Colombian Politics, 1863–1899* (University, Alabama: The University of Alabama Press, 1981), x, 134–135. James William Park, *Rafael Nunez and the Politics of Colombian Regionalism, 1863–1886* (Baton Rouge: Louisiana State University Press, 1985).

32. Russell H. Fitzgibbon, *Latin America: A Panorama of Contemporary Politics* (New York: Appleton-Century-Crofts, 1971), 319–322; *The Constitutions*, 160–162. Kent Eaton, "The Link between Political and Fiscal Decentralization in South America," in Alfred P. Montero and David J. Samuels, eds., *Decentralization and Democracy in Latin America* (Notre Dame: University of Notre Dame Press, 2004), 122–154.

33. Stuart, *The Governmental*, 99.

34. Alicia Hernandez Chaves, "Federalismo y gobernabilidad en Mexico," in Marcello Carmagnani, ed., *Federalismos latinoamericanos: Mexico/Brasil/Argentina* (Mexico: Fondo de Cultura Economica, 1993), 263–299.

35. Joseph L. Love, *Rio Grande do Sul and Brazilian Regionalism, 1882–1930* (Stanford: Stanford University Press, 1971); *Sao Paulo in the Brazilian Federation, 1889–1937* (Stanford: Stanford University Press, 1980). John D. Wirth, *Minas Gerais in the Brazilian Federation, 1889–1937* (Stanford: Stanford University Press, 1977). Robert

M. Levine, *Pernambuco in the Brazilian Federation, 1889–1937* (Stanford: Stanford University Press, 1978). Jose Maria Bello, *A History of Modern Brazil, 1889–1964* (Stanford: Stanford University Press, 1966).

36. Fitzgibbon, *The Constitutions*, 530–534; *Latin*, 57–60. Busey, *Latin*, 28–46, quote from 20.

37. Botana, *El orden*, xxviii–xxxvi, 48–49.

38. Fitzgibbon, *The Constitutions*, 181–188. Gibson, *The Constitutions*, 311–313, quote from 311.

39. Stuart, *The Governmental*, 39, 41, 84–85, 112.

40. Analogies were later drawn between the suicide of Balmaceda and that of President Salvador Allende in the face of the military uprising of 1973. Bravo Lira, *Historia de las instituciones*, 266–278, quote from 271. Harold Blakemore, *British Nitrates and Chilean Politics, 1886–1896: Balmaceda and North* (London: Athlone Press, 1974). Maurice Zeitlin, *The Civil Wars in Chile (or the Bourgeois Revolutions that Never Were)* (Princeton: Princeton University Press, 1984). William S. Stokes, *Latin American Politics* (New York: Thomas Y. Crowell Company, 1959), 422–426. Mathew Soberg Shugart and John M. Carey, *Presidents and Assemblies: Constitutional Design and Electoral Dynamics* (Cambridge: Cambridge University Press, 1992), 113–114. Julio Heise González, *Historia de Chile: El período parlamentario, 1861–1925*, 2 vols. (Santiago: Editorial Andrés Bello, 1974). Arturo Valenzuela, *Political Brokers in Chile: Local Government in a Centralized Polity* (Durham: Duke University Press, 1977), 193–220. For city government under the 1925 constitution, only the lowly members of the council were elected by direct vote, and even aliens could cast ballots in these elections if they had resided in Chile for five years and met the voting qualifications of literacy and twenty-one years of age. Fitzgibbon, *The Constitutions*, 140–144, 152–156, 160–163.

41. C. H. Haring, *Empire in Brazil: A New World Experiment with Monarchy* (Cambridge: Harvard University Press, 1966). Robert Packenham, "Functions of the Brazilian National Congress," in H. Weston Agor, ed., *Latin American Legislatures: Their Role and Influence* (New York: Praeger, 1971), 259–292. Love, *Rio Grande*; *Sao Paulo*. Wirth, *Minas*. Levine, *Pernambuco*.

42. Espiell, *Las constituciones*. Jorrin and Martz, *Latin*, 227–237.

43. Dieter Nohlen, "Elections and Electoral Systems in the Americas," in Dieter Nohlen, ed., *Elections in the Americas: A Data Handbook*, 2 vols. (New York: Oxford University Press, 2005), II, 1–58, especially 12. Fitzgibbon, *The Constitutions*, 518–519.

44. Stuart, *The Governmental*, 69–72.

45. Stokes, "Parliamentary," 461–463.

46. Smith, *Argentina*, xviii–xix, 10–12, 18–19, 21, 26–32, 61–63, 87, 92–103. Paula Alonso, *Between Revolution and the Ballot Box: The Origins of the Argentine Radical Party in the 1890s* (Cambridge: Cambridge University Press, 2000), 162–166. Davis,

Warnings, 77. Darío Cantón, *Elecciones y partidos políticos en la Argentina: Historia, interpetación y balance: 1910–1966* (Buenos Aires: Siglo Veintiuno Argentina Editores, S.A., 1973), 22, 29; *El parlamento argentino en épocas de cambio: 1890, 1916 y 1946* (Buenos Aires: Editorial del Instituto, 1966). Karen L. Remmer, *Party Competition in Argentina and Chile: Political Recruitment and Public Policy, 1890–1930* (Lincoln: University of Nebraska Press, 1984).

47. Fitzgibbon, *The Constitutions*, 175–183, 191.

48. Heise González, *Historia*. Arturo Valenzuela and Alexander Wilde, "Presidential Politics and the Decline of the Chilean Congress," in Joel Smith and Lloyd D. Musolf, eds., *Legislatures in Development: Dynamics of Change in New and Old States* (Durham: Duke University Press, 1979), 189–215. Stokes, *Latin*, 426. Fitzgibbon, *The Constitutions*, 144–152, quote from 145.

49. Carlos Malamud, "Introducción," in Carlos Malamud, ed., *Legitimidad, representación, y alternancia en España y América Latina: Las reformas electorales (1880–1930)* (Mexico: Fondo de Cultura Economica, 2000), 7–16.

50. Botana, *El orden*, xviii–xxviii, 43.

51. Smith, *Democracy*, 184–185.

52. Malamud, "Introducción," in Malamud, *Legitimidad*, 7–16.

53. Sonia Alda Mejías, "La consolidación de la 'república restrictiva' ante 'las demasias de la representación popular' en la Guatemala del siglo XIX," in Malamud, ed., *Legitimidad*, 292–314.

54. Marta Irurozqui, "Sobre leyes y transgresiones: Reformas electorales en Bolivia, 1826–1952," in Malamud, ed., *Legitimidad*, 262–291.

55. Fitzgibbon, *The Constitutions*, 372–374. Nohlen, "Elections," II, 12.

56. Graham, *Patronage*, 182–206. Herbert S. Klein, "Participación política en Brasil en el siglo xix: Los votantes de San Pablo en 1880," in Antonio Annino, ed., *Historia de las elecciones en Iberoamérica, siglo xix: De la formación del espacio político nacional* (Buenos Aires: Fondo de Cultura Economica, 1995), 453–468. Marianne L. Wiesebron, "Elecciones en el Brasil 1880–1900: Bom Jardim y Afogados de Ingazeira (Pernambuco). Relación del poder local con el poder estatal," in Annino, *Historia*, 409–452. Joseph L. Love, "Political Participation in Brazil, 1881–1969," *Luso–Brazilian Review*, 7:2 (December, 1970), 3–24. Jose Murilo de Carvalho, *Teatro de sombras: A política imperial* (Sao Paulo: Vertice, 1988).

57. Gabriella Chiaramonti, "Andes o nación: La reforma electoral de 1896 en Peru," in Annino, *Historia*, 315–346; "Construir el centro, redefinir el ciudadano: Restricción del sufragio y reforma electoral en el Peru de finales del siglo XIX," in Malamud, ed., *Legitimidad*, 230–261.

58. Stuart, *The Governmental*, 70, 119–123. Carmen McEvoy, *La utopía republicana: Ideales y realidades en la formación de la cultura política peruana (1871–1919)* (Lima: Fondo Editorial de la Pontifica Universidad Catolica, 1997), 121–445.

59. Gibson, *The Constitutions*, 312. Fitzgibbon, *The Constitutions*, 168, 173, 194. Eduardo Posada Çarbo, ' Fraude al sufragio: La reforma electoral en Colombia, 1830–1930," in Malamud, ed., *Legitimidad*, 208–229.

60. Bryce, *South*, 541.

61. Whitaker, "The Pathology," 260. Carbo, "Fraude," 208–229. Irurozqui, "Sobre," 262–291. J. Samuel Valenzuela, "La ley electoral de 1890 y la democratización del régimen político chileno," in Malamud, ed., *Legitimidad*, 130–161.

62. Delpar, *The Red*, 151–169. Charles W. Bergquist, *Coffee and Conflict in Colombia, 1886–1910* (Durham: Duke University Press, 1978), 96–97.

63. Aspasia Camargo, "La federación sometida. Nacionalismo desarrollista e inestabilidad democrática," in Carmagnani, *Federalismos*, 300–362, especially 302–303. Victor Nunes Leal, *Coronelismo, enxada e voto. O municipio e o regime representativo no Brasil* (Sao Paulo: Editora Alfa-Omega, 1975). Graham, *Patronage*. Love, *Rio Grande; Sao Paulo;* "Political." Wirth, *Minas*. Levine, *Pernambuco*.

64. Julio Heise González, *El período parlamentario, 1861–1925: Democracia y gobierno representativo en el período parlamentario (Historia del poder electoral)*, 2 vols. (Santiago: Editorial Universitaria, 1982), II, 58–65; *Historia*, II, 200–205, 227–275. Remmer, *Party*, 82–83. The 1925 Constitution kept the same qualifications for voters. Fitzgibbon, *The Constitutions*, 140. Valenzuela, "La ley," 130–161; *Democratización*, 35–41; "Building," 234–250. Michael Monteon, *Chile in the Nitrate Era: The Evolution of Economic Dependence, 1880–1930* (Madison: the university of Wisconsin Press, 1982), 51–61.

65. Vanger, *José*, 185–186, quote from 176–177; *The Model*.

66. Botana, *El orden*, 15, 174–189. David Rock, *State Building and Political Movements in Argentina, 1860–1916* (Stanford: Stanford University Press, 2002), 27–30. Austin F. Macdonald, *Government of the Argentine Republic* (New York: Thomas Y. Crowell Company), 1942, 85–88. Robert A. Dahl, *Polyarchy: Participation and Opposition* (New Haven: Yale University Press, 1971), 137.

67. Natalio R. Botana, "El federalismo liberal in Argentina: 1852–1930," in Carmagnani, *Federalismos*, 224–262; *El orden*, 50–51, 75–77, 107–115, 189–202. Macdonald, *Government*, 106–107. Rock, *Politics*, 27–28.

68. Thomas F. McGann, *Argentina, the United States, and the Inter-American System, 1880–1914* (Cambridge: Harvard University Press, 1957), 25.

69. Quote is from McGann, *Argentina*, 26.

70. McGann, *Argentina*, 30.

71. Rock, *Politics*, 29.

72. Busey, *Latin*, 26–27.

73. Deborah J. Yashar, *Demanding Democracy: Reform and Reaction in Costa Rica and Guatemala, 1870s–1950s* (Stanford: Stanford University Press, 1997), 41–56. Mejías, "La consolidación," 292–314; quote from 301.

74. Irurozqui, "Sobre," 262–291.

75. Edward S. Herman and Frank Brodhead, *Demonstration Elections* (Boston: South End Press, 1984). One U.S. envoy to Haiti explained to President Wilson that "elections as understood in America do not exist in Haiti. Elections being simply a continuation of military system under which the country is governed." A constitution drafted by the State Department was approved in 1918 in a farcical plebiscite by 98,225 to 768 votes. Drake, "From Good Men," 17–18, quote from 17.

76. Nohlen, "Elections," I, 12, 28. Yashar, *Demanding*, 55–56. Charles D. Ameringer, *Democracy in Costa Rica* (New York: Praeger, 1982), 19–25.

77. In most cases, Argentina permitted foreign residents to vote in local elections, but few participated; nevertheless, immigrant participation in many municipal elections from the 1880s onward provided a first step in their political incorporation. Botana, *El orden*, xi–xiii, 10–13, 54–55, 189–202. Dahl, *Polyarchy*, 138–140. In discussing Argentina, Carlos Waisman has referred to these systems as "Whig democracies," typical in agrarian societies, with very limited competition and participation. Carlos H. Waisman, "Argentina: Autarkic Industrialization and Illegitimacy," in Larry Diamond, Juan J. Linz, and Seymour Martin Lipset, eds., *Democracy in Developing Countries: Latin America*, 4 vols. (Boulder, 1989), IV, 59–110, quote from 83. Donald Denoon, *Settler Capitalism: The Dynamics of Dependent Development in the Southern Hemisphere* (New York: Oxford University Press, 1983).

78. The working class was defined as journeymen, sailors, masons, carpenters, gardeners, tailors, rural laborers, bakers, shoemakers, coach-drivers, coopers, and blacksmiths; the middle class as journalists, brokers, musicians, commissions agents, manufacturers, and merchants; the upper class as accountants, cattle owners, notaries, lawyers, engineers, doctors, and professors. Since all such stratification categorizations were approximations, it might be that this classification overstated the upper class and understated the middle. Alonso, *Between*, 150–161.

79. Botana, *El orden*, vii–xvii, 65. Romero, *A History*, 165–226. Hilda Sabato, *The Many and the Few: Political Participation in Republican Buenos Aires* (Stanford: Stanford University Press, 2001), 110–115, 180–181.

80. Cantón, *Elecciones*, 80–85. Botana, *El orden*, 258–283. Waisman, "Argentina," 83. Alonso, *Between*. Rock, *Politics*, 26, 34–39, 59–64. Matthew B. Karush, *Workers or Citizens: Democracy and Identity in Rosario, Argentina (1912–1930)* (Albuquerque: University of New Mexico Press, 2002). Carlos Malamud, "La efimera reforma electoral de 1902 en Argentina," in Malamud, ed., *Legitimidad*, 103–129. Daniel James, "Uncertain Legitimacy: The Social and Political Restraints Underlying the Emergence of Democracy in Argentina, 1890–1930," in George Reid Andrews and Herrick Chapman, eds., *The Social Construction of Democracy, 1870–1990* (New York: New York University Press, 1995), 56–70.

81. A couple of provinces gave women the vote in the 1920s, which they could do on their own for provincial and municipal but not federal elections. Macdonald, *Government*, 107–124. Waisman, "Argentina."

82. Botana, *El orden*, xi–xiii. Cantón, *Elecciones*, 30–45, 81–85. Macdonald, *Government*, 107–124.

83. Dahl, *Polyarchy*, 133–140. Torcuato S. Di Tella, *Latin American Politics: A Theoretical Approach* (Austin: University of Texas Press, 1990), 125–128. Botana, "El federalismo," 248–250. Cantón, *Elecciones*, 30, 43–45. In the United States, under universal male suffrage, the percentage of registered voters casting ballots in presidential elections averaged 69% from 1840 to 1872, 77% from 1876 to 1900, and then fell to 65% from 1900 to 1916, and to 52% in the 1920s. Richard Oestreicher, "The Two Souls of American Democracy," in Andrews and Chapman, *The Social*, 118–134, especially 125.

84. Richard J. Walter, *Politics and Urban Growth in Buenos Aires, 1910–1942*, (Cambridge: Cambridge University Press, 1993), 62–63. Paula Alonso, "Voting in Buenos Aires, Argentina, Before 1912," in Posada-Carbo, *Elections*, 181–200, especially 181–189. Cantón, *El parlamento*, 121.

85. Conservative preservation of the senate and rural provinces was also later engineered by Pinochet in Chile, to safeguard rightwing strongholds during a democratic opening to reformist groups, a not uncommon gambit in Latin America. Waisman, "Argentina." Rock, *Politics*. Davis, *Warnings*, 79–81. Smith, *Argentina*. Karush, *Workers*. Cantón, *El parlamento*. Remmer, *Party*.

86. Cantón, *Elecciones*, 10–11, 29.

87. Valenzuela, "La ley," 130–161.

88. Although Alessandri barely lost the popular vote, he won the electoral vote. Heise González, *Historia de Chile*, II, 123–125, 176, 215. René Millar Carvacho, *La elección presidencial de 1920* (Santiago: Editorial Universitaria, 1981). Ricardo Donoso, *Alessandri, agitador y demoledor. Cincuenta años de historia política de Chile*, 2 vols., (Mexico: Fondo de Cultura Economica, 1954). Paul W. Drake, *Socialism and Populism in Chile, 1932–52* (Urbana: University of Illinois Press, 1978), 41–65. Remmer, *Party*.

89. Alonso, "Voting," 192–194; *Between*. Cantón, *Elecciones*, 20. Macdonald, *Government*, 106–107.

90. Rock, *Politics*, 103–104. Remmer, *Party*, 87–135.

91. Heise González, *Historia*, II, 282–297. Remmer, *Party*, 61–86, 112–135. Bravo Lira, *Historia de las instituciones*, 272–274. Timothy R. Scully, *Rethinking the Center: Party Politics in Nineteenth- and Twentieth-Century Chile* (Stanford: Stanford University Press, 1992).

92. Bergquist, *Coffee*, 225–229, 247. Robertson, *History*, 346–348. Eduardo Posada-Carbo, "Limits of Power: Elections under the Conservative Hegemony in Colombia, 1886–1930," *Hispanic American Historical Review*, 77:2 (May, 1997), 245–279.

93. Robertson, *History*, 242–244.

Notes to Chapter 6

1. Leonard Binder, et al., *Crises and Sequences in Political Development* (Princeton: Princeton University Press, 1971). Ruth Berins Collier and David Collier, *Shaping the Political Arena: Critical Junctures, the Labor Movement, and Regime Dynamics in Latin America* (Princeton: Princeton University Press, 1991). Paul W. Drake, "International Crises and Popular Movements in Latin America: Chile and Peru from the Great Depression to the Cold War," in David Rock, ed., *Latin America in the 1940s: War and Postwar Transitions* (Berkeley: University of California Press, 1994), 109–140.

2. Paul W. Drake, *Socialism and Populism in Chile, 1932–52* (Urbana: University of Illinois Press, 1978); "Requiem for Populism?" in Michael Conniff, ed., *Latin American Populism in Comparative Perspective* (Albuquerque: University of New Mexico Press, 1982), 217–245; "Comment," in Rudiger Dornbusch and Sebastian Edwards, eds., *The Macroeconomics of Populism in Latin America* (Chicago: The University of Chicago Press, 1991), 35–40; "Chilean Populism Reconsidered, 1920s–1990s," in Michael L. Conniff, ed., *Populism in Latin America* (Tuscaloosa: The University of Alabama Press, 1999), 63–74. Steve Stein, *Populism in Peru: The Emergence of the Masses and the Politics of Social Control* (Madison: The University of Wisconsin Press, 1980). Torcuato Di Tella, "Populism and Reform in Latin America," in Claudio Veliz, ed., *Obstacles to Change in Latin America* (London: Oxford University Press, 1965), 47–74. Fernando Henrique Cardoso and Enzo Faletto, *Dependency and Development in Latin America* (Berkeley: University of California Press, 1971). María Moira Mackinnon and Mario Alberto Petrone, eds., *Populismo y neopopulismo en América Latina: El problema de la Cenicienta* (Buenos Aires: Editorial Universitaria de Buenos Aires, 1998).

3. Peter H. Smith, *Democracy in Latin America: Political Change in Comparative Perspective*, (New York: Oxford University Press, 2005), 28–31, 70–72.

4. Jonathan Hartlyn and Arturo Valenzuela, "Democracy in Latin America since 1930," in Leslie Bethell, ed., *Latin America: Politics and Society since 1930* (Cambridge: Cambridge University Press, 1998), 3–66. Smith, *Democracy*, 348–351. According to another classification for South America in these years mainly based on the extent of legal participation of voters and parties, "restricted democracies" took hold in Colombia from 1936 to 1949 and 1958 to 1990, Venezuela 1958 to 1968, Ecuador 1948 to 1961, Peru 1939 to 1948 and 1956 to 1968, Chile 1932 to 1970, Argentina 1958 to 1966, and Brazil 1945 to 1964. Meanwhile "full democracies" without restrictions flourished in Venezuela from 1968 to 1990, Bolivia 1952 to 1964, Chile 1970 to 1973, Argentina 1946 to 1951 and 1973 to 1976, and Uruguay 1942 to 1973. Dietrich Rueschemeyer, Evelyne Huber Stephens, and John D. Stephens, *Capitalist Development and Democracy* (Chicago: University of Chicago Press, 1992), 160–162.

5. Although various scholars come up with different tallies of regime types over time, depending on the criteria, classifications, and close calls, virtually everyone

agrees on the main trends and major cases. Paul W. Drake, "From Good Men to Good Neighbors," in Abraham Lowenthal, ed., *Exporting Democracy* (Johns Hopkins University Press, 1991), 3–40; "Debt and Democracy in Latin America, 1920s–1980s" in Barbara Stallings and Robert Kaufman, eds., *Debt and Democracy in Latin America* (Boulder: Westview Press, 1988), 39–58. Brian Loveman, *For la Patria: Politics and the Armed Forces in Latin America* (Wilmington: Scholarly Resources, 1999), 75, 102. Smith, *Democracy.*

6. Fernando Limongi and Adam Przeworski, "Democracy and Development in South America, 1946–1988," *Estudios/Working Papers* (Instituto Juan March de Estudios e Investigaciones) (February, 1994), 1–32.

7. Mikael Bostrom, "Political Waves in Latin America," *Ibero Americana Nordic Journal of Latin American Studies,* 19:1 (1989), 3–19. William Lytle Schurz, "Government," in Asher N. Christensen, ed., *The Evolution of Latin American Government* (New York: Henry Holt and Company, 1951), 11–52, especially 44–45. Russell H. Fitzgibbon, "The Pathology of Democracy in Latin America: A Political Scientist's Point of View," in Christensen, *The Evolution,* 270–284, especially 278–284. Adam Przeworski, Michael E. Alvarez, Jose Antonio Cheibub, and Fernando Limongi, *Democracy and Development: Political Institutions and Well-Being in the World, 1950–1990* (Cambridge: Cambridge University Press, 2000), last calculations in paragraph from 40, 48.

8. Leslie Bethell and Ian Roxborough, eds., *Latin America between the Second World War and the Cold War, 1944–1948* (Cambridge: Cambridge University Press, 1992).

9. "Latin America is ready for democracy. Its people have fought bitter battles in recent years to prove this fact. However, the struggle to establish democratic government on a firm basis still goes on." Charles O. Porter and Robert J. Alexander, *The Struggle for Democracy in Latin America* (New York: The Macmillan Company, 1961), 1. Tad Szulc, *Twilight of the Tyrants* (New York: Henry Holt and Company, 1959), especially 3–9, 18–22. Smith, *Democracy,* 28.

10. Many book titles conveyed an apocalyptic tone. Karl M. Schmitt and David D. Burks, eds., *Evolution or Chaos: Dynamics of Latin American Government and Politics* (New York: Frederick A. Praeger, 1963). Mildred Adams, ed., *Latin America: Evolution or Explosion?* (New York: Dodd, Mead, and Company, 1963). John J. TePaske and Sydney Nettleton Fisher, eds., *Explosive Forces in Latin America* (Columbus: Ohio State University Press, 1964). John Gerassi, *The Great Fear in Latin America,* revised ed. (New York: Collier Books, 1966). James Petras and Maurice Zeitlin, eds., *Latin America: Reform or Revolution?* (Greenwich: Fawcett, 1968). Thomas C. Wright, *Latin America in the Era of the Cuban Revolution* (New York: Praeger, 1991). Miguel Jorrin and John D. Martz, *Latin American Political Thought and Ideology* (Chapel Hill: The University of North Carolina Press, 1970), 280–313.

11. Tony Smith, "The Alliance for Progress: The 1960s," in Lowenthal, *Exporting,* 71–89. Loveman, *For,* 172–173, 186. Jerome Levinson and Juan de Onis, *The Alliance*

that *Lost Its Way: A Critical Report on the Alliance for Progress* (Chicago: Quadrangle Books, 1970). Smith, *Democracy*, 28. Porter and Alexander, *The Struggle*, 44–141. Schmitt and Burks, *Evolution*, 175–239. Guillermo A. O'Donnell, *Modernization and Bureaucratic Authoritarianism; Studies in South American Politics* (Berkeley: Institute of International Studies, 1973).

12. Nancy Bermeo, *Ordinary People in Extraordinary Times: The Citizenry and the Breakdown of Democracy* (Princeton: Princeton University Press, 2003).

13. W. Rex Crawford, "The Pathology of Democracy in Latin America: A Sociologist's Point of View," in Christensen, *The Evolution*, 105–111. Sanford A. Mosk, "The Pathology of Democracy in Latin America: An Economist's Point of View," in Christensen, *The Evolution*, 161–180. R. A. Humphreys, "Democracy and Dictatorship," in Christensen, *The Evolution*, 317–332, especially 328–332. John J. Johnson, *Political Change in Latin America: The Emergence of the Middle Sectors* (Stanford: Stanford University Press, 1958). Hugh M. Hamill, Jr., ed., *Dictatorship in Spanish America* (New York: Alfred A. Knopf, 1965).

14. J. Lloyd Mecham, "Latin American Constitutions," in Peter G. Snow, ed., *Government and Politics in Latin America* (New York: Holt, Rinehart and Winston, Inc., 1967), 144–157, quote from 156.

15. Schurz, "Government," 46–48.

16. See the first chapter of this book for fuller discussions and citations on these theories. For brief coverage, see Paul W. Drake, "Latin America in the Changing World Order, 1492–1992" in Roberto G. Rabel, ed., *Latin America in a Changing World Order* (Dunedin, New Zealand: University of Otago, 1992), 18–36.

17. Schmitt and Burks, *Evolution*, 175–239. O'Donnell, *Modernization*. H. E. Chehabi and Juan J. Linz, *Sultanistic Regimes* (Baltimore: John Hopkins University Press, 1998).

18. Among 15 criteria, these surveys gave the most weight to free and competitive elections; the second-most to freedom of press and speech and assembly, effectiveness of parties and the legislature, and civilian control over the military; the third-most to education, standard of living, national unity, political values, absence of foreign domination, independent judiciary, accountability for public funds, advanced social legislation, quality of government administration, and quality of local government; and the least weight to freedom from Church control of politics. Although a very heterogeneous and ambiguous list of variables, at least it was maintained consistently throughout the surveys. This sampling of Latin American specialists was highly subjective, quantifying qualitative judgments with mushy criteria. Nevertheless, it provided one benchmark with more than one iteration. Russell H. Fitzgibbon and Kenneth F. Johnson, "Measurement of Latin American Political Change," in Snow, *Government*, 261–277. Philip Kelly, "Measuring Democracy in Latin America: the Fitzgibbon Index," in Philip Kelly, ed., *Assessing Democracy in Latin America: A Tribute*

to Russell H. Fitzgibbon (Boulder: Westview Press, 1998), 3–11. Kenneth F. Johnson and Ben G. Burnett, "Stability-Instability in Latin American Politics," in Ben G. Burnett and Kenneth F. Johnson, eds., *Political Forces in Latin America: Dimensions of the Quest for Stability* (Belmont, California: Wadsworth Publishing Company, Inc., 1968), 511–524, especially 513–514. A broader international quantitative analysis of democracies during the years 1900–1950 ranked Chile fifth, trailing Canada, England, the United States, and Switzerland but leading more industrialized nations like France, Italy, and Germany. Weston H. Agor, *The Chilean Senate: Internal Distribution of Influence* (Austin: The University of Texas Press, 1971), 5. Another wider international survey of democracies in 1960 concluded that Chile was the one with the most unequal distribution of land, whereas democracies were generally more common in countries with more equal land distribution. The author found Chile high on contestation but low on participation, because of suffrage restrictions. The high concentration of land and the high level of political disputation led to escalating conflicts in the countryside that destabilized Chilean democracy. Robert A. Dahl, *Polyarchy: Participation and Opposition* (New Haven: Yale University Press, 1971), 84–85.

19. This entire section on political ideas draws on Jorrin and Martz, *Latin*, 249–254, 405–426. Morris J. Blachman and Ronald G. Hellman, eds., *Terms of Conflict: Ideology in Latin American Politics* (Philadelphia: Institute for the Study of Human Issues, 1977). Sandra McGee Deutsch, *Las Derechas: The Extreme Right in Argentina, Brazil, and Chile, 1890–1939* (Stanford: Stanford University Press, 1999), 143–339. Brian Loveman and Thomas M. Davies, Jr., eds., *The Politics of Antipolitics: The Military in Latin America* (Wilmington: Scholary Resources Inc., 1997).

20. Edward J. Williams, *Latin American Christian Democratic Parties* (Knoxville: The University of Tennessee Press, 1967).

21. Robert J. Alexander, *Prophets of the Revolution: Profiles of Latin American Leaders*, (New York: The Macmillan Company, 1962). Harry Kantor, *The Ideology and Program of the Peruvian Aprista Movement* (Berkeley: University of California Press, 1953). Víctor Raúl Haya de la Torre, *A donde va Indoamérica?* (Santiago: Ediciones Ercilla, 1935); *El antiimperialismo y el APRA* (Santiago: Ediciones Ercilla, 1936).

22. Fidel Castro, "Fidel Castro's Concept of the Goals of the Revolution and the Threat from Abroad, 1960," in Fredrick B. Pike, ed., *Latin American History: Select Problems* (New York: Harcourt, Brace & World, Inc., 1969), 404–405. Drake, *Socialism*. Julio Faundez, *Marxism and Democracy in Chile, from 1932 to the Fall of Allende* (New Haven: Yale University Press, 1988).

23. Gerald E. Fitzgerald, *The Constitutions of Latin America* (Chicago: Henry Regnery Company, 1968), xiii. William W. Pierson and Federico G. Gil, *Government and Politics of Latin America* (New York: McGraw-Hill Book Company, Inc., 1955), 161. Keith S. Rosenn, "The Success of Constitutionalism in the United States and its Failure in Latin America," in Kenneth W. Thompson, ed., *The U.S. Constitution and*

the Constitutions of Latin America (Lanham: University Press of America, 1991), 53–96, especially 87–94.

24. Mecham, "Latin," 144–157. Alexander T. Edelmann, *Latin American Government and Politics: The Dynamics of a Revolutionary Society*, revised ed. (Homewood, Illinois: The Dorsey Press, 1969), 383–387. Austin F. Macdonald, *Latin American Politics and Government* (New York: Thomas Y. Crowell Company, 1949).

25. The inclusion of workers' rights in the other constitutions of Latin America began with Uruguay (1932 and 1934), followed by Peru (1933), Brazil (1934 and 1946), Colombia (1936), El Salvador (1939), Nicaragua (1939), Paraguay (1940), Panama (1940), Cuba (1940), Bolivia (1945), Ecuador (1946), Venezuela (1947), Costa Rica (1949), Argentina (1949 and 1957), Guatemala (1954), Honduras (1957), and the Dominican Republic (1960). The Chilean Constitution of 1925 contained only summary provisions on social rights, but social legislation was well developed during this period. Jacques Lambert, *Latin America: Social Structure and Political Institutions* (Berkeley: University of California Press, 1967), 276–280. George I. Blanksten, "Constitutions and the Structure of Power," in Harold Eugene Davis, ed., *Government and Politics in Latin America* (New York: The Ronald Press Company, 1958), 237–239. Bernardino Bravo Lira, *Historia de las instituciones políticas de Chile e Hispanoamérica* (Santiago: Editorial Andrés Bello, 1986), 314–117. José Miranda, *Reformas y tendencias constitucionales recientes de la América Latina (1945–1956)*, (Mexico: Instituto de Derecho Comparado, Universidad Nacional Autonoma de Mexico, 1957), 287–291, 296–303. Mecham, "Latin," 145–146.

26. Macdonald, *Latin*, 357.

27. Fitzgibbon, *The Constitutions*, 713–761. Hector Gros Espiell, *Las constituciones del Uruguay (Exposición, crítica y textos)* (Madrid: Ediciones Cultura Hispanica, 1956), 75–99, 217–294.

28. Leonardo Pasquel, *Las constituciones de América*, 2 vols (Mexico, 1943), I, 168–169.

29. James L. Busey, *Latin America: Political Institutions and Processes* (New York: Random House, 1964), 100–113, 132–140.

30. Miranda, *Reformas*, 231–270. Fitzgibbon, *The Constitutions*. Pierson and Gil, *Government*, 195–206.

31. Manuel Alcántara Saez, *Sistemas políticos de América Latina*, 2 vols., 2nd ed. (Madrid: Tecnos, 1999), II, 92–115. Mary A. Clark, "Costa Rica: Portrait of an Established Democracy," in Roderic Ai Camp, ed., *Citizen Views of Democracy in Latin America* (Pittsburgh: University of Pittsburgh Press, 2001), 73–89. Charles D. Ameringer, *Democracy in Costa Rica* (New York: Praeger Publishers, 1982), 30–35.

32. In the four officially federal republics of Argentina, Brazil, Mexico, and Venezuela, the governors and provincial legislatures were normally elected. However, the governors in the first three countries were subject to intervention by the central

government and in Venezuela were appointed by the president. Pierson and Gil, *Government*, 296–312. William S. Stokes, "Latin American Federalism," in Snow, *Government*, 158–173. C. H. Haring, "Federalism in Latin America," in Christensen, *The Evolution*, 335–342. Blanksten, "Constitutions," 229–232. Macdonald, *Latin*, 646–647. Busey, *Latin*, 149–152. Miguel Jorrín, *Governments of Latin America* (New York: D. Van Nostrand Company, Inc., 1953), 142–143. Russell H. Fitzgibbon, *Latin America: A Panorama of Contemporary Politics* (New York: Appleton-Century-Crofts, 1971), 196–210.

33. Pierson and Gil, *Government*, 296–312. R. Andrew Nickson, *Local Government in Latin America* (Boulder: Lynne Rienner Publishers, 1995), 16–19.

34. Pierson and Gil, *Government*, 226–227. Hartlyn and Valenzuela, "Democracy," 16–17.

35. Matthew Soberg Shugart and John M. Carey, *Presidents and Assemblies: Constitutional Design and Electoral Dynamics* (Cambridge: Cambridge University Press, 1992), 33–36. Waldino Cleto Suárez, "El poder ejecutivo en América Latina; Su capacidad operativa bajo regimenes presidencialistas de gobierno," *Revista de Estudios Políticos*, 29 (1982), 109–44. Terry L. McCoy, "Congress, the President, and Political Instability in Peru," in Weston H. Agor, ed., *Latin American Legislatures: Their Role and Influence* (New York: Praeger Publishers, 1971), 325–368, especially 326–338.

36. For example, from 1932 to 1973 in Chile, presidential elections took place every six years, congressional every four, and municipal on a separate three-to-four-year cycle. None of the three types of elections were held simultaneously. Alan Angell, Maria D'Alva Kinzo, and Diego Urbaneja, "Electioneering in Latin America," in Roderick Ai Camp, ed., *Democracy in Latin America: Patterns and Cycles* (Wilmington: Scholarly Resources, 1996), 183–206, especially 194. Harold E. Davis, "The Presidency," in Davis, Government, 252–289, especially 264–267. Fitzgibbon, *The Constitutions*, 301–308. Fitzgerald, *The Constitutions*, 73–102. Macdonald, *Latin*, 394–396, 646–647. Busey, *Latin*, 146. Mecham, "Latin," 146.

37. Fitzgibbon, *Latin*, quote from 412–414; *The Constitutions*, 682–683. James Payne, *Labor and Politics in Peru: The System of Political Bargaining* (New Haven: Yale University Press, 1965).

38. Edelmann, *Latin*, 413.

39. Robert H. Dix, "The Colombian Presidency: Continuities and Changes," in Thomas V. DiBacco, ed., *Presidential Power in Latin American Politics* (New York: Praeger Publishers, 1977), 72–95, quote from 74.

40. Davis, "The Presidency," 275–277. Pierson and Gil, *Government*, 208–241. Fitzgibbon, *The Constitutions*, 668–696.

41. Whereas many political scientists in the 1980s and 1990s argued that presidents were too domineering in Latin America, one U.S. analyst suggested in the 1970s that the problem in Peru was that the president was not strong enough to override

an obstructionist congress. McCoy "Congress," in Agor, *Latin*, 342–356. Asher N. Christensen, "The Role and Organization of Legislative Assemblies in Latin America," in Christensen, *The Evolution*, 446–453. Stokes, "Parliamentary," 454–467; *Latin American Politics* (New York: Crowell, 1959), 386. Robert E. Scott, "Legislatures and Legislation," in Davis, *Government*, 208–241, 290–332, especially 322–329. Jorrin, *Governments*, 77–96. Rosendo A. Gomez, "Latin American Executives: Essence and Variation," in Snow, *Government*, 174–186. Macdonald, *Latin*, 8–11, 175. Fitzgibbon, *Latin*, 200–202, 411–416; *The Constitutions*, 104–105.

42. Shugart and Carey, *Presidents*, 36, 141–142. Alfredo Vázquez Carrizosa, *El poder presidencial en Colombia* (Bogotá: Enrique Dobry, 1979). Jonathan Hartlyn, "Presidentialism and Colombian Politics," in Juan J. Linz and Arturo Valenzuela, eds., *The Failure of Presidential Democracy: The Case of Latin America* (Baltimore: The Johns Hopkins University Press, 1994), 220–253.

43. Fitzgibbon, *The Constitutions*, quote from 599. Mecham, "Latin," 149.

44. Fitzgibbon, *The Constitutions*, 678; *Latin*, 414–415.

45. Macdonald, *Latin*, 519.

46. Fitzgerald, *The Constitutions*, 76.

47. Loveman, *For*, 175. Jose Nun, "The Middle-Class Military Coup," in Claudio Veliz, ed., *The Politics of Conformity in Latin America* (New York: Oxford University Press, 1967), 66–118.

48. Fitzgibbon, *Latin*, 311.

49. Mecham, "Latin," 157–156. Paul W. Drake and Mathew D. McCubbins, eds., *The Origins of Liberty: Political and Economic Liberalization in the Modern World* (Princeton: Princeton University Press, 1998).

50. Arturo Valenzuela and Alexander Wilde, "Presidential Politics and the Decline of the Chilean Congress," in Joel Smith and Lloyd D. Musolf, eds., *Legislatures in Development: Dynamics of Change in New and Old States* (Durham: Duke University Press, 1979), 189–215. Shugart and Carey, *Presidents*, 174–183, 280–281. Fitzgibbon, *Latin*, 311–319.

51. Dix, "The Colombian"; *Colombia: The Political Dimensions of Change* (New Haven: Yale University Press, 1967); *The Politics of Colombia* (New York: Praeger Publishers, 1987). *Pasquel, Las constituciones*, I, 163–192. Shugart and Carey, *Presidents*, 184–185. Fitzgibbon, *Latin*, 375–376.

52. William Columbus Davis, *Warnings from the Far South: Democracy versus Dictatorship in Uruguay, Argentina, and Chile* (Westport: Praeger, 1995), 24–29, 36. Gross Espiell, *Las constituciones*, 75–99, 109–121, 217–294, 371–462. Juan Maestre Alfonso, 2 vols., *Constituciones y leyes políticas de América Latina, Filipinas, y Guinea Ecuatorial* (Sevilla: E.E.H.A., 1989), I, 251–236; II. Weston H. Agor, "Introduction," xxiii–xlviii, in Agor, *Latin*, xxxii–xxxiv. Ronald H. McDonald, "Legislative Politics in Uruguay: A Preliminary Statement," in Agor, *Latin*, 113–138, especially 120–121.

Rolando Franco, *Democracia a la uruguaya* (Montevideo: El Libro Libre, 1984). Fitzgibbon, *Latin*, 463–469; *The Constitutions*, 713–761. Pierson and Gil, *Government*, 212–215. Shugart and Carey, *Presidents*, 97–99.

53. Panama also prescribed a lapse of two terms before a president could be reelected. Fitzgibbon, *The Constitutions*, 259, 628. Pierson and Gil, *Government*, 232. Fitzgerald, *The Constitutions*, 73–102. Macdonald, *Latin*, 646–647.

54. Miranda, *Reformas*, 278–283, 304–305. Macdonald, *Latin*. Fitzgibbon, *The Constitutions*, 398, 426, 431.

55. Fitzgibbon, *The Constitutions*, 45.

56. Fitzgibbon, *The Constitutions*, 338–344.

57. Davis, "The Presidency," 265–267. Schurz, "Government," 25–26. Russell H. Fitzgibbon, "Executive Power in Central America," in Christensen, *The Evolution*, 401–413.

58. Prohibitions on travel abroad originated with the Cadiz constitution of 1812. As further examples, the Nicaraguan constitution of 1939 forbade the president from departing the country without congressional permission during his tenure and "after his term is concluded, if there are pending court proceedings against him for official offenses." The Peruvian constitution of 1933 prohibited the president from going overseas without congressional approval or refusing to return to Peru after a trip. The Dominican constitution of 1947 required congressional authorization for the president to be in a foreign country for more than thirty days. The Guatemalan constitution of 1945 mandated congressional acquiescence to leave the country not only for the president but also for the vice president and the president of the congress. Fitzgibbon, *The Constitutions*, 76–77, 306, 338–344, 420, 682–683, Nicaraguan quote from 581.

59. Fitzgibbon, *Latin*, 312, 314. Mecham, "Latin," 147–148. Miranda, *Reformas*, 294–296.

60. Macdonald, *Latin*, quote from 520. Fitzgibbon, *The Constitutions*, 104–105. Brian Loveman, *The Constitution of Tyranny: Regimes of Exception in Spanish America* (Pittsburgh: University of Pittsburgh Press, 1993).

61. Fitzgibbon, *The Constitutions*, 338–344, quote from 339.

62. On balance, civil liberties were more limited than in the United States, even under democratic governments. For example, governments feared that particularly vociferous opponents might become subversive and delegitimize them, so they enforced strict rules against defaming, libeling, or just disrespecting public officials in publications, speeches, or actions. Gomez, "Latin," 80–81. Mecham, "Latin," 145. Miranda, *Reformas*, 287–303. Pierson and Gil, *Government*, 192–195. Loveman, *The Constitution*.

63. Alcántara, *Sistemas*, II, 92–115. Clark, "Costa Rica."

64. Hartlyn and Valenzuela, "Democracy," 17–23.

65. Scott, "Legislatures," 290–332. In the 1960s, both Nicaragua and Venezuela made former presidents senators for life, as Pinochet would later do in Chile. Edelmann, *Latin*, 441. In an attempt to buttress civilian rule, the Cuban Constitution of 1940 required deputies and senators not to have been in the armed forces for at least two years before their candidacy. The Dominican Republic's constitution of 1947 only required senators and deputies to be over 18. Fitzgibbon, *The Constitutions*, 68, 251–253, 301–304, 419.

66. One reason that Mexico did not allow legislators immediate reelection was to impede the president from keeping his cronies in the congress year after year. However, the main impact was that he could reward more clients with seats and that few legislators were experienced enough to counter the chief executive. Scott, "Legislatures," 307–317. In its 1946 constitution, Ecuador established the novel system of "functional senators" for 12 of its 55 seats. They were to be members of and elected by the following groups: public universities, private education, journalism and scientific and literary societies, the armed forces, agriculture, commerce, labor, and industry, these last four with one each from the coast and the highlands, reflecting the regional bipolarity of the country. Fitzgibbon, *The Constitutions*, 70–71, 329–330. Pierson and Gil, *Government*, 246–251. Mecham, "Latin," 146–149. Schurz, "Government," 31. Dieter Nohlen, "Elections and Electoral Systems in the Americas," in Dieter Nohlen, ed., *Elections in the Americas: A Data Handbook*, 2 vols. (New York: Oxford University Press, 2005), I, 1–58, especially 12. Ricardo Cruz-Coke, *Geografía electoral de Chile* (Santiago: Editorial del Pacífico, 1952), 55–67.

67. Weston H. Agor, "Introduction," in Agor, *Latin*, xxiii–xlviii. Pierson and Gil, *Government*, 243–265.

68. Scott, "Legislatures," 290–332. Fitzgibbon, *The Constitutions*. Gomez, "Latin," 102–105. Pablo González Casanova, *La democracia en México* (México: Ediciones ERA, 1965), 185.

69. Miranda, *Reformas*, 278–305.

70. Michael Coppedge, *Strong Parties and Lame Ducks: Presidential Partyarchy and Factionalism in Venezuela* (Stanford: Stanford University Press, 1994), 179.

71. Marvin Alisky, "Peru," in Burnett and Johnson, *Political*, 289–312. Fitzgibbon, *The Constitutions*, 678; *Latin*, 414–415. McCoy, "Congress," 325–368, especially 326–338.

72. Lee C. Fennell, "Congress in the Argentine Political System: An Appraisal," in Agor, *Latin*, 139–172. Peter Ranis, "Profile Variables among Argentine Legislators," in Agor, *Latin*, 173–258, especially 178–180, 203–205. Fitzgibbon, *Latin*, 203–206, 222–223.

73. Any congressional slates falling below the electoral quotient elected no deputies, while those rising above it could elect as many representatives as there were quotients divisible into its total tally. The seats went to the most popular parties and

298   *Notes*

then to the candidates from those parties that received the most votes. If any quotients were left over, they accrued in descending order to the parties that had elected at least one candidate and that had the largest number of surplus votes after cashing in all their quotients. Robert Packenham, "Functions of the Brazilian National Congress," in Agor, *Latin*, 259–292. Glaucio Ary Dillon Soares, "The Politics of Uneven Development: The Case of Brazil," in Seymour Martin Lipset and Stein Rokkan, eds., *Party Systems and Voter Alignments: Cross-National Perspectives* (New York: The Free Press, 1967), 467–496, especially 468, 484, 492–493. Busey, *Latin*, 109–113.

74. Agor, *The Chilean*, xvii, 3, 6–7, 19–22, 31–33. Fitzgibbon, *Latin*, 315–318.

75. Gary W. Hoskin, "Dimensions of Conflict in the Colombian National Legislature," in G. R. Boynton and Chong Lim Kim, *Legislative Systems in Developing Countries* (Durham: Duke University Press, 1975), 143–180; "Dimensions of Representation in the Colombian National Legislature," in Agor, *Latin*, 403–460. Ernest A. Duff, "The Role of Congress in the Colombian Political System," in Agor, *Latin*, 369–402, especially 369–378, 381–391. Agor, "Introduction," xxv–xxvi. Padgett and Murtra, "Colombia," 231–266. Dix, "The Colombian," 76–81.

76. The courts in Chile retained significant independence, partly because the supreme court and others controlled the list of nominees from which the president could appoint judges. Helen L. Clagett, "Law and Court Systems," in Davis, *Government*, 333–367. Fitzgibbon, *Latin*, 311–314, 318–319. Macdonald, *Latin*, 646–647.

77. Lambert, *Latin*, 293–295. Pierson and Gil, *Government*, 273, 280–281. Mecham, "Latin," 148. Keith S. Rosenn, "The Protection of Judicial Independence in Latin America," *Inter-American Law Review* 19:1 (1987), 1–35. Juan E. Vargas Viancos and Jorge Correa Sutil, *Diagnóstico del sistema judicial chileno* (Santiago: Corporación de Promoción Universitaria, 1995).

78. James A. Gardner, *Legal Imperialism: American Lawyers and Foreign Aid in Latin America* (Madison: University of Wisconsin Press, 1980). Steve Lowenstein, *Lawyers, Legal Education, and Development: An Examination of the Process of Reform in Chile* (New York: International Legal Center, 1970). The Allende administration used "Audiencias Populares," created by the supreme court, to bring judicial services to larger segments of the population. Jack Spence, *Search for Justice: Neighborhood Courts in Allende's Chile* (Boulder: Westview Press, 1979). Neal P. Panish, "Chile Under Allende: The Decline of the Judiciary and the Rise of a State of Necessity," *Loyola of Los Angeles International and Comparative Law Review* 9 (1987), 693–709.

79. The use of amparo spread from Mexico to Honduras (1936), Costa Rica (1950), Panama (1956), Argentina (1957), El Salvador (1960), Guatemala (1966) and then to Bolivia, Paraguay, and Ecuador (1967). Keith S. Rosenn, "Judicial Review in Latin America," *Ohio State Law Journal 35 (1974)*, 785–819. Kenneth L. Karst and Keith S. Rosenn, *Law and Development in Latin America: A Case Book* (Berkeley: University of

California Press, 1975). Russell H. Fitzgibbon, "Constitutional Development in Latin America: A Synthesis." *American Political Science Review* 39 (1945). 511–522.

80. Brian Loveman, *The Constitution*. Pierson and Gil, *Government*, 266–294. Gomez, "Latin," 107–108.

81. Mark J. Osiel, "Dialogue with Dictators: Judicial Resistance in Argentina and Brazil," *Law and Social Inquiry* 20:2 (1995), 481–560. Alejandro Carrio, *La Corte Suprema y su independencia* (Buenos Aires: Abeledo-Perrot, 1996). Rosenn, "The Protection." Fitzgibbon, *Latin*, 206–207.

82. Karst and Rosenn, *Law*. Osiel, "Dialogue." Martin Feinrider, "Judicial Review and the Protection of Human Rights under Military Governments in Brazil and Argentina," *Suffolk Transnational Law Journal* 5:2 (1981), 171–199.

83. The military regime also used "integrated lawyers," or temporary judges who were subject to re-appointment every two years, in the courts of appeal and the supreme court. Under Pinochet, the supreme court rejected all but 10 of the 5,400 writs of habeas corpus filed by the Vicaría de Soldaridad on behalf of victims between 1973 and 1983. The International Commission of Jurists, *Chile: A Time of Reckoning, Human Rights and the Judiciary* (Geneva: Centre for the Independence of Judges and Lawyers, 1992). Vargas and Correa, *Diagnóstico*.

84. A. J. McAdams, ed., *Transitional Justice and the Rule of Law in New Democracies* (Notre Dame: University of Notre Dame Press, 1997).

85. The entire sections on elections and parties rely on Frank R. Brandenburg, "Political Parties and Elections," in Davis, *Government*, 186–224; Asher N. Christensen, "The General Nature of Political Parties in Latin America," in Christensen, *The Evolution*, 501–507; and Macdonald, *Latin*, 82–83, 90–91, 249–252, 319, 359, 394, 646–647. For the above paragraphs, also see Stokes, *Latin*, 335–347. Edward J. Williams and Freeman J. Wright, *Latin American Politics: A Developmental Approach* (Palo Alto: Mayfield Publishing Company, 1975), 316–317. Fitzgibbon, *The Constitutions*, 83–85. Hartlyn and Valenzuela, "Democracy," 33–35.

86. The countries disallowing voting by the armed forces were Guatemala, Honduras, Cuba, the Dominican Republic, Venezuela, Colombia, Ecuador, Peru, Argentina, Paraguay, and Brazil. Fitzgibbon, *The Constitutions*, quote from 326.

87. Miranda, *Reformas*, 270–276, 283–285, 291–293.

88. Nohlen, "Elections," I, suffrage data on 12; II, 12. Smith, *Democracy*, 185–186. Joseph L. Love, "Political Participation in Brazil, 1881–1969," *Luso-Brazilian Review*, 7:2 (December, 1970), 3–24. Schurz, "Government," 31–32. Yashar, *Demanding*, 121–122. Pierson and Gil, *Government*, 339–346.

89. Eight countries adopted compulsory voting in this period. Nohlen, "Elections," I, 12. Fitzgibbon, *The Constitutions*, 88, 246–248, 675, quote on Paraguay from 657–658. Gomez, "Latin," 50–51. Smith, *Democracy*, 186–187.

90. This general study showed that high voter turnout correlated with low levels of political violence and low levels of government durability. So high participation seemed to be good for public order but not for government stability. G. Bingham Powell, Jr., *Contemporary Democracies: Participation, Stability, and Violence* (Cambridge: Harvard University Press, 1982), 13–15, 25–27. Nohlen, "Elections," I, 28.

91. Hartlyn and Valenzuela, "Democracy," 34–39. Enrique C. Ochoa, "The Rapid Expansion of Voter Participation in Latin America: Presidential Elections, 1845–1986," in *Statistical Abstract of Latin America* 25 (Los Angeles: UCLA, 1987), 869–891. Dieter Nohlen, *Sistemas electorales y partidos políticos*, 2nd ed. (Mexico: Fondo de Cultura Economica, 1998), 24–34.

92. In this period, five more countries officially legislated secret voting. Nohlen, "Elections," I, 12.

93. Gomez, "Latin," 51.

94. In Ecuador's tribunal, three members were appointed by congress, two by the president, and two by the supreme court. Fitzgibbon, *The Constitutions*, 269–270, 326, 598–599, Cuban quote from 248.

95. Angell, D'alva Kinzo, and Urbaneja, "Electioneering." Rein Taagepera and Matthew Soberg Shugart, *Seats and Votes: The Effects and Determinants of Electoral Systems* (New Haven: Yale University Press, 1989), 25. Arturo Valenzuela, *Political Brokers in Chile: Local Government in a Centralized Polity* (Durham: Duke University Press, 1977). Shugart and Carey, *Presidents*, 243–245.

96. Nohlen, *Sistemas electorales*, 24–34.

97. Busey, *Latin*, 26–28. González Casanova, *La democracia*, especially 180–181.

98. Padgett and Murtra, "Colombia," 231–266. Dix, *Colombia; The Politics*. Jonathan Hartlyn, *The Politics of Coalition Rule in Colombia* (New York: Cambridge University Press, 1987).

99. Yashar, *Demanding*. Piero Gleijeses, *Shattered Hope: The Guatemalan Revolution and the United States, 1944–1954* (Princeton: Princeton University Press, 1991).

100. Jorrin and Martz, *Latin*, 254–267. Lars Schoultz, *The Populist Challenge: Argentine Electoral Behavior in the Postwar Era* (Chapel Hill: The University of North Carolina Press, 1983). Darío Cantón and Jorge Raúl Jorrat, "Continuity and Change in Elections in the City of Buenos Aires, 1931–1954," *Latin American Research Review*, 33:3 (1998), 137–160. Carlos H. Waisman, *Reversal of Development in Argentina: Postwar Counterrevolutionary Policies and Their Structural Consequences* (Princeton: Princeton University Press, 1987). Bermeo, *Ordinary*, 178–220.

101. Designed by a directly elected constitutional assembly, the 1946 Constitution restored many aspects of the 1891 system, although with a more open democracy. It created weak federalism, strong central government powers including intervention in the states, a highly presidential system with vast appointive and legislative and fiscal

attributes as well as an item veto, suspension of individual liberties during crises, provisions for social rights similar to those in the 1917 Mexican constitution, and so many convoluted exceptions to so many clauses that wide latitude remained for maneuver by the chief executive. Busey, *Latin*, 100–105, 110–113. Thomas E. Skidmore, *Politics in Brazil, 1930–1964: An Experiment in Democracy* (New York: Oxford University Press, 1967). Love, "Political," 3–24. Bermeo, *Ordinary*, 69–99. O'Donnell, *Modernization*.

102. Yashar, *Demanding*. Ameringer, *Democracy*, 30–35.

103. Herbert Klein, *Bolivia: The Evolution of a Multi-Ethnic Society*, 2nd ed. (New York: Oxford University Press, 1992). James M. Malloy, *Bolivia: The Uncompleted Revolution* (Pittsburgh: University of Pittsburgh Press, 1970). Christopher Mitchell, *The Legacy of Populism in Bolivia: From the MNR to Military Regime* (New York: Praeger, 1977). Merilee S. Grindle and Pilar Domingo, eds., *Proclaiming Revolution: Bolivia in Comparative Perspective* (Cambridge: Harvard University Press, 2003).

104. John D. Martz, *Acción Democrática: Evolution of a Modern Political Party in Venezuela* (Princeton: Princeton University Press, 1966). Coppedge, *Strong*.

105. Arturo Valenzuela, *The Breakdown of Democratic Regimes: Chile* (Baltimore: Johns Hopkins University Press, 1978). Bermeo, *Ordinary*, 138–176. Faundez, *Marxism*. Drake, *Socialism*.

106. Jorge Montaño, *Partidos y política en América Latina* (Mexico: UNAM, 1975), 11–20. Hartlyn and Valenzuela, "Democracy," 31–33. Pierson and Gil, *Government*, 314–317. Gomez, "Latin," 48–49. Macdonald, *Latin*, 173. One of the weakest party systems persisted in Brazil. Soares, "The Politics," 467–496.

107. Pierson and Gil, *Government*, 336–339. Christensen, "The General," 505–508. Miranda, *Reformas*, 286–287. Fitzgibbon, *The Constitutions*, 247.

108. Shugart and Carey, *Presidents*, 174–183, 280–281. Beginning in 1865, the Colorados held the executive branch for 93 years, a record for a party in Latin America and perhaps the world. Fitzgibbon, *Latin*, 376, 461. Donald W. Bray, "Uruguay," in Burnett and Johnson, 429–446. Ending the rare military dictatorship of Gustavo Rojas Pinilla (1953–57), the Colombian constitutional reform of 1957 (of the enduring 1886 constitution) forged a pact to preserve peace between the two dominant political parties by establishing a bipartisan government from 1958 to 1974, the National Front. Not wanting to reignite their civil war that had led to the dictatorship, the Liberals and Conservatives agreed to share power in all branches of government. They also promised to alternate the presidency every four years. Although restoring a limited democracy and providing stability, this arrangement made many Colombians feel marginalized from political participation and representation. Dix, "The Colombian," 80–82. George I. Blanksten, "The Politics of Latin America," in Gabriel A. Almond and James S. Coleman, *The Politics of the Developing Areas* (Princeton: Princeton University Press, 1960), 455–531, especially 479–481.

109. Giovanni Sartori, *Parties and Party Systems: A Framework for Analysis* (Cambridge: Cambridge University Press, 1976), 131–141, 159–163, quote from 162. Valenzuela, *The Breakdown.*

110. Pierson and Gil, *Government*, 314–336. Williams, *Latin.* Porter and Alexander, *The Struggle*, 25–37. Alexander, *Prophets.* Lambert, *Latin*, 200–221. Russell H. Fitzgibbon, "The Party Potpourri in Latin America," *Western Political Quarterly*, 10:1 (March, 1957), 3–22. Gary W. Wynia, *The Politics of Latin American Development*, 2nd ed. (Cambridge: Cambridge University Press, 1984), especially 74–81.

111. The closing words to one standard anthology reflected the sense of crisis: "Democracy, the United States, and moderates throughout the hemisphere are on trial. The outcome remains uncertain everywhere." Schmitt and Burks, *Evolution*, 261. Wright, *Latin.*

112. Bermeo, *Ordinary*, 100–176. Mitchell A. Seligson, "Political Culture and Democratization in Latin America," in Camp, *Democracy*, 67–90.

113. O'Donnell, *Modernization.* David Collier, ed., *The New Authoritarianism in Latin America* (Princeton: Princeton University Press, 1979). Howard J. Wiarda, ed., *Politics and Social Change in Latin America: The Distinct Tradition* (Amherst: University of Massachusetts Press, 1974). Bermeo, *Ordinary.*

Notes to Chapter 7

1. The best comprehensive book covering this period is Peter H. Smith, *Democracy in Latin America: Political Change in Comparative Perspective* (New York: Oxford University Press, 2005), 156.

2. Arend Lijphart, *Democracies: Patterns of Majoritarian and Consensus Government in Twenty-One Countries* (New Haven: Yale University Press, 1984), 37–40. Raymond D. Gastil, *Freedom in the World: Political Rights and Civil Liberties, 1980* (New York: Freedom House, 1980), especially 27.

3. The point about the greater importance of "long-term historical factors" and "socioeconomic problems" rather than the character of outgoing dictatorships or transitions was made by one of the pioneers of transition studies. By the late 1990s, he considered only the historic strongholds of Chile, Uruguay, and Costa Rica as institutionalized democracies obeying most of the formal rules. Guillermo O'Donnell, *Counterpoints: Selected Essays on Authoritarianism and Democratization* (Notre Dame: University of Notre Dame Press, 1999), 133–194, quotes from 160. The foundational work on transitions is Guillermo O'Donnell, Philippe C. Schmitter, and Laurence Whitehead, eds., *Transitions from Authoritarian Rule* (Baltimore: The Johns Hopkins University Press, 1986). Samuel P. Huntington, *The Third Wave: Democratization in the Late Twentieth Century* (Norman: University of Oklahoma Press, 1991), 270–271. Manuel Alcántara Saez, *Sistemas políticos de América Latina*, 2nd ed., 2 vols. (Madrid, Editorial Tecnos, S.A., 1999). Paul W. Drake, "The International Causes of Democra-

tization, 1974–1990" in Paul W. Drake and Mathew D. McCubbins, eds., *The Origins of Liberty: Political and Economic Liberalization in the Modern World* (Princeton: Princeton University Press, 1998), 70–91. Paul W. Drake and Eduardo Silva, eds., *Elections and Democratization in Latin America, 1980–85* (La Jolla, California: Center for Iberian and Latin American Studies, 1986). Frances Hagopian, "Conclusions: Government Performance, Political Representation, and Public Perceptions of Contemporary Democracy in Latin America," in Frances Hagopian and Scott P. Mainwaring, eds., *The Third Wave of Democratization in Latin America: Advances and Setbacks* (Cambridge: Cambridge University Press, 2004), 319–362.

4. For criteria, criticisms, and qualifications for these surveys, see this book's previous chapter. Although many scholars would debate the precise ranking of particular countries, most would agree with the general clustering of the highest and lowest places, especially over more than five decades. For the late 1970s, matching the rankings with socioeconomic data showed a strong correlation between democracy and higher socioeconomic status, especially per capita GNP and consumption of telephones, electricity, tractors, and newspapers, as well as public education expenditures, literacy, life expectancy, urbanization, and lower infant mortality rates. Other variables, such as racial homogeneity, population density and growth rates, and size of territory, did not correlate with the democratic rankings. Philip Kelly, "Measuring Democracy in Latin America: The Fitzgibbon Index," in Philip Kelly, ed., *Assessing Democracy in Latin America: A Tribute to Russell H. Fitzgibbon* (Boulder: Westview Press, 1998), 3–11; "Democracy in Latin America: Update of the Fitzgibbon Survey," *LASA Forum*, 33:1 (Spring, 2002), 10–13. Per usual, most experts outside this survey agreed that the most democratic political systems prevailed in Costa Rica, Uruguay, and Chile and the least in Paraguay and Haiti. Guillermo O'Donnell, "Democracia, desarrollo humano, y derechos humanos" in Guillermo O'Donnell, Osvaldo M. Iazzetta, and Jorge Vargas Cullell, eds., *Democracia, desarrollo humano y ciudadanía: Reflexiones sobre la calidad de la democracia en América Latina* (Santa Fe, Argentina: Homo Sapiens Ediciones, 2003), 25–148, especially 88–89.

5. Extending Smith's data from 1978 through 2006, democracies lasted an average of 21 years. Smith, *Democracy*, 41–43. Paul W. Drake, "Debt and Democracy in Latin America, 1920s–1980s," in Barbara Stallings and Robert Kaufman, eds., *Debt and Democracy in Latin America* (Boulder: Westview Press, 1989), 39–58.

6. In the 1990s, however, Peru became increasingly authoritarian under Fujimori. Huntington, *The Third*, 258–270. Drake, "Debt."

7. Smith, *Democracy*, 313–345. Brian Loveman, "'Protected Democracies': Antipolitics and Political Transitions in Latin America, 1978–1994," in Brian Loveman and Thomas M. Davies, Jr., eds., *The Politics of Antipolitics: The Military in Latin America* (Wilmington: Scholarly Resources, Inc., 1997), 366–397; *For la Patria: Politics and the Armed Forces in Latin America* (Wilmington, Delaware: Scholarly Resources, Inc.,

1999). Kenneth M. Roberts, *Deepening Democracy: The Modern Left and Social Movements in Chile and Peru* (Stanford: Stanford University Press, 1998). Paul W. Drake and Eric Hershberg, "The Crisis of State-Society Relations in the Post-1980s Andes," in Paul W. Drake and Eric Hershberg, eds., *State and Society in Conflict: Comparative Perspectives on Andean Crises* (Pittsburgh: University of Pittsburgh Press, 2006), 1–40.

8. Kurt Weyland, "Clarifying a Contested Concept: Populism in the Study of Latin American Politics," *Comparative Politics*, 34:1 (October, 2001), 1–22; "Neopopulism and Neoliberalism in Latin America: Unexpected Affinities," *Studies in Comparative International Development*, 31 (Fall, 1996), 3–31; "Neoliberal Populism in Latin America and Eastern Europe," *Comparative Politics*, 31:4 (July, 1999), 379–401; "Populism in the Age of Neoliberalism," in Michael L. Conniff, ed., *Populism in Latin America* (Tuscaloosa: The University of Alabama Press, 1999), 172–190. Paul W. Drake, "Requiem for Populism?" in Michael Conniff, ed., *Latin American Populism in Comparative Perspective* (Albuquerque: University of New Mexico Press, 1982), 217–245; "Comment," in Rudiger Dornbusch and Sebastian Edwards, eds., *The Macroeconomics of Populism in Latin America* (Chicago: The University of Chicago Press, 1991), 35–40; "Chilean Populism Reconsidered, 1920s–1990s," in Michael L. Conniff, ed., *Populism in Latin America* (Tuscaloosa: The University of Alabama Press, 1999), 63–74.

9. Smith, *Democracy*, 338–345. Huntington, *The Third*, 208–316. Hagopian and Mainwaring, *The Third*. Scott Mainwaring, Guillermo O'Donnell, and J. Samuel Valenzuela, eds., *Issues in Democratic Consolidation: The New South American Democracies in Comparative Perspective* (Notre Dame: University of Notre Dame Press, 1992). Juan J. Linz and Alfred Stepan, *Problems of Democratic Transition and Consolidation: Southern Europe, South America, and Post-Communist Europe* (Baltimore: Johns Hopkins University Press, 1996). Elizabeth Jelin and Eric Hershberg, eds., *Constructing Democracy: Human Rights, Citizenship, and Society in Latin America* (Boulder: Westview Press, 1996). Felipe Aguero and Jeffrey Stark, eds., *Fault Lines of Democracy in Post-Transition Latin America* (Miami: North-South Center Press, 1998). O'Donnell, Iazzetta, and Cullell, eds., *Democracia*. Scott Mainwaring and Christopher Welna, eds., *Democratic Accountability in Latin America* (New York: Oxford University Press, 2003). Katherine Hite and Paola Cesarini, eds., *Authoritarian Legacies and Democracy in Latin America and Southern Europe* (Notre Dame: University of Notre Dame Press, 2004).

10. United Nations Development Programme, *Democracy in Latin America: Towards a Citizens' Democracy* (Buenos Aires: Aguilar, Altea, Taurus, Alfaguara, 2005), 154–161. Manuel Antonio Garretón, *Incomplete Democracy: Political Democratization in Chile and Latin America* (Chapel Hill: The University of North Carolina Press, 2003). Roberts, *Deepening*.

11. Alcántara, *Sistemas*, I, 74–79, 117–125, 169–176, 256–264; the responses for Central America were much the same as for South America and Mexico combined,

although 80% of Costa Ricans preferred democracy to any other form of government. II, 115–125.

12. Roderic Ai Camp, ed., *Citizen Views of Democracy in Latin America* (Pittsburgh: University of Pittsburgh Press, 2001), 9–18. Timothy J. Power and Mary A. Clark, "Does Trust Matter? Interpersonal Trust and Democratic Values in Chile, Costa Rica, and Mexico," in Camp, *Citizen*, 51–71.

13. Smith, *Democracy*, 285–310. Marta Lagos, "Public Opinion," in Jorge I. Dominguez and Michael Shifter, eds., *Constructing Democratic Governance in Latin America*, 2nd ed. (Baltimore: The Johns Hopkins University Press, 2003), 137–164.

14. O'Donnell, "Democracia," in O'Donnell, Iazzetta, and Cullel, eds., *Democracia*, 25–148, polling data on 90 and 137. United Nations Development Programme, *Democracy*, 131–135. Smith, *Democracy*, 333–335. Lagos, "Public," 152–155. www .Latinobarometro.org.

15. *www.Latinobarometro.org*. www.worldpublicopinion.org/pipa, March 8, 2007.

16. Huntington, *The Third*. Drake, "The International;" "The Hegemony of U.S. Economic Doctrines in Latin America," in Valpy Fitzgerald and Rosemary Thorp, eds., *Economic Doctrines in Latin America: Origins, Embedding and Evolution* (London: Palgrave MacMillan, 2005), 72–96. Laurence Whitehead, "Three International Dimensions of Democratization," in Laurence Whitehead, ed., *The International Dimensions of Democratization: Europe and the Americas* (New York: Oxford University Press, 1996), 3–25. Philippe C. Schmitter, "The Influence of the International Context upon the Choice of National Institutions and Policies in Neo-Democracies," in Whitehead, *The International*, 26–54. Scott Mainwaring and Anibal Perez-Linan, "Latin American Democratization since 1978: Democratic Transitions, Breakdowns, and Erosions," in Hagopian and Mainwaring, *The Third*, 14–62.

17. Similar to hegemony theory, the concept of international regimes refers to sets of formal and informal international norms, rules, conventions, expectations, and procedures favored by dominant powers and widely accepted by weaker countries. John Gerard Ruggie, ed., *The Antinomies of Interdependence: National Welfare and the International Division of Labor* (New York: Columbia University Press, 1983). Drake and Hershberg, "The Crisis."

18. Drake, "The International," 81. Abraham F. Lowenthal, ed., *Exporting Democracy* (Baltimore: Johns Hopkins University Press, 1991).

19. Drake, "The International." Huntington, *The Third*, 45–46, 59–108. Smith, *Democracy*, 111–133, 335–338; *Talons of the Eagle: Dynamics of U.S.-Latin American Relations*, 2nd ed. (New York; Oxford University Press, 2000). Kathryn Sikkink, "The Effectiveness of U.S. Human Rights Policy, 1973–1980," in Whitehead, *The International*, 93–124. Margaret E. Keck and Kathryn Sikkink, *Activists Beyond Borders: Advocacy Networks in International Politics* (Ithaca: Cornell University Press, 1998). Lars Schoultz, *Human Rights and United States Policy toward Latin America* (Princeton:

Princeton University Press, 1981). Thomas Carothers, *In the Name of Democracy: U.S. Policy toward Latin America in the Reagan Years* (Berkeley: University of California Press, 1991). Heraldo Muñoz V., *El fin del fantasma: Las relaciones interamericanas después de la guerra fría* (Santiago: Hachette, 1992). Jonathan Hartlyn, Lars Schoultz, and Augusto Varas, eds., *The United States and Latin America in the 1990s: Beyond the Cold War* (Chapel Hill: University of North Carolina Press, 1992). Francis Fukuyama, *The End of History and the Last Man* (New York: The Free Press, 1992). Stephan Haggard and Robert R. Kaufman, *The Political Economy of Democratic Transitions* (Princeton: Princeton University Press, 1995). Laurence Whitehead, "International Aspects of Democratization," in Guillermo O'Donnell, Philippe C. Schmitter, and Laurence Whitehead, eds., *Transitions from Authoritarian Rule: Comparative Perspectives* (Baltimore: The Johns Hopkins University Press, 1986), 3–46. Lowenthal, *Exporting*. Dankart A. Rustow, "Democracy: A Global Revolution?" *Foreign Affairs*, 69:4 (Fall, 1990), 75–91. Karen L. Remmer, "New Wine or Old Bottlenecks: The Study of Latin American Democracy," *Comparative Politics* 23:4 (July, 1991), 479–496. Terry Lynn Karl, "Dilemmas of Democratization in Latin America," *Comparative Politics* 23:1 (October, 1990), 1–22. Robert A. Pastor, ed., *Democracy in the Americas: Stopping the Pendulum* (New York: Holmes and Meier, 1989). Giuseppe Di Palma, *To Craft Democracies: An Essay on Democratic Transitions* (Berkeley: University of California Press, 1990), especially 183–200.

20. Scott Mainwaring and Anibal Perez-Linan, "Level of Development and Democracy: Latin American Exceptionalism, 1945–1996," *Comparative Political Studies*, 36:9 (November, 2003), 1031–1067; "Latin American."

21. Ruth Berins Collier, *Paths toward Democracy: The Working Class and Elites in Western Europe and South America* (New York: Cambridge University Press, 1999). Deitrich Rueschemeyer, Evelyne Huber Stephens, and John D. Stephens, *Capitalist Development and Democracy* (Chicago: University of Chicago Press, 1992). Paul W. Drake, *Labor Movements and Dictatorships: The Southern Cone in Comparative Perspective* (Baltimore: The Johns Hopkins university Press, 1996). Smith, *Democracy*, 53–62.

22. Drake, "Debt;" "The International." Karen L. Remmer, "Democracy and Economic Crisis: The Latin American Experience," in Camp, *Democracy*, 269–290. Huntington, *The Third*, 258–270. Smith, *Democracy*, 313–326. Loveman, "Protected"; *For*, 195–252.

23. This voluntaristic, contingent perspective on elite decision making permeated the most influential multivolume study of transitions toward democracy: O'Donnell, Schmitter, and Whitehead, *Transitions*. Linz and Stepan, *Problems*. Larry Diamond, Juan J. Linz, Seymour Martin Lipset, "Preface," in Larry Diamond, Juan J. Linz, and Seymour Martin Lipset, eds., *Democracy in Developing Countries: Latin America* (Boulder: Lynne Rienner, 1989), ix–xxviii. Adam Przeworski, *Democracy and the Market: Political and Economic Reforms in Eastern Europe and Latin America* (Cambridge: Cambridge University Press, 1991).

24. Huntington, *The Third*, 58. Roberts, *Deepening*. Jeffrey M. Puryear, *Thinking Politics: Intellectuals and Democracy in Chile* (Baltimore: Johns Hopkins University Press, 1994).

25. Kevin J. Middlebrook, ed., *Conservative Parties, the Right, and Democracy in Latin America* (Baltimore: Johns Hopkins University Press, 2000).

26. Nestor Kirchner (2003–2007) in Argentina, Alán García in Peru (2006–?), and Daniel Ortega (2007–?) in Nicaragua might also fit this moderate new left category or a mixed classification, but it is too soon to tell. Paul W. Drake and Peter Winn, "The Presidential Election of 1999/2000 and Chile's Transition to Democracy," *LASA Forum*, 31:1 (Spring, 2000), 5–9. Paul W. Drake, "El Nuevo escenario político," in *FLACSO: Nuevo gobierno: Desafíos de la reconciliación: Chile 1999–2000* (Santiago: FLACSO-Chile, 2000), 109–118. Eric Hershberg and Fred Rosen, eds., *Latin America After Neoliberalism: Turning the Tide in the 21st Century?* (New York: North American Congress on Latin America, 2006). Smith, *Democracy*, 1–6, 330–333.

27. Michael Coppedge, "Venezuela: Popular Sovereignty versus Liberal Democracy," in Dominguez and Shifter, eds., *Constructing*, 165–192. Michael Shifter, "Tempering Expectations of Democracy," in Dominguez and Shifter, eds., *Constructing*, 3–10. Steve Ellner and Daniel Hellinger, eds., *Venezuelan Politics in the Chávez Era: Class, Polarization, and Conflict* (Boulder: Lynne Rienner, 2003). Drake and Hershberg, eds., *State*. The quote comes from Teodoro Petkoff, a leading newspaper editor and supporter of the losing candidate. "Venezuelans Give Chávez a Mandate to Tighten His Grip," *New York Times*, December 5, 2006, A3.

28. Joe Foweraker, "Review Article: Institutional Design, Party Systems and Governability—Differentiating the Presidential Regimes of Latin America," *British Journal of Political Science* 28 (1998), 651–676.

29. Keith S. Rosenn, "The Success of Constitutionalism in the United States and its Failure in Latin America," in Kenneth W. Thompson, ed., *The U.S. Constitution and the Constitutions of Latin America* (Lanham: University Press of America, 1991), 53–96, especially 87–94.

30. Juan Maestre Alfonso, *Constituciones y leyes políticas de América Latina, Filipinas, y Guinea Ecuatorial*, 5 vols. (Sevilla: Imprenta E.E.H.A., 1989), II, 9–16, 47–106, 493–499. Alcántara, *Sistemas*, I, 158–164.

31. Maestre, *Constituciones*, II, 258–261, 337–490.

32. For an example of little change, when Argentina restored democracy in 1983, it simply reinstated the 1853 constitution and thereafter reformed it slightly in 1994. For an example of continuity with significant changes, Bolivia resurrected the 1967 constitution but reformed it substantially in 1994. Alcántara, *Sistemas*, I, 11–12, 290–294. Smith, *Democracy*, 156. Mainwaring and Shugart, *Presidentialism*, 440–460. William Columbus Davis, *Warnings from the Far South: Democracy versus Dictatorship in Uruguay, Argentina, and Chile* (Westport: Praeger, 1995), 140.

33. Donna Lee Van Cott, "Turning Crisis into Opportunity: Achievements of Excluded Groups in the Andes," in Drake and Hershberg, *State*, 157–188; ed., *Indigenous People and Democracy in Latin America* (New York: St. Martins, 1995); *The Friendly Liquidation of the Past: The Politics of Diversity in Latin America* (Pittsburgh: University of Pittsburgh Press, 2000). Nancy Grey Postero and Leon Zamosc, eds., *The Struggle for Indigenous Rights in Latin America* (Brighton, UK: Sussex Academic Press, 2004). United Nations Development Programme, *Democracy*, 102–107.

34. Alcántara, *Sistemas*, I, 383–388, 398–406.

35. Maestre, *Constituciones*, I, 343–403; progressive quotes from 349; solidarity quote from 363. Alcántara, *Sistemas*, I, 436–458.

36. Alcántara, *Sistemas*, II, 136–154, 174–222, 241–247, 264–293.

37. To detail all these rights, the 1988 document amassed 315 articles, much longer than previous Brazilian constitutions. Some other Latin American constitutions in this era also stretched to great length, with the Honduran entry reaching 379 articles. Aspasia Camargo, "La federación sometida. Nacionalismo desarrollista e inestabilidad democrática," in Marcello Carmagnani, ed., *Federalismos latinoamericanos: Mexico/Brasil/Argentina* (Mexico: Fondo de Cultura Economica, 1993), 300–362, especially 343–346. Alcántara, *Sistemas*, II, 241–247.

38. Alcántara, *Sistemas*, I, 337–345.

39. Alcántara, *Sistemas*, I, 179–202.

40. Miriam Kornblith, "Sowing Democracy in Venezuela: Advances and Challenges in a Time of Change," in Drake and Hershberg, *State*, 288–314.

41. R. Andrew Nickson, *Local Government in Latin America* (Boulder: Lynne Rienner Publishers: 1995), 7–29. Kent Eaton, *Politics Beyond the Capital: The Design of Subnational Institutions in South America* (Stanford: Stanford University Press, 2004). Alfred P. Montero and David J. Samuels, eds., *Decentralization and Democracy in Latin America* (Notre Dame: University of Notre Dame Press, 2004).

42. Alfred P. Montero and David J. Samuels, "The Political Determinants of Decentralization in Latin America: Causes and Consequences," in Montero and Samuels, *Decentralization*, 3–34. Nickson, *Local*, 24–29. Kent Eaton, "The Link between Political and Fiscal Decentralization in South America," in Montero and Samuels, *Decentralization*, 122–154; *Politics*. Kathleen O'Neill, *Decentralizing the State: Elections, Parties, and Local Power in the Andes* (Cambridge: Cambridge University Press, 2005). Alan Angell, Pamela Lowden, and Rosemary Thorp, eds., *Decentralizing Development: The Political Economy of Institutional Change in Colombia and Chile* (New York: Oxford University Press, 2001). Tim Campbell, *The Quiet Revolution: Decentralization and the Rise of Political Participation in Latin American Cities* (Pittsburgh: University of Pittsburgh Press, 2003). José E. Molina Vega and Janeth Hernández, "Sistemas electorales subnacionales," in Dieter Nohlen, Sonia Picado, and Daniel Zovatto, eds., *Tratado de derecho electoral comparado de América Latina* (Mexico: Fondo de Cultura Economica, 1998), 186–204.

43. Camargo, "La federación." German J. Bidart Campos, "El federalismo argentino desde 1930 hasta la actualidad," in Carmagnani, *Federalismos*, 363–396. Edward L. Gibson, "Federalism and Democracy: Theoretical Connections and Cautionary Insights," in Edward L. Gibson, ed., *Federalism and Democracy in Latin America* (Baltimore: The Johns Hopkins University Press, 2004), 1–28. Alberto Diaz-Cayeros, *Federalism, Fiscal Authority, and Centralization in Latin America* (Cambridge: Cambridge University Press, 2006). David J. Samuels, *Ambition, Federalism, and Legislative Politics in Brazil* (New York: Cambridge University Press, 2003). David J. Samuels and Scott Mainwaring, "Strong Federalism, Constraints on the Central Government, and Economic Reform in Brazil," in Gibson, *Federalism*, 85–130. Montero and Samuels, "The Political," 23. Eaton, *Politics*.

44. Nickson, *Local*, 61–68. Molina Vega and Hernández, "Sistemas," 188–204.

45. Alcántara, *Sistemas*, I, 326–328, 386–387, 456–457. Maestre, *Constituciones*, I, 343–403. O'Neill, *Decentralizing*, 89–205. Merilee S. Grindle, *Audacious Reforms: Institutional Invention and Democracy in Latin America* (Baltimore: The Johns Hopkins University Press, 2000). Michael Penfold-Becerra, "Federalism and Institutional Change in Venezuela," in Gibson, *Federalism*, 197–225. Fernando Carrión, ed., *Procesos de descentralización en la comunidad andina* (Quito: FLACSO, 2003).

46. Eaton, *Politics*, 36–37. Enrique Ochoa-Reza, "Multiple Arenas of Struggle: Federalism and Mexico's Transition to Democracy," in Gibson, *Federalism*, 255–296. O'Neill, *Decentralizing*, 229–235.

47. 47. Smith, *Democracy*, 139–155. Matthew Soberg Shugart and John M. Carey, *Presidents and Assemblies: Constitutional Design and Electoral Dynamics* (Cambridge: Cambridge University Press, 1992), 283–287. Scott Mainwaring and Matthew Soberg Shugart, eds., *Presidentialism and Democracy in Latin America* (New York: Cambridge University Press, 1997). Mark Penfield Jones, "Electoral Laws and the Survival of Presidential Democracies," Ph.D. Dissertation (University of Michigan, 1994), 48. Juan J. Linz and Arturo Valenzuela, eds., *The Failure of Presidential Democracy* (Baltimore: The Johns Hopkins University Press, 1994). Giovanni Sartori, *Comparative Constitutional Engineering: An Inquiry into Structures, Incentives, and Outcomes* (New York: New York University Press, 1994), 91–97. Rosenn, "The Success," 79–80. Przeworski, Alvarez, Cheibub, and Limongi, *Democracy*, 128–137. Lijphart, *Democracy*, 145–147.

48. Manuel Aragon Reyes, "Derecho electoral: Sufragio activo y pasivo," in Nohlen, Picado, and Zovatto, *Tratado*, 104–122, especially 114–115. Alcántara, *Sistemas*, I, 49–50.

49. In Bolivia, the presidential election was direct unless no one obtained an absolute majority, in which case the congress chose among the top three candidates, as the Chilean legislature used to do prior to 1973 among the top two, with the difference that the Bolivians did not follow the Chilean example of always picking the frontrunner.

In 1994, Bolivia reduced the congressional selection to the top two presidential candidates. Carey, "Presidentialism," 16–18. Nohlen, "Sistemas," in Nohlen, Picado, and Zovatto, *Tratado*, 179–181; "Elections and Electoral Systems in the Americas," in Dieter Nohlen, ed., *Elections in the Americas: A Data Handbook*, 2 vols. (New York: Oxford University Press, 2005), I, 1–60, especially 30–35. United Nations Development Programme, *Democracy*, 86. Alan Angell, Maria D'Alva Kinzo, and Diego Urbaneja, "Electioneering in Latin America," in Camp, *Democracy*, 183–206, especially 185. María Lourdes González, "Organos electivos: Composición y períodos electorales," in Nohlen, Picado, and Zovatto, *Tratado*, 59–64.

50. Dieter Nohlen, "La reelección," in Nohlen, Picado, and Zovatto, *Tratado*, 141–144, quotes from 141. Colomer, *Introducción*, 125. Shugart and Carey, *Presidents*, 87–91. Carey, "Presidentialism," 18–21. Smith, *Democracy*, 160–161.

51. Shugart and Carey, *Presidents*, 208–225. Carey, "Presidentialism," 14–15. Smith, *Democracy*, 159–160. Nohlen, "Elections," in Nohlen, *Elections*, I, 37–40. Jones, "Electoral."

52. Shugart and Carey, *Presidents*, 154–158. Mainwaring and Shugart, eds., *Presidentialism*. Smith, *Democracy*, 162–165. United Nations Development Programme, *Democracy*, 92–93

53. Maestre, *Constituciones*, II, 61–68. Peter M. Siavelis, *The President and Congress in Postauthoritarian Chile: Institutional Constraints to Democratic Consolidation* (University Park: The Pennsylvania State University Press, 2000).

54. Smith, *Democracy*, 162–165, 354–355. Brian Loveman, *The Constitution of Tyranny: Regimes of Exception in Spanish America* (Pittsburgh: University of Pittsburgh Press, 1993); *For*; "Protected," 374–377.

55. John M. Carey and Matthew Soberg Shugart, eds., *Executive Decree Authority* (Cambridge: Cambridge University Press, 1998). Catherine M. Conaghan and James M. Malloy, *Unsettling Statecraft: Democracy and Neoliberalism in the Central Andes* (Pittsburgh: University of Pittsburgh Press, 1994). Eric Magar, "The Clash of Two Bully Pulpits: Posturing, Bargaining, and Polarization in the Legislative Process of the Americas," Ph.D. Dissertation (University of California-San Diego, 2001). Scott Morgenstern and Benito Nacif, eds., *Legislative Politics in Latin America* (New York: Cambridge University Press, 2002). For provisions for executive-legislative relations in both the older and newer constitutions, see Mainwaring and Shugart, *Presidentialism*, 440–460. Loveman, *The Constitution*. Alcántara, *Sistemas*, I, 290–294. Davis, *Warnings*, 140.

56. This index was apparently created prior to Venezuela's adoption of a more presidentialist constitution in 1999. Matthew Soberg Shugart and Stephan Haggard, "Institutions and Public Policy in Presidential Systems," in Stephan Haggard and Mathew D. McCubbins, eds., *Presidents, Parliaments, and Policy* (New York: Cambridge University Press, 2001), 64–102, index on 80. Smith, *Democracy*, 162–174.

57. O'Donnell, *Counterpoints*, 160–173. Scott Morgenstern, "Towards a Model of Latin American Legislatures," in Morgensten and Nacif, eds., *Legislative*, 1–19. John M. Carey, "Presidentialism and Representative Institutions," in Dominguez and Shifter, eds., *Constructing*, 11–42. Drake and Hershberg, eds., *State*. Alcántara, *Sistemas*, I, 436–458 on Peru; II, 174 on Guatemala. Penfold-Becerra, "Federalism," 217–220. Catherine M. Conaghan, *Fujimori's Peru: Deception in the Public Sphere* (Pittsburgh: University of Pittsburgh Press, 2005).

58. Alcántara, *Sistemas*, II, 523–534.

59. Smith, *Democracy*, 201–209. Jones, "Electoral." Alcántara, *Sistemas*, I, 83–84. Barry Ames, *The Deadlock of Democracy in Brazil* (Ann Arbor: The University of Michigan Press, 2001).

60. Smith, *Democracy*, 263–284. United Nations Development Programme, *Democracy*, 113–118.

61. The Peruvian constitution of 1979 tried to shield the president by forbidding coups d'état. Maestre, *Constituciones*, I, 343–403. Drake and Hershberg, eds., *State*. Carey, "Presidentialism," *Constructing*, 12. Massive demonstrations also drove presidents Fernando de la Rúa from office in 2001 in Argentina and Jean Bertrand-Aristide in 2004 in Haiti. Smith, *Democracy*, 130–133, 327–335.

62. The quote comes from Bolivian political scientist César Rojas. Martín Garat, "Bolivia: Constituent Assembly Stalled," *Latin America Data Base*, 16:45 (December 8, 2006), 5.

63. Scott Morgenstern, "Explaining Legislative Politics in Latin America," in Morgenstern and Nacif, eds., *Legislative*, 413–445, data from 415–416; "Towards," 1–19; *Patterns of Legislative Politics: Roll-Call Voting in Latin America and the United States* (New York: Cambridge University Press, 2004). Gary W. Cox and Scott Morgenstern, "Epilogue: Latin America's Reactive Assemblies and Proactive Presidents," in Morgenstern and Nacif, eds., *Legislative*, 446–468. David Close, ed., *Legislatures and the New Democracies in Latin America* (Boulder: Lynne Rienner Publishers, 1995).

64. Smith, *Democracy*, 165–175. El Salvador's congress was fairly strong and had the same authority as its Ecuadorean counterpart to declare the president physically or mentally incompetent. Alcántara, *Sistemas*, I; II, 150–151. Nohlen, "Elections," in Nohlen, *Elections*, I, 32–34; II, 28–33; "Sistemas electorales parlamentarios y presidenciales," in Nohlen, Picado, and Zovatto, *Tratado*, 145–185. González, "Organos," 60. Aragon Reyes, "Derecho," 105–122. John M. Carey, *Term Limits and Legislative Representation* (New York: Cambridge University Press, 1996).

65. Richard Snyder and David J. Samuels, "Legislative Malapportionment in Latin America: Historical and Comparative Perspectives," in Gibson, *Federalism*, 131–172.

66. Siavelis, *The President*. Maestre, *Constituciones*, II, 68–70.

67. Angell, D'Alva Kinzo, and Urbaneja, "Electioneering," 193–198.

68. Shugart and Carey, *Presidents*, 112–113. Carey, "Presidentialism," 22–26.

69. Smith, *Democracy*, 201–204. Morgenstern, "Explaining," 430–433. Nohlen, "Sistemas," 177–179.

70. Smith, *Democracy*, 249–253. Mala N. Htun, "Women and Democracy," in Dominguez and Shifter, *Constructing*, 118–136. United Nations Development Programme, *Democracy*, 85–87.

71. United Nations Development Programme, *Democracy*, 87–89. Van Cott, ed., *Indigenous*.

72. Juan E. Méndez, Guillermo O'Donnell, and Paulo Sérgio Pinheiro, eds. *The (Un)rule of Law and the Underprivileged in Latin America* (Notre Dame: University of Notre Dame Press, 1999). Pilar Domingo and Rachel Seider, eds., *Rule of Law in Latin America: The International Promotion of Judicial Reform* (London: Institute of Latin American Studies, 2001). Susan Eva Eckstein and Timothy P. Wickham-Crowley, eds., *What Justice? Whose Justice? Fighting for Fairness in Latin America* (Berkeley: University of California Press, 2003). Eduardo Soto Kloss, *El recurso de protección: Origenes, doctrina y jurisprudencia* (Santiago: Editorial Juridica de Chile, 1982). Sergio Lira Herrera, *Recurso de protección: Naturaleza juridíca, doctrina, jurisprudencia, derecho comparado* (Santiago: Alborada S.A., 1990). Fix Zamudio and Cossio Díaz, *El poder judicial en el ordenamiento mexicano* (Mexico: Fondo de Cultura Economica, 1996).

73. Druscilla L. Scribner, "Limiting Presidential Power: Supreme Court-Executive Relations in Argentina and Chile," Ph.D. Dissertation (University of California-San Diego, 2004). United Nations Development Programme, *Democracy*, 93–95.

74. Experience with judicial councils in France, Spain, and Italy inspired similar institutions in Colombia (1955, 1971, 1991), Venezuela (1961, 1969, 1988), Peru (1969, 1979, 1993), El Salvador (1983, 1991), Panama (1987), Ecuador (1992), Paraguay (1992), Costa Rica (1993), Bolivia (1994), Argentina (1994), and Mexico (1994). Irwin Stotzky, ed., *Transition to Democracy in Latin America: The Role of the Judiciary* (Boulder: Westview Press, 1993). Keith S. Rosenn, "The Protection of Judicial Independence in Latin America." *Inter-American Law Review* 19:1 (1987), 1–35. Joel G. Verner, "The Independence of Supreme Courts in Latin America: A Review of the Literature." *Journal of Latin American Studies* 16:2 (1984), 463–506. Roberto Gargarella, "Recientes reformas constitucionales en América Latina: Una primera aproximación," *Desarrollo Económico* 36: 144 (1997), 971–990.

75. A. J. McAdams, ed. *Transitional Justice and the Rule of Law in New Democracies* (Notre Dame: University of Notre Dame Press, 1997). Jorge Correa Sutil, ed., *Situación y políticas judiciales en América Latina* (Santiago: Escuela de Derecho, Universidad Diego Portales, 1994). Edmundo Jarquin and Fernando Carillo, eds., *Justice Delayed: Judicial Reform in Latin America* (Washington, D.C.: Inter-American Development Bank, 1998). Linn A. Hammergren, *The Politics of Justice and Justice Reform in Latin America: The Peruvian Case in Comparative Perspective* (Boulder: Westview Press, 1998). William

C. Prillaman, *The Judiciary and Democratic Decay in Latin America: Declining Confidence in the Rule of Law* (Westport: Praeger, 2000). Mark Ungar, *Elusive Reform: Democracy and the Rule of Law in Latin America* (Boulder: Lynne Rienner, 2002). Rebecca Bill Chavez, *The Rule of Law in Nascent Democracies: Judicial Politics in Argentina* (Stanford: Stanford University Press, 2004). Gretchen Helmke, *Courts under Constraints: Judges, Generals and Presidents in Argentina* (Cambridge: Cambridge University Press, 2005).

76. The countries establishing ombudspersons included: Guatemala (1985), Mexico (1990–1992), El Salvador (1991), Colombia (1991), Costa Rica (1992), Honduras (1992–1995), Argentina (1993–1994), Bolivia (1994), and Ecuador (1996). Juan E. Méndez and Irene Aguilar, *El ombudsman y la protección de los derechos humanos en América Latina* (San José: Instituto Interamericano de Derechos Humanos, 1997). International Commission of Jurists, *Chile: A Time of Reckoning, Human Rights and the Judiciary* (Geneva: Centre for the Independence of Judges and Lawyers, 1992). Elisabeth C. Hilbink, "Legalism against Democracy: The Political Role of the Judiciary in Chile," Ph.D. Dissertation (University of California, San Diego, 1999). Edgardo Buscaglia, Maria Dakolias, and William Ratliff, *Judicial Reform in Latin America: A Framework for National Development* (Stanford: Stanford University Press, 1995).

77. Paul W. Drake and Eduardo Silva, "Introduction: Elections and Democratization in Latin America," in Drake and Silva, *Elections*, 1–8.

78. Nohlen, "Elections," in Nohlen, *Elections*, I, 25–42. United Nations Development Programme, *Democracy*, 78–84. Angell, Kinzo, and Urbaneja, "Electioneering," 183–206. Juan Jaramillo, "Los órganos electorales supremos," in Nohlen, Picado, and Zovatto, *Tratado*, 205–249.

79. Nohlen, "Elections," in Nohlen, *Elections*, I, 13–14, 29–30. Detlef Nolte, "La observación internacional de las elecciones," in Nohlen, Picado, and Zovatto, *Tratado*, 674–688. Kevin Middlebrook, ed., *Electoral Observation and Democratic Transitions in Latin America* (La Jolla: Center for U.S.-Mexican Studies, 1999). United Nations Development Programme, *Democracy*, 51.

80. Alcántara, *Sistemas*, I, 104–105, 339, 385; II, 174. Nohlen, "Elections," in Nohlen, *Elections*, I, 41–42. Bernhard Thibaut, "Instituciones de democracia directa," in Nohlen, Picado, Zovatto, *Tratado*, 65–88. Gary Hoskin, "Democratization in Latin America," *Latin American Research Review*, 32:3 (1997), 209–223. United Nations Development Programme, *Democracy*, 98–99.

81. Brian Loveman, "When You Wish upon the Stars: Why the Generals (and Admirals) Say Yes to Latin American 'Transitions' to Civilian Government," in Drake and McCubbins, *The Origins*, 115–145, here 132–135. Smith, *Democracy*, 186–187. Nohlen, "Elections," in Nohlen, *Elections*, I, 28. Manuel Aragon Reyes, "Derecho electoral: Sufragio activo y pasivo," in Nohlen, Picado, and Zovatto, *Tratado*, 104–122. Mario Fernández Baeza, "El voto obligatorio," in Nohlen, Picado, and Zovatto, *Tratado*, 123–139.

82. Angell, D'Alva Kinzo, and Urbaneja, "Electioneering," 189–193.

83. United Nations Development Programme, *Democracy*, 78–85.

84. Smith, *Democracy*, 188–192. Fernández Baeza, "El voto."

85. Paul W. Drake and Ivan Jaksic, eds., *The Struggle for Democracy in Chile*, revised ed. (Lincoln: University of Nebraska Press, 1995); *El Modelo chileno: Democracia y desarrollo en los noventa* (Santiago: LOM, 1999). International Commission of the Latin American Studies Association to Observe the Chilean Plebiscite, "The Chilean Plebiscite: A First Step Toward Redemocratization," *LASA Forum* 19:4 (Winter, 1989), 18–36.

86. Ochoa-Reza, "Multiple." Dieter Nohlen, "Mexico," in Nohlen, *Elections*, I, 439–478. Smith, *Democracy*, 62–64.

87. Smith, *Democracy*, 195–201, 327–345. Eric Hershberg and Fred Rosen, eds., *Latin America after Neoliberalism: Turning the Tide in the 21st Century?* (New York: The New Press, 2006).

88. Ronald H. McDonald and J. Mark Ruhl, *Party Politics and Elections in Latin America* (Boulder; Westview Press, 1989). Rein Taagepera and Matthew Soberg Shugart, *Seats and Votes: The Effects and Determinants of Electoral Systems* (New Haven: Yale University Press, 1989), 77–83. Scott Mainwaring and Timothy R. Scully, "Introduction: Party Systems in Latin America," in Scott Mainwaring and Timothy R. Scully, eds., *Building Democratic Institutions: Party Systems in Latin America* (Stanford: Stanford University Press, 1995), 1–36, here 28–33.

89. Smith, *Democracy*, 176–182. McDonald and Ruhl, *Party*. Michael Coppedge, *Strong Parties and Lame Ducks: Presidential Partyarchy and Factionalism in Venezuela* (Stanford: Stanford University Press, 1994). Francis Hagopian, "Democracy and Political Representation in Latin America in the 1990s: Pause, Reorganization, or Decline?" in Aguero and Stark, *Fault*, 99–144. Morgenstern, *Patterns*, 188–202. Scott P. Mainwaring, *Rethinking Party Systems in the Third Wave of Democratization: The Case of Brazil* (Stanford: Stanford University Press, 1999). Mainwaring and Scully, eds., *Building*. Drake and Hershberg, eds., *State*. Manuel Alcántara Saez and Flavia Freidenberg, "Organización y funcionamiento de los partidos políticos en América Latina," in Manuel Alcántara Saez and Flavia Freidenberg, eds., *Partidos políticos de América Latina*, 3 vols. (Salamanca: Ediciones Universidad de Salamanca, 2001), I, 11–30. Foweraker, "Review," 665–676.

90. All of the country data from this source exclude Cuba and Haiti from the group of 18 as undemocratic. United Nations Development Programme, *Democracy*, 85–87. Petra Bendel, "Los partidos políticos: Condiciones de inscripción y reconocimiento legal, democracia interna, etc.," in Nohlen, Picado, and Zovatto, *Tratado*, 384–409. Xiomara Navas, "La financiacion electoral: Subvenciones y gastos," in Nohlen, Picado, and Zovatto, *Tratado*, 454–488. Guatemala and El Salvador in the 1970s–1980s sometimes placed formal and informal obstacles in the way of leftwing

parties. Alcántara, *Sistemas*, I; II. Angell, D'Alva Kinzo, and Urbaneja, "Electioneering," 192–201.

91. Angell, D'Alva Kinzo, and Urbaneja, "Electioneering," 185–186.

92. Marcelo Cavarozzi and Manuel Antonio Garretón, "Introducción," in Marcelo Cavarozzi and Manuel Antonio Garretón, eds., *Muerte y resurrección: Los partidos políticos en el autoritarismo y las transiciones en el cono sur* (Santiago: FLACSO, 1989), 13–33. Roberts, *Deepening*. Drake, *Labor*, 180–193. Jorge G. Castañeda, *Utopia Unarmed: The Latin American Left after the Cold War* (New York: Alfred A. Knopf, 1993). Barry Carr and Steve Ellner, eds., *The Latin American Left: From the Fall of Allende to Perestroika* (Boulder: Westview Press, 1993). Katherine Hite, *When the Romance Ended: Leaders of the Chilean Left, 1968–1998* (New York: Columbia University Press, 2000). Steven Levitsky, *Transforming Labor-Based Parties in Latin America: Argentine Peronism in Comparative Perspective* (New York: Cambridge University Press, 2003).

93. Alcántara, *Sistemas*, I; II. Nohlen, "Elections," in Nohlen, *Elections*, I, 18–19. Morgenstern, *Patterns*, 1–25. Mainwaring and Scully, *Building*. Douglas A. Chalmers, Maria do Carmo Campello de Souza, and Atilio A. Boron, eds., *The Right and Democracy in Latin America* (New York: Praeger, 1992). Middlebrook, ed., *Conservative*. Marcus J. Kurtz, *Free Market Democracy and the Chilean and Mexican Countryside* (New York: Cambridge University Press, 2004). Donna Lee Van Cott, *From Movements to Parties in Latin America: The Evolution of Ethnic Politics* (New York: Cambridge University Press, 2005). Jennifer Collins, "Democratizing Formal Politics: Indigenous and Social Movement Political Parties in Ecuador and Bolivia, 1978–2000," Ph.D. Dissertation (University of California, San Diego, 2006).